Created and Directed by Hans Höfer

US★National Parks West

Edited by John Gattuso
Managing Editor: Martha Ellen Zenfell

Editorial Director: Brian Bell

APA PUBLICATIONS

ABOUT THIS BOOK

The national parks, wrote John B. Oakes of the *New York Times*, "are as sacred to most Americans as the flag, motherhood and apple pie." And nowhere is this more true than in the American West, where the parks protect some of the most sublime landscapes and abundant wildlife in the world.

Insight Guide: US National Parks West is the first of two books dedicated to America's national parks, and is part of the award-winning travel series created in 1970 by **Hans Höfer**, now chairman of Apa Publications. Each of the 190 titles encourages readers to celebrate the essence of a place rather than try to tailor it to their expectations, and is edited according to Höfer's conviction that, without insight, travel can narrow the mind rather than broaden it.

Höfer

The present project was conceived and produced by **John Gattuso**, editor of Stone Creek Publications in Hunterdon County, New Jersey. An Apa Publications' veteran whose credits include Insight Guides to *Philadelphia, US National Parks East, The Wild West*, and *Native America* plus *Insight Pocket Guide: New York City* and a half-dozen other titles, Gattuso tried to present the parks not only as a travel destination but as "a cornerstone of America's environmental conscience." He was aided in the overall direction of the book by Apa Publications' editor-in-chief of US titles, **Martha Ellen Zenfell**, who herself grew up in one of America's national parks.

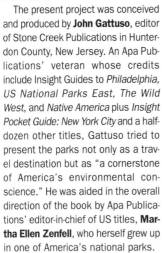

Gattuso

Zenfell

"The parks satisfy our basic need for wilderness," Gattuso says. "Few things are as moving as seeing the Grand Canyon or Rocky Mountains for the first time or having an unplanned encounter with a bison or grizzly bear."

For this book, Gattuso covered North and South Dakota as well as the history of the National Parks System. "The parks are not only beautiful and inspiring," he says, "they're one of the best travel values in the country."

When it came time to assemble a team of writers and photog-raphers, Gattuso searched for people who combined detailed knowledge of the parks with the sort of lucid journalistic style that is the hallmark of Insight Guides. **Nicky Leach** was a natural. A British-born writer and editor now based in Flagstaff, Arizona, Leach concentrated on the parks of southern Utah, which she describes as "the most intense landscapes in the Southwest." Leach's many publications include a comprehensive and award-winning guide to Southwestern parks.

Leach

The Pacific Northwest was covered by **Todd Wilkinson**, a writer and outdoorsman living in Bozeman, Montana. Wilkinson says he was attracted by the region's diversity. "Within a few hours you can hike from alpine tundra to lush rain forests, and then drive to the Pacific Coast."

Jeremy Schmidt, a writer and former park ranger based in Jackson Hole, Wyoming, wrote about Yellowstone, Grand Teton and Grand Canyon national parks. The Grand Canyon and the Tetons are like a "mirror image," he says. Travelers look down into the canyon or up at the mountains, but both "leave visitors gaping at the sheer scale of the landscape." Yellowstone, on the other hand, "has no particular focus. Its meadows, lakes and wildlife have a quieter, more subtle appeal."

Schmidt

Aitchison

Stewart Aitchison covered a number of topics, including geology,

Houk

wildlife and the California Desert. "My heart beats a little faster every time I head into the field," says Aitchison, "and if I can take a few folks with me, so much the better."

Elsewhere in the Southwest, **Rose Houk**, a writer, editor and former park ranger with several books to her credit, covered Great Basin National Park and prehistoric Indian sites. **George Hardeen**, a journalist and inveterate backpacker, penned lively chapters on outdoor recreation. **George Wuerthner**, whose words and pictures appear in the book, wrote about Big Bend National Park.

In California, **Steven Medley**, president of the Yosemite Association, was amply qualified to cover Yosemite National Park. **John Levine** trekked into the wildlands of northern California to write about Lassen Volcanic and Redwood national parks, and journalist **Eugene Rose** wrote about Sequoia and Kings Canyon National Parks. **Rita Ariyoshi**, a writer and photographer based in Honolulu, covered Hawaii.

To the north, Glacier National Park was covered by **Thomas Schmidt**, a dedicated outdoorsman and author of several books about the region. "Alaska's National Parks" was contributed by **Bill Sherwonit**, an outdoor writer based in Anchorage.

Till

The book's lush photography is the work of several talented people. Based in the red-rock country of Moab, Utah, **Tom Till** has published his work in countless calendars, books and magazines. "I like to capture ephemeral images, situations that only last a few seconds and then disappear," he says. "Those are the most challenging shots and often the most beautiful."

Lewis Kemper agrees. An outdoor photographer based in Sacramento, California, he says he likes going into the field "without knowing what to expect. When a good picture presents itself, it's like a gift." Kemper's "lifelong love of nature" started as a kid in Baltimore and followed him to Yosemite, where he studied with Ansel Adams. **Tom** and **Pat Leeson**, a husband-and-wife team from Vancouver, Washington, have specialized in wildlife photography since 1976. Their work has appeared in magazines such as *National Geographic* and *Audubon.*

Dugald Bremner is a former wilderness guide based in Flagstaff, Arizona. An editorial and commercial photographer, he works frequently for outdoor publications. **Art Wolfe** has photographed wildlife around the world. His credits include *National Geographic*, *Smithsonian*, *Stern*, *Audubon* and many books. **Larry Ulrich** has been a photographer for more than 20 years. He is the author of five books and contributes to major magazines and calendars. **Steve Bruno**'s work appears often in *Arizona Highways.*

John Running, **Bill Hatcher** and **Dave Edwards** – all based in Flagstaff, Arizona – contributed dazzling shots of outdoor recreation. Additional photographs were contributed by **Steve Mulligan, Kim Heacox, William Neill, Stephen Trimble, Gavriel Jecan, Larry Mayer, Kerrick James** and **Connie** and **Pat Toops**.

In Insight Guides' London editorial office, the manuscript was proofread and indexed by **Pam Barrett**. In the US, special thanks go to **Edward A. Jardim** for his invaluable editorial help, and to the many park rangers and naturalists who agreed to review the text for accuracy.

Bremner

Wolfe

CONTENTS

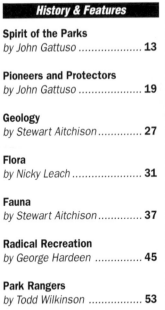

CONTENTS

Maps

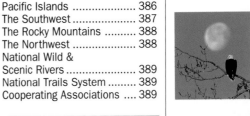

The national parks are a promise that Americans have made to themselves. As a people, they have resolved to protect a small portion of their precious wildlands from the ravages of "progress," to leave room for the bears and butterflies, wildflowers and ancient forests, to preserve as a "vignette of primitive America" the crown jewels of America's natural and cultural heritage.

But the parks are more than islands of nature. They are sanctuaries of the human heart. More than just pretty places where one can snap a few pictures, they are an acknowledgment of the human need for wilderness. These are places, as Colin Fletcher wrote of the Grand Canyon, where people can move "closer to rock and sky, to light and shadow, to space and silence." Where there's room for lone hikers to lose, or find, themselves; for mountaineers to test their mettle against the elements; for scientists to study the natural world in a nearly pristine environment; for ordinary visitors to gape at something greater than themselves and let their dreams run wild.

The wilderness of the American West has always attracted dreamers. Hope seems to rise where the sun sets – over the next mountain, across the plains, beyond the horizon. And perhaps dreams are the best way to understand the riveting, almost surreal, landscapes of the West. After all, what clear-thinking person would believe that rocks can flow like a fiery river as at Hawaii's Kilauea, that the very earth can boil and sputter as at Yellowstone, or that trees can turn to stone as at the Petrified Forest? What rational person could imagine the unearthly tablelands of South Dakota's Badlands, the improbable stone arches of the Colorado Plateau, the inconceivable span of the Grand Canyon?

To Native Americans, these landscapes are sacred ground. Landmarks like the Black Hills and Grand Canyon are part of a spiritual topography, an identification between land and people that comes with ancient tenure. Indians can point to mountains, rivers and canyons and declare, "This is where our people came from." They can point to the ruins of ancient villages and say, "These are the footprints of our ancestors."

"Every part of this soil is sacred in the estimation of my people," a Duwamish chief named Sealth said in 1854. "Every hillside, every valley, every plain and grove, has been hallowed by some sad or happy event in days long vanished." Years later, Chief Joseph of the Nez Perce expressed his attachment to the land in even more fundamental terms: "The earth and myself are of one mind. The measure of the land and the measure of our bodies are the same."

But to the young nation of immigrants whose spiritual attachments lay elsewhere, the West was terra incognita, an open book to be colored by foreign dreams and ideologies. And these dreams – or were they delusions? – took a toll on the land. Rivers were

Preceding pages: Exploring a slot canyon in southern Utah; Marble Canyon, Grand Canyon National Park; Colorado River kayaker; hang gliding from Glacier Point, Yosemite National Park. Left, a moose grazes on water plants beneath the snowcapped peaks of Alaska's Denali National Park.

dammed, wildlife exterminated, forests cleared, the earth torn open, streams fouled, and the soil exhausted and left to blow away.

And yet, through it all, the land remained, altered but enduring, reminding us of both its power and fragility and of the great need for stewardship. For if the parks are indeed a promise, they are equally a responsibility. Americans have an obligation to keep them whole and healthy for future generations. And the job isn't getting any easier. It's not that visitors don't care about the parks. In fact, if attendance is any indication, they may love them too much. Of the many problems that beset the parks, popularity – the sheer number of people – may prove to be the most serious. "We may love a place and still be dangerous to it," Wallace Stegner warned. "The best thing we have learned from nearly 500 years of contact with the American Wilderness is restraint, the willingness to hold our hand, to visit such places for our souls' good, but leave no tracks."

These precious places are certainly worth protecting. You may remember visiting a national park as a child and thrilling at the sight of a bison wallowing in the dust, or a black bear sauntering across a road, trying to get a peek at the tourists who were trying to get a peek at him. It's a feeling people don't forget, that keeps them coming back with friends and family and especially children. Because the parks are a gift, too. They're a gift that Americans give to themselves and to the world, and to generations of children who will experience the parks as they were meant to be experienced: wide-eyed and filled with wonder.

Right, humpback whale, Point Adolphus, Alaska.

PIONEERS AND PROTECTORS

The national parks may be the best idea America has ever had. Some people have suggested as much. But the urge to protect nature, to preserve vast stretches of wilderness for future generations, hasn't come easy.

As a nation of pioneers, Americans tend to imagine themselves as conquerors rather than protectors of nature. They revere the "can do" spirit of their pioneer forefathers and admire the courageous souls who set out in wagons across the Great Plains to carve new lives out of an unknown wilderness.

If you told an American in the early 19th century that the day would come in the not-so-distant future when his country would lack for wild places, he would probably think you were joking. Perched on the edge of a vast and untamed continent, Americans had more wilderness than they knew what to do with. "The happiness of my country arises from the great plenty of land," declared Albert Gallatin, the Secretary of the Treasury. His superior, President Thomas Jefferson, thought that the western lands contained "room enough for our descendants to the thousandth and ten thousandth generation." Indeed, many Americans regarded the land as an inexhaustible source of wealth in furs, timber, minerals and tillable soil.

And yet, despite the nation's optimism, there was deep ambivalence about nature, a sense of foreboding that went back at least as far as the Pilgrims. Peering into the New England woods, William Bradford, governor of Plymouth Colony, saw a "hideous and desolate wilderness of wild beasts and wild men." There was a moral imperative behind these words, an injunction to subjugate nature, to conquer wildness, and cast the devil out of Eden.

A "nation's park": Nearly 200 years later, as settlers struck out across the Great Plains, the urge to subdue nature began to take on larger proportions; it was no longer a simple necessity but a duty. Many saw it as America's

"manifest destiny" to occupy the continent from ocean to ocean and to bring the land and its native people under the dominion of the civilized world. According to President James Monroe, the vast wilderness occupied by Indians "requires a greater extent of territory… than is compatible with the progress and just claims of civilized life… and must yield to it."

And so the intruding settlers chopped and plowed and burned and hunted, wresting land from the native people and changing the

face of the earth with little regard for long-term effects. Americans "may be said not to perceive the mighty forests that surround them till they fall beneath the hatchet," the French historian Alexis de Tocqueville observed in 1832. "Their eyes are fixed upon another sight: The American people view its own march across these wilds, draining swamps, turning the course of rivers, peopling solitudes, and subduing nature."

In the same year, George Catlin, the American painter who chronicled the tribes of the West, realized that the wild country beyond the Mississippi River would soon be "tamed" by civilization. With uncanny foresight, he

Preceding pages: South Rim of the Grand Canyon, circa 1915. **Left**, Theodore Roosevelt and John Muir at Glacier Point, during Roosevelt's 1903 visit to Yosemite. **Right**, early tourists in the Grand Canyon.

proposed that the Great Plains be set aside in a "magnificent park."

"What a beautiful and thrilling specimen for America to preserve and hold up to the view of her refined citizens and the world, in future ages!" he wrote. "A *nation's park*, containing man and beast, in all the wild[ness] and freshness of their nature's beauty." Busy building a nation, most Americans weren't ready to hear what Catlin had to say.

There were exceptions, those who, like Catlin, found a deeper value in nature. On the East Coast, Emerson, Thoreau and Whitman looked to the natural world for spiritual renewal, for a sense of the divine. Thoreau suggested that small parks be set aside in

the peak of a 100-ft (30-m) fir in order to experience first-hand the rage of a windstorm, riding an avalanche above Yosemite Valley and calling it "the most spiritual and exhilarating of all the modes of motion," and hiking the Sierra for weeks with little more than bread and tea to sustain him. "Climb the mountains and get their good tidings," he advised his fellow Sierrans. "Nature's peace will flow into you as sunshine flows into trees. The winds will blow their own freshness into you and the storms their energy, while cares will drop off like autumn leaves."

By the time Muir first strode into Yosemite Valley, the idea for a national park had already begun to germinate. In 1864, four

every town so that residents would never be far from the healing power of living things. "In wildness is the preservation of the world," he wrote, suggesting that experiencing nature is a deep human need.

In the West, the cause of wilderness was championed with greatest passion by John Muir, co-founder of the Sierra Club and an inspired naturalist, writer, wanderer and organizer. Traipsing around the great mountain ranges of the West, particularly his beloved Sierra Nevada, Muir developed a vision of wilderness as an ecological and spiritual necessity. He sought union with the natural world as a living entity, climbing to

years before his arrival, the valley and nearby Mariposa Big Tree Grove had been granted to the state of California by the Congress of the United States to be "held for public use, resort, and recreation… inalienable for all time." Several years later, as reports of the beauty and endowments of the Yellowstone region began fascinating the rest of the nation, a campaign was mounted to preserve Yellowstone for public use. Because neither Montana nor Wyoming were yet American states, Yellowstone was placed under the supervision of the federal government which, in 1872, was empowered to "provide for the preservation, from injury or spoliation, of all timber, mineral deposits, natural curiosities, or wonders within said park, and their retention in their natural condition."

In California, John Muir was fighting to protect the Sierra. He campaigned against the spoliation of the forest by unrestrained logging and overgrazing sheep – which he called "hoofed locusts." Finally, in 1890, thanks in large part to his efforts, legislation creating Sequoia, General Grant (later incorporated into Kings Canyon) and Yosemite national parks was signed by President Benjamin Harrison. In 1892, Muir and others formed the Sierra Club to "explore, enjoy and protect the nation's scenic resources." And in 1906, after a 10-year battle with

historic or scientific interest such as the Petrified Forest, Mesa Verde, Devils Tower and Chaco Canyon, many of which have since been designated national parks.

Rape of Hetch Hetchy: But Muir's struggle to save Yosemite and, in a larger sense, to safeguard all national parks, wasn't over yet. In 1901, the city of San Francisco filed a request to dam the Tuolumne River in Yosemite National Park and drown the Hetch Hetchy Valley. Muir considered Hetch Hetchy among the most sublime locations in the Sierra, and he crusaded angrily against the proposal: "These temple destroyers, devotees of ravaging commercialism, seem to have a perfect contempt for Nature, and,

legislators and public opinion, the Yosemite Valley itself was surrendered by the state of California and incorporated into Yosemite National Park.

Meanwhile, several more areas of exceptional natural features were being designated national parks, including Mount Rainier, Crater Lake and Wind Cave. A new, conservation-minded chief executive, Theodore Roosevelt, pushed his administration for the creation of national monuments in areas of

Left, a member of the Hayden Expedition at Mammoth Hot Springs, Yellowstone, 1871. **Above**, rangers gather at Yosemite Falls, 1915.

instead of lifting their eyes to the God of the Mountains, lift them to the Almighty Dollar. Dam Hetch Hetchy! As well dam for water-tanks the people's cathedrals and churches, for no holier temple has ever been consecrated by the heart of man."

Hetch Hetchy was a divisive issue that is with us even today. Essentially, it boiled down to a struggle between two pivotal figures. One was Muir, who felt a moral imperative to protect wilderness for its own sake and on its own terms. The other was a charismatic and committed conservationist, Gifford Pinchot, who as President Roosevelt's chief forester, took a utilitarian view of wilderness – protection, yes, but protection for the sake of use. Pinchot regarded conservation as a deeply democratic movement, a way of reclaiming the wealth of federal lands from the lumber barons and land grabbers and distributing it more equitably. "People have not only the right but the duty to control the use of the natural resources, which are the great sources of prosperity," he declared.

It was Pinchot, in fact, who engineered some of the federal government's most important conservation policies, programs and legislation in the first years of the 20th century. Under Pinchot's guidance, Theodore Roosevelt set aside 130 million acres (52.5 million hectares) of national forest and 18

national monuments, and launched a system of wildlife refuges. Roosevelt, too, was a champion of wilderness. An avid outdoorsman, he had learned the lessons of conservation first-hand during a brief career as a rancher in North Dakota, and he was dedicated to protecting America's remaining wild places. "Leave it as it is," he said of the Grand Canyon, which he saved from developers by designating it as a national monument. "You cannot improve on it. Keep it for your children, your children's children, and for all who come after you as the one great sight which every American should see."

But for both Roosevelt and Pinchot,

conservation meant balancing economic use with preservation. Despite Muir's campaign, Roosevelt and Pinchot ultimately agreed to the dam, and Congress approved the flooding of Hetch Hetchy in 1913. Exhausted and disheartened, Muir died the following year.

The so-called rape of Hetch Hetchy, however, fired up supporters of the national parks. One of them, Stephen T. Mather, an influential Chicago entrepreneur, was invited to Washington by the Secretary of the Interior to take charge of park policy. Mather advocated a centralized park administration. And in August 1916, America's 35 national parks and monuments were placed under the supervision of the new National Parks Service. Mather was appointed director and, together with his young assistant Horace M. Albright, set about shaping the mission of the National Parks Service "to conserve the scenery and the natural and historic objects and the wild life therein and to provide for the enjoyment of the same in such manner and by such means as will leave them unimpaired for the enjoyment of future generations."

Mather and Albright began immediately to push for expansion, especially in the field of historic sites. By the 1930s, a dozen natural areas and more than 40 historic parks were added to the Park Service. And growth continues. Today, the National Parks Service manages more than 350 sites on 80 million acres (32.5 million hectares). Some parks, such as Ford's Theatre in Washington, DC, occupy less than an acre. Others, such as Gates of the Arctic and Wrangell–St Elias in Alaska, are larger than many states.

The number of visitors has expanded, too, from 6 million in 1942 to 72 million in 1960 to a phenomenal 375 million in 1990. And the Park Service expects an incredible half billion by the turn of the century. It would appear that John Muir's observation, made more than 80 years ago, rings truer than ever: "Thousands of tired, nerve-shaken, over-civilized people are beginning to find out that going to the mountains is going home; that wilderness is a necessity; and that mountain parks and reservations are useful not only as fountains of timber and irrigating rivers, but as fountains of life."

Left, Harry Yount, Yellowstone's first ranger. **Right**, Glacier Point, Yosemite, with Half Dome in the distance, circa 1880.

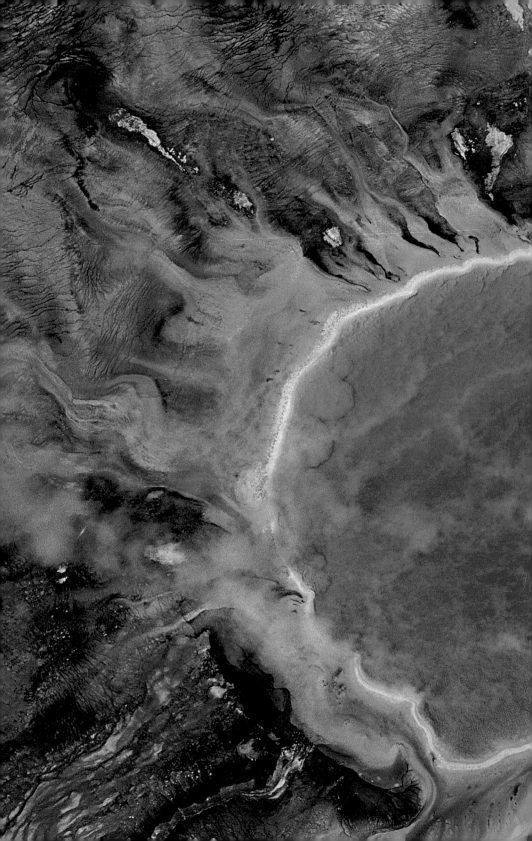

The national parks of the American West have been called a geologist's paradise. And so they are. From the gaping maw of the Grand Canyon to the volcanic mass of Mount Rainier, the rocks can, in their own way, speak. And the story they tell is nothing less than the creation of the earth.

Surveying the Western landscape, travelers are often gripped by a sense of timelessness. The "standing rocks" of the Colorado Plateau, the frozen peaks of Alaska, the sharp aretes of the Sierra Nevada seem unchanging, unmoving, eternal. And yet, compared to the age of the earth, these formations are little more than a blink of the geologic eye – lasting only a few millennia at most. Elsewhere, geologic events occur so quickly and with such force that one can't comprehend the magnitude of change. One has only to think of the devastation wrought by the eruption of Mount Saint Helens in 1980, the ongoing lava flows of Hawaii's Kilauea, debris-laden flash floods in the desert Southwest, and, to a lesser extent, the erosion of South Dakota's Badlands. These events remind us that no matter how stable the West's landscapes appear, they are only temporary features on the surface of a restless earth.

In the beginning: Some 4.6 billion years ago, the earth was a ball of cosmic gases and flowing, bubbling magma. Volcanic activity ruled this young world as the crust slowly congealed, producing gases such as hydrogen, methane ammonia and water vapor, which was released back onto the surface in the form of rain. For perhaps a billion years, endless torrents of rain cooled the earth's outer shell, filling low-lying areas with seas, lakes and rivers. Beneath the surface, the earth continued to churn, heaving and folding the newly formed crust. Great mountain ranges – some the size of the Himalayas – rose from the surface of what would become North America, only to be broken down by wind, ice and rain and replaced with yet other towering masses of rock. Debris gathered in

Preceding pages: Grand Prismatic Spring, Yellowstone National Park. **Left**, Castle Rock, Colorado River Canyon, Utah. **Right**, a stream cuts through a rock fissure in Zion National Park.

the lower elevations, and in time became the first sedimentary rocks.

Later, as the continental plate drifted and the climate changed, a succession of rivers, deserts, swamps and seas deposited thousands of vertical feet of sediment: windblown sand, mud, volcanic ash, seashells, skeletons and other organic matter destined to become sandstone, claystone, shale, limestone and other sedimentary rocks.

All the while, the North American plate continued to drift, constantly changing its

position relative to the equator and neighboring continents. At least 140 million years ago, one of the oceanic plates began to crash into the western margin of the continent. In Alaska, land masses (their exact origin is being debated and are therefore called "suspect terrain" by geologists) came rafting along on the oceanic plate and smashed into what is now the central part of the state. Sections of oceanic crust were ground into the geologic melange. Tremendous pressure and heat metamorphosed much of the rock as it was heaved into a series of complex mountain ranges such as the Alaska Range in Denali and Lake Clark national parks, the

Baird Mountains in Kobuk Valley National Park and the Endicott Mountains of Gates of the Arctic National Park. As a result, Alaska's geology is like a scrambled jigsaw puzzle, with pieces from different puzzles thrown into the mix. It's doubly difficult to understand because much of the land is hidden from view by dense growths of vegetation or massive, slow-moving glaciers.

Suspect terrain was also crashing into the ancestral West Coast, forcing sections of the ocean bed under the continental plate in a process called subduction. The friction of plate rubbing against plate melted subterranean rocks, turning them into great wads of molten magma. The magma rose in massive

mountain ranges of the world usually form along a plate boundary. The Rocky Mountains, however, march down the interior of a presumably stable continent. Some geologists believe that the rise of the Rockies is somehow related to the oceanic plate colliding with the West Coast, but the exact mechanism is still being debated. What is known is that by 70 million years ago, thrusts and uplifts were folding huge areas of ancient sediments and even older granite and metamorphic rock into the Rocky Mountains. Glaciers finished the job. The great sheets of ice plowed through the Rockies as well as the Cascades and Sierra Nevada. They widened valleys, gouged out bowl-like cirques, chis-

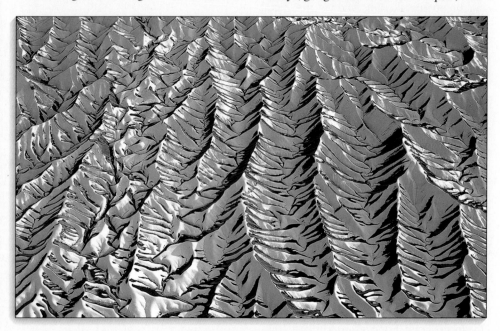

bubbles, cooled underground and, in some cases, small portions were eroded and exposed millions of years later as giant granite domes such as those in Yosemite National Park. Farther north, magma exploded onto the surface in great rivers of lava and showers of hot cinders that, over millennia, built up the Cascade Range in Washington, Oregon and northern California. Mount Rainier, Crater Lake, Olympic and North Cascades national parks contain volcanoes, craters, and lava flows that are a result of subduction.

Mountain building: While all this activity was going on along the coast, the Rocky Mountains were being pushed up. The major

eled sharp aretes and pinnacles, and deposited huge mounds of morainal debris before retreating between 6,000 and 8,000 years ago. Glacier, Grand Teton and Rocky Mountain national parks contain prime features of the mountain-building period.

The Great Plains were being lifted, too, although much more gently. An eastern outpost of the Rockies now known as the Black Hills was pushed toward the sky – an island of granite peaks in a sea of prairie. Streams gathered into rivers and flowed from the mountains onto the plains. They cut deeply into soft layers of rock and eroded the landscape into a complex and sometimes bizarre network of gullies, ravines, canyons and tables such as those at Badlands and Theodore Roosevelt national parks.

Between the Rockies and the great mountain ranges of the West Coast – the Sierra Nevada and Cascades – the continent was being stretched. The spreading of the land created long parallel faults in the crust. Between the faults, massive blocks of rock rotated slightly along their longest axis, forming mountain ranges with a typical profile: steep on one side, gradual on the other. Most of these ranges are separated by long, narrow valleys with no outlet to the ocean. During wetter climatic periods, the basins were filled with immense intermontane

age, a mile above sea level. Again, pressure from plate movements is thought to have caused the elevation. Why it didn't fold into mountains a mystery, but the answer may be hidden in tremendous faults in the oldest basement rocks that caused the region to lift en masse. Although little folding occurred, the Colorado River and its tributaries carved the plateau into a labyrinth of awesome canyons, mesas and majestic buttes. Many parks and monuments, including Grand Canyon, Bryce Canyon, Zion, Canyonlands, Arches and Capitol Reef natural parks, preserve remarkable pieces of the Colorado Plateau.

Hawaii is a hot spot – a center of thermal upwelling. Most volcanic and seismic activ-

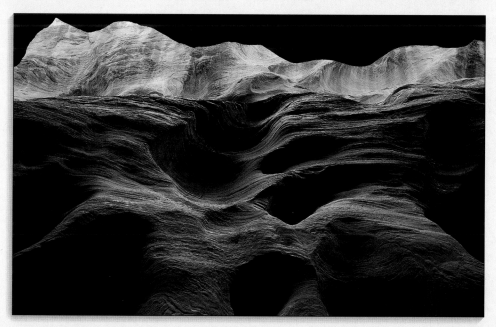

(mountain) inland lakes. The Great Salt Lake is but a remnant of one of the ancient bodies of water that covered much of the intermontane West. Great Basin National Park and Death Valley and Joshua Tree national monuments exhibit outstanding parts of the Basin and Range Geologic Province.

Amid all of this geologic chaos was a huge 130,000-sq. mile (336,698-sq. km) block of colorful, sedimentary real estate – the Colorado Plateau – which was uplifted, on aver-

Left, an aerial view of snow patterns in Utah's San Rafael Wilderness. **Above**, light filters into a slot canyon, Buckskin Gulch, Utah.

ity takes place along plate boundaries, but scattered across the globe are fairly permanent upwellings of molten rock (Yellowstone National Park is another example). On the big island of Hawaii, Kilauea and Mauna Loa, in Hawaii Volcanoes National Park, continue to pump hot glowing lava down their slopes. Offshore, magma is bubbling out of underwater vents. When the deposits rise above sea level, a new island will be formed; and as the Pacific Plate moves, the island will be rafted away. Why these hot spots stay put while the plate moves across them is a question which geologists continue to ponder.

The enormous diversity of landscapes in the American West is one of its enduring attractions. From forest-clad mountains and plateaus to sheltered canyons, arid deserts to frigid tundra, wind-swept coastal cliffs to dune-filled beaches, life-giving streams to sere salt flats, volcanic moonscapes to grassy prairies – this is a place where geology and climate continually shape the land into a jigsaw of distinct interlocking environments and micro-environments.

Legions of highly adapted flowers, trees and shrubs clothe the vast and varied contours of this changing panorama, with some species endemic to certain locations while others manage to gain a foothold almost everywhere. Nowhere in the United States are there more flowering plant species than in the West. Remote Hawaii is the only place in the world to have so many diverse species evolved from so few ancestors.

The western United States, from the Pacific Ocean to the Rockies, can be broadly divided into four regions: coast/beaches, deserts, mountains and wetlands. Alaska, far to the north, has the short summers and endless winters associated with the Arctic tundra. By contrast, the isolated Hawaiian Islands, in the middle of the Pacific, are warm year-round, with a generally humid, tropical climate. Geographic location, climate, sunlight, amount of water, elevation, soil type, exposure and plant and animal neighbors affect what will grow within each region and what it will look like, creating habitats where specific plant associations regularly occur, as well as ecotones, or overlapping habitats, within them.

Coast and sand dunes: Most of the West is affected by weather over the Pacific Ocean. The climate of Hawaii is dictated by trade winds that create warm and moist or hot and dry conditions, depending on where you are on each island. The western exposure is frequently dry and relatively unvegetated, while the east may support lush rain forests, filled with orchids, lobelias and other hot-

house rarities that benefit from daily rainfall hitting the world's tallest mountains (from the ocean bottom to the summits).

Moist Pacific winds journey eastward and buffet the coasts of Washington, Oregon and California, making this a challenging environment for plants. Many native flowers, such as sand verbena and sea asters, maintain low profiles, deep roots, fleshy leaves and a matted appearance in order to survive the sand dunes, high winds, salt spray, fog and inadequate water intake. On exposed cliffs,

cypresses and Monterey, Bishop and Torrey pines look like bonsai plants, their branches blown back by the wind and wrapped in wraithlike fog. Along the tinder-dry southern California coastal foothills, the gnarled miniature oaks for which this state is famous grow alongside manżanita and a variety of shrubs in a dense chaparral mix that scratches passing hikers.

The groves of tall redwood trees are happiest in foggy river valleys near the northern California and Oregon coasts. Like the ancient bristlecone pines of Utah's Cedar Breaks, the giant sequoias along the western Sierra Nevada, and the mixed conifer forests

Left, mule ear flowers, near the Colorado River. **Right**, fern fiddlehead, Hawaii Volcanoes National Park.

of Texas's Guadalupe Mountains, the redwoods were stranded here by the last Ice Age, and now grow in only a few locations. Other Ice Age relics are the glaciated vernal pools found only in California's grassy Great Valley, which sits between the coastal mountains and the imposing Sierra Nevada massif. Hundreds of species of wildflowers enjoy these soggy locations each spring.

The mountains: The mountains of the West, with their weathered pinnacles and domes, cooler temperatures and increased moisture, contain the greatest variety of vegetation, although some, like the Inyo and White Mountains of the Great Basin, are overshadowed by taller mountains that block rainfall.

ton's Mount Rainier remain snowcapped and dotted with glaciers year-round. The exposed location, thin soils and cold temperatures mean that only the hardiest of mosses, lichens and ground-hugging, woody-stemmed perennials can survive.

Below these boulder-strewn summits, in the alpine and sub-alpine zones, spruce, fir and various pines, such as lodgepole, whitebark, limber, Jeffrey and occasionally bristlecone, survive admirably by using water conservatively and retaining their waxy needles year-round. These conifers are gradually joined at lower elevations by silvery-barked aspens, ruddy maples, toothy oaks and other deciduous trees that leaf out in

Mountains of varying heights exist throughout the region, even in the hottest deserts, where they rise through the heat haze like islands amid salt flats and dry oceans of sand.

Washington's Olympic Mountains are the wettest peaks in the contiguous United States, home to the temperate Hoh Rain Forest, whose dripping glades foster a climax forest of western hemlock, Sitka spruce and western red cedar, and provide cover for deciduous underlings and shade-loving plants like leafy trillium. In the cool north, the treeline is often reached at 4,000 ft (1,219 m) – far lower than in the south – and giants like Alaska's Mount McKinley and Washing-

spring and die so colorfully in autumn. In one of nature's ironies, aspens are often the first to colonize the sub-alpine zone between 8,000 ft (2,438 m) and 10,500 ft (3,200 m), but are soon overshadowed by incoming conifers and forced to seek sunlight in clearings. An eye-popping array of bluebells, columbines, Indian paintbrushes, shooting stars, gentians, primroses, monkeyflowers, penstemons, sunflowers and other dazzlers bloom in waves from warm, damp May to August, splashing forests and meadows across the West with color. Although wildfires are frequently brought under control by nervous humans, many trees and flowering plants need fire in order to regenerate. The glorious rebirth of Yellowstone flora after the great fire of 1988 was ample evidence that nature knows best.

At about the 7,000- to 8,000-ft (2,134- to 2,438-m) mark, swaying forests of ponderosa pine make an appearance. Ponderosa reaches its greatest density south of the Grand Canyon where, alongside Gambel oak, it forms a transition zone between high desert and mountain. As elevation drops and water is more scarce, the ponderosa habitat disappears, making way for pygmy juniper and pinyon trees, dryland grasses, yuccas, rabbitbrush, sagebrush, woolly mullein and hardy paintbrushes, prickly poppies, sunflowers, globemallows and other flora that

Chihuahuan – owe their existence to the barrier of California's Sierra Nevada, which throws an enormous rain shadow across land to the east. No prevailing ocean influences moderate these low-lying regions, making the western deserts frighteningly hot in summer, frigid in winter, and subject to flash flooding during torrential thunderstorms that saturate easily eroded sandy soils. For any vegetation to make it here, it must tough out long droughts (deserts average only 10 inches/ 25.4 cm of rainfall a year, much of it coming in a short rainy season); it must compete effectively for water; and it must have mutually beneficial relationships with local and migratory birds, insects and other animals in

must be content with the thin, rocky soils of the high desert. The mesas, high plains and gullies of the Southwest, around the 6,000-ft (1,830-m) mark, are prime habitat for pinyon-juniper forests, as much a hallmark of the mile-high Colorado Plateau as redwoods in California, Joshua trees in the Mojave Desert, sagebrush in the Great Basin, and Sitka spruce in the Northwest and Alaska.

The deserts: The four great western deserts – the Mojave, Great Basin, Sonoran and

Left, globeflowers blossom along a Rocky Mountain stream. **Above**, tundra harebells, crowberry and cranberry in Denali National Park.

order to reproduce.

Tough-barked mesquite, palo verde, sagebrush, creosote bush, blackbrush and bitterbrush manage quite well, and some bushes, like iodinebush and saltbush, have made a specialty of salt flats where nothing else grows. But cacti are perhaps the best adapted to desert conditions. The giant, many-limbed saguaro of the Sonoran Desert is undoubtedly the most famous, yet more than a hundred cacti find their home in the western desert, among them teddybear cholla, prickly pear, beaver tail, pincushion, claret cup and hedgehog.

Cacti have expandable, gelatinous tissues

into which they suck up rainfall through shallow roots – a strategy that allows them to go up to a year without water. A waxy coating keeps the water in. Spines retain moisture and keep away thirsty neighbors. The cactus uses its broad trunk or paddles to photosynthesize sunlight, water and minerals into food. In spring, many species sprout a crown of large, creamy blooms attractive to nocturnal migratory bats and moths, which pollinate each cactus as they search for nectar. By late summer, bright, globular fruits appear – a delicacy for animals and humans alike. Some larger cacti also provide nesting sites for birds.

Agaves are another common sight, their

tall, thick spikes rising from a rosette of fleshy, sword-like "leaves." Yuccas have been particularly useful to desert dwellers, who use the roots for shampoo, the fibers for clothing, and the autumn fruits as a starchy food. The shaggy Joshua tree, the symbol of the Mojave Desert, is a well-known member of the yucca family.

The desert's low elevation allows wildflowers to begin blooming early. From February or March, brilliantly colored carpets of wildflowers enliven the subtle tones of the land, bringing admirers from near and far. No two years are likely to be the same, with different species awaiting just the right amount of rain to awaken. Some of the most beautiful flowers are spring annuals, such as poppies and owl's clover, which burst on the scene early during years of abundant rainfall. The Sonoran Desert is particularly noted for its floral displays.

Wetlands: Wetlands, or riparian areas, are found throughout the West, wherever springs, pools, streams, rivers and seeps are located. Recognizable from miles away by the ribbon of green that announces the presence of cottonwoods, willows, box elders and sedges, these shady groves provide water, shelter and food for a variety of plants and animals, including humans. Monkeyflowers, columbines, ferns and mosses form hanging gardens deep in the desert around the dripping sandstone bases of cliffs and along the riverbanks. Damp winters and spring runoff from the mountains awaken plants from Alaska to southern Texas, demonstrating the water's role as life-giver essential to the seasonal cycle of plants.

But water is now a precious commodity throughout much of the West, as native flora compete with ranching, agriculture, industry, recreation and other human endeavors for access to this scant but essential resource. Approximately 90 percent of riparian environments in California and Arizona have been lost through overdevelopment, and nearly all the West's major rivers have already been tapped. Damming, too, has its consequences. In the Grand Canyon, beach erosion along the Colorado River during dam operation has altered habitat for native plants and must now be restored. Introduced tamarisk is monopolizing many Southwestern waterways, crowding out other plants along washes and rivers that cannot tolerate the salty conditions this attractive but exotic intruder generates.

Looking at these natural gardens filled with trees, shrubs and flowers, it is interesting to consider that we would not be here at all if it weren't for plants, which give us oxygen, food, clothing and medicine, to say nothing of aesthetic pleasure. Our well-being is tied to theirs. Learn about them, fight for them, keep them in their native habitat; it's a fair exchange.

Left, Joshua Tree in bloom, Death Valley. **Right**, bear grass and lupine in a high-country meadow, Olympic National Park.

WILDLIFE

Wildlife is one of the great treasures of the national parks. Few things evoke the spirit of wildness like the sight of bald eagles snatching salmon from the frigid waters of the Katmai coast, bighorn rams butting heads in the Rockies, a cloud of Brazilian free-tailed bats spiraling out of caves in Carlsbad Caverns, thousands of caribou migrating across the vast tundra of Gates of the Arctic, or the howl of gray wolves echoing across Yellowstone after a 50-year silence.

In the contiguous western states alone, there are some 700 species of birds, 340 species of mammals, 250 species of reptiles and amphibians, and 300 species of fish. And the national parks shelter almost all of them. Some species, such as the resourceful coyote, mule deer and raven, are able to survive in a wide range of environments. Others, such as the Grand Canyon's Kaibab squirrel, Olympic marmot and rare Hawaiian honeycreepers, are limited to specific areas. Biologists recognize six major regions, or biomes, in western North America and a seventh in Hawaii: coniferous forest, woodland, chaparral, tundra, grassland, desert and tropical. From the torrid flats of the Sonoran Desert to the glacier-capped summit of Mount McKinley, the national parks represent the full range of animal habitats. In fact, more than 10 western parks have been named International Biosphere Reserves by the United Nations.

Coniferous forest and woodland: Coniferous forests take in a variety of environments, from the relatively open, dry ponderosa forests of the Southwest to the luxuriant old-growth "jungles" of the Olympic Peninsula. The cool, moist boreal forest extends from southern Alaska to the Rocky Mountains, where it overlaps with the drier montane forest. Rodents such as shrews, chipmunks, lemmings and voles are characteristic of the northern range and make tasty little morsels for a variety of predators such as fishers, lynx, black bears and grizzly bears. Moose, the largest member of the deer family, inhabit this community, too, as do woodland caribou, known for massive seasonal migra-

Left, the gray wolf, hunted almost to extinction, is returning to several park areas.

tions. Two endangered birds, the spotted owl and the northern goshawk, have become celebrities. The spotted owl, in particular, is at the center of a much publicized controversy between environmentalists and the timber industry over the fate of the Northwest's old-growth forest.

The relatively warmer and drier montane forest is found throughout the Rocky Mountains, the Sierra Nevada and parts of the Cascades as well as in large swaths of the intermontane West. Mule deer and elk are among the most frequently seen large mammals here. Consider yourself lucky if you spy a black bear, a mountain lion or a bobcat, which tend to stay hidden.

There tend to be fewer birds in the montane forest, but there's plenty of variety. Listen for the loud "shook-shook-shook" of large, blue Steller's jays, the "tsick-a-zee-zee-zee" of diminutive mountain chickadees, and the "kit-kit" of pygmy nuthatches, which are often seen gleaning insects from tree trunks and branches. Flycatchers snatch insects in midair and quickly return to their perch. Warblers let melodies drift down from the canopy. And male western tanagers, evening grosbeaks and red-capped Cassin's finch bring flashes of color to the understory. At night, you'll hear the mellow "hoot" of the flammulated owl or the single, whistle-like "hoo" of the northern pygmy owl.

Scattered woodlands of pinyon pine, pygmy juniper and evergreen oak are common throughout the West. Mule deer tend to browse in the woodlands in winter, and mountain lions and coyotes come to hunt. Bobcats pass through, too, and, before overhunting, grizzly bears were not uncommon. Of the rodents, the pinyon mouse is perhaps the most distinctive. It is the most arboreal of the deer mice, making its den in hollow juniper branches.

A bounty of seeds, nuts and berries attract a variety of bird life. You may hear the nasal buzz of blue-gray gnatcatchers, the rapid-fire tapping of Lewis or ladder-backed woodpeckers and, in the considerably drier chaparral, the catlike call of the rufous-sided towhee. The ash-throated flycatcher and western bluebird dart into the air hunting insects, the plain titmouse and bushtit spend hours gleaning bugs from the foliage, and both the pinyon and scrub jay cache pine nuts against the long winter months. There's no lack of color here, either. Among the most flamboyant is the handsome male Scott's oriole, which sports a black head and back and a contrasting yellow breast.

Grasslands: As the song says, grasslands are where "the buffalo roam and the antelope play," although any biologist will tell you that American buffalo are properly called bison and antelope are pronghorn. The massive bison herds that once roamed the Great Plains – more than 60 million animals – were systematically exterminated in the late 19th

ing nearly led to the extinction of their main predator, the black-footed ferret. You'll find prairie-dog towns at several parks; efforts to restore ferrets are currently under way.

Grassland birds are primarily ground-nesters, although a few, like the ferruginous hawk, find an occasional tree for nesting. The lovely, flute-like song of the western meadowlark can be heard most summer mornings. And, if you're lucky, you may hear the "booming" of prairie chickens during courtship. The male's elaborate displays include inflated throat, or gular, sacs and erect, horn-like neck feathers. The sharp-tailed grouse also has inflatable gular sacs but makes a single, low "coo-coo" accompa-

century. Had it not been for the efforts of conservationists at Yellowstone National Park and elsewhere, the shaggy beasts might have been lost forever. Today, remnant herds remain at Yellowstone, Wind Cave, Badlands and several other parks and reserves. Swift-running pronghorns didn't fare much better. Vast numbers of them died when the range-land was fenced in the latter part of the 19th century. Fortunately, herds at Wind Cave, Theodore Roosevelt, Grand Teton and other parks have increased thanks to transplanta-tion and better management.

Highly social prairie dogs were targeted for eradication, too, and large-scale poison-

nied by quill-rattling and foot-shuffling. The long-billed curlew and upland sandpiper are shorebirds that summer in the grasslands. The curlew uses its long, sickle-shaped bill to probe the soil for invertebrates. You may see a short-eared owl coursing back and forth close to the ground looking for prey, or a burrowing owl "still-hunting" – waiting motionless until a rodent or large insect happens by. Although they don't actually nest in grasslands, golden eagles, turkey vultures and various hawks can be seen pa-trolling the skies. You may spot black-billed magpies, too, especially along watercourses, but like most raptors, they nest in trees.

The desert: Survival in the searing heat and bone-dry conditions of the Mojave, Sonoran and Chihuahuan deserts requires special adaptations. Don't expect to see very much animal life during the day. Most mammals are nocturnal, although a few, such as the antelope ground squirrel, can tolerate soaring daytime temperatures. Other rodents, such as kangaroo rats and pocket mice, never have to drink water; they produce it metabolically from high-carbohydrate seeds. In the cooler deserts of the Great Basin and Colorado Plateau, you'll find Nuttall's cottontails, kangaroo mice, sagebrush voles and pygmy rabbits, which feed almost exclusively on sagebrush.

There is a conspicuous lack of large mammals here. Mountain lions and bobcats tend to be nocturnal and secretive, coyotes are usually shy, and desert bighorn sheep remain extremely rare despite efforts to reintroduce them into several Southwestern parks. At the first hint of a spring dawn, however, bird calls pierce the clear desert air. From a hidden *tinaja* comes the hollow "coah, coo, coo, coo" of a mourning dove, followed by the harsh "who cooks for you?" of a white-winged dove. In canyons, listen for graceful notes tripping down the scale – a canyon wren in love. Along dry washes, the brown-crested flycatcher calls with a sharp "whit," curve-billed thrashers and Abert's towhees scratch the dirt looking for a meal, and black-tailed gnatcatchers flit about. Keep your eyes and ears open for a black phainopeplas eating mistletoe berries, or a tiny Lucy's warbler singing from the top of a mesquite tree. You may see a family of plump, grayish Gambel's quail scurry between the bushes, or hear the drumming of a woodpecker in a grove of tall saguaros. Suddenly, a greater road runner races by chasing a lizard.

High on the cliffs, lone peregrine falcons survey their domain. Nearly wiped out by pesticides in the contiguous United States, the falcons have made a strong comeback in remote desert regions. As the day heats up, vultures catch a thermal and spiral upward, their keen sense of smell alert for carrion. A red-tailed hawk cruises by looking for an unsuspecting squirrel or rabbit. Ravens cartwheel and tumble in the cloudless sky. And

after nightfall, great horned owls and tiny elf owls come out to hunt, while lesser nighthawks glide through the air scooping insects into their large mouths.

Deserts are also home to a rather unpleasant variety of creepy crawlies – rattlesnakes, tarantulas, scorpions, millipedes and Gila monsters. Rattlesnakes can't tolerate high ground temperatures and usually spend the day under a ledge or shady bush. The large hairy tarantulas sometimes seen in the fall are usually males looking for a mate. They almost never bite humans, even when molested. Scorpions, too, have little interest in people, although their sting packs a wallop. Consider yourself lucky if you happen upon

a Gila monster, North America's only poisonous lizard. They do not have fangs but have to chew on their victims – mostly small rodents and lizards – in order to work in the poison. If you keep your hands and feet where you can see them, it's unlikely you'll be bitten or stung.

Tundra: Alaska's tundra is the richest in North America. Here, the most abundant mammal is the mouse-like lemming. Every three to four years, the lemming population peaks, providing a bountiful food supply for arctic foxes, gray wolves and grizzly bears. No, lemmings don't rush headlong into the sea, but high populations do cause frenzied

<u>Left</u>, Alaskan grizzly bear. <u>Above</u>, bighorn sheep rams perform a dominance ritual known as bowing.

dispersals and animals may drown while crossing rivers or lakes. Other mammals include arctic shrew, arctic hare, arctic ground squirrel, tundra vole, polar bear, weasel, wolverine, and barren ground caribou.

In the lower 48 states, alpine tundra covers a relatively small area atop mountain peaks, and there are only a few characteristic species. Collared pika, hoary marmots, singing voles, mountain goats and bighorn sheep are found in the tundra of the Rockies, Cascades and Sierra Nevada. Pikas, relatives of the rabbit, pile grasses into little haystacks that sustain them with food through the harsh winter. Marmots, on the other hand, build up a thick layer of fat for their long winter

hibernation. Other mammals such as black bears, weasels, badgers, elk (or wapiti) and mule deer sometimes range through the alpine tundra in summer.

Arctic birds generally rely on ponds and lakes for food and nest sites. Few sounds are more haunting then the falsetto wail and yodel of loons. A variety of shorebirds, such as plovers and sandpipers, populate the Alaskan coast. Flocks of red-necked phalaropes feed on the water, sometimes spinning like tops to stir up insect larvae and crustaceans. Herring gulls dive for fish, glacous gulls prey on young birds and lemmings, and jaegers – dark, hawk-like seabirds – harass

gulls and terns. The arctic tern makes the longest migration in the animal kingdom; it nests in the Arctic and spends its winters in the Antarctic.

Some arctic birds, such as the small Lapland longspur, snow bunting, horned lark and water pipit, search among short plants for beetles, craneflies, mosquitoes and seeds. They keep a wary eye out for the snowy owl, which often hunts by day. One of the first birds of prey to arrive on the tundra in the spring is the rough-legged hawk, which follows melting snow north into Alaska. Other raptors include gyrfalcons, North America's largest, which tend to fly low in their hunt for large birds, and bald eagles, which gorge on spawning salmon.

Hawaii: In terms of biodiversity, the tropics are the richest habitat on the planet. The Hawaiian islands are so isolated, however, that they make a rather incomplete example. Native species have been substantially reduced since the arrival of humans, and introduced species have proliferated. An endemic bird family, Hawaiian honeycreepers, is perhaps the world's best example of "adaptive radiation"—a process by which one species evolves into many in order to take advantage of different ecological niches. Tragically, more than a third of honeycreeper species are extinct. Introduced species have been so successful that in most parks and lowland areas all the vertebrates and most plants and insects are non-natives.

Part of the problem is that park boundaries reflect political rather than ecological boundaries. Although we like to believe that the parks are preserving animal communities, these "islands of life" are often isolated, threatened by development, and too small to be entirely self-sustaining. There seems to be some hope, however, in recent discussions of "greater ecosystem management," which protects wildlife in large areas surrounding national parks.

It's a powerful idea and well worth considering. There's something about wild animals that stirs the human soul. They reflect the wildness in ourselves. They remind us that we're only a small part of the natural world, one species of hundreds, that roam the magnificent landscapes of the American West.

Left, moose cow and calf in Denali National Park. **Right**, ladybugs, Yosemite Valley.

During the week, Bob Kerry is a mild-mannered, middle-aged lawyer. But on weekends, he's a rock jock – a member of the growing cadre of athletes who get a kick out of scaling sheer rock walls. You may see them clinging to the side of a canyon at mind-numbing heights, looking like tiny specks against the massive stone face. The most radical are "free climbers," those who use no safety ropes. And when it comes time to bed down during an overnight climb, they simply attach a hammock to the rock and dangle in the breeze.

Rock jocks: Rock climbers are part of a new breed of high-octane athletes that includes river runners, hang gliders, cavers, mountain bikers and others who approach the outdoors with daring spirits and an eagerness to test their limits. Some navigate rafts or kayaks through churning white water, or burn up their thighs on mountain bikes. Others ride the wind in giant kites or explore silent passages beneath the earth's surface.

More than ever, people want a first-hand experience of wilderness, and that means total immersion. Athletes are out for a good time, to be sure. But they're looking for something more, too – adventure, achievement, excitement and, to borrow a phrase from John Muir, a way of "getting in touch with the nerves of Mother Nature."

"Everybody does it for different reasons," says Kerry, who has been rock climbing for 12 years. He calls himself a "lifelong adrenalin junkie," but says that other rock climbers do it for the exercise, a sense of accomplishment, and a feeling that both their minds and bodies are in top condition.

During a recent climb in the Grand Canyon, for example, Kerry made a tricky ascent of an 80-ft (24-m) crack known as a chimney. "It's an awfully scary feeling because you're not standing on any footholds," he says. "If you relax your body even for a moment, you just drop straight down. You don't have any handholds or footholds to

keep you up. All you have is the tension on either side of your body."

Controlling fear in these situations, he explains, is what separates novices from experienced climbers. "There's something inside you that puts a chill in your brain. All you can see are the little edges in the rock, and you just continue to go up." Climbing is good therapy, too, and a hell of a lot cheaper than consulting a shrink. It teaches you how to eliminate distractions and focus completely on what you're doing. And clinging to a rock

several hundred feet above the ground has a way of putting life's mundane problems in their proper perspective. As Kerry puts it, "you're going to die if you fall even 50 feet… The rest is immaterial, really."

If climbing doesn't get you high enough, consider flying. Once the domain of steely-nerved 20-year-olds, the sport of hang gliding has come of age. According to Bill Holmes, an instructor in the sport, the age of many first-time flyers is now well over 30.

The change is due in part to innovations in hang gliding's design and technique. "Our danger factor is way down," says Holmes, declaring that the "flexwing" is now among

Preceding pages: white water adventure on the Colorado River. **Left,** rappelling at Deer Creek Falls, Grand Canyon. **Right,** boulder climbing at California's Joshua Tree National Monument.

the safest forms of aviation. "We make a joke about the good old days when sex was safe and hang gliding was dangerous."

After a few lessons in "ground school," Holmes wastes no time getting his students airborne. "My philosophy is to get students as high as we can as quickly as we can, and give them enough altitude to make three mistakes." After about a dozen lessons, he says, his students can be soaring at an altitude of 15,000 ft (4,572 m) for an hour or more.

And he does make it sound appealing. The sensation, he says, "is purely sexual." The constant buzz of surface life gives way to the sound of wind rippling across the wings and a sense of peace and awareness that is hard to

Warner, who runs a bike touring company in Moab, Utah, considered by freewheelers to be the capital of the world when it comes to mountain biking. Located in the red rock country of southeastern Utah, the area is crosshatched with thousands of miles of dirt roads left behind by miners and ranchers, giving bikers plenty of spare room to spin their wheels.

"The riding is excellent because the scenery is excellent," Warner says. "You can go from an elevation of 4,000 feet (1,219 m) at the Colorado River to almost 14,000 feet (4,267 m) on the snowcapped peaks of the La Sal Mountains." For him, mountain biking combines the best aspects of hiking and

find anywhere else. "It's so intimate up there that the hawks share the thermals with you," he says. He especially enjoys flying in the evening, when smooth air currents, or "wonder wind," let hang gliders "float around for two or three hours while the sun sets," catching "marshmallowy thermals" and soaring above snowy mountaintops.

Freewheeling: If you prefer less elevated kicks, think about mountain biking, described by *Newsweek* magazine as a "mode of transportation that combines the strenuousness of push-ups with the comfort of falling down a flight of steps in a shopping cart."

"The self-powered thing is cool," says Lou

skiing – access to the hills and downhill speed – and leaves behind the worst one – slow travel.

In national parks, biking is allowed only on paved or dirt roads and a few designated trails. Still, it's a great way to see the country without fogging up the atmosphere and to reach remote locations that you might otherwise miss on foot. And who says it has to be fast and bumpy? Biking at a nice slow pace lets the landscape unfold in glorious detail.

Reading the river: The West is braided with some of the most powerful and scenic waterways in North America. Whether you thread a kayak through icebergs in Alaska's Glacier

Bay, canoe beneath the Teton Range in Wyoming, or shoot the rapids of the Colorado River in the Grand Canyon, the opportunities for waterborne adventure are as varied as the West itself.

Larry Rice, a wildlife biologist and avid outdoorsman, finds that traveling by water is among the quickest and easiest ways of getting into the backcountry. "Canoeing and kayaking let you enter a wilderness area almost effortlessly, without the restraints or encumbrances of a heavy backpack. It's a more contemplative form of travel and permits a quicker change of scenery than hiking. It tends to free the mind without the numbing sensation of heavy equipment on your back."

He's quick to point out that traveling by water doesn't preclude hiking. In fact, combining the two can make the experience more rewarding. "Letting the power of the river, rather than your legs, carry you into the backcountry frees up a lot of energy to make camp and take day hikes. You can really experience the best of both worlds – river running and hiking – in one trip."

He also finds it's easier to get close to wildlife in a small watercraft. Animals tend to be "less frightened and more curious" when they're approached in a kayak or canoe. He recalls drifting near a perplexed grizzly bear on the Upper Missouri River in Montana, paddling past seals among the ice floes of Alaska's Glacier Bay and, in a truly magical episode that he describes as a "wildlife nugget," encountering gray whales off the coast of Baja California.

"Four adult whales were spyhopping (poking their heads vertically out of the water) around my kayak, doing a kind of ballet with me at the center of the circle… I remember looking into their dark black eyes; it was one of those transcendental moments. I was looking at them, they were looking at me, and for a moment there was almost a spanning of the species."

It's at times like these, Rice says, that he feels "really privileged to be in that kind of environment, a real wilderness beyond sight and sound of civilization, where you either sink or swim on your own skills and experience."

For some people, like Colorado River guide Jenny Gold, river running is a lifelong passion. Gold works as a river guide around the world at least 10 months a year. She says there's a hard-to-define romance in river life, a freedom that can't be found anywhere else. Most trips last a week or two or longer, so there's plenty of time to get close to the elements, to experience rock, sky and wildlife in an unspoiled environment and, most importantly, to learn how to "read the river."

"Water has a way of teaching you things," she explains. "There's a lot of finesse involved in allowing the river to take you where you want to go without fighting it." Gold says a good river guide knows instinc-

tively how to clear the mind and assess a potentially dangerous situation: the speed and direction of the boat, the waves bouncing off boulders, rocks hidden beneath the surface, and the condition of water downstream. Above all, she says, a river runner needs to stay humble. "You find out fast that no matter who you are or what you do, you'll never be more powerful than the river."

Descending order: Much the same can be said about caving – spelunking, as it used to be known. Caves have a way of surprising even the best-prepared and best-trained cavers. Serious cavers are particular about what they do and how it's done. Generally speaking, they take pains to distance themselves from weekend thrill-seekers. They particularly despise being portrayed as subterranean daredevils engaged in some sort of Indiana Jones adventurism. They emphasize that caving is not for everyone and definitely not something you want to jump into without proper instruction.

"Caving is safe if practiced with the proper equipment and the proper training," says Jay Jansen, a volunteer spokesman for the National Speleological Society. "It can be dangerous if the proper equipment is not used or if people don't know what they're doing. That's the bottom line." And he should know. Every year society members are called upon

to pull out of caves people who went in with a cotton clothesline after being inspired by something they saw on television.

Cavers also tend to be secretive about the locations of their caves, and for good reason. As elsewhere, vandalism and damage – intentional or not – is taking a toll on the underworld. Even experienced cavers may damage or destroy underground formations that have taken thousands of years to form and are completely irreplaceable. "Caves are non-renewable resources and can be damaged easily even by people who think they know what they're doing," Jansen says.

The society has 150 caving clubs around the country, and urges attendance at one of their meetings. Or, to learn about caving, visit any one of several national parks. At Wind Cave and Carlsbad Caverns, for example, you can sign up for a ranger-led "exploration tour" that will introduce you to some of the charms and challenges of caving. You may be surprised at just how fascinating (and exhausting) caving can be. There's something alluring about being in a dark, quiet place so far removed from the outside world. And as a ranger explained, it gives people an entirely new way of "experiencing the earth… People are so disconnected from the planet to begin with, and this is one way of bringing that connection back."

Take a hike: Finally, if you're just trying to get away from it all and don't have a lot of time or resources, consider hiking. The Western parks are wrinkled with intriguing canyons and mountains and scatter-shot with lakes, rivers, meadows and forests. There are easy trails, difficult trails and, in some areas, no trails at all. All it takes to get started are a few commonsense essentials like a sturdy pair of shoes, the proper clothing, food, water and a decent map. Hiking can be done by just about anyone at any pace. And like the more radical sports, it's as much mental as physical. The sound of the trail crunching underfoot slows the mind, speeds the heart and clears away distractions so that you can really focus on the world around you.

"The tendency nowadays to wander in wilderness is delightful to see," wrote John Muir, who was not only a great naturalist and writer but a great hiker as well. He'd take to the Sierra Nevada for days with little more than a few biscuits and a blanket. Hiking took him to the place where his inspiration was born. There is peace to be found, he wrote, in "sauntering in rosiny pinewoods or in gentian meadows… jumping from rock to rock, feeling the life of them, learning the songs of them, panting in whole-souled exercise, and rejoicing in deep, long-drawn breaths of pure wildness."

Since those words were written, millions have come to the national parks to find their own inspiration and, as Muir envisioned, to renew themselves with the enchanting power of nature.

Left and **right**, camping and climbing in the Southwest's red-rock country.

For more than 75 years, national park rangers have been identified with a single article of clothing and a challenging mission. Like English Bobbies or Canadian Mounties, a distinctive *chapeau* sets them apart. The Smokey Bear hat is a holdover from the 19th century when the United States Cavalry patrolled Yellowstone and the life-style of park rangers was modeled after the military.

Rangers then were almost always men who lived in crude barracks, ate communal meals, were frequently transferred from post to post, and kept long working days that began before the crack of dawn and ended after sundown. "Rangers loved their jobs and put their commitment to the resource – whether it was natural or cultural – before everything else," says Rick Gale, a 36-year veteran of the agency, who is based in Boise, Idaho. "You weren't in it for the money. If you worked for the National Park Service you understood that you were no longer your own master and accepted it. You gave your life to the park and in return you always had a piece of it with you in your heart."

Esprit de corps: Gale's introduction to national parks began as it did with many of his 21,000 colleagues – as a "Park Service brat." He is a product of the esprit de corps that makes the National Park Service one of the most distinguished branches of public service. He was born near Virginia's Colonial National Historic Park in 1936 to a father who spent his career as a park ranger. By the time he graduated from high school, the young Rick Gale had already lived in Wyoming's Grand Teton, Arizona's Petrified Forest and New Mexico's Carlsbad Caverns.

And the legacy continues. Gale's eldest daughter works for the park police in San Francisco and her husband for Point Reyes National Seashore. Gale's middle daughter and son-in-law are a procurement clerk and chief ranger, respectively, at Idaho's Nez Perce National Historic Park; and his youngest daughter has worked as a backcountry ranger in the Grand Canyon.

The ranger romance: Western park rangers in particular cut a romantic figure in the public eye. Clad in their wide-brimmed hats, gray service shirts and forest-green pants, the park ranger is an icon of the wilderness. "My favorite ranger story involves a legendary veteran ranger who was called on the radio by one of his subordinates," writes author Paul Schullery. "The younger ranger thought he needed advice on some sticky law

enforcement situation he was embroiled in. The senior ranger's advice was simple and complete: just remember who you are, and what you stand for."

Schullery says the ranger mystique continues to this day. "When you arrive at a [park entrance] gate," he notes, "you have every right to expect you will be greeted by one of these singular figures, and usually you are. If he or she is doing good work, the greeting will be friendly, and the information will be accurate. If he or she is a really good ranger, the information will be given with pride."

Some of the more famous park rangers over the years include a former president,

Preceding pages: park rangers gently guide an evacuation litter over the edge of a bluff. **Left,** a ranger posts an avalance warning sign in Yellowstone National Park. **Right,** a welcoming smile at Denali National Park.

Gerald R. Ford, and the late environmental writer Edward Abbey, who spent several summers at a fire lookout tower. In 1916, the inaugural year of the Parks Service, agency director Stephen Mather summarized the varied demands on a ranger: "They are a fine, earnest, intelligent, and public-spirited body of men, the rangers," he said. "Though small in number, their influence is large. Many and long are the duties heaped upon their shoulders. If a trail is to be blazed, it is 'send a ranger.' If an animal is floundering in the snow, a ranger is sent to pull him out; if a bear is in the hotel, if a fire threatens a forest, if someone is to be saved, it is 'send a ranger.'"

Over the past few decades, however, the

Park Service has undergone a period of modernization – in its responsibilities, demography, infrastructure and, to some extent, its values. The world is infinitely more complex than in the halcyon days when park rangers in Yellowstone or Yosemite patrolled the backcountry on horseback looking for poachers. Most wildland parks are no longer remote sanctuaries far removed from bustling cities. Urban areas have encroached upon the doorsteps of many parks. Despite manpower shortages and budget cuts, today's rangers are called on to confront drug dealers, thieves and well-armed poachers; they carry out search-and-rescue missions, direct traffic, fight fires, manage wildlife, conduct research, and cope with the needs of more than 375 million visitors.

The Park Service's oldest ranger, a living legend named Carl Sharsmith, has spent 60 of his 90 summers as a seasonal ranger-interpreter at Yosemite. Sharsmith says that what he savors most about the experience is the camaraderie of the old days "when everybody knew one another."

One profound change in the Park Service since Sharsmith's salad days is the inclusion of women and minorities. The first woman to be a permanent ranger was Herma Baggley, who came to Yellowstone in 1927, which was 55 years after the creation of the park. Today, about one-third of the Park Service's employees are women, one-tenth African-American and one-twentieth Hispanic.

The internal landscape: There's no way to describe the typical ranger. Each one is different, bound only by a passion for the job. The best way to become acquainted with a ranger is to approach one and chat either at a park visitor center or at one of the enormously popular camp-fire talks or ranger walks delivered daily at most parks.

"Ranger walks can set you on the high road to adventure as well as give you new insights into the world of animals," writes Art Miller, who went on ranger walks throughout Glacier National Park and later chronicled his experience in *The Park Ranger Guide to Wildlife*. "Our ranger-guide was Mike Wacker, a sturdily-built outdoorsman and a member of the Blackfeet Indian tribe. Mike was working as a ranger for the summer, and then planned to return to the University of Wisconsin to complete his bachelor's degree in geology." In fact, most rangers have at least an undergraduate degree, and about a third have a master's degree or Ph.D.

The agency has also tried to ensure that rangers reflect the ethnic ties of an area. At Badlands National Park, Canyon de Chelly National Monument and Little Bighorn National Battlefield, for example, Native American rangers are employed to interpret the history of the area from their perspective; at the Booker T. Washington National Monument, black rangers man the information desks and develop exhibits on Washington's role in African-American culture. At Coronado National Memorial near the Mexican border, interpreters explain the history of the trail to Spanish-speaking visitors. Much has been accomplished, but officials confess that still more needs to be done to bring equality to the system.

In 1983, sociologist Darryll Johnson and three colleagues conducted an in-depth survey in order to gain insight into the modern ranger. While an overwhelming majority of rangers professed dedication to the goals and principles of the Park Service, they cited formidable challenges such as low wages, poor housing conditions and an antiquated system of relocation. Generally speaking, they are less willing to accept the rigid military type of lifestyle that was standard during the agency's early years. For example, only about

changes in morale. There's a general dissatisfaction in the way things are going because each year we are having to do more with less. It stems from the frustration of knowing that you need to do more to protect the resource yet you don't have the money or field resources or manpower to get the job done. And yet, you won't find a prouder group of people in government. They will try to get the job done in any way they can."

In the end, what distinguishes park rangers is a personal commitment to the parks themselves. It's something that former rangers Kim and Melanie Heacox (who met as rangers at Glacier Bay Park and married in 1986) describe as an "internal landscape – a love of

half said they approved of a policy that causes most rangers to be transferred several times over the course of their careers.

"Younger people coming into the service have different values than the dinosaurs now at the tail end of our careers," Gale says. "I'm not sure the agency or anybody else has kept up with them. I think some of the changes are manifested in the unwillingness to sacrifice family for the job. We are also seeing some

Left, Herma Baggley, the first permanent female ranger at Yellowstone, 1929. **Above**, a fallen sequoia dwarfs members of the Sixth Cavalry in Yosemite's Mariposa Grove of Big Trees, 1899.

the land that runs so deep it's almost Thoreauvian." There are problems, Kim says, but there are also benefits, such as a sense of community among staff members and "the sheer magic of being in the parks."

"The Park Service becomes your second family," Heacox says. "As a young person, you're put into an environment where everybody shares the same values." In the best cases, it becomes a place where people "develop a special bond with each other."

There's a special bond with the land, too, that grows stronger every time "you put on a backpack, get away from it all, and remind yourself why you're there."

Inner Gorge

Tonto Platform

Isis Temple

Cheops Pyramid

Plateau Point

Colorado River

It's an American tradition. Load the kids and camping gear into the car and take off for the national parks.

There are more than 350 sites in the national park system. Only about 100 are officially designated national parks, although the others – national monuments, memorials, recreation areas, historic sites and the like – tend to be called "parks," too. Together they welcome nearly 400 million visitors every year, and the number keeps growing. And the visitors are not all Americans. Surveys at some parks indicate that as many as 15–30 percent are foreign tourists. People from every continent and from every walk of life are drawn to the splendor of America's parklands. Whether it's Yosemite Valley or the Statue of Liberty, the Alaskan wilderness or a Civil War battlefield, the National Parks Service is dedicated to preserving America's natural and cultural heritage and making it accessible to the people of the world.

In the West, the park system is dominated by large wilderness areas. These are landscapes of mythic proportions – the Rocky Mountains, the Badlands, the Grand Canyon, Yellowstone, Yosemite, Death Valley – places of such power and resonance that they have become icons of American wilderness.

For some people, just gazing at these awesome panoramas is satisfying enough. Indeed, most visitors never venture more than a few steps from their cars. They tour the scenic drives, stop at pullouts and overlooks, and perhaps explore a few unpaved backcountry roads. But for more ambitious travelers, those who want a close-up look at the parks' natural wonders or, even more challenging, a genuine wilderness experience, the national parks offer a variety of options.

In addition to a schedule of campfire talks and ranger-led tours, many sites have relatively short, easy, interpretive trails that acquaint visitors with elements of the park's natural and cultural history. More adventurous visitors can strike out on a network of well-maintained trails for day hikes of various lengths and difficulty. Backpackers can explore the parks for several days or even weeks, taking advantage of backcountry campsites.

And that's just the beginning. There are more ways to experience the parks than there are parks to experience. How about horseback riding in the badlands of Theodore Roosevelt National Park? Mule-packing in the Grand Canyon? Rafting the Rio Grande through Big Bend? Skiing beneath 2,000-year-old sequoias in Kings Canyon? Biking the red-rock country of southern Utah? Scaling columns of hardened magma at Devils Tower? Or squirming through subterranean passages at Carlsbad Caverns?

The parks are an American treasure unrivaled elsewhere in the world. Use them. Cherish them. And protect them.

Preceding pages: hiking Utah's canyonlands. **Left**, understanding the Grand Canyon.

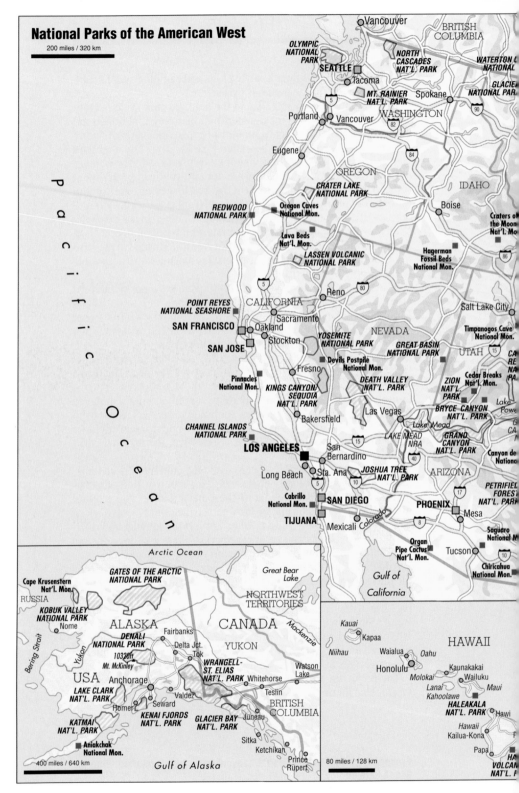

National Parks of the American West

200 miles / 320 km

Vancouver

BRITISH COLUMBIA

OLYMPIC NATIONAL PARK

NORTH CASCADES NAT'L. PARK

WATERTON L. NATIONAL

SEATTLE

Tacoma

Spokane

GLACIE NATIONAL PAR.

MT. RAINIER NAT'L. PARK

Portland

Vancouver

WASHINGTON

Eugene

OREGON

IDAHO

CRATER LAKE NATIONAL PARK

Boise

REDWOOD NATIONAL PARK

Oregon Caves National Mon.

Craters of the Moon Nat'l. Mo.

Lava Beds Nat'l. Mon.

LASSEN VOLCANIC NATIONAL PARK

Hagerman Fossil Beds National Mon.

Pacific

Reno

Salt Lake City

POINT REYES NATIONAL SEASHORE

CALIFORNIA

Sacramento

NEVADA

Timpanogos Cave National Mon.

SAN FRANCISCO

Oakland

Stockton

YOSEMITE NATIONAL PARK

GREAT BASIN NATIONAL PARK

UTAH

SAN JOSE

Devils Postpile National Mon.

Fresno

DEATH VALLEY NAT'L. PARK

ZION NAT'L. PARK

Cedar Breaks Nat'l. Mon.

CA RE NA PA.

Pinnacles National Mon.

KINGS CANYON/ SEQUOIA NAT'L. PARK

BRYCE CANYON NAT'L. PARK

Lake Powe

Bakersfield

Las Vegas

Lake Mead

GRAND CANYON NAT'L. PARK

G CA

CHANNEL ISLANDS NATIONAL PARK

LAKE MEAD NRA

Canyon de Nationa

LOS ANGELES

San Bernardino

ARIZONA

Ocean

Long Beach

Sta. Ana

JOSHUA TREE NAT'L. PARK

PETRIFIEL FORES NAT'L. PARK

Cabrillo National Mon.

SAN DIEGO

PHOENIX

Mesa

17

TIJUANA

Mexicali

Colorado

8

TUCSON

Saguaro National M

Arctic Ocean

Great Bear Lake

Gulf of California

Chiricahua National Mon.

Cape Krusenstern Nat'l. Mon.

GATES OF THE ARCTIC NATIONAL PARK

NORTHWEST TERRITORIES

RUSSIA

KOBUK VALLEY NATIONAL PARK

Nome

ALASKA

DENALI NATIONAL PARK

Fairbanks

CANADA

YUKON

Mackenzie

Kauai

Kapaa

HAWAII

Niihau

Waialua

Oahu

10320ft. Mt. McKinley

Delta Jct.

Tok

Honolulu

Kaunakakai

Bering Strait

USA

Anchorage

WRANGELL- ST. ELIAS NAT'L. PARK

Whitehorse

Watson Lake

Molokai

Wailuku

Lanai

Maui

Yukon

LAKE CLARK NAT'L. PARK

Valdez

Teslin

Kahoolawe

Homer

Seward

BRITISH COLUMBIA

HALEAKALA NAT'L. PARK

Hawi

KATMAI NAT'L. PARK

KENAI FJORDS NAT'L. PARK

GLACIER BAY NAT'L. PARK

Juneau

Hawaii

Kailua-Kona

Aniakchak National Mon.

Sitka

Ketchikan

Papa

HA VOLCAN NAT'L.

400 miles / 640 km

Gulf of Alaska

Prince Rupert

80 miles / 128 km

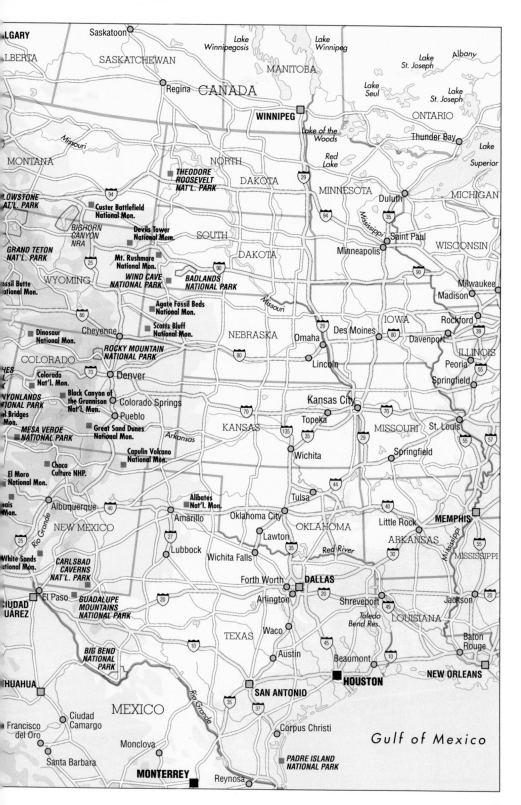

LGARY
Saskatoon
LBERTA
SASKATCHEWAN
Regina
CANADA
MANITOBA

Lake Winnipegosis
Lake Winnipeg
Lake St. Joseph
Albany

WINNIPEG
ONTARIO

Lake of the Woods
Thunder Bay
Lake Superior

Lake Seul
Lake St. Joseph

MONTANA
Missouri

NORTH DAKOTA

THEODORE ROOSEVELT NAT'L. PARK

Red Lake

MINNESOTA
Duluth
MICHIGAN

29
94

OWSTONE AT'L. PARK

Custer Battlefield National Mon.

Mississippi
Saint Paul
WISCONSIN

BIGHORN CANYON NRA

Devils Tower National Mem.

SOUTH DAKOTA

Minneapolis
35

GRAND TETON NAT'L. PARK

Mt. Rushmore National Mon.
25

WIND CAVE NATIONAL PARK
90

BADLANDS NATIONAL PARK
90

Milwaukee
Madison

ossil Butte ational Mon.

WYOMING
80

Agate Fossil Beds National Mon.

Missouri

IOWA
Rockford
39

Dinosaur National Mon.

Scotts Bluff National Mon.

NEBRASKA
29
Des Moines
80
Davenport

ILLINOIS

Cheyenne

ROCKY MOUNTAIN NATIONAL PARK

Omaha
Peoria
55

COLORADO
Colorado Nat'l. Mon.
70
Denver

80
Lincoln

Springfield

HES L

Black Canyon of the Grunnison Nat'l. Mon.
Colorado Springs

KANSAS
Kansas City
70
St. Louis

NYONLANDS TIONAL PARK
l Bridges Mon.

Pueblo

Topeka
135
35

MISSOURI
57
55

MESA VERDE NATIONAL PARK

Great Sand Dunes National Mon.

Arkansas

Wichita
Springfield

El Moro National Mon.

Capulin Volcano National Mon.

44

Chaco Culture NHP.

Tulsa

Alibates Nat'l. Mon.

ais Mon.
Albuquerque
40
Amarillo

Oklahoma City
OKLAHOMA
40
Little Rock
MEMPHIS

NEW MEXICO

27
Lawton

ARKANSAS
Mississippi
55
MISSISSIPPI

25
Rio Grande
Lubbock

Wichita Falls
35
Red River

30

White Sands ational Mon.

CARLSBAD CAVERNS NAT'L. PARK

Forth Worth
DALLAS
20
Jackson
20

IUDAD UAREZ
El Paso

GUADALUPE MOUNTAINS NATIONAL PARK
20
Arlington
Shreveport
49
LOUISIANA

HUAHUA

BIG BEND NATIONAL PARK

TEXAS
Waco
10
Austin
45
Beaumont
10
Baton Rouge

Toledo Bend Res.

HOUSTON
NEW ORLEANS

MEXICO
Rio Grande
SAN ANTONIO
35
37

Francisco del Oro
Ciudad Camargo

Corpus Christi

Gulf of Mexico

Monclova

Santa Barbara

MONTERREY
Reynosa

PADRE ISLAND NATIONAL PARK

California and Pacific Islands

50 miles / 80 km

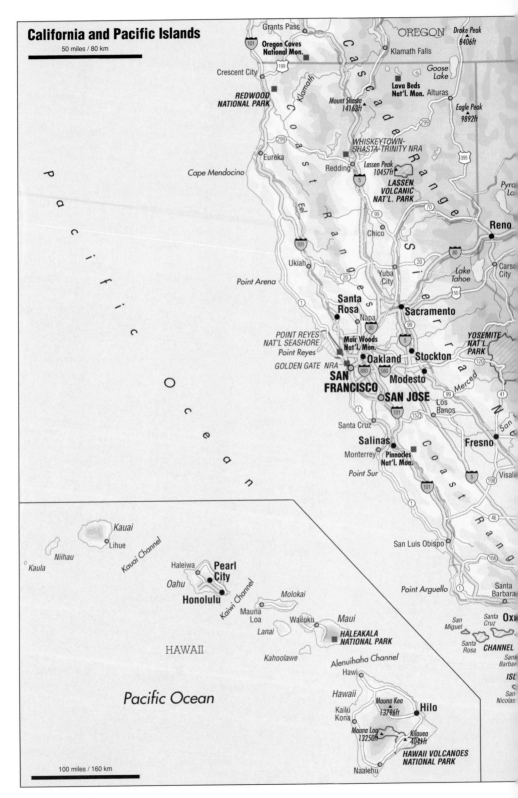

OREGON

Grants Pass
Oregon Caves National Mon.
Klamath Falls
Drake Peak 8406ft

Crescent City
Goose Lake

Lava Beds Nat'l. Mon.
Alturas

REDWOOD NATIONAL PARK
Mount Shasta 14163ft
Eagle Peak 9892ft

Eureka
Cape Mendocino
WHISKEYTOWN-SHASTA-TRINITY NRA
Redding
Lassen Peak 10457ft
LASSEN VOLCANIC NAT'L. PARK

Chico
Reno

Ukiah
Yuba City
Lake Tahoe
Carson City

Point Arena
Santa Rosa
Sacramento
Pyra Lo

POINT REYES NAT'L SEASHORE
Point Reyes
Napa
Muir Woods Nat'l. Mon.
GOLDEN GATE NRA
Oakland
Stockton
YOSEMITE NAT'L. PARK

SAN FRANCISCO
Modesto
SAN JOSE
Los Banos

Santa Cruz
Merced

Salinas
Monterrey
Pinnacles Nat'l. Mon.
Fresno

Point Sur
Visali

San Luis Obispo

Point Arguello
Santa Barbara

HAWAII

Kauai
Lihue
Niihau
Kaula
Kauai Channel

Haleiwa
Pearl City
Oahu
Honolulu
Kaiwi Channel

Molokai
Wailuku
Maui

Mauna Loa
Lanai
Kahoolawe

San Miguel

Santa Cruz

Santa Rosa

HALEAKALA NATIONAL PARK

CHANNEL

San Barbar

ISL

Alenuihaha Channel
Hawi

Hawaii

San Nicolas

Kailua Kona
Mauna Kea 13796ft
Hilo

Pacific Ocean

Mauna Loa 13250ft
Kilauea 4011ft

HAWAII VOLCANOES NATIONAL PARK

Naalehu

100 miles / 160 km

Pacific Ocean

CALIFORNIA AND PACIFIC ISLANDS

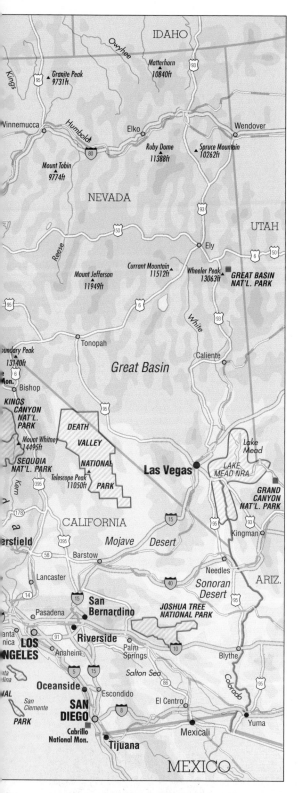

California is graced with snowcapped mountains and torrid deserts, ancient forests and desert islands, with sun-baked playas and rain-drenched coasts, and with the highest and lowest points in the contiguous United States.

The crown jewel is Yosemite National Park, a magical tableau of granite domes, leaping water, wildflower meadows and old-growth forests that attracts over 4 million visitors every year. You'll find a less-traveled pocket of the Sierra among the sheer canyons of Sequoia and Kings Canyon National Parks, where backpackers can explore 800 miles (1,287 km) of trails in a rugged wilderness best known by black bears and mule deer. All three parks are home to the mighty sequoias, the largest living things on the planet.

A mountain refuge of a different sort awaits at Lassen Volcanic National Park. Among dense stands of mountain hemlock, Douglas fir, and lodgepole pine, Lassen Peak is surrounded by bubbling mudpots and steaming fumaroles – evidence of its explosive past.

The giant sequoia's cousin, the coast redwood, dominates Redwood National Park, hugging the surf-pounded shore, where one can spot seals, sea lions, sea otters and migrating gray whales.

Far to the south, the Channel Islands are a marine life sanctuary, too. Only 7 miles (11 km) from the mainland, the tiny, wind-tossed archipelago is a vital outpost for sea mammals, seabirds and several native land animals.

Inland, three parks protect the fragile plant and animal communities of the California Desert, a land of unrelenting heat and aridity that sustains a surprising variety of life.

In far-off Hawaii, rare native plants and animals are protected at Haleakala and Hawaii Volcanoes, where the mighty Kilauea pumps fiery lava into the sea.

And American Samoa is a world of turquoise lagoons, sheer volcanic ridges, lush rain forests and pristine coral reefs exploding with life.

YOSEMITE

The essence of Yosemite is rock. Everywhere, granite creates a rough gray canvas upon which are painted brilliant jade forests, sparkling silver lakes and streams, and multihued flowers, leaves and grasses. Rock dominates. Towering cliffs, solitary spires, subtle domes, jumbled piles of boulders, and thin, undulating ridges make up a landscape sculpted over the ages by ice, water and wind. Together, ubiquitous granite with various metamorphic and volcanic rocks form what geologist King Huber calls "Yosemite's foundation."

Water runs on this rock. Two major rivers, the Merced and the Tuolumne, take life in Yosemite, then course resolutely across its breadth. Along their route, they create rapids, pools and several of the free-leaping waterfalls for which the park is famed. Glaciers gouged out hundreds of high country lakes, and in spring, scores of minor tributaries collect melting snow and send it downhill in tendrils of icy water, producing seasonal cascades and ephemeral falls.

This remarkable terrain is vitalized by an abundance of living creatures, from the world's largest trees to diminutive pocket gophers to microscopic fungi to several endangered birds, mammals and plants. An original commissioner for the park, Frederick Law Olmsted, writing in 1865, was among the first to recognize in Yosemite "the value of the district... as a museum of natural science and the danger, indeed the certainty, that without care many of the species of plants now flourishing upon it will be lost and many interesting objects be defaced or obscured if not destroyed." Olmsted was prescient. Yosemite serves as an environmental test station, gauging the health of the natural world. And what the gauge has been showing lately is that the park is vulnerable to a number of external threats, including air pollution, acid rain and development at its doorstep.

Despite its wealth of scenic and natural wonders, it is now the human presence that overshadows all else in Yosemite. Euro-Americans did not begin visiting the park in meaningful numbers until late in the 19th century; in 1899 only 4,500 "tourists" were counted in Yosemite. Now about 4 million visit the park each year. This onslaught has at times resulted in congestion, resource damage and crowding, and has brought into urgent focus the conflict between the use and protection of this spectacular national treasure.

The simple years: This crush of humans is, indeed, new to Yosemite. For hundreds of years it supported a modest native population that enjoyed a relatively simple lifestyle. Anthropologists believe that, about 3,500 years ago, Native Americans, characterized as Southern Miwok, first occupied the region. Because they were "prehistoric," we know little about them. At the same time, archaeological studies show that few cultural changes occurred in the Yosemite Miwok lifestyle during the 600 years before outsiders arrived.

Few of the Yosemite Miwoks, or

Preceding pages: mesquite tree skeleton. *Left,* El Capitan reflected in Merced River. *Right,* black bear cub.

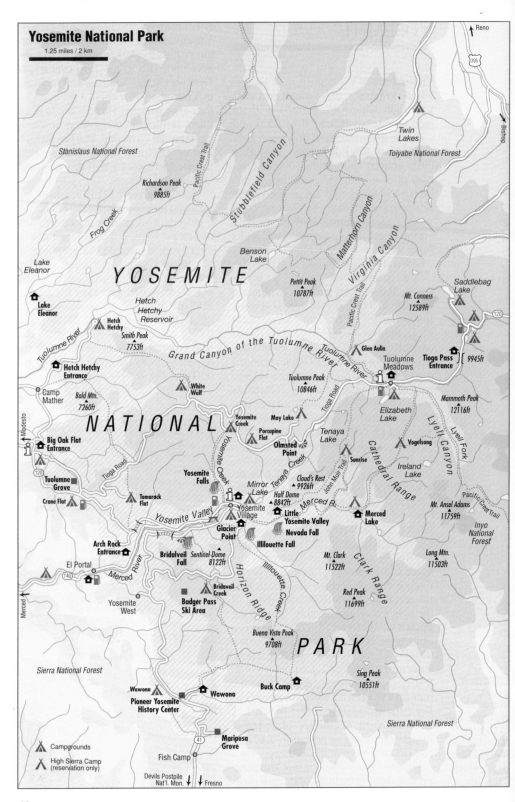

Yosemite National Park

1.25 miles / 2 km

↑ Reno

395

Stanislaus National Forest

Richardson Peak
9885ft

Pacific Crest Trail

Stubblefield Canyon

Twin
Lakes

Toiyabe National Forest

Bishop →

Matterhorn Canyon

Virginia Canyon

Lake
Eleanor

Y O S E M I T E

Benson
Lake

Pettit Peak
10787ft

Pacific Crest Trail

Mt. Conness
12589ft

Saddlebag
Lake

Lake
Eleanor

Hetch
Hetchy
Reservoir

Hetch Hetchy

Smith Peak
7753ft

Tuolumne River

Grand Canyon of the Tuolumne River

Tuolumne River

Glen Aulin

Tuolumne
Meadows

Tioga Pass
Entrance 9945ft

120

Hetch Hetchy
Entrance

Camp
Mather

Bald Mtn.
7260ft

N A T I O N A L

White
Wolf

Tuolumne Peak
10846ft

Tioga Road

Elizabeth
Lake

Mammoth Peak
12116ft

Modesto

Big Oak Flat
Entrance

Yosemite
Creek

May Lake

Lyell Fork

120

Tuolumne
Grove

Tioga Road

Porcupine
Flat

Olmsted
Point

Tenaya
Lake

Vogelsang

Lyell Canyon

Crane Flat

Tamarack
Flat

Yosemite
Falls

Mirror
Lake

Cloud's Rest
9926ft

Tenaya Creek

Sunrise

John Muir Trail

Cathedral Range

Ireland
Lake

Pacific Crest Trail

Yosemite Creek

Half Dome
8842ft

Merced R.

Mt. Ansel Adams
11759ft

Inyo
National
Forest

Yosemite Valley

Yosemite
Village

Little
Yosemite Valley

Merced
Lake

Arch Rock
Entrance

Glacier
Point

Nevada Fall

El Portal

140

Bridalveil
Fall

Sentinel Dome
8122ft

Illilouette Fall

Mt. Clark
11522ft

Clark Range

Long Mtn.
11503ft

Merced River

Bridalveil
Creek

Horizon Ridge

Illilouette Creek

Red Peak
11699ft

Merced

Yosemite
West

Badger Pass
Ski Area

Buena Vista Peak
9708ft

P A R K

Sierra National Forest

Wawona

Pioneer Yosemite
History Center

Wawona

Buck Camp

Sing Peak
10551ft

Sierra National Forest

▲ Campgrounds

⋏ High Sierra Camp
(reservation only)

41

Mariposa
Grove

Fish Camp

Devils Postpile
Nat'l. Mon. ↓ ↓ Fresno

Ahwahneechees, were full-time residents of the park region. A number of permanent villages were established in Yosemite Valley, but most of the inhabitants moved down to the western foothills in winter. Yosemite's high country was visited primarily during the summer for hunting and trading with eastern neighbors. The Ahwahneechees exchanged acorns, arrows, manzanita berries and baskets for obsidian, salt, insect larvae (a popular food), pinyon pine nuts and more.

The Gold Rush in 1849 shattered the Ahwahneechees' world. Miners flooded into the foothills. The Ahwahneechees raided a few mining camps but didn't have much of a chance against the well-armed intruders. In 1851, a group of volunteers known as the Mariposa Battalion was formed to subdue the Indian "marauders." While pursuing the Indians into their mountain stronghold, they became the first white men to set foot in Yosemite Valley.

Lafayette Bunnell, a member of the Battalion, wrote glowingly of his first glimpse of the place. "None but those who have visited this most wonderful valley can even imagine the feelings with which I looked upon the view that was there presented… a peculiar exalted sensation seemed to fill my whole being, and I found my eyes in tears with emotion." Those who followed in his footsteps had similarly passionate reactions, and before long the wonders of Yosemite were being proclaimed throughout the world.

The first park: Yosemite's attractions were quickly recognized to have enormous commercial potential. Fortunately, the profit-driven schemes of early settlers and developers never reached full realization thanks to the efforts of several conservation-minded individuals. Acting to safeguard Yosemite Valley and the nearby Mariposa Grove of Big Trees, they convinced Congress to establish the Yosemite Grant in 1864. Although not designating a national park as such, the act created a reserve (to be administered by the state of California) that was the first federally protected natural area in the world.

In the ensuing years, Yosemite's fame grew, along with a public awareness that the greater region surrounding the valley was likewise an invaluable scenic and natural resource which deserved to have governmental protection. Thanks largely to the efforts of conservationist John Muir and his colleagues, Yosemite National Park, encompassing an area greater than 1,200 sq. miles (1,931 km), was created in 1890. In 1906, the larger national park and the state grant were combined to form the park that we know today.

Yosemite has come a long way from its early, peaceful days. In a world of endless urbanization, freeways and shopping malls, it is an inspiring, liberating, almost irresistible natural place. Its popularity has spawned both special problems and a devoted constituency. The park is a mecca for rock climbers, photographers, hang gliders, fishermen, artists, backpackers, recreational vehicle owners, mountain bikers, shoppers, birders, horseback riders, rafters and others. And every visitor has a different

A shaft of light illuminates Horsetail Fall.

expectation about how Yosemite should be used and managed.

The park is also popular because it provides security and comfort. Yosemite is the most revisited park in the United States, probably because, in our world of constant flux and tension, it is a fixed point of unchanging, rock-solid beauty. Wallace Stegner wrote, "The massive shapes that time, weather, and ice have carved out of the walls are so grandly simple, the broad flat forested meadow-breasted river-veined valley is so gentle, that we are invited in, not shut out. We are never overpowered. I know of no natural scenery on so grand a scale that makes a watcher feel at once so reverent and so safe."

Heart of the Sierra: Yosemite National Park is mostly wilderness, accessible only on foot. The portion of the park that can be visited by automobiles can be divided into three sections: **Yosemite Valley**; the area south of Yosemite Valley which includes **Wawona** and the **Mariposa Grove of Big Trees**; and the area north of Yosemite Valley which

encompasses **Tioga Road** and **Tuolumne Meadows**.

Yosemite Valley, only 7 sq. miles (18 sq. km) and a tiny fraction of the park's whole, offers more startlingly beautiful scenery than perhaps anywhere else in the world. An array of breathtaking waterfalls, sheer granite cliffs, imposing rock formations and the sinuous Merced River come together in sheer perfection. For most, the valley is the main attraction of the park; 80 percent of visitors travel to Yosemite Valley at some point in their trip.

There are three routes into the valley, which is the perfect place to begin a first visit to the park: from the west, take Highway 140 through Mariposa; from the northwest, take Highway 120 through Groveland; and from the south, take Highway 41 through Fish Camp. All traffic is routed onto a 12-mile (19-km) one-way loop which circles Yosemite Valley.

As you enter the valley, a panorama of unparalleled beauty unfolds. To the south, lacy **Bridalveil Fall** drops 620 ft (190 m) from a "hanging valley." Bridalveil's gentle charm is almost overpowered by the granite bulk of **El Capitan** at the valley's opposite side. "El Cap," one of the world's largest rock monoliths, is so steep that its only denizens are feathered (peregrine falcons, swifts and other avians) or fearless (rugged climbers who often spend seven days or more scaling the stone face). In spring, watch for wispy **Horsetail Fall** on El Capitan's eastern shoulder. Past Bridalveil, the almost architectural formations of **Cathedral Rocks** and **Spires** grace the south wall. Beyond El Capitan rises a trio of triangular rock shapes, one atop the next, known as the **Three Brothers**. The tallest of the group, **Eagle Peak**, offers one of the best views from the valley's north rim. Across the valley, **Sentinel Rock**, a four-sided granite column, stands guard over this mountain paradise. When the road finally permits a clear view to the north, you'll marvel at inimitable **Yosemite Falls** as its white water plunges nearly a half-mile (1 km) in three sections. The falls are most spec- **Dragonfly.**

tacular during the spring runoff, but are often little more than a trickle by late summer. (The famous journalist Horace Greeley, glimpsing the bare trickle one autumn, cried "humbug!" and went away unimpressed.)

As the road progresses eastward, picnicking is available at **Cathedral Beach** and **Sentinel Beach**, both under the trees on the sandy banks of the Merced River, and at other locations along the way. There are also plenty of pullouts for serious sightseeing, wandering along the base of dizzying cliffs, or just sitting on a rock to soak in the scene.

Yosemite Valley's developed area, where campgrounds, lodges, restaurants and stores are to be found, is located at its eastern end. The **Valley Visitor Center** offers a slide show, information services, exhibits, a bookstore and more. Most ranger-led interpretive programs originate here, and next door there's the **Indian Cultural Museum**, **Fine Arts Gallery** and **Indian Garden**.

To explore further in Yosemite Valley's eastern end, use of the free

Lupine leaves near Cascade Falls.

Yosemite Shuttle Bus is recommended. The buses operate year-round, servicing 19 different stops, and visit many locations that are off-limits to private automobiles. The shuttle bus can be boarded in front of the visitor center, or at campgrounds, hotels and other convenient spots. On the bus route, **Happy Isles Nature Center** (stop number 16) offers something for the whole family. Located near the banks of the **Merced River**, the nature center is designed for kids, and offers many exhibits and programs for them, including a Junior Ranger program. Happy Isles is also the trailhead for the hike to **Vernal** and **Nevada Falls**. In spring, the walk up the **Mist Trail** is a drenching experience; mist blown from Vernal Fall rains down on the daring hikers who attempt the trip. It's only 2 miles (3 km) to the top of Vernal and about twice that distance to the overlook of Nevada Fall.

Among other notable locations on the shuttle bus route are Mirror Lake, the Ahwahnee Hotel and Lower Yosemite Fall. From shuttle stop 17, a mile-long

walk leads to **Mirror Lake** (once a bona fide lake, now a wide spot in the stream), the still surface of which reflects the imposing face of **Half Dome**, which sits in silent repose high above. There's more hiking up **Tenaya Canyon** (a 3-mile/5-km loop up one side of Tenaya Creek and down the other) and shallow pools in the creek – useful for cooling off.

The shuttle also stops at the classic **Ahwahnee Hotel**, a handsome structure in the rustic style that provides elegant accommodations in this remote, mountain setting. The grand lounge, decorated in a Native American motif and complete with a walk-in, two-sided fireplace, is worth a visit, and a meal taken under the vaulted ceiling and chandeliers in the dining room will long be remembered.

No one should pass up the walk to **Lower Yosemite Fall**. Climb off the shuttle bus at stop number 7 and make the easy stroll to the bridge at the base of the lower fall. It's particularly impressive in spring when the volume of water

is at its greatest. When there's a full moon, a nighttime excursion to this vantage point is utterly enchanting. It's one of the few places in the world where you can experience a prismatic phenomenon known as a "moon-bow" which appears in the watery spray.

For more sightseeing, the park concessionaire offers an open-air tour of the valley throughout the day. The trams leave from most lodging units; there's a transportation desk in **Yosemite Village** for information and tickets. For those more athletically inclined, bicycles may be rented at **Curry Village** or **Yosemite Lodge** to explore the valley's 9 miles (14 km) of biking trails.

South of the valley: The Wawona area with its Mariposa Grove of Giant Sequoias is a logical next stop. The route heads south over the **Wawona Road** (Highway 41), providing access to two key attractions along the way. About 2 miles (3 km) out of the valley, you'll reach **Tunnel View**, a glorious panorama of granite cliffs, thundering waterfalls and rock monoliths. It is easily the most photographed view in the park.

Farther south, the road takes a side route to **Glacier Point**, a lookout on the rim of Yosemite Valley affording a remarkable perspective on the valley floor, the north wall, Tenaya Canyon, Half Dome and the High Sierra stretching to the north and east. The trip is about 30 miles (48 km) off the main route but well worth the detour. Besides the view, there are geologic exhibits, ranger talks, a snack bar and gift shop. The moderate 1-mile (1½-km) hike from Glacier Point to nearby **Sentinel Dome** is recommended for those desiring a 360° view from the roof of the south rim. The wildflowers can be dazzling in spring and summer, and the top of the dome offers a great vantage point for watching the sun rise or set.

The meadow known as Wawona is historically rich and rife with recreational opportunities. Originally a stagecoach stop on the route to Yosemite Valley, Wawona is home to the oldest resort-hotel in California. The **Wawona Hotel** is a rambling, whitewashed series of buildings first developed in 1879. It

Moonrise over Yosemite's granite cliffs.

has undergone a thorough restoration, and its rooms are nicely appointed, comfortable and modern. Hotel amenities include an inviting dining room, old-time piano music in the lounge, a swimming tank and a nine-hole golf course (where mule deer often graze). For a perfect getaway, relax and watch the world go by from the hotel's vine-clad, covered porches.

The park's past is also the theme of Wawona's **Pioneer Yosemite History Center**. The center is a collection of significant old buildings that were moved from various locations in Yosemite. In summer, park rangers dressed in period costumes engage in "living history" demonstrations. When funding allows, there are stagecoach rides, a working blacksmith, a bookshop and other activities. A gas station, post office, grocery store and gift shop are near the center.

The biggest draw of Yosemite's south end is the world-famous **Mariposa Grove of Trees** – a stand of some 500 giant sequoias. About 7 miles (11 km)

from Wawona, the Mariposa Grove contains many trees more than 2,000 years old. The **Grizzly Giant** is renowned for its huge girth and gnarled grandeur. The famous **Wawona Tunnel Tree** stood here until it toppled under a heavy snow in 1969.

The trees in the Mariposa Grove can be reached by foot (it's a 2½-mile/4-km hike to the upper grove) or via the open-air tram tour provided by the concessionaire most of the year. Stops include the Grizzly Giant, the fallen Tunnel Tree and the **Mariposa Grove Museum**. Recommended walks in the grove include the moderate 1-mile (1½-km) trail to the promontory at **Wawona Point** and the easy 2-mile (3-km) return from the museum to the parking lot. You'll see frenetic chickarees (small squirrels) and a colorful array of wildflowers, including lupine, paintbrush, azaleas and the unusual red-spiked snow plant.

North of the valley: The opposite end of the park is home to Yosemite's fabled high country – a rugged landscape bi-

A windblown Jeffrey pine atop Sentinel Dome.

sected by the Tioga Road, which is usually open from Memorial Day to the end of September. From Yosemite Valley, follow the **Big Oak Flat Road** 13 miles (21 km) to **Crane Flat**, where you can pick up the Tioga Road for the stunning 35-mile (56-km) drive to **Tuolumne Meadows**.

From Crane Flat, it's about a mile walk down to **Tuolumne Grove**, the park's second largest stand of sequoias. If you don't have time to see the Mariposa Grove, this is a good place for an introduction to the colossal trees. Listen for the hoot of the great horned owl or the drumming of the blue grouse. Farther up the Tioga Road (about 14 miles/23 km from Crane Flat), **White Wolf** offers camping and overnight lodging amid lodgepole pines and a lovely spray of shooting stars, paintbrush and owl's clover.

The road winds ever higher, crossing Yosemite Creek and climbing to the glacier-scoured highlands near the head of Tenaya Canyon, where you'll find **Olmsted Point**, a large turnout over-

looking an enormous expanse of granite including **Cloud's Rest** and the back side of Half Dome. To the east, the view of **Tenaya Lake** and the peaks ringing Tuolumne Meadows is superb. This is a likely spot to come face to face with a fat, furry, yellow-bellied marmot. A rock-loving mammal, the marmot prefers higher elevations and has developed a taste for tourist handouts, which makes for a poor diet. Do the marmots a favor and let them find their own food.

The road passes Tenaya Lake (there's good picnicking and swimming at its northeast end) before finally dropping into Tuolumne Meadows proper. This "meadow in the sky" sits at 8,600 ft (2,621 m) in one of the most picturesque alpine regions in the world. At the height of the season, the huge meadow complex is vibrant with the blooms of wildflowers like mountain pride, elephant's heads, Lemmon's paintbrush and columbine. The hiking is tremendous, with abundant day-hike and backpacking opportunities in every direction, including a relaxing stroll along the Tuolumne River in **Lyell Canyon**, a moderate 4½-mile (7-km) round-trip to **Elizabeth Lake**, or a 1½-mile (2-km) scramble to the top of **Lembert Dome**. Other popular activities include fishing, camping and swimming. In summer, Tuolumne becomes the center of rock-climbing activities in the park. **Yosemite Mountaineering School** has a branch here as well as in Yosemite Valley and offers climbing lessons at all levels of experience. To the east, the road exits the park through **Tioga Pass**, at 9,945 ft (3,031 m), the highest paved road in the Sierra Nevada.

Those departing Yosemite through its eastern gate should consider visiting **Devils Postpile National Monument**, about 60 miles (96 km) southeast of the park. The monument is home to a remarkable geological formation made up of 40- to 60-ft- (12- to 18-m) high balsaltic columns formed about 100,000 years ago. There are trails to the postpile, to soda springs and to the imposing Rainbow Falls. Devils Postpile is usually closed by heavy snowfall between November and May.

Meditating on Half Dome in the distance.

JOHN MUIR

John Muir played host to two especially famous visitors during his long years in Yosemite Valley. The first, in May 1871, was Ralph Waldo Emerson, the placid philosopher of transcendentalism who ranks among the most renowned Americans of the 19th century. The other, more than three decades later, was Theodore Roosevelt, the dynamic young president of a new century who touted the virtues of "the strenuous life" and shared Muir's enthusiasm for the great outdoors.

Emerson arrived only two years after Muir first encountered, and had been smitten by, the Sierra Nevada. During their brief sojourn in the California valley, Emerson's 12-member party put up at Leidig's Hotel. The tall, lanky and bearded Muir screwed up his courage, visited the hotel (only 38 and still unknown, he was taken for a "local menial") and delivered a note inviting Emerson to join him in the wild.

Surprisingly, Emerson took up the offer. He rode out the next day to Muir's "hang-nest," a ramshackle cabin in the woods, and together the young Western naturalist and the 68-year-old sage of Concord, Massachusetts spent the day communing with the wonders of Creation. Muir was delighted by Emerson's receptivity for such phenomena as the venerable sequoias and he invited his guest – who had so famously extolled "Nature" in his written works – to abandon the dubious comforts of hotel accommodations and to camp out.

Emerson consented, but alas, his traveling companions, male and female, vetoed his decision, fearing that he might be too frail to withstand life in the raw. And so, on May 11, Emerson's party took their leave at Mariposa Grove, riding slowly away on horseback, the philosopher trailing behind somewhat wistfully as he waved to the naturalist. We're told that the prophetic Emerson said of Muir: "There is a young man from whom we shall hear."

It was a different story with Theodore Roosevelt. Thirty-two years later, Muir was a nationally prominent champion of the wilderness. President Roosevelt had, in fact, proposed the visit to him, and TR was, at 44, a robust type who liked nothing more than to venture into untamed country. Muir wrote afterwards that he "fairly fell in love with him."

Muir's rapport with the habitat impressed TR and fueled the president's enthusiasm for conservation measures. On their last morning together, the pair awoke under a dusting of snow. The "grandest day of my life," Roosevelt proclaimed when he rode back to join his party.

Ralph Waldo Emerson and John Muir corresponded but never met again. In 1893, the naturalist visited Concord and laid flowers at the graves of both Emerson and Henry David Thoreau, whom we now regard, like Muir, as an American patron saint of conservation.

Upon Muir's own death, on Christmas Eve in 1914, Roosevelt paid public tribute to his "dauntless soul" and said of him that he was "brimming over with friendliness and kindliness." Coincidentally, it was a teen-aged Teddy Roosevelt who, many years before, had rowed Emerson to shore during a chance encounter on a sailing trip along the Nile in Egypt. Thus did the lives of three famous Americans intersect. ∎

John Muir in Yosemite, 1907.

REDWOOD

"This generation has received, as a free inheritance from past ages, a hoard of forest wealth," wrote landscape architect Frederick Law Olmsted. "But if any of the future generations for thousands of years to come are to have the opportunity of enjoying the spiritual values obtainable from such primeval forests, this generation must exercise the economic self-restraint necessary for passing on some portion of this inheritance, instead of 'cashing-in' on it all."

Olmsted could very well have been talking about **Redwood National Park**, which was established in 1968 to protect northern California's redwood forest from logging. Here, one of the few remaining groves of coastal redwood, *Sequoia sempervirens*, grows just a few minutes' walk from the relentlessly pounding surf of the Pacific Ocean. The giants rise prodigiously, some to a height of more than 300 ft (91 m). Roosevelt elk graze in nearby prairies, seals and sea lions splash in the waves, salmon and trout swim in streams and rivers, and a wide range of bird life inhabit the shore and forest.

Fifty miles (80 km) long from north to south and totaling more than 110,000 acres (44,515 hectares), Redwood National Park incorporates three California state parks: **Prairie Creek**, **Del Norte Coast** and **Jedediah Smith.** The lumber business is still active in the area surrounding the national park, but gone are the days when old-growth forests were wantonly harvested.

From forest to sea: As you approach the parks along US Highway 101 from the south (by way of Eureka), your first stop should be the **Redwood Information Center**. Here you can learn just about anything you need to know about the park. Talk to the ranger on duty or examine the center's exhibits and maps. During the winter whale-watching season there is a telescope set up at the center for viewing the mammals' migratory activity offshore. Excellent trail maps are available at the center and include information on trails in both the national and state parks.

As you leave the information center and continue north along Highway 101, you'll catch your first glimpse of the "wilds" of Redwood. Impressive Roosevelt elk – many weighing more than 1,000 lbs (454 kg) – graze on the prairies, often right beside the highway. Native to the area, the animals once roamed from the central California valley to the north's Mount Shasta. Like other indigenous wildlife, their numbers have diminished over the years. If you stop to watch them, they may look up momentarily, but most will simply ignore you as long as you keep your distance. The male elk's giant rack of antlers is there for good reason and the elk will charge if they feel threatened.

The tiny logging town of **Orick** is the first sign of civilization north of the national park visitor center. Dominated by a strip of redwood souvenir stands, the town boasts a grocery store and a few motels and restaurants.

For a good introduction to the natural

features of the area, be sure to take a walk along the **Lady Bird Johnson Grove Nature Loop Trail**. The trail begins 2 miles (3 km) up Bald Hills Road, just north of Orick. The ride is extremely steep and may be difficult for motor homes and trailers. The self-guided nature trail is under a mile long and can be covered in less than an hour, even if you stop at all the numbered sights recommended by the user-friendly pamphlet available at the trailhead. The grove was the site of the 1968 dedication of the park, attended by Lady Bird Johnson and her husband, President Lyndon B. Johnson, as well as Richard M. Nixon and the then governor of California, Ronald Reagan.

If time allows, consider visiting the **Tall Trees Grove** in the southern end of the park. During the summer, a shuttle bus transports visitors down the rugged 7-mile (11-km) road to the **Tall Trees Trailhead**.

Otherwise, a limited number of private-vehicle permits are distributed on a first-come, first-served basis. The ac-cess road travels through an extensively logged area where reforesting is an apparent work-in-progress. Once at the trailhead, expect to spend several hours exploring the area: hiking down the steep 3-mile (5-km) trail, spending time in the Tall Trees Grove where the tallest known tree stands (367 ft/112 m), and allowing plenty of time for the hike back out. During the summer, park rangers lead tours and discussions on logging damage and reforestation methods. At other times, an interpretive brochure is available for self-guided tours of the grove.

Generally speaking, the trails of Redwood National Park are wider and shorter than those of the adjacent state parks, which tend to run longer and venture deeper into the forested wilderness. From the south, 12,500-acre (5,059-hectare) **Prairie Creek** is the first state park you'll encounter. The trailheads for many of this area's nature trails are located next to the parking lot of the **Prairie Creek Visitor Center**. Stop at the center for more details about

Left and right, blood star; Douglas iris and crimson columbine.

80

the trails, or just put one foot in front of the other and start hiking.

For an interesting day hike, take the **James Irvine Trail**, **Miner's Ridge Trail** or **Prairie Creek Trail** through the lush redwood forest. Keep your eyes open as you pass the creek: salmon and steelhead may be visible. Beneath the towering redwood and fir trees, plant life along these trails includes various ferns – which flourish in the moist, shaded environment of the forest – and redwood sorrel, with its clover-like leaves green on top and red on the underside. Many trails interconnect; you can extend your hike or cut it short depending on time and energy.

A unique feature of Prairie Creek is its **Revelation Trail**. Designed for blind as well as sighted hikers, the trailhead is located just south of the visitor center and offers many "sights" that can be experienced through the other senses. Wooden and rope handrails run the length of the trail and a Braille guide describes attractions along the way.

Other trails within the Prairie Creek park are found along the **Drury Scenic Parkway**, just off Highway 101. Short hikes along **Little Creek Trail**, **Ten Taypo Trail** and **Hope Creek Trail** take from 10 minutes to an hour and offer quick surveys of old-growth redwood forests for hikers interested in the "woodsy" experience.

Besides the forest, Redwood's other spectacular attribute, the Pacific Coast, is accessible to hikers via the **Coastal Trail**, which runs the length of the national park. In Prairie Creek State Park, the trail can be reached from **Davison Road**, **Gold Bluffs Campground**, **Ossagon Trail** and **Carruthers Cove Trail** (at low tide only).

Be sure to make a mental note of where you entered the beach. Once you're on the sand, it's difficult to distinguish entry points.

The Coastal Trail is an excellent place for picnicking, tide pool exploration, birding and whale-watching. In the north part of the national park, the coast can be reached on the **Flint Ridge Trail**, **Hidden Beach Trail**, **DeMartin Camp-**

Freewheeling on a park road.

grounds, **Damnation Creek Trail** and the **Crescent Beach Trail**.

Leaving Prairie Creek State Park, heading north on 101, your next stop should be the **Klamath** area. This was once a precious fishing and hunting region for the Yurok Indians, but their numbers were severely reduced by miners who ruined the fisheries and burned Yurok villages. Today, Klamath and the neighboring community of Klamath Glen provide access to the **Klamath River**, a favorite among salmon and steelhead fishermen. The annual **Summer Salmon Festival** features a salmon barbecue and displays of traditional Yurok arts and crafts.

Into the ancient forest: Also in the Klamath area are the **Trees of Mystery**, as featured in "Ripley's Believe It Or Not," where huge likenesses of the mythical Paul Bunyan and his Blue Ox, Babe, and chainsaw-sculpted trees attract thousands of tourists each year. Farther north along the Klamath River is the tiny town of **Requa**, another important historic Yurok settlement.

You will find a variety of restaurants and lodging in both Klamath and Requa.

Moving north, the next state park you'll visit is **Del Norte Coast Redwoods State Park**. Its 6,400 acres (2,590 hectares) make it the smallest of the three parks. It boasts a variety of foliage, from old-growth redwoods to wild rhododendrons (growing much taller than their suburban counterparts). Several trails lead from the forest to the sea allowing you to sample the variety of the area. Along the relatively challenging **Damnation Creek Trail**, which begins near Highway 101 north of False Klamath Cove, you'll hike through old-growth spruce, redwood and Oregon grape and end up at a hidden sea cove replete with offshore sea stacks and tide pools. You can also reach a stretch of the Coastal Trail by way of **Enderts Beach Road** south of Crescent City.

For excellent birding and views of second-growth redwood forest, take the nearly 4-mile (6-km) **Hobbs Wall Trail**, named for the Hobbs Wall Company, a primary enterprise of the Del Norte timber industry back in the 1860s. The trail is accessible from Highway 101. For a shorter hike in Del Norte Park, the **Nature Loop Trail** begins across from Mill Creek Campground and makes a 20-minute loop through redwood forest. Notable along the trail is the madrone tree, recognizable by its red bark.

If you find yourself with questions in need of answers as you head up 101, stop off at the **Crescent Beach Information Center**. Two miles (3 km) farther up the highway, you'll come to the town of **Crescent City**. Park headquarters is at 2nd and K streets. Crescent City offers plenty of dining and lodging as well as markets, museums and historic attractions.

Proceed north on Highway 101 until you come to the junction of Highway 199, your gateway to the third of the state parks, **Jedediah Smith Redwoods State Park**. This 9,200-acre (3,723-hectare) park is ideal for hiking, camping, picnicking, fishing or swimming in the **Smith River**, California's only undammed river system. An alternative approach to the park is via **Howland**

Acorn woodpecker.

Hill Road, an unpaved artery offering a scenic route through the lush redwood forest and access to **Stout Grove**, site of the park's largest measured redwood tree, 340 ft (104 m) tall and 16 ft (5 m) in diameter. This state park was named for mountain explorer Jedediah Smith, who led a party of 20 men across the area in 1828 in a grueling effort to reach the Pacific Coast.

There are a number of excellent hiking trails within Jedediah Smith Park. For specific details, you can visit the **Hiouchi Information Center** on Highway 199. The visitor center is open spring, summer and fall. For an easy 2-mile (3-km) hike, take the **Simpson-Reed** and **Peterson Loop trails** on 199; each can be covered in about 20 minutes. Several species of fern and skunk cabbage adorn the trails beneath the spectacular old-growth redwoods, many of them with large burls. Another short hike, offering a quick sampling of the region, is the **Lieffer Loop** and **Ellsworth Loop trails**. The trailheads are about a half-mile north of Highway 199, along Walker Road. The trails contain some steep grades along a moss-laden path through big leaf maple and old-growth redwood forest.

For a longer hike, try the **Boy Scout Tree Trail** along Howland Hill Road, which can be covered in about 4 hours round-trip. The trail forks about 3 miles (5 km) in. The right fork leads to the Boy Scout Tree, the left to **Fern Falls**. Excellent for birding, the hike is sure to reveal winter wrens, Steller's jays and Allen's hummingbirds. As an historical note, Chinese gold mines operated along this route during the 1800s.

Besides the motels and inns in Orick, Klamath and Crescent City, visitors have the option of camping at one of the four campgrounds which are located within the state parks. Most of these campgrounds have a table, a grill and a cupboard, plus hot showers, restrooms and disposal stations. Camping facilities tend to fill up fast during the summer months, so advance reservations are needed. Drop-in camping is usually no problem from November through April.

Indian paintbrush, Redwood meadow.

LASSEN

Few places testify to the awesome power of nature like **Lassen Volcanic National Park**. Tucked away in a remote corner of the southern Cascade Range, this 106,000-acre (42,897-hectare) park is still very much in the throes of creation – a place where the very earth bubbles and sputters and where the explosive power of volcanism has left behind a trail of destruction and rebirth.

One of the least-visited national parks in the continental US, Lassen is also a place of precious solitude. Even during the summer months, when Yosemite National Park is mobbed with tourists, Lassen offers plenty of opportunities to escape into the wilderness where your only company is likely to be mule deer, chipmunks and an occasional black bear. And because the elevation ranges from 5,000 – 10,000 ft (1,524 – 3,050 m), you can explore a variety of life zones in a short period of time, from crystal-clear lakes, wildflower meadows and dense coniferous forests at the lower elevations to the treeless snowfields atop 10,457-ft (3,187-m) Lassen Peak.

Lassen Peak owes its existence to an ancient volcano, 11,500-ft (3,505-m) Mount Tehama, which stood in the southwest corner of the park before collapsing 350,000 years ago. Little of Tehama remains today; its crater, or caldera, was scraped away by successive waves of glaciers, leaving behind only a few jagged peaks (including Brokeoff Mountain and Mount Diller). Lava continued to flow, however, creating the younger peaks to the north. Of these, Lassen Peak is the highest and the last to erupt. The cataclysm began with a blast of steam and ash in May 1915 and reached its climax with devastating waves of debris and lava that wiped out a patch of forest 3 miles (5 km) long. Although it has been dormant since 1921, Lassen remains a geologic hot spot where bubbling mudpots and hot-water springs are getting hotter – a sign that more activity may be on the way.

The western half of the park can be surveyed by automobile via **Lassen Park Road**. This, the park's one paved road, can be covered in about an hour or two, which makes it ideal for those on a limited schedule. It loops around three sides of Lassen Peak and offers access to trails, lakes and geothermal features. There are numbered markers along the route, indicating some 67 points of interest. Most of the road is closed between November and May, when it's used as a cross-country skiing trail.

To hell and back: Enter from the south and drive directly to the **Sulphur Works**, where you can stroll along the well-signed boardwalk through an area of sulfurous mudpots and fumaroles. This was the heart of ancient Mount Tehama, and it still brims with awesome geothermal power. The parking area also serves as the starting point of the gradually ascending trail to **Ridge Lakes**.

Back along the park road, proceed approximately 4.5 miles (7 km) to the **Bumpass Hell Nature Trail**, catching your first view of Lassen Peak, due north. The nature trail, less than a 3-mile (5-km) round-trip, was named for mountain man Kendall Vanhook Bumpass, who discovered the hydrothermal area in 1865 and lost a leg from burns when he stepped into a boiling mudpot. Bumpass later described the mishap as his "easy descent into hell."

This is one of the park's most popular trails, with views of deep-blue **Lake Helen**, impressive glacier-carved rock formations, hemlock trees and pinemat manzanita, as well as the hot spot itself at the end of the trail. Remarkably, a few species of bacteria and algae manage to grow in the hot, acidic water – its between 125°F (52°C) and 196°F (91°C).

The next notable stop along the park road is Lassen Peak. The huge parking lot at the foot of the mountain is testimony to the popularity of the **Lassen Peak Trail**. The round-trip hike to the summit is almost 5 miles (8 km) in length and ascends from an elevation of 8,450 to 10,457 ft (2,576–3,187 m). The air is relatively thin here, so go slowly. In season, you'll see plenty of wildflowers – including irises, violets, lupines and monkeyflowers – and be-

Preceding pages: new snow on Pyrite Lake. **Left,** the summit of Mount Lassen.

fore reaching the summit, you'll probably trudge through patches of snow. Once on top, if the weather is clear, you'll be treated to views of **Mount Shasta** to the north and **Sutter Butte** to the south.

The mountain was named for Danish guide Peter Lassen, an explorer of questionable skill. General John Bidwell, a friend, confided that Lassen "was a singular man, very industrious, very ingenious, and very fond of pioneering – in fact, of the latter, very stubbornly so. He had great confidence in his own power as a woodsman, but strangely enough, he always got lost." As the story goes, he once mistook Lassen Peak for Shasta Peak and inadvertently led a party of murderously angry pioneers 200 miles (322 km) out of their way.

Back in the car, the road winds along the eastern side of Lassen Peak past red fir, lodgepole and western white pine to **Summit Lake**, the starting point for a number of good day hikes to **Echo** and **Twin lakes**, **Horseshoe Lake** and **Cluster Lakes**. The next stop is **Emigrant**

Pass, a 19th-century pioneer trail and the best place to view the **Devastated Area**, a section of forest that was virtually destroyed when Lassen Peak blew its stack in 1915. The eruptions sent lava spilling down the mountainside, blew down a 3-mile (5-km) patch of trees, and smothered the entire area in mud and ash.

Proceeding northwest, you'll come to **Hot Rock**, a 300-ton (272-metric ton) remnant of the mudflow of May 19, 1915. This boulder, one of the many which was transported from Lassen's summit more than 4 miles (6 km) away, is one of the larger rocks that descended the mountain.

As you near the park boundary, you'll see **Chaos Jumbles** north of **Chaos Crags**, a group of plug dome mountains. Chaos Jumbles was formed about 300 years ago after a series of avalanches were triggered by a steam explosion on the northwest face of Chaos Crags. Just before reaching the north entrance station, the road is flanked by lovely **Reflection** and **Manzanita lakes**, created in the wake of Chaos Jumbles.

Into the wilderness: For adventure beyond the park road, try exploring the hiking trails in the eastern half of the park. The Butte Lake, Juniper Lake and Warner Valley regions are excellent starting points for day hikes. For longer stays, campgrounds are located near major trailheads.

To reach the **Butte Lake** area, follow Highway 44 for 11 miles (18 km) east after it splits with Highway 89 and take the unpaved road south to the Butte Lake ranger station. There are four trailheads at the Butte Lake parking lot. A short hike to **Bathtub Lake** can be broken up by a refreshing summer swim. Another hike, a bit longer and more strenuous, leads to **Prospect Peak** along part of the Cinder Cone Nature Trail.

The **Cinder Cone Nature Trail** offers a variety of routes, depending on how much time you want to spend, what sights you want to see, and how much physical exertion you're looking for. The Cinder Cone was a volcano that shot lava, or tephra, straight up. The lava shattered in mid-air and piled up

Balsamroot blossoms at Little Hot Springs.

around the vent. Hiking the nearly symmetrical Cinder Cone takes three to four hours, is quite strenuous, and features black lava formations, devastated tree stumps and multicolored ash fields along an 800-ft (244-m) ascent. Alternative routes along the same trail go as far as **Snag Lake** to the south.

To reach the **Juniper Lake** area by car, head west along Feather River Drive just off Highway 36. Go about a half-mile to a fork in the road and angle right all the way to the Juniper Lake ranger station. Most trails from this area can be hiked in a single day, although some are longer and more strenuous than others.

Hikes to 8,048-ft (2,453-m) **Mount Harkness**, **Inspiration Point**, **Horseshoe Lake**, **Crystal Lake**, **Indian Lake**, **Swan Lake** and **Snag Lake** offer a variety of scenery and physical workouts. The trail east to **Jakey Lake** and **Red Cinder Cone** (another volcano) takes you into some of Lassen's least traversed backcountry.

There are hundreds of other hiking possibilities at Lassen, including the **Pacific Crest Trail**, which intersects trails from Butte and Juniper lakes. You can devise other variations by consulting a park map or, if you are proficient with a compass and topographic map, you can head cross-country. Permits are required for backcountry camping.

Remember to bring adequate water, food and warm clothing. Temperatures can be extreme, and the weather often changes at a moment's notice. Signs warning campers to keep food out of reach of bears should be taken seriously; they've been known to help themselves to a midnight snack.

Lodging in the park is limited to the secluded, scenic **Drakesbad Guest Ranch** – the only working dude ranch located within a national park – just west of **Warner Valley** campgrounds. The inn opened in the mid-19th century as a hot-springs spa and now offers a modest lodge, cabins and bungalows (most with no electricity; reservations required). The park's campgrounds are open from April to September on a first-come, first-served basis.

A boardwalk protects visitors from steaming springs, Bumpass Hell.

SEQUOIA AND KINGS CANYON

Sequoia and **Kings Canyon National Parks** are the twin jewels of California's towering Sierra Nevada. Here, under the gaze of the Golden State's highest peaks, a tiara of snowcapped mountains stand guard over alpine lakes. Sparkling streams flow through canyons rimmed with dense forests. Foothills and meadows sustain wildflowers and wildlife. And, of course, visitors can touch the famed sequoias, the largest living things on the face of the earth – some more than 3,000 years old.

Located along the western flank of the southern Sierra Nevada, the 1,350-sq. mile (3,496-sq. km) parks rise out of the highest and most rugged section of California. Surveying the Sierra from the summits of Mount Brewer and Mount Tyndall, a member of the 1864 Brewer Expedition described a land of "thin ridges topped with pinnacles sharp as needles, successions of great-greater-like amphitheaters with crowning precipices. Over-sweeping snow fields and frozen lakes, everywhere naked and shattered granite…"

Creating the park: This rugged mountain terrain was once the homeland of the Monache Indians, who made summer camps in the high country to gather acorns, hunt deer and small game, and occasionally cross the crest of the Sierra Nevada to trade with Paiute Indians in the Owens Valley. The Gold Rush of 1849 put a swift end to all that. Miners swarmed into the Sierra by the thousands, ruthlessly uprooting native people wherever they went. Loggers and stockmen quickly followed, indiscriminately felling trees, overgrazing mountain meadows and scattering game.

In the 1870s, John Muir, then a voice in the wilderness, began speaking out against the destruction, and soon afterward a newspaperman, George Stewart, took up the cause and began sounding the alarm to conservationists throughout California. The word finally reached Washington, and in 1890 Sequoia and General Grant (now in the western unit of Kings Canyon) national parks were created. Damage was still being done outside the parks, however, and it wasn't until 1940 that the Kings River country was protected within Kings Canyon National Park. Today, Sequoia and Kings Canyon are among the most pristine units in the National Park System.

Sequoia and Kings Canyon tend to be backcountry parks. Ninety percent of the land is accessible by trail only, and none of its 2,600 lakes and ponds can be reached by car. And yet, less than 5 percent of visitors are backcountry users. Bill Tweed, a Park Service veteran, describes the parks as "wilderness islands in a sea of urban California."

"These are parks that you have to hike to really enjoy," he says, and with 800 miles (1,287 km) of trails, there's plenty of opportunity to venture into the wilderness. Among the most famous is the **John Muir Trail**, which stretches 219 miles (352 km) along the crest of the Sierra Nevada from Yosemite Valley to **Mount Whitney**, the highest peak in the contiguous United States, which rises

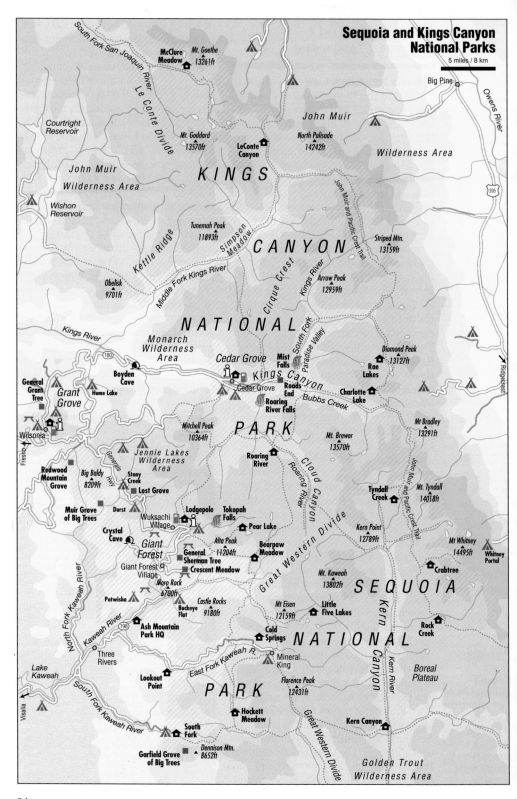

Sequoia and Kings Canyon National Parks

at the parks' borders. The Muir Trail is generally regarded as the most spectacular segment of the longer **Pacific Crest Trail**, which runs between the Mexican and Canadian borders. Another major trail, the **High Sierra**, runs 71 miles (114 km) from Crescent Meadow to Mount Whitney's 14,495-ft (4,418-m) summit. There is also a maze of secondary trails which fan out across the mountains and canyons, providing a variety of rewarding, high-mountain experiences for hikers at just about any level of skill and fitness.

Motorists can enjoy the wonders of Sequoia and Kings Canyon, too. Two major roads link the parks together, affording spectacular views of the big trees, deep canyons and other scenic wonders. Most visits begin at the Ash Mountain entrance where Highway 198 from Visalia becomes the **Generals Highway**, a 47-mile (76-km) long scenic road that winds through some of the parks' most stunning landscapes. Your first stop should be the **Foothills Visitor Center**, about a mile (1.5 km) from the park border, where you can consult with rangers about special tours and events, and check weather conditions – which is extremely important during fall and winter when sudden snowfalls can make roads impassable.

From Ash Mountain, elevation 1,500 ft (457 m), the Generals Highway climbs steeply out of the foothills, passing several vista points along the way. About 15 miles (24 km) from the visitor center, the **Four Guardsmen** – a quartet of stately sequoias – introduce visitors to the "big trees." The **Giant Forest**, centerpiece of Sequoia National Park, is a mile beyond. Here, standing at an elevation of 6,500 ft (1,981 m), are the largest organisms in the world, *Sequoiadendron giganteum*, the giant sequoia. Hundreds of the huge trees dominate the landscape, their massive, rust-colored trunks rising in solemn majesty. This is a relict species. Its ancestors once grew throughout western North America before climatic and geologic changes left them stranded in the southern Sierra. The oldest have been standing here for at least 2,500 years. The ancient trees are so magnificent, so utterly huge, that few first-time visitors are prepared for the introduction.

In summer, there are a wide range of visitor services at **Giant Forest Village**, including a store, restaurant and lodge. A small kiosk provides information on nature walks and other ranger-led activities. Near the cafeteria, **Moro Rock-Crescent Meadow Road** leads through the sequoias to **Crescent Meadow**, one of the gems of the Giant Forest area. The trees are truly spectacular. There's even a downed tree visitors can drive their cars through – a popular "photo opportunity." Crescent Meadow is also an idyllic spot for those who want to get off the beaten path. In summer, park interpreters guide visitors around wildflower meadows and to the **log cabin** of **Hale Tharp**, the first white pioneer to settle in the Giant Forest.

A turnoff in the same road leads to **Moro Rock**, a 6,700-ft (2,042-m) granite monolith with glorious views of Alta Peak, the Great Western Divide and the Kaweah River basin. A long, steep stair-

Tokopah Falls.

way climbs to the summit. Several easy, foot trails radiate out of Giant Forest Village, making loops of various lengths through the lush meadows and sequoia groves. Here, visitors can take a few hours or an entire day to experience the big trees close up, occasionally spotting a black bear or mule deer browsing in the brush.

Beyond Giant Forest Village, the highway winds a short way through a forest of pines, firs and sequoias to the famed **General Sherman Tree**, the world's largest living thing. This monarch boasts a diameter of 30 ft (9 m) and rises 274 ft (84 m) into the Sierra sky. It contains approximately 52,000 cubic ft (1,472 cubic m) of lumber – enough for about 85 average-sized homes. One of its upper branches is about 6 ft (2 m) in diameter and 80 ft (24 m) long – bigger than many trees. **Congress Trail** starts at the Sherman Tree and makes a pleasant, 2-mile (3-km) loop through the sequoia grove where, in summer, you're likely to see or hear Steller's jays, Clark's nutcrackers, juncoes, white-headed woodpeckers and chickadees, among other native birds.

Back on the road, the Generals Highway winds toward a rugged mountain canyon known as **Tokopah Valley**, where you'll find the **Lodgepole Visitor Center**, several stores and a large campground on the Marble Fork of the Kaweah River. An easy 2-mile (3-km) trail runs along the canyon to **Tokopah Falls**, a spectacular 100-ft (30-m) cascade that thunders down a rocky chute.

Entering Kings Canyon: North of Lodgepole, the highway passes **Wuksachi Village**, where the Park Service plans to relocate aging visitor facilities now scattered in Giant Forest. The road exits the park at **Lost Grove** and winds through Sequoia National Forest for about 11 miles (17 km) before entering the western unit of Kings Canyon National Park. Just past the park boundary, near Quail Flat, a rough, 2-mile (3-km) long road (closed in winter) runs out to **Redwood Mountain Grove**, the largest stand of *Sequoiadendron giganteum* in the country. Redwood Mountain is a park

A hiker on Muir Pass.

unto itself, containing thousands of sequoias of varying size. And unlike the more popular groves, there are no railings around the trunks – it's a tree hugger's paradise.

Continue north on the Generals Highway, bypassing the intersection of Highway 180. Drive on to **Grant Grove**, where you'll find a visitor center, campground, general store, gas station and other conveniences. Half a mile past the visitor center, a left turn takes you down a hillside to the famed **General Grant Tree**. Over 267 ft (81 m) tall and 107 ft (33 m) around, it's the third largest in the world and has been designated the nation's Christmas tree. Every December hundreds of people from the surrounding area gather here for a brief Christmas service. For more adventurous drivers, a steep, narrow road leads 2½ miles (4 km) to **Panoramic Point**. A quarter-mile trail leads to the overlook with sweeping vistas of the surrounding peaks.

The 30 miles (48 km) between Grant Grove and Cedar Grove (across Sequoia National Forest) are officially designated a National Scenic Byway and constitute one of the most spectacular drives in the West. The road plummets nearly 4,500 ft (1,372 m) to the depths of the majestic **Kings River Canyon**. In the upper elevations, you'll pass stumps of sequoias felled by loggers a century ago – a reminder of the destructive practices that led to the founding of the parks. Beyond, the highway provides sweeping views of the deepest canyons in the country.

The road re-enters Kings Canyon National Park and leads to **Cedar Grove** in the dramatic, glacially-shaped Kings Canyon where you'll find a ranger station, general store, gas station, campgrounds and lodging (summer only). The east end of the canyon offers a wide range of hiking trails from easy to extreme. A stop at **Roaring River Falls** is at the top of most visitors' lists. A pleasant quarter-mile stroll, the falls are worth at least a 30-minute visit and a half roll of film. A mile up the road, the self-guiding **Cedar Grove Motor Nature**

A natural arch frames Mount Whitney and Lone Pine Peak.

Trail runs down the north side of the river, offering a less strenuous way to enjoy Kings Canyon.

Road's End lies another 3 miles (5 km) up the canyon. At **Zumwalt Meadow,** a self-guiding trail leads to the opposite bank of the Kings River over a suspension bridge. For the meek mountaineer, the popular **Mist Falls Trail** is an 8-mile (13-km) round-trip along the south fork of the majestic Kings River; the trail climbs 800 vertical ft (244 m) in 4 miles (6 km). **Paradise Valley**, about another half-mile up the trail, is a lovely spot for a picnic or an afternoon stroll.

Off the beaten path: Visitors with enough time and a sense of adventure should consider wandering off the main roads and journeying into the parks' wilderness areas, if only for a day or two. An easy introduction might be a half-day excursion to **Crystal Cave** (summer only), at the end of a narrow mountain road just south of Giant Forest Village. You must buy tickets in advance at the Lodgepole or Foothills

visitor centers for an hour-long tour of the cave, which was carved by water out of subterranean marble. In places, stalagmites and stalactites, formed drop by drop over thousands of years, are joined into single columns. The cave remains at a constant 55°F (13°C) year-round.

Elsewhere in Sequoia, you can take the steep, partially paved road to **Mineral King** (summer only), a stunning region of high valleys, sheer mountain sides and isolated alpine lakes. The access road is off Highway 198 just southwest of the Ash Mountain entrance. It takes about 90 minutes to drive to the ranger station near the end of the road; camping sites are available nearby but fill rapidly on weekends. Take it slowly, especially if you're not yet acclimated to the high altitude. Trails in this area start at an elevation of 7,500 ft (2,286 m) and climb steeply in a long series of switchbacks. Although extremely strenuous, the effort is well-rewarded. Awaiting you along the trails are dazzling displays of lupine, Indian paintbrush, orchid and shooting star, turquoise lakes in glacier-carved basins, excellent wildlife-watching, sweeping views at every turn, and a seemingly endless supply of solitude.

Free permits are required for overnight backpacking trips. Reservations are advised for some trails and campgrounds, so check with park headquarters several weeks in advance. The park is open year-round, but deep snow makes several side roads impassable in winter, although the Generals Highway from Ash Mountain to Lodgepole is almost always open. Call ahead for road conditions if you are planning a winter visit, and be sure you are equipped with chains, ice scraper, collapsible shovel and other necessary snow gear.

Both Sequoia and Kings Canyon National Parks offer a variety of winter activities, and travelers who are willing to brave the snow and chilly temperatures will be able to appreciate the parks in an entirely different light. Skiing or snowshoeing among the big trees, for example, is magical, especially after a fresh snowfall, when sounds are muffled by a trackless white blanket.

Left, the Marble Fork of the Kaweah River. Right, the General Sherman sequoia, the world's largest living thing.

GENERAL SHERMAN

THE CALIFORNIA DESERT

The California Desert is actually the meeting place of three deserts: the Mojave, the Sonoran and the Great Basin. Sprawling across 39,000 sq. miles (101,010 sq. km) under the rain shadow of the Sierra Nevada and San Bernardino mountains, it is the hottest, driest place in North America, with summer temperatures exceeding 115°F (46°C).

"This is where the bones of the earth stick through," says Eldon Hughes, director of the California Desert Protection League. So much of the land is devoid of vegetation that the earth's folds, faults and raw surfaces are in plain view. From scorching salt flats to jagged mountain crests, the California Desert is naked geology.

There are three large federal parks in the California Desert: **Death Valley National Park**, **Joshua Tree National Park**, and **Mojave National Preserve**. Harsh and unrelenting, this is nonetheless a land of subtle, almost surreal, beauty and a surprising variety of life. Because of extreme heat and aridity, desert wildlife is largely nocturnal. At dusk, when temperatures drop, the acute silence of day is broken by the distant yapping of a coyote, the hooting of a great horned owl, or the croaking of tree frogs hidden in secret springs.

Many animals avoid the hottest part of the day by burrowing underground or seeking shade under rocks and plants. Some estivate (become dormant) for the entire summer or during droughts. Others, like the kangaroo rat, produce water metabolically from high-carbohydrate seeds. A few species, such as mourning doves and California quail, can tolerate extraordinary levels of dehydration.

Other animals that have adapted to the harsh desert environment include road runners, peregrine falcons and kit fox. Bobcats, bighorn sheep and desert tortoises, a protected species, are more rarely seen.

Ocotillo, creosote bush and other desert plants slow evaporation by reducing the size of their leaves or dropping them entirely during the driest part of the year. Many desert plants, such as Joshua trees, have thick, waxy leaves to impede water loss. The sponge-like tissues of cactus soak up moisture during brief downpours. Most desert wildflowers – such as locoweed, purple lupine and desert primrose – bide their time during dry spells and then explode into bloom after a good soaking, sometimes lasting only a few days before drying out. Juniper, pinyon and bristlecone pines stand in the higher elevations; palm trees, cottonwoods and mesquite crowd the few oases – prime places for viewing wildlife.

Death Valley: The name alone conjures visions of oppressive heat, blinding sunlight, bleached skeletons. A portion of the Mojave Desert, Death Valley is a 140-mile (225-km) long trough set between steep mountain walls of virtually naked rock. The shallow Pleistocene lake that once filled the valley slowly evaporated, leaving behind salt pans, cracked mud flats and undulating dunes. To the west, the deeply eroded walls of

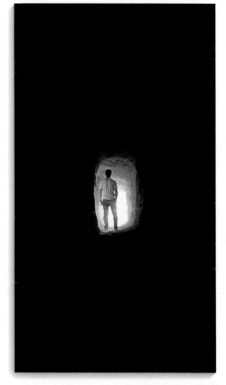

Preceding pages: Mojave Desert sunrise. **Left**, the Amargosa Range. **Right**, abandoned mine shaft at Twenty Mule Team Canyon.

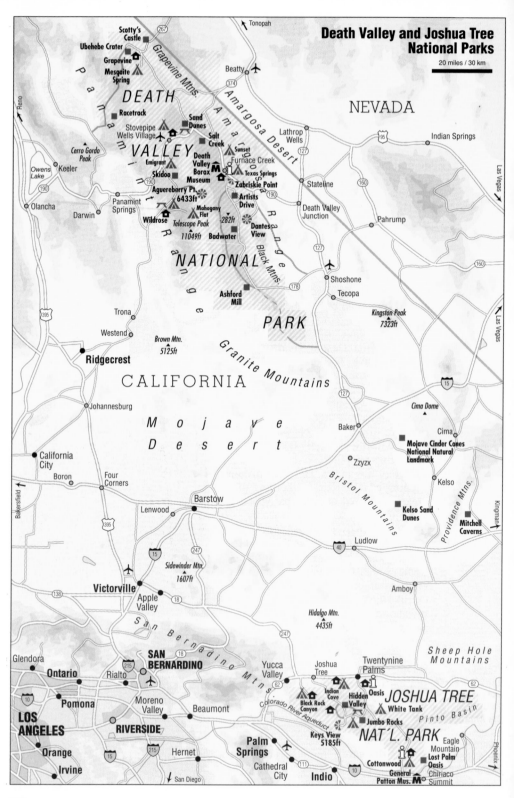

Death Valley and Joshua Tree National Parks

20 miles / 30 km

NEVADA

Tonopah

Scotty's Castle
267
Ubehebe Crater
Grapevine
Mesquite Spring
Beatty
374

Reno

DEATH

Racetrack

Sand Dunes

Stovepipe Wells Village

Salt Creek

Sunset

Lathrop Wells
127
95
Indian Springs

Cerro Gordo Peak

VALLEY

Emigrant
Skidoo
Death Valley Borax Museum
Furnace Creek
Texas Springs
Zabriskie Point

Las Vegas
160

Owens Lake
Keeler
190
Olancha

Aguereberry Pt. 6433ft
Panamint Springs
Darwin

Artists Drive

Stateline
Death Valley Junction

Pahrump

Mahogany Flat
282ft
Wildrose
Telescope Peak 11049ft
Badwater
Dantes View

NATIONAL

127

160

395

Black Mtns.
178
Shoshone
Tecopa

Las Vegas

Trona

Ashford Mill

PARK

Kingston Peak 7323ft

Westend

Brown Mtn. 5125ft

Granite Mountains

Ridgecrest

15

CALIFORNIA

Johannesburg

Mojave Desert

Cima Dome

Baker

Cima

California City

Mojave Cinder Cones National Natural Landmark

Boron
Four Corners

Zzyzx

Kelso

Barstow

Bristol Mountains

Bakersfield

Lenwood

395

247

15

Ludlow
40

Kelso Sand Dunes

Providence Mtns.

Mitchell Caverns

Kingman

Sidewinder Mtn. 1607ft

Victorville
138
Apple Valley
18

Amboy

San Bernardino Mtns.

Hidalgo Mtn. 4435ft

247

Sheep Hole Mountains

Glendora

SAN BERNARDINO
18

Yucca Valley
62

Joshua Tree

Twentynine Palms
Oasis

62

Ontario
215
Rialto

Moreno Valley

Beaumont

Black Rock Canyon
Indian Cove
Hidden Valley
White Tank

JOSHUA TREE

Pinto Basin

LOS ANGELES
10
Pomona
RIVERSIDE
215

Colorado River Aqueduct

Jumbo Rocks

NAT'L. PARK

Orange
Irvine
15

Hernet

Palm Springs
111

Keys View 5185ft

Cottonwood
General Patton Mus.

Eagle Mountain
Lost Palm Oasis
Chiriaco Summit

Phoenix

San Diego

Cathedral City

Indio
10

the **Panamint Range** tower to an elevation of 11,000 ft (3,353 m), while to the east the **Amargosa Range** reaches 8,000 ft (2,438 m).

Furnace Creek is a hub of tourist activities and the best place to start a tour. The **Furnace Creek Visitor Center** and nearby **Borax Museum** will supply you with plenty of background information on the area's human and natural history, and rangers are always available to advise you on camping, hiking and regularly scheduled tours. If you plan on staying for a few days, the Mediterranean-style **Furnace Creek Inn** (reservations required well in advance) is an oasis of creature comforts with fine dining, shopping, swimming, golfing, and more.

You can get your first good overview of Death Valley about 3 miles (5 km) southeast on Highway 190 at **Zabriskie Point**, which overlooks a multihued panorama of sun-baked peaks and ridges. About a mile farther south, an unpaved road loops through the wrinkled landscape and subtle colors of **Twenty Mule Team Canyon**, named after the wagon teams that once hauled ore through mountain passes. Continue on Highway 190 to the 13-mile (21-km) spur road to **Dantes View**, a 5,475-ft (1,669-m) perch overlooking the salt flats at **Badwater** which, at 282 ft (86 m) below sea level, is the lowest spot in the United States.

Double back toward Furnace Creek and then head south on Highway 178, stopping for an easy mile-long walk through colorful layered formations along the **Golden Canyon Trail**. Pick up the one-way **Artists Drive** loop about 7 miles (11 km) farther south; the short, winding drive takes you through a rainbow region of colored rocks eroded from the lake-bed over thousands of years. Continuing south on Highway 178, you'll pass a short dirt road to **Devils Golf Course**, a vast expanse of knobby salt formations rising from the earth. Just beyond, a spur road on the left leads to the **Natural Bridge Canyon Trail**, a mile- (2-km) long walk to a 50-ft (15-m) high stone bridge carved by water gushing over the dry falls at the end of the trail. The highway continues

south through Badwater and eventually swings west into the **Black Mountains** at **Ashford Mill**, where the ruins of an old gold-processing operation are scattered across the stark landscape. There are hundreds of abandoned mining sites throughout the park; many have not yet been made safe for visitors. Never enter mine shafts or abandoned buildings without conferring with park rangers.

Return to Furnace Creek Visitor Center and head north on Higway 190 to the **Harmony Borax Interpretive Trail**, where you can explore the remains of a cleanser-processing plant dating to the 1880s. About 10 miles (16 km) farther north, the short, easy **Salt Creek Interpretive Trail** explains the life history of the endangered pupfish, a tiny relict species found in only a few locations in the West. It is about another 5 miles (8 km) on Highway 190 to the shifting patterns of the **Sand Dunes**, where giant piles of wind-scoured quartz grains, some as high as 80 ft (24 m), are continually sculpted by the wind.

You can stop for gas, food and lodg-

ing at **Stovepipe Wells Village** and then make a long, winding side trip through **Emigrant Canyon** which, like most roads in the park, was once used by miners to haul ore and equipment. Dirt spur roads (four-wheel-drive recommended) lead to **Skidoo** ghost town and to 6,433-ft (1,961-m) **Aguereberry Point**. The main road finally winds through **Wildrose Canyon**, where a row of 30-ft (9-m) beehive-shaped kilns were once used to make charcoal for silver smelters across the Panamint Valley. You can start two long, strenuous hikes from this area. The 9-mile (14-km), round-trip **Wildrose Peak Trail** climbs through pinyon and juniper forest to spectacular views at the 9,064-ft (2,763-m) summit. Starting at Mahogany Flat Campground, **Telescope Peak Trail** (expect snow from October to April) makes a rough 3,000-ft (914-m) gain over 7 miles (11 km) before reaching the ancient bristlecone pines at the summit. At 11,049 ft (3,368 m), Telescope Peak is the highest point in the park and offers magnificent views of both Badwater, the lowest point in the country, and 14,495-ft (4,418-m) **Mount Whitney**, the highest peak in the contiguous United States.

Finally, you'll find Death Valley's most popular attraction, **Scotty's Castle**, in the far north of the park, about 45 miles (72 km) from Stovepipe Wells Village. Scotty's Castle is a magnificent, 25-room, Spanish-style villa that was started as a retreat in 1922 by Albert M. Johnson, a Chicago millionaire. It was looked after and later occupied by Johnson's unlikely friend, a former prospector, cowboy, mule driver, tale-spinner and self-promoter extraordinaire by the name of Walter Scott – otherwise known as Death Valley Scotty. The interior, still decorated with fine art and furnishings, is a virtual chronicle of pre-Depression opulence. Tours are given hourly in season. About 8 miles (13 km) away, the gaping maw of **Ubehebe Crater** – about a half-mile (1 km) across and 500 ft (152 m) deep – was blasted out of the earth's crust several thousand years ago by a volcanic eruption.

Scotty's Castle.

If you have more time, consider exploring some of the park's backcountry trails and roads. From Ubehebe Crater, for example, it's a 25-mile (40-km) drive on a rough dirt road (four-wheel drive recommended) to the **Racetrack**, where rocks seem to move across the *playa* on their own power. (Geologists think the rocks are actually blown by high winds across a fine layer of ice or slippery clay.) Other popular backcountry drives include spectacular **Titus Canyon**, **Echo Canyon**, **Cottonwood Canyon** and **West Side Road**, which leads to several remote canyons popular among experienced hikers. Because of the high temperatures, hiking in lowlands during summer can be extremely dangerous. Remember to bring at least a gallon of water per person per day (more if possible), and be aware of potential flash floods while hiking in canyon bottoms.

Joshua Tree: Explorer John C. Fremont happened upon a Joshua Tree in 1844 and called it "the most repulsive tree in the vegetable kingdom." But to a colony of California Mormons journeying to Utah, the tree's outstretched branches resembled arms beckoning them across the desert to the promised land. The tufts of shaggy leaves reminded them of the beard of an Old Testament patriarch; they named the tree – a member of the lily family – after Joshua, who led the Israelites into the land of Canaan.

Established as a national monument in 1936, the park not only preserves a portion of the Mojave Desert's Joshua Tree forest but several long fingers of the Sonoran Desert that penetrate the lower valleys. More than 90 percent of the park is classified as wilderness, but two paved roads and several dirt roads provide access to some of the most scenic areas.

Entering from the north, your first stop should be the **Oasis Visitor Center** in Twentynine Palms, where exhibits explain the natural and cultural history of the region and where books and maps help you get oriented. From the visitor center, follow the park road about 8 miles (13 km) to a fork in the road and bear right. The road swings through

Left, Furnace Creek fan palm. **Right**, cactus blossom.

Queen and Lost Horse valleys, passing the fantastic granite formations of Jumbo Rocks, Hidden Valley (a legendary cattle rustler's hideout) and the Wonderland of Rocks – favorite areas for rock climbers, who can often be seen scaling boulders.

For a couple of interesting side trips, take a left on the Geology Tour Road about a half-mile (1 km) past the Jumbo Rocks Campground. The self-guiding tour is 18 miles (29 km) long on a rough dirt road into some of the park's most fascinating terrain (four-wheel drive is recommended.) A right turn off the main road into Queen Valley leads to a network of dirt roads that lace through boulders and Joshua Trees. A second left off the main road just past the Ryan Campground takes you to 5,185-ft (1,580-m) Keys View in the Little San Bernardino Mountains where, on a clear day, you can see the Salton Sea and Coachella Valley.

There are several excellent day hikes in the western flank of the park. Short nature trails at Hidden Valley, Barker Dam, Cap Rock, Skull Rock and elsewhere introduce first-time visitors to the fragile desert ecology and traces of early human habitation. Longer trips include the 3-mile (5-km) round-trip to the top of 5,461-ft (1,665-m) Ryan Mountain, the 4-mile (6-km) round-trip to the ruins of Lost Horse Mine, and the 16-mile (26-km) round-trip Boy Scout Trail through the stunning Wonderland of Rocks.

Return to the fork in the road and head south. As the road descends, you begin to enter the hotter, drier Colorado Desert (a subdivision of the Sonoran), scattered with a sparse growth of teddy-bear cholla, spidery ocotillo, creosote bush and smoke trees. You can take a short walk through some of the area's characteristic vegetation at the Cholla Cactus Garden and, about 2 miles (3 km) farther along, the Ocotillo Patch. About 15 miles (24 km) farther down you'll reach another small oasis: Cottonwood Spring, and the Cottonwood Visitor Center.

A fairly taxing, 7½-mile (12-km) trail

Zabriskie Point, Death Valley.

(round-trip) leads from the nearby campground to **Lost Palms Oasis**, the largest in the park and a great place for spotting seldom-seen wildlife like bighorn sheep. You can make a 3-mile (5-km) round-trip to **Mastodon Peak** from the campground, too. The views are superb, an excellent way to end the day. There are no accommodations within the park, but tent and RV sites are available at several campgrounds, most on a first-come, first-served basis.

Mojave: In 1980, Congress designated a 1½-million-acre (607,017-hectare) chunk of the desert a national scenic area, the first of its kind. About the size of Delaware, **Mojave National Preserve** is dominated by crags of limestone, dolomite, rhyolite and granite, glistening salt flats, coal-black lava flows, tawny dunes and big, blue sky.

Several paved and unpaved roads crisscross the preserve. On the western side, **Ivanpah-Lanfair Road** is one of the best places to see the threatened desert tortoise, especially in the spring. The road – mostly unpaved – passes abandoned mines in the **New York Mountains**, named for their skyscraper turrets, home to desert bighorn sheep.

Farther west, **Essex-Black Canyon Road** leads from Interstate 40 to the **Providence Mountains** which contain **Mitchell Caverns**, an intricate network of some 40,000 limestone caves. Ranger-led tours of the caverns are conducted daily from mid-September to mid-June. The self-guiding, half-mile **Mary Beal Nature Trail** begins near the visitor center. **Black Canyon Road** runs north through the weird, volcanic landscapes of **Hole-in-the-Wall** and **Wild Horse Mesa** and then into the pinyon – juniper woodlands of **Mid Hills**. At dusk, watch for the black-tailed jackrabbit.

Any place with a name like **Zzyzx** (pronounced *zizz-ex*) deserves a visit. To get there, take Interstate 15 about 60 miles (97 km) east of Barstow and then drive south 4 miles (6 km) along the shore of **Soda Lake**, usually a dry lake bed, to the **Desert Studies Center**. During the 1940s and 1950s, this old cavalry outpost site was a health club

Joshua trees, symbol of the Mojave.

run by Dr Curtis Springer. Rather eccentric, the good doctor apparently wanted the last word on everything, hence Zzyzx. In 1976 the resort was turned into a university research station. A spring-fed pond and nearby marshes shelter the rare Saratoga Spring pupfish and Mojave tui chub.

A few miles farther east, **Kelbaker Road** threads through a desolate area of cinder cones and lava beds now designated as **Mojave Cinder Cones National Natural Landmark**. Stop at **Kelso**, site of the grand, Spanish-style, Union Pacific Railroad depot built in 1924. Farther along, you pass the 600-ft (183-m) high **Kelso Dunes**, third highest dune system in the country and one of the so-called "singing dunes" that hum or boom when in motion. The road then climbs through a boulder-choked pass separating the Granite and Providence Mountains and descends toward Interstate 40. Double back to Kelso and turn right onto **Kelso-Cima Road**, which curves northward past **Cima Dome**, a gently sloping geologic "blister" of monzonite, a granite-like rock, that covers 75 sq. miles (194 sq. km). You'll also pass one of the finest Joshua Tree forests in California. Some people say it's even more impressive than Joshua Tree National Park.

Along the way, you'll cross the **Mojave Road**, a 140-mile (225-km) Indian trade route that connected the Colorado River with Camp Cady on the lower Mojave River. It was later used by the Spanish priest Francisco Garces, mountain men like Jedediah Smith, merchants, settlers and the United States mail. Portions of the trail are still passable by four-wheel-drive or on foot. Adventurous travelers can still visit the crumbling ruins of **Fort Piute**, built in 1867 to protect mail wagons.

There are no accommodations in the preserve, but motels can be found in Baker, Barstow, Needles and Nipton, where the Hotel Nipton once served as a refuge for the silent-film star Clara Bow. There are also tent and RV campsites at Mid Hills, Hole-in-the-Wall and Providence Mountains.

The desert is a haven for rock climbers; park plaque.

SHOOTING NATURE

Photography and national parks go hand in hand. In fact, early conservationists used photographs to persuade government officials to set aside parklands. Now millions of tourists tote cameras into the parks to shoot family pictures, landscapes, sunsets and wildlife. No matter what your intentions or level of expertise, photography is a wonderful way of connecting with the beauty and grandeur of America's national parks.

Before venturing into the parks, keep a few basic tips in mind: First, know your camera. Don't borrow or buy a new camera the day before your trip and expect to be proficient with it right away. Shoot a few rolls of film before you leave. Try different settings and get familiar with the camera's functions. Check the batteries and be sure you have plenty of film before you leave. Nothing is more disappointing than missing that long-awaited eruption of Old Faithful or a chance encounter with wildlife.

For most amateur photographers, a lot of complicated equipment isn't necessary. A simple, inexpensive camera will fill the photo album just as well as (and sometimes better than) a fancy one. If you have an adjustable camera, learn a little about depth of field. In short, the smaller apertures (lens openings f8, f11 and f16) give the greatest amount of depth of field. They allow objects in the foreground and background to appear sharp in the picture, even if they don't look sharp through the camera.

If you're thinking about additional equipment, consider a polarizing filter. It helps to darken the sky and makes the clouds look more distinct. It also reduces glare from reflective surfaces such as leaves, eyeglasses and water.

A tripod is always a good investment. Blurry pictures are more often caused by camera shake than by poor focus. A telephoto lens will come in handy, too, especially if you want to photograph wildlife. A zoom lens that is 80mm to 200mm or 75mm to 300mm will do the trick in most cases.

Remember, light is a photographer's true medium. You're not taking a picture of an object but the light that reflects off that object. Study the colors of sunset and sunrise. Find out exactly when the sun and moon rise and set, as well as their positions on the horizon. Scout out locations ahead of time and try to anticipate how the light will fall on your subject. Generally speaking, the "magic hours" of dawn and dusk cast a warm glow on the landscape. Bright sunlight tends to cast dark, well-defined shadows which often make rather unflattering portraits. Use the even light of overcast skies to shoot close-ups of flowers and other natural elements.

Ask rangers where to find the best places to photograph wildlife. Be patient. As you learn more about an animal's behavior, you'll be in a better position to anticipate a good shot. If you don't have a telephoto lens, don't try to get too close. Crowding most animals will only scare them away. Never try to sneak up on animals or use food to lure them closer.

Most importantly, have fun. Experiment with various shutter speeds, lenses, filters and angles. Use photography as a gateway to the natural world. Keep your eyes open, enjoy the parks, and bring home some memories to share with others. ■

Setting up a shot, Death Valley.

CHANNEL ISLANDS

One of America's richest national parks – and, ironically, one of its least visited – consists of five islands off the coast of southern California. In fact, it is such an exceptional place that the United Nations has recognized it as an International Biosphere Reserve.

Whales. Dolphins. Sea lions. Twenty-five species of shark. Birds of all kinds that nest in its cliffs. Many people find it remarkable that a wilderness so remote and ecologically significant as this tiny archipelago should endure so close to the southern California megalopolis.

The five islands are **Santa Barbara**, **Anacapa**, **Santa Cruz**, **Santa Rosa** and **San Miguel**. When the mist lifts from the sea, the park's mirage-like profile is a focal point for the people of the city of Santa Barbara across the channel, who take a proprietary view of the place. The larger islands deliver serenity for backpackers who choose to explore them, but unrelenting winds, lack of fresh water and penetrating spells of heat or cold can make exploration a challenge.

Created in 1980, the park has been spared mammoth crowds largely because you can't get there by car. Transportation from the mainland is via commercial boat or chartered flight in a small plane that lands at dirt airfields on Santa Cruz, Santa Rosa and San Miguel.

The **Santa Barbara Channel** serves as a vital migration corridor for marine animals, ranging from whales to sea lions. During the spring and fall pods of gray whales – some of the earth's largest creatures – navigate the channel during a 10,000-mile (16,093-km) journey that takes them from calving grounds off Mexico's Baja Peninsula to feeding areas in the Bering Sea, and back again. Until overharvesting took its toll, the coves of the Channel Islands produced vast quantities of sea anemone, sea urchins and abalone, which are central to the diet of threatened sea otters.

Scientists say the upwelling of cold sea currents from the northern Pacific combine here with tropical waters from the south to create ideal conditions for marine life. The Channel Islands are to the California coastline what the Galapagos are to Ecuador, a rare place where marine and terrestrial influences have conspired to create a novel, irreplaceable environment. Solitude is the park's saving grace.

Some 18,000 years ago, the islands (except Santa Barbara) were so near the mainland that wildlife could swim the channel during periods of low tide. Biologists believe that imperial mammoths, foxes and flightless geese emigrated to a single super island known as Santarosae. But when northern glaciers melted, the sea level rose, leaving expatriated colonies cut off from the mainland. Eventually, as many island organisms are apt to do, they evolved into endemic subspecies, "dwarfed" by the limitations of their habitat and dwindling food supply.

Evidence of these events can be found in 12,000-year-old fossils of dwarfed mammoths as well as living species

Preceding pages: a colony of California sea lions. Left, San Miguel Island. Right, giant coreopsis.

such as island foxes and spotted skunks that are quite a bit smaller than their mainland counterparts.

Santa Barbara: To visit the islands, start at park headquarters on Spinnaker Drive at the harbor in **Ventura**. The visitor center will acquaint you with the islands' cultural and natural history. It also stocks several useful books and a detailed trail map. Island Packers, a privately-owned park concessionaire, offers daily boat and hiking tours to the park.

Santa Barbara, situated 52 miles (84 km) south of Ventura, is often thought of as the "lost Channel Island" because it drifts apart from the others. Camping is allowed on Santa Barbara with advance reservations, and the **Canyon View Nature Trail** leads to a network of hiking routes totaling 5½ miles (9 km). Take advantage of the ranger-led nature walks.

Santa Barbara provides critical refuge for elephant seals in winter and California sea lions in spring. It also yields excellent birdwatching opportu-

nities; there are, among others, American kestrels, Xantus murrelets, horned larks, brown pelicans and barn owls. After the winter rains, grasses sprouting from island rock are covered with magnificent yellow coreopsis, a tree with giant daisy-like blossoms, that can climb up to 10 ft (3 m) high.

To the northwest, the land forms of Anacapa mark a dramatic entrance to the Channel Islands archipelago. Austere and brooding, Anacapa gets its name from the Indian word "Eneepah," which means deception or mirage. Appropriately, it's not one island but three, stretching a total of 5 miles (3 km). The smallest and most visited of the island trio is **East Anacapa**.

These isles, located 13 miles (21 km) from Ventura Harbor, are prime territory for scuba diving and snorkeling among the intertidal pools. The coves are rich with marine life and nourished by forests of kelp that attract sea otters, seals, crustaceans, and sea anemone, as well as whales. The sole campground is on East Anacapa where there's a 1½-

Anacapa Island Lighthouse.

mile (2-km) nature trail. A favorite destination is the **old lighthouse**. Rangers here lead free nature tours. Above **West Anacapa**, which is closed to visitors, endangered brown pelicans ride the air currents and coast into their rookeries with freshly caught fish.

Santa Cruz and Santa Rosa: Santa Cruz, the biggest island in the park, is owned by the Nature Conservancy, a private conservation organization, which offers day hikes and overnight camping permits to small groups of backpackers and kayakers. Long, arid and mountainous, Santa Cruz is blessed with a variety of sites. One of them, **Painted Cave**, is a cavern accessible only by boat and is a popular side trip for kayakers. Snaking in and out of the tide pools, harbor seals and federally protected sea otters are frequent visitors. Ashore there are many lizards and birds.

Humpback whales migrate near the Channel Islands.

The highest summit is 2,450-ft (747-m) **Devils Peak**. Except for a small piece owned by the federal government, the island is strictly off-limits to unregistered guests, though the Conservancy

has made several options available for those who want to explore it. The **Santa Barbara Natural History Museum** and Island Packers will coordinate your itinerary and tell you which hiking trails and campsites are open. To visit Nature Conservancy lands on Santa Cruz island get permission from Conservancy in advance, or show up at the Santa Barbara Natural History Museum.

Second largest in the chain, **Santa Rosa** measures 15 miles (24 km) long and 10 miles (16 km) wide, enough terrain for a multi-day excursion, even though most visitors spend only an afternoon. Following the winter rainy season, the highlands of Santa Rosa turn luminous with blooming wildflowers. Moisture brings a vernal rejuvenation. This mountainous island is crisscrossed by a series of dirt roads that offer a direct overland connection between the ranger station at **Beechers Bay** and **Johnson's Lee** near an abandoned military base on the other side of the island.

Someday these pathways could become a centerpiece for hiking, horse-

back riding and mountain biking along a hut-to-hut circuit. There is currently a daily limit of 500 visitors, although the number is seldom reached except in spring. Make sure you take advantage of the ranger-led nature tours. The island can be an inhospitable outpost in late summer when the dry Santa Ana winds desiccate the landscape and turn it brown, but the island becomes green again between late March and early July. Although the highest named summit, **Soledad Peak**, climbs only 1,574 ft (480 m), the jutting, rounded slope creates a dramatic silhouette against the sky. An unnamed peak about a mile to the west is the tallest point at 1,589 ft (484 m).

Until the early 19th century, Santa Rosa was home to the Chumash Indians, and remains of several villages are scattered across strategic promontories. Hundreds of midden sites where Indians disposed of abalone shells have a ghostly presence.

An internationally-acclaimed collection of Chumash artifacts is on perma-nent display at the Santa Barbara Natural History Museum, an essential introduction for anyone trying to understand the Chumash world, but remember, removing artifacts or natural objects from the islands is a federal crime.

For most of the 20th century, the island's native wildlife has shared the mountainous *arroyos* with the elk and mule deer that were relocated here by private hunters, as well as cattle. The Park Service reached an agreement with local ranchers to continue grazing their cattle here. Each year, the animals are brought to and from the mainland in an old wooden vessel, the *Vaquero*, that is the last of its kind.

San Miguel: Pounded by heavy winds and rough seas, San Miguel is both the most difficult island to reach and the most enchanting. There is one campground here, limited to 30 people, so call park headquarters well in advance to reserve a site. The island is widely recognized as a premier spot for viewing six species of seals and sea lions at the **Point Bennett** cliffs. To get there, it's necessary to make a 15-mile (24-km) round-trip from **Cuyler Landing**. A strange relic found on both San Miguel and Santa Rosa are the caliche forests, and there is one here, near the **Point Bennett Trail**. The branches of individual trees appear to be made of stone. Actually, the weird protrusions were created by minerals that made a natural cast around living bushes. When the plants died, the shells remained.

San Miguel is reputed to hold the body of Juan Rodriguez Cabrillo, the Portuguese explorer who "discovered" California in 1542. "Experts disagree on this subject," writes Marla Daily in her book, *California's Channel Islands*. "It is known that Cabrillo wintered at San Miguel Island in 1542 during which time he broke either an arm or a leg which later became infected. Knowing he was a dying man, Cabrillo turned his expedition over to his chief pilot Bartolomé Ferrer. On January 3, 1543, Cabrillo died as a result of his injury, and many say he was buried on the island." There is an honorary tombstone to him at **Cuyler Harbor**.

Left, a sea otter cracks a clam on a rock. **Right**, silver lotus and common mullein, Santa Cruz Island.

HAWAII AND AMERICAN SAMOA

Kilauea, the world's only drive-up volcano, is the red-hot heart of **Hawaii Volcanoes National Park**. Located on the island of Hawaii, it also happens to be the world's most active volcano, having erupted continuously for more than a decade. In its current rampage, Kilauea has added some 300 acres (121 hectares) to the largest island in the Hawaiian chain. It has also destroyed more than 180 island homes, including the entire village of Kalapana, and it devoured the famous Black Sand Beach at Kaimu.

Hawaii Volcanoes National Park was founded in 1916 to protect the natural wonders of Kilauea and its fuming neighbor, **Mauna Loa Volcano**. The 377-sq. mile (976-sq. km) preserve encompasses the summit calderas of both Kilauea and Mauna Loa (currently quiet) and sections of the **Kalapana Coast**, just down slope of Kilauea.

The composition of Hawaiian lava is such that eruptions are usually not as explosive as in other parts of the world. Consequently, when a Hawaiian volcano erupts, instead of heading for the nearest escape route, people tend to pack a picnic and head for the park to see the most spectacular fireworks on earth. On a Saturday night, crowds can number in the thousands when Kilauea is really pumping.

Park rangers are heroic in their efforts to help people see the eruption safely, often marking new walking trails several times a day as the lava changes course. A visit is like securing front row seats at the dawn of creation.

The volcano appears most awesome at night, when the fires rage against the darkened sky. Right after sunset, there is an eerie rosy glow, almost celestial, as Hawaii continues to be born in the flames. The shoreline expands visibly as each wave of lava seethes into the sea. Towering billows of steam rise for miles along the cooking coast. In the most recent phase of Kilauea's eruption, lava has been flowing in blazing cascades down the side of the mountain. Motorists on **Chain of Craters Road** can sometimes see the great falls of fire from their car windows.

River of fire: Every visit to the park should begin at the **Kilauea Visitor Center**, just inside the park entrance. (Until recently there was a visitor center at Wahaula on the coast, but it was destroyed by lava. Interestingly, the nearby Wahaula Heiau, an ancient temple ruin, was spared. The lava flow went right up to the temple walls, parted, and passed around it, leaving a locket of trees and old stone walls on the black bosom of the landscape.)

At the visitor center, the day's activities, such as free guided nature walks, are posted, along with the latest eruption information. Anyone planning an overnight backcountry hike should register, so rangers know where campers are in the event of an emergency.

Every hour on the hour, a film on the park and the volcanoes' most impressive eruptions is aired in the center's theater. The best orientation, however,

is the 11-mile (18-km) spin around **Crater Rim Drive**, which skirts the huge steaming craters of **Kilauea Iki**, **Halemaumau** and others.

Chain of Craters Road, which goes to the coastal section of the park, is now a dead end, closed off by lava. It is in this area, at Kamoamoa, that the rivers of fire are sometimes so close that people poke them with sticks and watch them instantly ignite. Unless rangers are present, however, it is best not to approach the active flows; they may also be moving beneath the earth's crust, which can collapse.

At the park's **Thomas A. Jaggar Museum**, perched on the lip of Kilauea's summit caldera, instruments are linked to the next-door **Hawaiian Volcano Observatory**, where scientists monitor Kilauea's every tremble. At the museum, hands-on exhibits tell the whole fascinating story of volcanology and Hawaii's fiery sea mountains. The islands were formed as the Pacific Plate beneath the Pacific Ocean inched its way across a stationary hot spot in the earth's mantle. Magma, molten rock beneath the earth, broke through the plate, forming first one volcano and then another as the plate shifted over the hot spot. Over time, the accumulated lava became the Hawaiian islands.

The process, which started at least 70 million years ago, continues. Not only is the Big Island still growing, an entirely new island is being formed off the coast, southwest of Kilauea. From the bowels of the earth, lava is being pumped out upon the ocean bed, where it solidifies, forming pillows and mounds. In about 200,000 years, the lava mass will be tall enough to break the surface of the waves and begin its long climb toward the sky – and Hawaii will have a new island: Loihi.

"Kilauea is changing constantly, like a jigsaw with moving parts," says David Clague, the volcano observatory's chief scientist. "The other day I was talking by radio to a road crew and I could hear what sounded like gunshots – it was rocks cracking, bursting from volcanic pressure."

A road engulfed by lava.

Science, however, has its limits. Exhibits at the Jaggar Museum acknowledge the ancient primal power of Pele, goddess of the volcano. Pele is considered to be responsible for the volcano's creative energy and its behavior. Many people say she still dwells in Halemaumau Crater, and there is always someone who claims to see her right before a major eruption. She is sometimes perceived as a beautiful lady dressed in red, with flowing hair the color of flames. Other times she may take the form of an old woman walking a white dog.

Offerings of flowers, rocks and *ti* leaves are left for her along park trails and at the edge of the crater. Anyone gathering *ohelo* berries, the cranberry-like fruit that grows at Kilauea, throws the first handful into the crater, for the fruit, like the crimson *ohia lehua* blossom, is sacred to Pele. In a modern twist to the Pele tales, it is claimed that the goddess has developed a taste for hooch – gin specifically – so that, too, is tossed into the volcanic stew.

In 1790, Pele ignored all tribute and,

End of the road.

in a rare explosive outburst, destroyed the army of Chief Keoua as he and his men marched to do battle with Kamehameha, the chief destined to unite the Hawaiian islands into one nation. All that's left of the warriors now are the ghostly tracks etched into hardened ash in the black sands of the Ka'u desert, visible from the **Mauna Iki Trail** (off Hawaii 11, about 9 miles/14 km from the visitor center).

Hope and devastation: Hawaii Volcanoes National Park is more than hellfire and brimstone, however. Even if the volcano were to take a break, the park would still be well worth a visit. "When people come to Kilauea, they want to see red – 'Where's the lava?' they ask," says park ranger Mardie Lane. "It's our job to help visitors understand not only the science of volcanoes but the Hawaiian culture, the native plants and wildlife that don't exist anywhere else on the planet. I'd like everyone who comes here to promise themselves, 'I will park my car and get out and walk.'"

The park offers unusual hiking trails,

each revealing different facets of this utterly fascinating terrain. The **Kilauea Iki Trail** descends 400 ft (122 m) through a jungle of tree ferns, then meanders across the floor of Kilauea Iki Crater, warming the toes of hikers with heat from the magma that is burning 300 ft (91 m) below the surface. Sulfurous steam escapes through trailside vents.

Devastation Trail is a boardwalk laid out on glistening jet cinders. Skeletons of trees are bleached white by time and sun. Fifteen years ago there was barely a vestige of vegetation beside the boardwalk. Now the trail is cheered by tawny grasses, clumps of wildflowers, the scarlet *ohia lehua* blossoms, and lavender polyganum.

The 15-minute **Thurston Lava Tube Loop** is a journey through a lava tunnel that once surged with magma. The 11-mile (18-km) **Crater Rim Trail** circles the summit, beginning at the visitor center. The most interesting section leads from Chain of Craters Road through native forest, across hard black lava flows, and ends at the rim of **Kanea-kakoi Crater**. Along the way are eerie tree molds formed when a lava flow rushed through the forest, splashed around trees and hardened in their shape. What's left are phantasmagoric black sculptures, some 10 ft (3 m) high.

Nearby, tender new fronds of *amau* fern poke from lava chinks, finding a determined foothold. Native *ohia* trees take root in the impossible terrain. Some are only a foot or two high and already bursting in brilliant red flowers. It's a scene that whispers more than any pop-psychology paperback about encouragement, hope, endurance, triumph over adversity, and beauty from ashes.

The most strenuous trek in the park is the 4-day round-trip trek to the top of 13,250-ft (4,038-m) **Mauna Loa** volcano. It is recommended only for experienced backpackers equipped to face snow, wind and high-altitude hiking. A shorter but equally demanding round-trip trail to the summit begins at the **Mauna Loa Weather Observatory.** Permits are required for both trips. In winter months, the upper slopes of

Ruins of an ancient village...

Mauna Loa are usually blanketed with snow. The mountain is so large that the entire Sierra Nevada range could fit nicely inside. It is said that Poliahu, goddess of the snow and nemesis of Pele, resides atop Mauna Loa. Through the ages the two have carried on their feud, using weapons of fire and ice.

Many of the plants at the park are rare and endangered, the last stand for some embattled species. When the Hawaiian volcanoes emerged from the ocean, they were sterile and lifeless. At the rate of one successful new species every 40,000 years, seeds and spores of plants arrived in the jet streams and the ocean currents and as gifts of migratory birds. In utter isolation, farther from a land mass than any place else on earth, the plants and birds evolved into a unique biota.

Within the park, in the middle of lava flows, are areas called *kipuka*, which were unmolested by the flows and left as pristine islands of life. Some are quite large and offer refuge to endemic flora and fauna. A hiking trail off **Mauna Loa Road** traverses hilly **Kipuka Puaulu** through stands of *ohia lehua*, with their scarlet blossoms, and *koa* trees, once the king of the Hawaiian forest. The great voyaging canoes that carried early Hawaiians as far as Tahiti were carved from *koa* logs.

Along the **Kipuka Trail** are occasional benches so hikers can pause and listen to a symphony heard nowhere else – the honeyed notes of the apapane, the little red bird with white britches who drinks nectar from the *lehua* blossom; the warbling of the *iiwi*; and the big police whistle of the tiny *omao*.

The *nene*, a native goose rescued from the brink of extinction, can once again be spotted waddling among the ferns and trees of the park, often with a line of goslings in tow. Signs warn motorists to brake for one of the world's rarest birds.

Remember: it's important to stay on marked trails. Vegetation can hide dangerous cracks and fissures. Walking at night is risky because it's easy to stumble onto steam vents, lava crevices or sharp outgrowths. People who help themselves to the flashlights which rang-

… and a stark volcanic landscape.

ers use to illuminate paths endanger other visitors. Extreme caution should be exercised when approaching an active flow or vents emitting toxic fumes. Pregnant women, infants and people with heart or lung problems should stay away from these areas.

Visitors who want to enter this haunting place can stay in heated cabins at **Namakani Paio Campgrounds**, or at **Volcano House**, the only lodge in the park. The lodge sits at the rim of Kilauea caldera with views of the vast steaming pit. During summit eruptions, it's sometimes possible to sip cocktails while watching the most spectacular dinner show in the world.

House of the Sun: Haleakala National Park on the island of Maui protects parts of the world's largest dormant volcano. At 10,023 ft (3,055 m), **Haleakala**, which means House of the Sun, rises a mile above any other Maui peak. Its "crater" – actually a high, eroded valley filled with small cinder cones – is an awesome sight: 21 miles (34 km) in circumference, 3,000 ft (914 m) in depth.

Gazing down into its immensity, Mark Twain wrote, "I felt like the last Man, neglected of the judgement and left pinnacled in mid-heaven, a forgotten relic of a vanished world."

Haleakala last erupted in 1790 and left behind a landscape so unearthly that American astronauts trained here for the first moon landing. The 28,655-acre (11,596-hectare) park encompasses the summit as well as a portion of the Kipahulu Coast. Some areas are virtually unexplored, and new species of birds and plants are still being found. The park has been designated by the United Nations as one of only a few Significant Natural Areas of the World.

There are magnificent views of the wilderness area at **Leleiwi**, **Kalahaku** and **Puu Ulaula Summit** along the tortuous 11-mile (17-km) park road, as well as at the visitor center, which is perched on the rim. But, as always, the best way to experience Haleakala is on foot. The park offers more than 30 miles (48 km) of hiking trails, some going right into the "crater" where there are

Waves break along bluffs, the Kipahulu Coast.

campgrounds and a few cabins (reservations required).

Just beyond the park entrance is the **Hosmer Grove Nature Walk**, an easy half-mile trail that loops through stands of native and exotic trees planted here about 80 years ago by experimental forester Ralph Hosmer. This is also one of the last refuges of honeycreepers (*iiwi*, *amakihi*, *apapane* and *alauahio*), among the rarest birds in the world.

About 4 miles (6 km) from Hosmer Grove, you'll find the trailhead of **Halemau'u Trail**, which crosses rolling hill country to the volcano rim. From there it descends down switchbacks to **Holua Cabin** on the volcano floor, about a 1,000-ft (305-m) drop. Experienced hikers can continue 6 miles (10 km) to **Paliku Cabin**. Here, you can pick up **Kaupo Trail**, a strenuous, rocky descent which is used as an exit.

The most popular route into the park is the **Sliding Sands Trail**, which begins at the visitor center just below the summit and plunges down a steep 6-mile (10-km) incline to **Kapalaoa Cabin**

Palikea stream cascades to the sea.

on the valley floor. (Hiking up the loose cinder trail is extremely fatiguing, so consider cutting the hike short or exiting on Halemau'u Trail.)

Along the way are stands of endangered silversword, the rare silver plant that grows only at Haleakala; it blooms only once, then dies. Silversword glows with light and cradles tiny drops of water on its wands. Surprisingly, it is a member of the sunflower family that has adapted to this lunar-like environment and acquired an eerie beauty.

The immense cinder cone **Puu O Maui** dominates the landscape, along with the neighboring cones of **Kamoalii**, **Puu O Pele** and the multihued crater of **Kalua O Ka O'o**. The colors run from russet, sienna and umber streaked with yellow, purple and red to a pale silver and delicate pea green. Nature has painted the landscape with bold strokes of black augite crystals, red cinders and sparkling green olivine. The shades change with the angle of the sun, and the effect is simply electrifying.

The shoreline **Kipahulu** section of

the park is a complete contrast to the stark drama of the summit. Ice-cold **Palikea Stream** cascades to the sea in a series of falls with large plunge pools. Popular as swimming spots, the pools are surrounded by rolling grasslands and lush rain forest. The 2-mile (3-km) **Waimoku Falls Trail** reveals a great variety of tropical scenery in a brief hike through a thick bamboo forest to the foot of a tall cascade plunging from the side of the volcano.

In both the summit and Kipahulu sections of the park, rangers conduct hikes and guided nature walks. Concessionaires outside the park offer horseback expeditions into the volcano.

National Park of American Samoa: Located 2,300 miles (3,701 km) south-southwest of Hawaii, American Samoa is a United States territory of five volcanic islands and two coral atolls. The national park, established October 31 1988, is one of America's newest and encompasses nearly 9,000 acres (3,642 hectares) in three units on widely separated islands. The 5,000-acre (2,023-hectare) parcel on **Ta'u Island** is mostly undisturbed rain forest. The beautiful sea cliffs drop from the top of **Lata Mountain**, the highest peak in the territory. The **Tutuila Island** section of the park is also rain forest with highly scenic shoreline. **Ofu Island** contains the beach considered to be the loveliest in Samoa and also one of the most exceptional coral reefs in the Pacific. Within this unique rain forest environment – the only one of its kind in the United States – the park protects a remarkable variety of wildlife including dozens of tropical birds and fish, tortoises, the Pacific boa and the rare flying fox, which is actually a large bat.

Because of the communal nature of land tenure in Samoa, most of the parklands are still under the jurisdiction of the local villages. Entering the park may require special permission, and some areas may be closed to visitors. Contact the regional park office in Honolulu for details well in advance.

<u>Right</u>, steam billows from lava as it flows into the ocean.

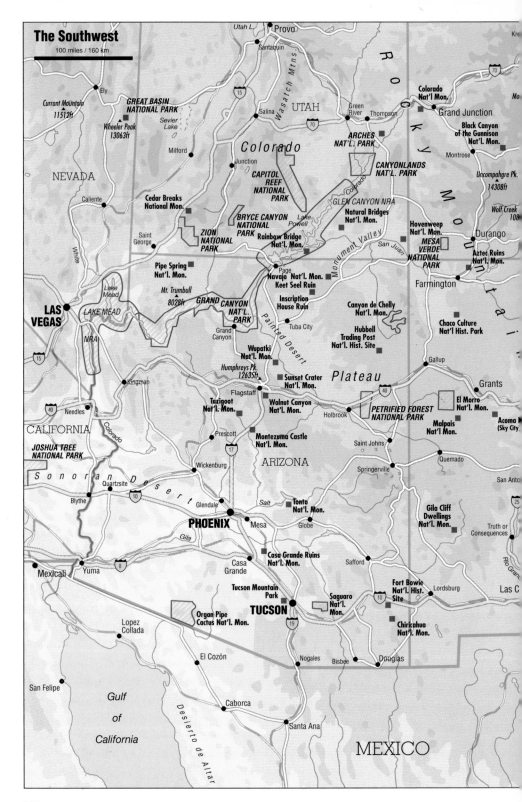

The Southwest

100 miles / 160 km

UTAH

Utah L.
Provo
Santaquin
Salina
Green River
Thompson
Colorado Nat'l. Mon.
Grand Junction
Kre
Mo

Ely
Current Mountain 11512ft
GREAT BASIN NATIONAL PARK
Wheeler Peak 13063ft
Sevier Lake
Milford
Junction

NEVADA

Caliente
Saint George

Colorado

CAPITOL REEF NATIONAL PARK

Lake Powell

ARCHES NAT'L. PARK

CANYONLANDS NAT'L. PARK

Montrose

Black Canyon of the Gunnison Nat'l. Mon.

Uncompahgre Pk. 14308ft

Wolf Creek 108

GLEN CANYON NRA

Colorado

Cedar Breaks National Mon.

BRYCE CANYON NATIONAL PARK

Rainbow Bridge Nat'l. Mon.

Natural Bridges Nat'l. Mon.

Hovenweep Nat'l. Mon.

Durango

ZION NATIONAL PARK

Saint George

Pipe Spring Nat'l. Mon.

San Juan

MESA VERDE NATIONAL PARK

Aztec Ruins Nat'l. Mon.

Monument Valley

Lake Mead

Mt. Trumbull 8028ft

Page

Navajo Nat'l. Mon.
Keet Seel Ruin

Farmington

LAS VEGAS

GRAND CANYON NAT'L. PARK

Inscription House Ruin

Canyon de Chelly Nat'l. Mon.

Chaco Culture Nat'l. Hist. Park

LAKE MEAD NRA

Grand Canyon

Painted Desert

Tuba City

Hubbell Trading Post Nat'l. Hist. Site

Wupatki Nat'l. Mon.

Gallup

Grants

Humphreys Pk. 12635ft

Sunset Crater Nat'l. Mon.

Plateau

Kingman

Flagstaff

Tuzigoot Nat'l. Mon.

Walnut Canyon Nat'l. Mon.

Holbrook

PETRIFIED FOREST NATIONAL PARK

El Morro Nat'l. Mon.

Acoma (Sky City)

Needles

CALIFORNIA

Prescott

Montezuma Castle Nat'l. Mon.

Saint Johns

Malpais Nat'l. Mon.

Colorado

JOSHUA TREE NATIONAL PARK

Wickenburg

ARIZONA

Springerville

Quemado

San Anto

S o n o r a n   D e s e r t

Quartzsite

Blythe

Glendale

Salt

Tonto Nat'l. Mon.

Gila Cliff Dwellings Nat'l. Mon.

Truth or Consequences

PHOENIX

Mesa

Globe

Safford

Gila

Casa Grande Ruins Nat'l. Mon.

Fort Bowie Nat'l. Hist. Site

Lordsburg

Las C

Mexicali

Yuma

Casa Grande

Tucson Mountain Park

Saguaro Nat'l. Mon.

Rio Grand

Lopez Collada

Organ Pipe Cactus Nat'l. Mon.

TUCSON

Chiricahua Nat'l. Mon.

El Cozón

Nogales

Bisbee

Douglas

San Felipe

Gulf of California

Caborca

Santa Ana

Desierto de Altar

MEXICO

White

ROCKY MOUNTAINS

THE SOUTHWEST

From the red rock country of southern Utah to the torrid flats of the Chihuahuan Desert, few places rival the natural beauty of the American Southwest. Here the Colorado Plateau rises like a great block of stone that's been sculpted by water and wind into a dreamscape of canyons, mesas, spires and arches. At the heart of the plateau, the great maw of the Grand Canyon opens to the Colorado River. With more than 4 million visitors a year, this is the most popular park in the Southwest. But even here, there are vast expanses of wilderness where a backpacker is more likely to see a coyote, mule deer or rattlesnake than another human.

To the north, several large parks in southern Utah preserve a geologic fantasy-land of "hoodoos," balanced rocks and natural bridges. Once the home of the ancient Anasazi, whose remarkable pueblos are preserved at Mesa Verde, Chaco Canyon and many other parks, the Colorado Plateau now attracts flocks of rock climbers, mountain bikers, river runners and other recreationists who want to immerse themselves in the unparalleled beauty of canyon country.

Beyond the plateau, in Nevada's Snake Range, Great Basin National Park is a mountainous pocket of the massive Basin and Range region. To the south, the Sonoran Desert stretches into Mexico, broken by stark peaks and *bajadas*. Three parks – Saguaro, Organ Pipe and Chiricahua national monuments – protect the fragile balance of life in this supremely arid environment.

To the east, in the Chihuahuan Desert, travelers can explore the strange underworld of Carlsbad Caverns and the peaceful high country of the Guadalupe Mountains. Tucked into a graceful bow in the Rio Grande, Big Bend encompasses 1,100 sq. miles (2,849 sq. km) of the Chihuahuan Desert surrounding the rugged beauty of the Chisos Mountains.

GRAND CANYON

John Hance, a Grand Canyon pioneer and tourist guide, used to tell clients about a fierce snowstorm that howled into northern Arizona with snow so thick you couldn't see from one end of a mule to the other. Even so, Hance had work to do, so he put on snowshoes and headed out – a foolish thing to do. Before long he was hopelessly lost. Still he plodded on, and pretty soon the weather began to break. Patches of blue sky appeared above, and then, to his horror, little patches of ground appeared below – way down below.

The storm was so thick, it seems, that Hance had walked out over the canyon edge and was supported only by clouds. And now, as the clouds broke up, he was in danger of falling to his earthly reward. He never ran so hard in his life, he said, and barely made it back to the rim before the last of the clouds evaporated.

Bunyanesque: A tall tale? John Hance was full of them. It seems that the Grand Canyon encourages these Bunyanesque exaggerations, and he was a master at crafting stories to match its unparalleled landscape. Many of his listeners believed him – the canyon, after all, is a landscape where it seems anything might happen. Who can vouch for reality in a place where solid rock so abruptly meets airy space? A place so deep that, as Hance used to say, it takes seven days to see all the way to the bottom? Like many of his tales, this one also contains a grain of truth. You can stare all day and still not make sense of the wondrous landscape. You can see, but you cannot quickly comprehend.

It takes at least a week. Only after days of looking and listening and reading will patterns begin to emerge. Specific rock layers become familiar. Details of the geologic story become clear. Things once invisible become obvious. A sheer cliff face, for example, may seem featureless until your eye suddenly picks out a raven's nest perched on a ledge. Or a small stone building, a prehistoric storage structure, appears

like magic beneath a distant rock overhang. It was there all along, but to see it required an experienced eye.

In the same way, a sense of scale can be developed. Looking way down to the bottom of the canyon, where the river shows a glimmer of white water, you see a few tiny, bright-colored ovals flash in and out of view. Through binoculars, these reveal themselves to be river boats, 20 ft (6 m) long, loaded with people crashing through waves big enough to swallow them from sight. Suddenly the canyon acquires a human dimension.

It helps to know a few facts and figures. The canyon is 277 miles (446 km) in length, measured along the Colorado River from Lees Ferry to the Grand Wash Cliffs on Lake Mead. If you add tributaries, many of which are great canyons in their own right, the length stretches to thousands of miles. The canyon's depth and width vary. Grand Canyon Village, for example, is just under 7,000 ft (2,134 m) elevation. Twelve miles (19 km) away on the North Rim, Bright Angel Point stands at 8,145

Preceding pages: on the edge of the abyss. **Left,** the view from Yaki Point, South Rim. **Right,** dories on the Colorado River.

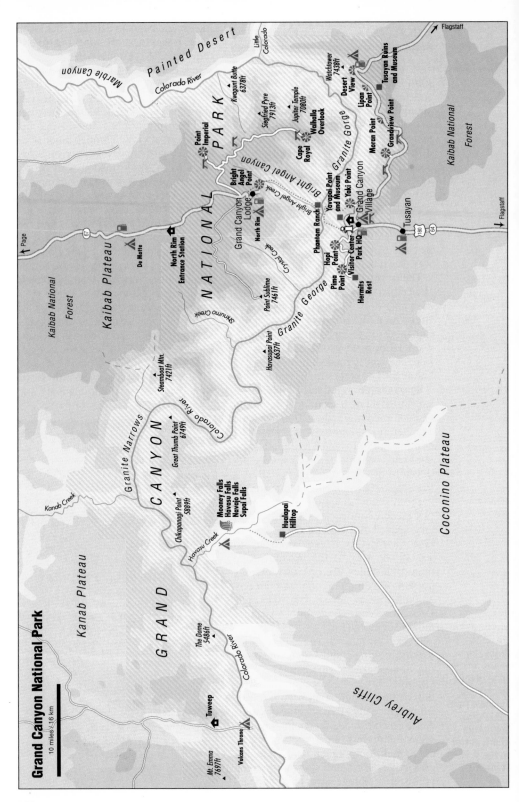

Grand Canyon National Park

10 miles/√16 km

Painted Desert

Marble Canyon

Colorado River

Little Colorado

→ Flagstaff

Kwagunt Butte 6378ft

Siegfried Pyre 7913ft

Jupiter Temple 7080ft

Walhalla Overlook

Watchtower 7438ft

Desert View

Tusayan Ruins and Museum

Lipan Point

Point Imperial

NATIONAL PARK

Cape Royal

Granite Gorge

Moran Point

Grandview Point

Bright Angel Point

Bright Angel Canyon

Bright Angel Creek

Yavapai Point and Museum

Yaki Point

Grand Canyon Village

Kaibab National Forest

→ Page

67

De Motte

North Rim Entrance Station

Kaibab Plateau

Grand Canyon Lodge

North Rim

Crystal Creek

Phantom Ranch

Park HQ

Visitor Center

Hopi Point

Pima Point

Hermits Rest

Tusayan

180

64

→ Flagstaff

Kaibab National Forest

Point Sublime 7461ft

Shinumo Creek

Havasupai Point 6637ft

Granite George

Steamboat Mtn. 7421ft

Colorado River

Granite Narrows

Great Thumb Point 6749ft

GRAND CANYON

Kanab Creek

Chikapanagi Point 5889ft

Mooney Falls
Havasu Falls
Navajo Falls
Supai Falls

Hualapai Hilltop

Coconino Plateau

Havasu Creek

The Dome 5486ft

Colorado River

Kanab Plateau

Tuweep

Mt. Emma 7697ft

Vulcans Throne

Aubrey Cliffs

ft (2,483 m). Between them, at river level, Phantom Ranch breathes the relatively thick air of 2,400 ft (732 m). The greatest relief from rim to river is below Point Imperial on the North Rim, which stands 6,000 ft (1,829 m) above the canyon bottom. In its roadless western reaches, which are visited by almost no one, the inner canyon is less deep but considerably narrower.

The climate varies widely, too. Whereas the North Rim gets about 27 inches (69 cms) of rain a year, the average is only 15 inches (38 cms) for the South Rim and less than 7 inches (18 cms) in the canyon bottom. On a typical day in May, temperatures on the South Rim go from 78°F (26°C) down to 36°F (2°C), while at the river, the high will be 98°F (37°C) with an overnight low of 73°F (23°C). And as much as 200 inches (508 cms) of snow falls on the North Rim during winter, while at the river a dusting is a rarity.

Creating the canyon: How the canyon was carved is no mystery: it was eroded. Virtually all the rock that once occupied this space has been carried off by water, primarily the Colorado River. In a geologic sense, it wasn't such a great task; after all, the Mississippi River has carried off a far greater volume of sediment, creating a "canyon" that spreads from the Rockies to the Appalachians. Simple erosion is easy to understand. What challenges geologists even today, however, is that in doing its work the river performed a seemingly impossible trick – it cut through the Kaibab Plateau, a 3,000-ft (914-m) high bulge in the earth's surface. Rivers normally flow around such highlands, not through them. What happened here?

Once it was thought that the plateau rose up beneath the ancient, pre-existing Colorado River; in other words, the river carved the canyon as the land was lifted. This seemed to be a logical explanation until other evidence showed that only 6 million years ago, the Colorado River as it flows today did not exist, and therefore, neither could the Grand Canyon. Thus, the Kaibab Plateau reached its current elevation millions of years before the river began its great work.

Other theories have come and gone. Nowadays, the most widely accepted idea involves not one but two rivers, going back to when a small river, the ancestral Colorado, wandered across an open landscape, flowing eventually toward the northwest into what is now Nevada. A second river flowed into the Gulf of California. Gradually, as rivers will do, the second river eroded into the highlands at its source, lengthening its reach toward the northeast until finally it broke through a critical divide, tapped into the drainage of the ancestral Colorado, and captured that river's water.

All this took place some 5½ million years ago. One river was born from two – a new river with a steep gradient, fed by snowmelt from the Rocky Mountains – and the carving of the Grand Canyon began in earnest.

For geologists, the rock itself is the most revealing feature of the canyon. Lying in largely undisturbed layers, the great mass of exposed stone describes nearly 2 billion years of North American history. Starting from the top, the

Playing in the mud on the Little Colorado River.

youngest is the Kaibab Limestone, loaded with fossil seashells that even an untrained eye can easily find. At the bottom lies the so-called basement rock of the canyon: the 1.7-billion-year-old Vishnu complex, a fine-grained, black rock with red marbling that is beautiful even to a layman's eye.

Between the Vishnu and the Kaibab lies the rest of the story, as told by layers of mostly sedimentary rocks, including limestone, sandstone and mudstone. Geologists read them like the neatly stacked pages of a vast history book.

Just as the rock layers form distinct levels, so do the canyon's so-called life zones. As a general rule, the deeper you go into the canyon the warmer and drier it becomes. Consider, for example, a trek from the park's highest point on the North Rim down the Kaibab Trail to the river. Your journey will begin at over 9,000 ft (2,743 m) among aspen, spruce and fir. This forest is home to mule deer, coyotes, mountain lions, wild turkey and the unusual white-tailed Kaibab squirrels. As the plateau slopes down toward the rim, conditions become warmer. The forest grades into species like pinyon, juniper and mountain mahogany – plants capable of withstanding the formidable combination of cold winters and hot, dry summers.

Spilling off the North Rim into the canyon, forest plants mix for some distance. At about 5,000 ft (1,524 m), trees vanish altogether, giving way to a scrubland of blackbrush, yucca, Mormon tea and various cacti. Animals common to this zone are lizards, jackrabbit, desert bighorn sheep, coyotes and a host of small rodents – notably the kangaroo rat, a mouse-sized creature that hops on hind legs like its Australian namesake.

The canyon goes deeper still, to elevations between 2,000 ft (610 m) and 3,000 ft (914 m). Here we find the barrel cacti, ocotillo and mesquite trees that are so familiar in southern Arizona. Temperatures at the canyon bottom rise above 120°F (49°C) at times, and while thunderstorms drench the forested rim, this zone can remain parched for months at a time. From a human point of view, it would be a cruel landscape were it not for the river and its many tributary streams. To a hiker descending a long dusty trail there is no greater earthly miracle than the sudden appearance of desert water, flowing cool and clear over smooth rock. Water bursts from springs, seeps out of gravel in canyon bottoms, and supports lush oases of vegetation, including willows and big, shady cottonwood trees. The streams are home to beavers, dippers, herons, rainbow trout, frogs and other undesertlike creatures.

Canyon culture: The park was established in 1919 and enlarged in 1975, but human habitation goes way back. As early as 5,000 years ago, desert nomads left animal figurines made of split willow twigs in canyon caves. They were placed carefully, ceremonially, giving rise to the suggestion that they had something to do with hunting rituals. About 2,000 years ago, the Anasazi appeared on the scene. A society of farmers, they lived in permanent communities of stone houses. These were the same Puebloan people who built, among others, the

River runners get swamped at Lava Falls.

famous cliff dwellings of Mesa Verde. In the canyon, they built no large structures, but their legacy survives in practically every nook and cranny.

The first Europeans to see the Grand Canyon were Spanish, in 1540 – a scant two generations after Christopher Columbus' epic voyage of discovery to the New World. They were treasure-seekers, members of Coronado's futile expedition in search of the fabulous Seven Cities of Cibola. One of Coronado's lieutenants, Garcia Lopez de Cardenas, was guided by Indians to the South Rim. Surviving accounts of that first visit are sketchy. The Spanish were duly impressed by the size of the place, but they saw the canyon chiefly as a barrier to further exploration and they left with no recorded regrets.

Some three centuries later, Europeans again encountered the Grand Canyon. They were also explorers and adventurers, dreamers and scoundrels, but this time some of them stayed. A few built reputations here, but others lost everything. The most famous explorer was John Wesley Powell, a geologist who led the first descent down the Colorado River through the canyon. Partly through Powell's influence, the canyon became the focus of American geology and signaled a growing appreciation of the desert landscape.

Touring the park: Today, most visitors arrive at the **South Rim** and spend their time along the roads and trails that skirt the abyss. Visitor services are clustered at **Grand Canyon Village**. Here you'll find lodging, restaurants, shops, park headquarters, the visitor center and other facilities. Two main trails begin near here. Both the **Bright Angel** and the **Kaibab** trails descend into the canyon, eventually reaching the river at **Phantom Ranch**. To walk or ride a mule to the bottom, and spend a night there, is an unforgettable experience but one that requires planning. Make reservations well in advance.

Many of the buildings at Grand Canyon Village are of historic significance. The genteel **El Tovar Hotel** was built in 1905, when most tourists arrived by train – which is still possible, thanks to the recently reorganized **Grand Canyon Railway** which runs from Williams, Arizona, to the South Rim of the Grand Canyon. Nearby, the **Bright Angel Lodge** houses a small museum. The lodge was designed by Mary E.J. Colter, who also drew plans for other distinctive structures at the canyon, including **Lookout Studio**, a fine example of how buildings can blend with their surroundings, and **Hopi House**, a fanciful representation of native pueblos. Colter also built **Desert View Watchtower**, near the east entrance, and **Hermits Rest**, a charming little structure at the end of the **West Rim Drive**.

The South Rim is essentially one grand viewing stand. But several points provide more expansive panoramas. A good place to begin is **Yavapai Point**, where a geologic museum perched on the canyon's brink explains the canyon's major features. From there, consider touring the West Rim Drive. During summer, this road is closed to private vehicles; the park operates free shuttle buses. Although it means leaving your car be-

Kayaking at Deer Creek Falls.

hind, the system makes it simple to combine walking with riding. Visitors can hop on and off the bus as they wish.

Going in the other direction is the **East Rim Drive**, which is open all year to private vehicles. Among worthwhile stops are **Grandview Point**, **Moran Point** and **Lipan Point**, each offering a different perspective. Keep in mind that the eyes become fatigued when confronted by mile after mile of this strange landscape. It's a good idea to take the canyon a bit at a time – better to spend three leisurely hours at one viewpoint than to race from one to the next. A good way to keep the canyon from blurring into sameness is to pick a single prominent landmark and try to locate it from various points along the rim.

Also along the East Rim Drive is **Tusayan**, the remains of a prehistoric pueblo that was home to a small group of perhaps 30 people some 800 years ago. A small archaeology museum displays ancient artifacts typical of the canyon. Several times a day, rangers conduct guided tours of the ruin, ex-plaining different aspects of life at the Grand Canyon so many centuries past.

To the North Rim: Near the East Entrance, **Desert View** provides limited visitor services, including a campground and the Desert View Watchtower. At this point the Colorado River, having maintained a southerly course for many miles, turns hard to the west and enters the deepest section of the canyon. From here, the North Rim is only a few miles away as the raven flies but over 180 miles (290 km) by auto. Leaving the park, the highway drops some 3,000 ft (914 m) past the impressive gorge of the **Little Colorado River** before turning north across the **Navajo Reservation**, through the **Painted Desert**, past the towering **Echo Cliffs**, to the spectacular **Navajo Bridge**. From its deck to the green river is 467 dizzying feet (142 m).

A short distance from the bridge, at Marble Canyon Trading Post, a road leads north to **Lees Ferry** – historically significant as the only feasible crossing for hundreds of miles in either direction; geologically significant as the of-

Sunset at the Watchtower, South Rim.

142

ficial beginning of the Grand Canyon.

From **Marble Canyon**, the main road turns abruptly toward the west and climbs to the heights of the **Kaibab Plateau**. The transition from treeless desert to deep forest is dramatic. Squirrels replace lizards, deer bound through the shadows of giant ponderosa pines, and snowbanks last well into June. The word Kaibab comes from two Paiute words, *kaiuw* (mountain) and *a-vwi* (lying down). Indeed, the plateau feels like a "mountain lying down," alpine in character but with no definite summit. It makes for pleasant driving, with car windows open, its occupants breathing in the smell of piney woods.

The **North Rim** is the less visited side of the Grand Canyon, partly because the access road is closed by snow for about six months every year, partly because the roads on this side do not parallel the rim for long distances. No one feels disappointed here. The canyon views are, if anything, more spectacular and the uncrowded atmosphere is quite appealing in comparison to the jostling crowds of the South Rim. Most visitors will go straight to the **Grand Canyon Lodge**, a superb stone-and-log building surrounded by cabins, some perched right on the canyon brink. A short, paved trail takes you along a knife-edged ridge to the tip of **Bright Angel Point**. This path rivals anything anywhere in the national park system for sheer drama, and ends at yet another grand vista.

For many visitors, it comes as a surprise that what is seen from here is not the Grand Canyon proper but a tributary called **Bright Angel Canyon**. That such an enormous gulf can be just one auxiliary branch can be hard to accept. To reach the main canyon, follow **Cape Royal Road** to its end at **Cape Royal**. Although only 23 miles (37 km) in length, this excursion can take at least half a day, stopping at **Point Imperial** and other viewpoints along the way.

Today, as ever, at the heart of the canyon runs the **Colorado River** – creator and prime mover of this remarkable landscape. It is said that if you know the river, you know the canyon. Beginning

Pinyon skeleton at Desert View.

far upstream in the snowy mountains of Colorado, the river draws strength from tributaries like Wyoming's Green River, pouring cold and clear into Utah's red rock country. Here it becomes warm in the summer sun, and picks up the sediment for which it was named. *Colorado* is a Spanish word for red. The river once flowed red all the way to the Gulf of California. It built a great delta there, until a series of dams diverted the water to booming cities.

The most recent obstruction, **Glen Canyon Dam**, stands just above the Grand Canyon and contains **Lake Powell**. Emerging from the depths of the lake, the old red river now flows cold and green. Like a string of jade among the red sandstones, it is beautiful to look at, but the dam-controlled river environment is very different from what it once was. In permanently cold water, a new assortment of fish and insects has replaced native species. With no new sand flowing downstream, the beaches are disappearing. And with the disappearance of spring floods, vegetation

has grown more dense, with different species dominating the scene.

These effects fuel a heated controversy between demands that the natural river environment be maintained and the need for electrical power from the dam. Through the adjustment of flow rates, some of these effects can be mitigated, but others will bear on the canyon as long as the dam remains.

Meanwhile, Lake Powell is the centerpiece of **Glen Canyon National Recreation Area**, administered by the Park Service and devoted almost exclusively to power-boating. There's a visitor center at the dam, and it's worth going in just to see the superb scale model of the region. This is also the starting point for tours of the dam. Those who knew Glen Canyon before it was flooded still regard its inundation as one of the great environmental losses of the century. It was a unique place, unlike any other canyon on earth, characterized by soaring walls of sandstone carved in liquid shapes. The Colorado flowed warm and shallow through a child's fantasy of shape and color. Side canyons hundreds of feet deep and only a few yards wide opened into huge amphitheaters beneath the desert surface.

Most of that is gone now, but the lake has its own appeal. The serpentine shoreline provides thousands of coves and beaches alternating with sheer cliffs and great domes of smooth, white sandstone. The water is deep blue and pleasantly warm in summer. Road access is limited to several marinas, the largest of which is **Wahweap**, near the dam. Tour boats ply the lake to various sites, including **Rainbow Bridge National Monument**, where visitors marvel at the most graceful and perhaps largest natural bridge on earth.

At the other end of Grand Canyon, **Lake Mead National Recreation Area** also centers on a reservoir, this one created by the Hoover Dam. Aside from the lake, interest here centers on the unusual richness of desert flora and fauna. Three distinct desert regions come together here – the Mojave, Sonoran and Great Basin. The result is rewarding for anyone interested in wildlife.

Left, Lake Powell, near Padre Bay. **Right**, scaling a slot canyon.

CANYONLANDS

Utah's **Canyonlands National Park** sprawls at the physical and emotional center of the huge province known as the Colorado Plateau. Here, across an enormous, tilted, tiered and carved rock stage, one of nature's longest-running dramas plays every day – an epic in which rock, river, weather and finely tuned living things all have equal roles.

Stewart Udall, who as Secretary of the Interior was midwife to the congressional bill that created Canyonlands in 1964, described the region as "a vast area of scenic wonders and recreational opportunities unduplicated elsewhere on the American continent or in the world." You will certainly need to plan your trip to this 527-sq. mile (1,365-sq. km) park carefully, as it is divided into four quite separate units – Island in the Sky, the Needles, the Maze, and the converging Green and Colorado rivers – all of which deserve equal consideration.

If you have only a day, the 6,000-ft (1,829-m) plateau of **Island in the Sky**, situated in the northern part of Canyonlands between the Y of the two rivers, offers sweeping views of the entire park, a visitor center, interpretive talks, a tiny campground (no water), and short, rugged hikes to salt domes, arches and other geologic features.

The road to this unit begins 10 miles (16 km) north of Moab, then southwest from Highway 191 for another 25 miles (40 km). Float trips above the confluence of the Green and Colorado rivers – one of the most pleasurable ways to experience the park – are popular, as are mountain biking and four-wheel-driving. Concessionaires, located primarily in Moab or Green River, can arrange these. These businesses are contracted by the National Parks Service to manage a variety of services, including lodging, restaurants, gift shops and tours.

If you want to head into canyon country, drive south 40 miles (64 km) on Highway 191, then another 35 miles (56 km) on Highway 211 into the highly rewarding **Needles District**, where a dizzying array of sandstone arches, fins, buttes, spires and canyons rival ancient Anasazi ruins and rock art for beauty and abundance. The Needles maintains a visitor center and a pleasant campground (water from April to September), primitive backcountry campsites, and a number of four-wheel-drive and primitive hiking trails.

The remote **Maze District**, once described as "a 30-square-mile puzzle in sandstone," can only be reached by foot or four-wheel-drive from west of the park (or from the river) and is best left for future visits. But if you're well-equipped with water, food and backpacking supplies and willing to spend more time, the pristine Maze contains a rich variety of rocks, desert landscapes and rock art.

For "river rats," there's no better way to go into the heart of this convoluted canyon country than to follow in the wake of John Wesley Powell, who made daring runs down the **Green** and **Colorado** rivers in 1869 and 1871–72. Below the river confluence, the swollen

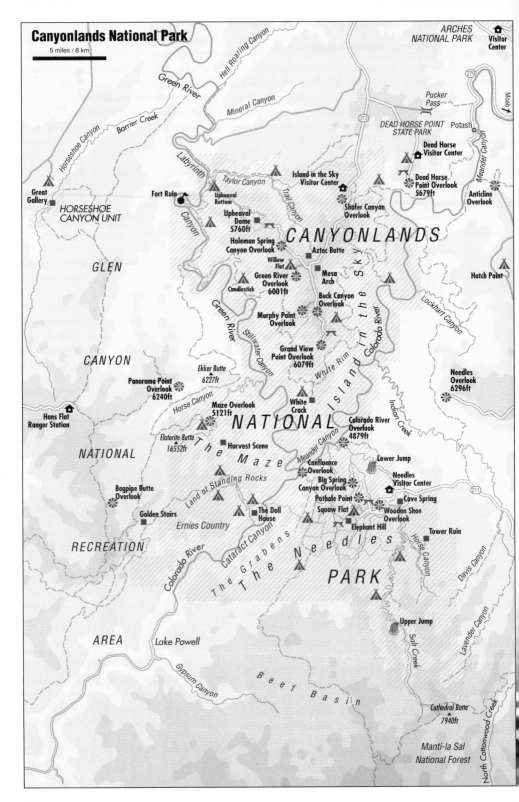

Canyonlands National Park

5 miles / 8 km

ARCHES
NATIONAL PARK

Visitor
Center

Green River

Hell Roaring Canyon

Moab

279

Mineral Canyon

Pucker
Pass

Potash

313

DEAD HORSE POINT
STATE PARK

Dead Horse
Visitor Center

Horseshoe Canyon

Barrier Creek

Labyrinth

Taylor Canyon

Island in the Sky
Visitor Center

Dead Horse
Point Overlook
5679ft

Great
Gallery

HORSESHOE
CANYON UNIT

Fort Ruin

Upheaval
Bottom

Trail Canyon

Shafer Canyon
Overlook

Anticline
Overlook

Canyon

Upheaval
Dome
5760ft

CANYONLANDS

Meander Canyon

GLEN

Holeman Spring
Canyon Overlook

Aztec Butte

Willow
Flat

Mesa
Arch

Hatch Point

Candlestick

Green River
Overlook
6001ft

Buck Canyon
Overlook

Lockhart Canyon

CANYON

Green River

Murphy Point
Overlook

White Rim

Island in the Sky

Colorado River

Grand View
Point Overlook
6079ft

Stillwater Canyon

Needles
Overlook
6296ft

Ekker Butte
6227ft

Panorama Point
Overlook
6240ft

Horse Canyon

White
Crack

NATIONAL

Indian Creek

Maze Overlook
5121ft

Colorado River
Overlook
4879ft

Hans Flat
Ranger Station

Elaterite Butte
16552ft

Harvest Scene

The Maze

Meander Canyon

Lower Jump

NATIONAL

Land of Standing Rocks

Confluence
Overlook

Needles
Visitor Center

211

Bagpipe Butte
Overlook

Big Spring
Canyon Overlook

Cave Spring

Golden Stairs

The Doll
House

Pothole Point

Squaw Flat

Wooden Shoe
Overlook

Ernies Country

Tower Ruin

RECREATION

Colorado River

Cataract Canyon

The Grabens

The Needles

Elephant Hill

Horse Canyon

Davis Canyon

PARK

Lavender Canyon

AREA

Lake Powell

Gypsum Canyon

Beef Basin

Upper Jump

Salt Creek

North Cottonwood Creek

Cathedral Butte
7940ft

Manti-la Sal
National Forest

Colorado erupts into roaring white water for the 14 miles (23 km) that link sheer-walled **Cataract Canyon** with **Lake Powell**. River running here is carefully monitored by the Park Service, and only experienced river runners may attempt the trip.

Island in the Sky: Rock is the leitmotif of Canyonlands. To try to understand its scope, drive south from **Island in the Sky Visitor Center** to **Grand View Point**, which is the best place to survey the 360° panorama that unfolds before you. Hidden in the northeast are the soaring red rock landmarks of Arches National Park. To the east rise the tall, laccolithic crags of the **La Sal Mountains**, imposing yet inviting. Closer to the park, beneath **Dead Horse Point State Park**, loop the famous "goosenecks" of the Colorado River, marking the park's eastern border.

To the west, the equally contorted Green River winds through **Labyrinth Canyon**, its narrow meanders forming the shared boundary with Glen Canyon National Recreation Area.

To the southwest the **Henry Mountains** obstruct the view of Capitol Reef National Park, their great bulk looming beyond the Maze. The view south absorbs more than 100 miles (160 km) of drifting tablelands and swirling canyons, including the junction of the Colorado and Green rivers, bound on either side by the eroded sandstones of The Needles and the tortuous passages of The Maze. Just below this sky island is the **White Rim Trail**, a circuitous, 100-mile (160-km) dirt trail that was used by prospectors mining uranium in the colorful Chinle Formation in the 1950s. This popular four-wheel-drive route follows a bench of White Rim Sandstone through prime bighorn sheep land.

The scenic drive offers several places for stopping and hiking. Short trails to **Aztec Butte** and **Mesa Arch** are marked by rock cairns along the Navajo Sandstone slickrock. Plants struggle to survive in the thin soils found in this arid environment – in cracks in the rock and in fragile, "brown sugar" patches of cryptobiotic soil that will eventually allow pinyons, junipers, blackbrush and grasses to take hold. Watch where you walk; your footsteps have a huge impact here. Adaptable reptiles, such as whiptailed lizards, and ground squirrels, canyon mice and other gnawing creatures are found on the plateau. They make fine fare for peripatetic coyotes and gray foxes and alert sky patrollers, such as eagles, ravens and red-tailed hawks.

The rocks in this park contain a color-coded record of sediment deposited over the past 300 million years, in a succession of seas, beaches, deserts, rivers and streams. But the accounting is not complete; more than a vertical mile of recent strata has already been borne away by the youthful enthusiasm of the Colorado and Green rivers, which began scouring the land as the massive Colorado Plateau was forced up. The topography is forever changing. As the sediment-laden rivers cut their paths, and ground water, ice, snow and wind break down the rocks, it is possible that the eroded beauty of Canyonlands will one day be merely a memory.

One of the best ways to confront the

A hardy sunflower blooms in the desert.

geologic processes that brought Canyonlands into being is to hike the short trail to **Upheaval Dome**, a short way from the main road in Island in the Sky. Just below you is a 1,500-ft (457-m) crater filled with a jumble of rocks, which is believed by many geologists to be a collapsed salt dome. The 11 layers of sedimentary rocks on display in Canyonlands sit uneasily on a layer of salt thousands of feet thick – the remnant of evaporated seas that lay trapped here 300 million years ago.

As overlying sediments pressed down on this salt – the Paradox Formation – it liquidized and began to move away from the weight. Highlands blocked it on the east, so it flowed west until it encountered ancient fault blocks that forced the salt to bulge upward, forming the cracked salt domes you see throughout the large Paradox Basin. Ground water began to seep into the fractures, dissolving the salt and deepening the joints through many layers of sedimentary rocks. This weathering of sandstone has created memorable features throughout the park – some of the most spectacular are found among the highly eroded Cedar Mesa Sandstone in The Needles.

The Needles: The turnoff for **The Needles** lies 14 miles (23 km) north of Monticello on Highway 191, where a paved road follows **Indian Creek Canyon** to **Squaw Flat**, one of those rare places in Canyonlands blessed with deeper soils that allow Indian rice grass, galleta and other useful grasses to establish themselves. The road passes **Pothole Point**, where depressions in the rock trap life-giving rainwater. Good views of the narrow spires of The Needles can be seen from here.

The road ends at **Big Spring Canyon Overlook**, where a trail to the **Confluence Overlook** begins. From **Squaw Flat Campground**, a 3-mile (5-km) unpaved spur leads to **Elephant Hill**, and, thence, a dirt road takes you to the collapsing fins of the **Grabens** near the river and foot trails enter The Needles themselves. The 5-mile (8-km), round-trip **Chesler Park Trail**, through a meadow dotted with eroded rocks,

Heading for information.

makes a good hike from Elephant Hill. The canyons and meadows of The Needles support many wood rats, chipmunks, squirrels, kangaroo rats and other rodents, as well as horned larks and black-throated sparrows.

There are a number of places along the scenic drive to turn off and explore. One four-wheel-drive road, beginning at the **Needles Visitor Center**, takes you north to the **Colorado River Overlook**. A short, unpaved spur south of the pavement leads to **Cave Spring Trail**, which preserves a historic cowboy line camp beside a spring. The camp is a reminder that much of Canyonlands was grazed heavily by cattle and sheep from the late 1800s until well into this century. From Cave Spring, you will need a four-wheel-drive vehicle (or a sturdy pair of legs) to explore portions of **Salt Creek** or its main tributary, **Horse Canyon**, where hidden Indian ruins make the trip worthwhile.

Ancient art: Remnants of the Anasazi Indians, who lived here between AD 1 and 1300, abound. Horse Canyon contains the Anasazi masonry structures of **Tower** and **Keyhole ruins**, as well as the **Thirteen Faces**, red-and-white pictographs painted on the sandstone walls. When possible, the Anasazi farmed along ephemeral washes, now overgrown with willow, tamarisk and cottonwood, but they continued to hunt small game and supplement meals with seeds, nuts and edible plants. Surplus grain was stored in tightly lidded granaries built into hard-to-reach ledges.

Rock paintings found in these canyons portray large, mysterious-looking, anthropomorphs, both shield-shaped and triangular, bejeweled and brightly painted in red, white and sometimes blue. (**All-American Man** is one of the most famous pictographs.) Images of human figures, game animals and numerous symbols were also pecked into the walls. Here as elsewhere, you may look but not touch rock art. Disturbing artifacts is strictly prohibited. Scientists speculate that when life here became too tough sometime in the 1200s, the Anasazi moved to farmlands along the

Fording the river.

Rio Grande and the Little Colorado, where their descendants, still live.

An even earlier culture has also been identified in Canyonlands: the Archaic people who hunted and gathered here between 10,000 and 2,000 years ago. Signs of their passage are preserved in 3,000-year-old, ghostly Barrier Canyon-style pictographs found along the 6½-mile (10-km), round-trip hike to the **Great Gallery** in Horseshoe Canyon. Horseshoe Canyon is in the **Maze District**, which has been kept primitive and difficult to access by overland route. (**Robber's Roost**, where Butch Cassidy and his cattle-rustling cohorts hid out, is nearby.) You can go as far as **Hans Flat Ranger Station**, on a 46-mile (74-km) unpaved road, but then you need a four-wheel-drive vehicle and a good pair of legs – yours or a horse's.

Several long unpaved roads traverse wild country dotted with strangely named landmarks, which, in true Western style, arose from differing perspectives of native people, early adventurers and poetic travelers. A road leads north to Horseshoe Canyon, south to **Bagpipe Butte Overlook**, then east along the **Flint Trail** to **Ernies Country** and the **Land of Standing Rocks**. From here you can hike through the **Doll House** above the river confluence and down into **Spanish Bottom**

For a look into The Maze, backtrack to the **Golden Stairs**, then drive northeast to the **Maze Overlook** or hike the 14-mile (23-km) **North Trail Canyon** to the overlook. A 3-mile (5-km) trail leads into The Maze itself, where Archaic pictographs known as the **Harvest Scene** reward your efforts. This is the park's most pristine experience – a place where quiet desert residents, such as kit foxes, coyotes and mountain lions, are bolder, and unexpected seeps deep in the canyons nourish throngs of maidenhair ferns, mosses, monkeyflowers and columbines. This is rugged, beautiful country but, without preparation, it is treacherous. Talk to the park rangers before attempting a trip.

Right, rainbow over Salt Creek, Needles district.

ARCHES

"This is a landscape that has to be seen to be believed," marveled writer Ed Abbey, one of the Southwest's most passionate advocates, "and even then, confronted directly by the senses, it strains credulity."

Indeed. Yet, one of the pleasures of a trip across the Colorado Plateau is the way its ever-changing topography pushes us to understand our surroundings according to different rules, to change our sense of what is normal. **Arches National Park**, with its world-renowned population of carved, salmon-colored arches, fins, spires, pinnacles and balanced rocks, is a case in point. Here, the very landmarks for which this park is famous are windows through which we experience the natural world in a new way.

This 114-sq. mile (295-sq. km) desert park, 5 miles (8 km) north of Moab, Utah, is home to more than 1,700 natural arches and many other strangely eroded red rock giants. Unlike neighboring Canyonlands, which requires many visits to appreciate, Arches is small enough to experience in a day by way of its paved scenic drive, pullouts – where a driver can take a breather and take in the view – and many short trails, but large enough to warrant longer explorations into the backcountry, where its wild nature becomes apparent.

Arches boasts the largest number of natural sandstone arches in the world, with many more being formed all the time – the fortuitous result of location, geology and water erosion. You might think that the explanation for the large number of shape-shifting rocks in this place is complicated, but you would be wrong. The key to this odd convention of geologic landmarks is salt – a common enough commodity which here has given rise, quite literally, to this high-relief landscape.

The geologic story: The salt that lies below Arches was deposited 300 million years ago when a succession of large, shallow seas lay landlocked by highlands to the east. As the climate gradually dried, the seawater evaporated, leaving behind salt deposits thousands of feet thick in an enormous depression known as the **Paradox Basin**. Eventually, the highlands (known as the **Uncompahgre Uplift**) began shedding debris into the basin, which compacted there, cemented by calcium carbonate and other minerals. Its tremendous weight bore down on the underlying Paradox deposits, causing the salt, which is somewhat "plastic," to flow west, away from the burden. The movement stalled when the salt ran up against ancient fault blocks.

One of the most obvious of these faults can be seen near the visitor center, where a 2,500-ft (762-m) displacement along the **Moab Fault** has exposed the fossiliferous strata of the ancient Honaker Trail Formation on the opposite side of the valley – a rare glimpse of the rocks that make up the park's basement.

Unable to move farther, the salt layer domed up through the 12 layers of rocks

lying on top of it, cracking the rocks and weakening the strata. Joints appeared along these fault lines, giving ground water a chance to enter and dissolve the salt. Undermined by this erosion, the salt domes began to collapse. The low-lying **Salt** and **Cache valleys** and the parallel lines of formations sweeping across them are testimony to this ongoing weakening of loosely cemented sedimentary rocks. It's not difficult to understand what happened next. The evidence can be found everywhere in Arches. Once water, ice and snow went to work on the rock, deepening and widening joints, all manner of oddly carved stones gradually emerged, of which the delicate spans of reddish-brown sandstone, known as natural arches, are some of the most interesting.

For a look at the many different types of arches and carved phenomena in the park, take the 18-mile (29-km) scenic drive from the visitor center to Devils Garden, stopping to hike along the short trails that wind through this oversized Zen garden of standing stones.

The first weathered rocks you come to are the skyscraper-like monoliths in **Park Avenue**, so named because of the way their sheer walls jostle the skyline. Nearby, in the **Courthouse Towers**, are **Sheep Rock**, the **Organ**, the **Tower of Babel**, and the **Three Gossips**, soaring giants composed of iron-rich Entrada Sandstone, the principal rock layer in the park. Different rates of erosion in the three "members" of Entrada Sandstone are responsible for the majority of features, with the lower Dewey Bridge Member crumbling easily beneath the harder Slick Rock Member.

The uppermost layer, the white Moab Member, can be seen capping some of the higher landmarks. Underlying the Entrada are the swirling beds of cream-colored Navajo Sandstone, whose Sahara-like origins can easily be seen just beyond Courthouse Towers in the humped shapes of "petrified" sand dunes. In this open landscape, you get a great view of the 12,000-ft (3,658-m), snowcapped **La Sal Mountains**, great laccoliths with hearts of lava, exposed

Desert denizen, a side-blotched lizard.

160

by erosion in forested crags and peaks that dominate the eastern sky.

Park rangers recommend that you drive at least as far as the **Windows Section**, for it is here that you can see single and double arches, windows, buttes and the gravity-defying **Balanced Rock**, sitting beside the 2½-mile (4-km) paved spur road. Between May and August, this is a good area to see Indian paintbrush, larkspur, sand verbena and other wildflowers.

Just beyond The Windows, you can stop and take in much of the park at **Panorama Point**. The canyon of the **Colorado River** is visible on the southeast border of the park. The green belt of willows, tamarisks and cottonwoods that grows along the waterway seems like a mirage on the other side of this sparsely vegetated salt valley, where only salt-tolerant plants like pickleweed and seepweed can grow. You can get a better feel for the Colorado River along Highway 128, which parallels the river just outside the park. Travelers on the Spanish Trail in the 1830s and 1840s forded the Colorado River just beyond modern-day **Moab**. This sleepy little community was founded by Mormon missionaries who came to convert the Ute Indians in 1855, although Indian resistance prevented them from settling there before the 1870s. Today, the town makes an excellent jumping-off point for nearby parks.

After Panorama Point, a road turns northeast for 3 miles (5 km), crossing an area of collapsed rocks of the more recent Dakota, Morrison and Mancos formations. The road ends at a viewpoint overlooking **Delicate Arch**, the world-famous symbol of Utah's red rock country. Delicate Arch is actually not very tall – only 45-ft (14-m) high – but its location on the lip of a slickrock bowl gives it a dramatic bearing. For a close-up look, climb the steep trail to the arch (1½ miles/2 km each way) – one of the most rewarding hikes in the park. The trail begins at a rudimentary cabin, the 1906 **Wolfe Ranch**, which was home to a rather antisocial Civil War veteran named John Wesley Wolfe and his son. Wolfe came here for his health in 1888,

Delicate penstemon blossoms.

but it's hard to understand what could have prompted him to settle in such a remote outpost, so far from society. Maybe that was exactly the point. Writer Ed Abbey, who spent several seasons as a backcountry ranger in Arches in the late 1950s, and who wrote eloquently of his experiences in the classic *Desert Solitaire*, apparently relished his isolation. The canyon country seems to attract loners who value silence and the harmony of the desert.

Desert fire: A few miles farther and you reach the flaming rock fins known as **Fiery Furnace**, which explode with vibrant color at sunset. In spring, summer and fall, park rangers lead popular early-evening hikes through this deeply eroded rockscape. If time permits, sign up for this three-hour hike; it's one of the most spectacular backcountry hikes in the park. But it's not a good idea to hike it alone. There is no marked trail through the radiating rocks, so it is quite easy to lose your way.

Beyond Fiery Furnace a left turn onto an unpaved road leads 8 miles (13 km)

across **Salt Valley** to **Klondike Bluffs**, whose **Marching Men** formations so impressed prospector Alexander Ringhoffer that he persuaded the railroad to conduct tours to the spot in 1923. Arches was named a national monument just six years later. (It did not become a national park until 1971.) Klondike is now one of the least visited places in the park. If you do decide to drive there, don't start out when rain is expected. Desert flash floods are common here and frequently wash out roads. Ask a ranger before venturing into areas likely to funnel flood waters.

The scenic drive ends at **Devils Garden**, where the park's densest array of arches and fins makes a fitting climax to any visit to the park. Several easy trails meander among its soaring spans. **Sand Dune Arch** shelters a large sand dune at its base; **Skyline Arch** became famous when a rockfall in November 1940 doubled its size. A 1-mile (1½-km) trail from the road leads to **Landscape Arch**, a 306-ft (93-m) spall of "desert varnished" beige rock, thought to be the longest natural arch in the world. You may continue from Landscape Arch along an unimproved trail to two other formations – **Double O Arch** (1 mile/ 1½ km) and the **Dark Angel** (½ mile/1 km). A short side trail leads to massive **Navajo Arch** and the twin openings of **Partition Arch**. Devils Garden has a pleasant little campground, but you will need to get there early in the day to scoop up a spot. While out hiking, stay on the trails. The desert floor is dotted with dark patches of cryptobiotic soil, composed of mosses, lichens, fungi and algae that retain moisture, protect against erosion, and provide nitrogen and other nutrients in which plants can grow. Once stepped on, this fragile, new soil, on which so much new life depends, is destroyed for decades.

Temperatures at this 3,960–5,653-ft (1,207–1,723-m) elevation are very hot in summer, and thunderstorms and torrential rain are apt to swoop in suddenly. In winter, it is surprisingly frigid, with sub-freezing night-time temperatures. The dry-rocked landscape is occasion- **Indian paintbrush.**

ally transformed under a glittering white blanket of snow. Colors seem deeper and more intense.

The secret of survival: Plants and animals must be very choosy about where they live in this difficult environment, jealously guarding their special places in an ongoing bid for survival. Desert creatures are generally nocturnal, venturing out only when the desert cools down. You are likely to hear the yip of coyotes at night, as they and their gray fox neighbors trot great distances across the park in search of jackrabbits, cottontails, ground squirrels and other rodents. Rattlesnakes, collared lizards and other reptiles, which are unable to control body temperatures, doze beneath rocks and bushes at midday. The sheerest of cliffs make good perches for lazy-winged golden eagles and red-tailed hawks, while in shadowed canyons, the joyous song of the tiny canyon wren bounces off seeping sandstone walls decorated with colorful water-loving plants. Hardy junipers do better than pinyon trees on exposed surfaces, cling-ing tenaciously to naked rocks like drowning men atop life rafts.

For an interesting comparison with Arches National Park, consider visiting **Natural Bridges National Monument**, off Highway 191, south of Moab. This small park unit preserves three natural bridges composed of Cedar Mesa Sandstone, which were cut by a tributary of the Colorado River. One of the bridges, **Sipapu**, is second in size to Rainbow Bridge in Glen Canyon, the world's largest known natural bridge. The difference between a natural arch and a natural bridge is that an arch is weathered into existence by the elements; a natural bridge is carved by flooded streams and rivers filled with debris cutting through their meanders. The famous "goosenecks" seen throughout canyon country are the result of meandering streams that became deeply entrenched when the Colorado Plateau began rising. As you might expect, natural bridges and goosenecks are constant companions in canyon country; watch out for them.

Fiery furnace.

CAPITOL REEF

For many people, the desert Southwest seems like a vast dry ocean that stretches endlessly in every direction, its rocky floor occasionally interrupted by broad troughs, tablelands, snowcapped mountains, maze-like canyons and island communities of wildlife.

But in Utah, the paradox of ocean imagery amid intensely arid land goes one step farther, for here, rolling in long, colorful, petrified breakers across a desert basin is one of the most dramatic geologic features on the American continent: the **Waterpocket Fold**, a 100-mile (160-km) long warp on the earth's surface that neatly bisects southeastern Utah, from volcanic Thousand Lake Mountain in the north to man-made Lake Powell in the south. In between, **Capitol Reef National Park** preserves 75 miles (120 km) of the Waterpocket Fold and the plants, animals and artifacts of Indian and pioneer settlers who have made the area their home.

Capitol Reef is one of the lesser-known parks in the Southwest – a plus for geology fans who are put off by the crowds at Grand Canyon and Zion. It is halfway between Bryce Canyon and Canyonlands national parks and is easily reached from Highway 12 to the south or from Highway 70 to the north. Highway 24 cuts across the park, following the winding **Fremont River** beneath tall sandstone cliffs, which open into a series of humpbacks, known to the Paiutes as "the sleeping rainbow," at the eastern exit. Roads on either side of the Waterpocket Fold swing south from Highway 24, providing numerous possibilities for exploring the park by car, bicycle or on foot.

Rainbow rocks: Most visitors are intrigued by the Waterpocket Fold. How did it come to be here? Scientists believe that it was created about 65 million years ago, when a period of geologic activity began wrenching the low-lying landscape of western America into its present contorted form. It is generally thought that massive movements along the junction of the Pacific and North American plates around that time forced up the Sierra Nevada in California and continued to reverberate eastward, squeezing the miles of sedimentary rocks that had accumulated across the Southwest. The monolithic Colorado Plateau rose slowly under this pressure, and a series of steep, north–south-oriented monoclines, or folds, began to form across its surface, of which the Waterpocket Fold is one of the most spectacular examples.

The exposed rock surfaces soon became vulnerable to weathering. In this region, wind and water erosion carved the rainbow-colored cliffs, spires, natural bridges, arches and hogbacks that characterize Capitol Reef today.

Because it follows the Waterpocket Fold, the park is much longer than it is wide and can be divided roughly into three sections: the rugged, remote northern section of **Cathedral Valley** paralleling the northeastern exposure of the Fold; the accessible **Escarpment** section, encompassing park headquarters

at **Fruita**, the Fremont River and a particularly scenic portion of the Fold; and the southernmost section of the park, above Bullfrog Basin in Glen Canyon, where the great rock waves of the Waterpocket Fold reach 1,500 feet (457 m) in height and are cut by a labyrinthian network of deep canyons.

This is a park that inspires strong emotions. It is remote, overscaled and desperately hot and dry in the summer (unless you find yourself caught in a summer downpour, when most of the park's scant 7 inches (17.8 cm) of precipitation falls). To keep cool in summer, either view the park from your car or stick to one of the day hikes off the scenic drive and Highway 24, such as **Capitol Gorge**, **Grand Wash**, the **Goosenecks**, **Sunset Point** or **Hickman Bridge**. The tree-lined banks of the Fremont River also provide shade on days when the temperature approaches 100°F (37°C). If you hope to explore the park on foot, bring adequate weather protection, water, food and backpacking equipment with you – they are not avail-

able in the park. There are numerous places where you can hike and camp off-trail. Plan your trip carefully before venturing out by obtaining a free backcountry map from rangers at the visitor center.

Mormon settlers: If you haven't been to Capitol Reef before, start your visit at park headquarters in Fruita, which sits next to the emerald belt of cottonwoods, tamarisks and willows along the Fremont River. This old Mormon community (elevation 5,500 feet/1,676 m) grew up in the 1880s, comprising 12 families, some of whom were polygamists wishing to live quiet, self-supporting lives away from the glare of government disapproval. (Names like **Cohab Canyon** linger, commemorating these early settlers.) With a reliable water source at hand, the residents were able to harvest plentiful supplies of apricots, peaches, cherries and apples, which they used for their own consumption or sold to neighboring towns, transient miners, cowboys and even outlaws (Butch Cassidy and his Wild Bunch were customers). Cattle ranching also took place at Capitol Reef, evidence of which may still be seen in the park.

These adherents to the Church of Jesus Christ of Latter-Day Saints prospered as nearby communities struggled. They built wagon roads across the nearly impassable ridges and smooth domes of the Waterpocket Fold, which received its name because of the way depressions in the smooth "slickrock" filled with life-giving water when it rained. The settlers' preoccupation with land and government shows in names such as Capitol Reef. In their eyes, the central section of the Fold welled up like an ocean reef, while one of its larger domes seemed like a dead-ringer for the US Capitol. Other unusually eroded rocks sparked equally descriptive names – Chimney Rock, Golden Throne, Egyptian Temple and the Castle.

These early European settlers were keen to attract visitors to this remote area of Utah, which, in typically grand fashion, they dubbed Wayne Wonderland (Capitol Reef is in Wayne County). It was a combination of their boosterism

Chimney Rock.

and continuing political pressure at the state level that directly led to Capitol Reef being designated a national monument in 1937 and a national park in 1971. Today, all that remains of Fruita are its turn-of-the-century schoolhouse, a barn, a couple of houses and the orchards. The last of the residents were bought out in the late 1960s. They have been supplanted by Park Service employees who operate park headquarters, a visitor center and a small campground, which sits among the original orchards (you are welcome to pick fruit for your own consumption but you must pay for larger quantities).

Desert life: The river and the shallow pools at the base of seeping sandstone walls provide an oasis where trees and water-loving plants, such as columbines, monkeyflowers and ferns, grow. They are also popular haunts for mule deer, warblers, ringtail cats, frogs and other desert denizens who come to drink and splash during cool desert evenings and mornings. In winter, you can sometimes surprise a mountain lion or bob-cat, emboldened by the lack of visitors.

It is a mistake to imagine that the desert is devoid of life. In reality, the many creatures, large and small, that live here have adapted to a life beneath rocks, have burrowed underground, or hidden in narrow canyons, where sunlight and human visitors rarely interrupt their privacy.

Towering nearly 1,000 feet (305 m) above the river are the vertiginous cliffs of red Wingate Sandstone, narrow ledges of maroon Kayenta, and creamy Navajo slickrock domes that give the Fold its awesome ramparts. On these slippery surfaces, pinyon and juniper trees struggle with the elements, sending roots into pockets of soil. These dune-deposited rocks were laid down in a vast desert roughly 200 million years ago and, over time, compressed into mineralized rocks several miles thick. A 13-mile (21-km) scenic drive from Fruita takes you through the dramatic western exposure of the Waterpocket Fold into **Grand Wash** and **Capitol Gorge**, two water-carved, sheer-walled canyons. Along

Kicking back.

the drive, older rocks of the Shinarump Conglomerate, Chinle and Moenkopi formations appear, their ancient origins in sluggish streams and rivers during the time of the dinosaurs.

There are many places where you can stop and hike along trails leading to overlooks, arches, remote canyons and slickrock wilderness. To the east loom the 11,000-ft (3,353-m), lava-intruded **Henry Mountains**, the last range to be named in the United States, and to the west, the great bulk of **Boulder Mountain**. You are never far from cool forests of ponderosa, fir and spruce, or from icy mountain streams.

Abundant evidence of geologic activity is on view in the northern section of the park. Here the enormous drainage area of **Cathedral Valley** fans southeast from the base of **Thousand Lake Mountain**, where more recent volcanism and glaciation have built and sculpted the high country beyond Capitol Reef. In this extremely arid section of the park, accessible only on foot or by four-wheel-drive, thick layers of red Entrada Sandstone have been whittled by erosion into 500-ft (152-m) spires that seem to guard this bleak landscape. The exposed location is home to only the hardiest desert plants. Burrowing creatures such as kangaroo rats, jackrabbits and cottontails have found a way to survive here. They form the diet of gray foxes, coyotes, mountain lions, golden eagles, ravens and other peripatetic desert dwellers.

In this remote spot, there is one primitive campground close to **Upper Cathedral Valley Overlook**, and another at Elkhorn in Fishlake National Forest, outside the park limits.

For "desert rats" used to the rigors of hiking over naked slickrock, the southernmost tip of the Fold is the most alluring. It can be reached via the **Notom-Bullfrog** dirt road, which runs down the east side of the Fold all the way to **Bullfrog Marina** at **Lake Powell**, or by turning off at Boulder along Highway 12 and crossing the famous **Burr Trail**, a prospector's route to the canyons.

On this southern exposure of the Waterpocket Fold, the national park meets the wilderness that surrounds the **Escalante River** and its canyons and the true meaning of canyon country becomes apparent. The best way to explore it is to hike south from where the Burr Trail meets the Notom-Bullfrog Road, through 16-mile (26-km) **Muley Twist Canyon**, where early travelers joked that the canyon zigzagged so sharply that their mules had to twist to get through. This route takes you through steep canyon narrows to an exceptionally wild area of the park around **Lower Hall's Creek**, where a ferry took 19th-century pioneers across what used to be the Colorado River.

The Escalante area also harbors beautiful rock art created by prehistoric Anasazi and Fremont Indians. Deep in the canyons are panels depicting, among other things, tall, bejeweled shaman-like anthropomorphs carrying shields and surrounded by bighorn sheep and other game. Look but don't touch. These beautiful images are one of the highlights of this unusual park and protecting them is everyone's responsibility.

Left, bikers can explore back roads. **Right**, the Fruita schoolhouse is a remnant of an early Mormon village.

BRYCE CANYON

Some landscapes are so remarkable that many people are never the same again after seeing them. **Bryce Canyon** in southern Utah is one such place. A geologic fantasyland of Kodacolor dreaming spires, natural bridges, gravity-defying arches, precariously balanced rocks and sky-filled windows, carved deeply into the soft, limestone cliffs of the Paunsaugunt Plateau – this is one national park you'll long remember.

To the Paiute people who have lived in the region for centuries, the remarkable geomorphic forms of Bryce Canyon came into being in legendary times, when the animal people so displeased powerful Coyote that he punished them by turning them to stone. Ebenezer Bryce, a Scottish Mormon who homesteaded the **Paria Valley** below the cliffs in 1875–6, is said to have been more prosaic about the series of carved amphitheaters towering above him, complaining that it was "a hell of a place to lose a cow!" In fact, Bryce Canyon can be explained by the erosive action of water, snow and ice on the east-facing edge of a lofty plateau. The ending to Bryce's story is always changing, as gravity and erosion continue sculpting this natural masterpiece.

The **Pink Cliffs** of Bryce Canyon form the sixth and uppermost "step" of a geologic Grand Staircase, which ascends in color-coded formation – oldest to youngest – from the Grand Canyon to the Paunsaugunt Plateau, a distance of more than a hundred miles. The rocks, which were pushed up, cracked and broken into plateaus by movement along faults more than 13 million years ago, originated as sediments laid down over millions of years, when a succession of inland seas, lakes, rivers, streams and even a dune-filled desert covered the Southwest. Over time, the sediments hardened into rock, colored by manganese and iron. Today, weathering has oxidized these minerals into the blues, reds, purples and yellows that bathe the rocks in a wash of pastel hues.

Bryce's Pink Cliffs are the youngest sedimentary rocks in the area, the result of silts, sands and the limey skeletons of creatures that lived in the ephemeral freshwater lakes that formed here 60 million years ago, when geologic activity elevated the Colorado Plateau. Millions of years later, when southern Utah began to split into its characteristic plateaus, these rocks, known as the **Claron Formation**, were exposed to the action of water speeding down the eastern edge of the Paunsaugunt Plateau. In what is today a semi-arid country, there is an irony in the role water has played in creating the eerie "hoodoos" and other "rock-candy" formations that crowd the amphitheaters of Bryce Canyon.

Exploring the park: But this is not a landscape simply to gape at; it begs to be explored. Plan to spend at least a day here to take full advantage of the many interesting summer ranger programs and exhibits at the visitor center, as well as the different experiences to be had in this 6,600–9,100-ft (2,012–2,774-m) elevation park. Bryce has two pleasant

Preceding pages: lightning arcs across the desert sky. Left, mountain lions occasionally range through the park. Right, cross-country skiing at Yovimpa Point.

campgrounds as well as the rustic **Bryce Canyon Lodge** (closed in winter), built in the 1920s by the Utah Parks Company. The lodge is on the Register of Historic Places and is very popular; guests should book six months to a year ahead. Day-trippers can get a flavor of the place at the gift shop and restaurant. Other accommodations may be found along local highways outside the park.

You can view the park's highly eroded cliffs from your car during an 18-mile (29-km) scenic drive that follows the edge of the 8,000-ft (2,438-m) plateau through forests of ponderosa pine and summer wildflowers, such as Indian paintbrush, skyrocket gilia and penstemon. The drive takes in 13 overlooks whose names exude romance. Among them are **Fairyland Point**, **Sunrise Point**, **Sunset Point** and **Inspiration Point**. The highest spot in the park is **Rainbow Point** (9,105 ft/2,775 m). Here the ponderosa gives way to sub-alpine conifers, such as white fir and blue spruce. In particularly exposed areas at this high elevation, rare bristlecone pines grow, some more than 1,000 years old.

In the evenings, you will encounter mule deer grazing by the side of the road; in the daytime, rodents like ground squirrels and prairie dogs are commonly sighted. Out of sight but not out of mind are the shy mountain lions that prey on deer – their numbers diminished by destruction of habitat, but their presence still felt on the plateau. The skies are patrolled by red-tailed hawks and ravens, whose languid, circuitous flight is in sharp contrast to the quick, darting forays of cliff swallows.

In the forests, jays jabber loquaciously in the pines, their iridescent blue feathers flashing among green needles. The wildlife at the 6,600-ft (2,012-m) canyon bottom varies considerably from that on the moister, cooler rim. Pinyon and juniper trees grow alongside sagebrush, clinging tenaciously to pockets of soil in bare rock ledges. Runoff comes and goes swiftly here; there is little to hold it as it courses down steep precipices toward the **Paria River**, and thence to the Colorado River.

Dawn breaks over rocky "hoodoos" in the Queen's Garden area.

176

A closer look: Even if you have only a short time, get out of your car and hike down into the amphitheaters along one of the superb intersecting trails, which start from the overlooks. From **Sunrise Point**, you can descend the steep cliffs along the 1½-mile (2-km), round-trip called **Queen's Garden Trail** and, if you wish, join up with the **Navajo Loop Trail** (1½ mile/2-km round-trip), which drops down from **Sunset Point** and proceeds through the clustered formations of **Silent City**. Don't forget that you're climbing a mountain in reverse.

The steep ascent from Queen's Garden is 320 ft (98 m); from the bottom of Navajo Loop, 520 ft (159 m). Carry water and don't be in too much of a rush. Hiking through these strange carved rocks is one of life's great novelties. You won't soon forget the sight of an out-of-place Douglas fir yearning toward the sunlight from a narrow corridor on Navajo Loop Trail, nor should you miss taking a guided moonlit hike among these phantasmagoric rocks, if you visit at the right time of year.

If you want a longer hike, the strenuous, 5-mile (8-km) **Peekaboo Loop** starts at Bryce Point and meanders through the amphitheaters' otherworldly formations. The **Rim Trail** is a fairly flat 5½-mile (9-km) hike overlooking the amphitheaters between **Fairyland Point** and **Bryce Point**.

For overnight trips, the **Under-the-Rim Trail** runs 22 miles (35 km) from Bryce Point to **Yovimpa Point** through some of the most remote and wildlife-rich country in the park. Be sure to consult the park rangers before attempting long backcountry hikes. Note that permits are required for overnight backpacking.

Although its high elevation made year-round residence here difficult, the region was used by prehistoric Indians – possibly early Basketmaker Anasazi and later Pueblo Anasazi – who were adept dryland farmers and knew how to utilize the area's plants and animals. These early inhabitants were superseded by nomadic Paiutes, who, like their predecessors, ventured into the high country

Leave no footprints.

in summer to hunt game and gather pine nuts and other plants.

Mormon settlers, such as Bryce, whose name came to be associated with these spectacular cliffs, generally kept their eyes down and concentrated on wresting a living from the land around **Tropic**, in the Paria Valley. It was left to explorers such as Major John Wesley Powell to chart the maze of canyonlands in the 1870s and report back on what he had seen. A member of his party labeled the area "one of the wonders of the world" and spread the word. In 1924, the state of Utah pressed Park Service director Stephen Mather and his assistant Horace Albright to create what was dubbed Utah National Park. Bryce Canyon National Park was created in 1928.

This small park is open year-round and is particularly magical under a fresh snowfall. Snowshoeing and cross-country skiing are encouraged, but snowmobiling is allowed only outside park limits. Modern paved roads now make visiting Bryce Canyon easy. You can approach from I-15 via Panguitch, drive up Highway 89 from Kanab, or take the spectacular Scenic Highway 14 from Cedar City. From Highway 89, take State 12 into the park.

Cedar Breaks: You mustn't miss glorious **Cedar Breaks National Monument**, atop the 10,000-ft (3,048-m) Markagunt Plateau, west of Bryce Canyon, which is reached by a short spur (closed from October to May) from Highway 14. This tiny gem preserves another highly eroded amphitheater of Claron Formation rock, but because the amphitheater is deeper, the coloration somewhat different, and descent into it discouraged, it complements a trip to Bryce rather than takes the place of it.

Cedar Breaks is perhaps best known for its extravagant wildflower displays, including lupine sneezeweed, yarrow and sunflowers, which begin adorning the meadows in July, shortly after the park reopens. Summer brings a rush of wildlife, which ranges from scurrying pikas, chipmunks, squirrels and marmots to stealthy mountain lions and coyotes. Mule deer browse on lush high-country meadows. Ravens and violet-green swallows swoop past colorful cliffs, and chattery Clark's nutcrackers and Steller's jays feast on the seasonal bounty of pine nuts.

A 5-mile (8-km) scenic drive follows the rim of the amphitheater and provides many pleasant overlooks from which to view Cedar Breaks. **Alpine Pond Trail** (1 mile/1½ km long) takes you through a cool, moist forest of spruce and fir.

A completely different hike skirts the rim of the amphitheater, past a large stand of thousand-year-old bristlecones clinging to bare rock at **Spectra Point**, and out along the **Wasatch Ramparts** (4-mile/6-km round-trip). Be sure to stay on marked trails. Cedar Breaks protects a fragile environment; off-trail hiking is discouraged. The park operates a welcoming visitor center and a small campground (open seasonally).

Other campgrounds on national forest lands can be found outside the park. Don't hurry through; this is some of the most spectacular high country to be found anywhere in the West.

Bristlecore pines are among the oldest living things.

Maintaining the Balance

Mining on the borders of Yellowstone. Gridlock in Yosemite. Graffiti in Petroglyph. Theft of artifacts from Chaco Canyon. Air pollution in Sequoia. Proposed dams on Zion's Virgin River. Loss of native species. Poaching of protected animals. Budget cuts, crumbling facilities, and increased policing.

More than a century after Yellowstone became the country's first national park, several of America's 357 parks are in crisis – many victimized by their own success in drawing visitors; others impacted by human activity just outside their borders.

No longer are many national parks islands of calm cut off from the outside world. They are increasingly at the mercy of an overcommercialization that Ed Abbey, an influential environmental writer, criticized as "industrial tourism."

A lot has changed since the Parks Service was founded in 1916. The Vail Agenda, a self-critical report commissioned by the service in 1991, highlighted many of the problems facing park rangers, including excessive paperwork, long hours, low pay, substandard housing, low morale, and an inability to attract qualified staff. Yet, despite these problems, a 1993 survey of 20,000 park visitors found consistently high ratings for Parks Service personnel.

Grand Canyon National Park, with nearly 5 million visitors annually, has reached crisis point. In 1993, it produced a sophisticated workbook detailing several alternative management plans for the park, and it held town meetings to encourage public input. Other parks are looking for ways to attract more volunteers and better interaction with local communities. A revival of successful 1930s government programs, such as the Civilian Conservation Corps, which built many of the facilities in the parks, is another possibility. Some parks have also started cooperative ventures with private companies to improve park environments. Grand Canyon, for example, teamed up with Dow Chemical to sponsor a successful recycling program.

In the future, the public is likely to be asked to pay higher entrance fees, to pay for searches and rescues, and to submit to a reservation process at the more popular parks. They may even be asked to park outside the gates and enter by way of light rail, bus, bicycle or foot in order to lessen the impact on park resources. Visitor services may also be relocated outside park boundaries, a move that could save Grand Canyon and Yosemite national parks, which are in danger of being loved to death by the thousands of tourists who flock there daily.

Help is also on the way for beleaguered park biologists. In October 1993, an independent agency, the National Biological Survey, was created by Interior Secretary Bruce Babbitt. It is charged with taking inventory of all living creatures and their habitats on public lands – an enormous task. This information will encourage agencies, private organizations and individual landowners to cooperate in monitoring the health of entire ecosystems rather than on a species-by-species basis, an approach that may obviate the need for controversial endangered-species listings. For too long, we have assumed that our overworked Parks Service can do its job alone. In the future, we must share the responsibility for these national treasures. ∎

Graffiti spoils a magnificent view.

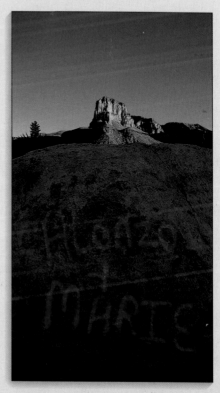

ZION

Set in the rocky heart of southern Utah's convoluted canyon country, **Zion National Park** is nature at its most eloquent: a dramatic juxtaposition of towering sandstone monoliths, narrow slot canyons, fast-flowing water, dense greenery and myriad wildlife.

From afar, the park's enormous buttes and domes rise like temples beckoning the faithful. From up close, its sheltering walls seem to offer a protected sanctuary. For the Mormon settlers who came here in the mid-1800s, this seemed to be Zion, "the Heavenly City of God." As a national park since 1919, Zion continues to draw millions of "worshippers" who marvel at the extraordinary geology and natural beauty found in these precipitous canyons.

Dramatically eroded sedimentary rocks are what give Zion its character and have led to its fame. Eight different rock strata may be found in the vicinity, all of which were deposited over a period of 200 million years, as geologic instability and changing climates and topography brought a succession of inland seas, lakes, rivers, streams, volcanic debris and even a dune-filled desert into the region. It is the latter that was responsible for the park's dominant rocks, the sheer, creamy-pink Navajo Sandstone cliffs, which reach 2,200 ft (671 m) in height in Zion.

Reading the rocks: The best way to "read the rocks" is to drive into Zion from the west, via Hurricane, along Highway 9, following the pretty **Virgin River** through spick-and-span villages into the park's South Entrance. From Hurricane, 25 miles (40 km) away, you drive over the dramatic **Hurricane Fault** in the Kaibab Limestone cliffs, whose marine sediments make up the rimrock of Grand Canyon, and into the **Virgin River Canyon**, encountering progressively younger rocks on the journey east. Near the community of **Virgin**, the banded Moenkopi Formation is visible. A little farther along, above the colorful gardens of charming little **Rockville**,

the multihued Chinle Formation forms crumbling hills scattered with dinosaur-era petrified wood.

At **Springdale**, the compacted red mud shales of the Moenave are visible beneath vermilion-colored Kayenta rocks that sometimes display dinosaur tracks. The sheer cliffs of Navajo Sandstone are now everywhere in sight, topped occasionally by the rounded bald domes of the Great White Throne and other landmarks. In the farther reaches of the park, younger Carmel Limestone and Dakota Formation appear on only the highest mountains.

The corrosive power of flash-flooding rivers, ephemeral waterfalls and seeping water is primarily responsible for the deep canyons, etched rock faces, smooth domes and colorfully streaked rocks found at Zion. Hard though it is to believe, the little **Virgin River** (a tributary of the Colorado River), which rises at 9,000 ft (2,743 m) on the tableland of the Markagunt Plateau just north of Zion, carved **Zion Canyon**. Beginning some 13 million years ago, the southern Colo-

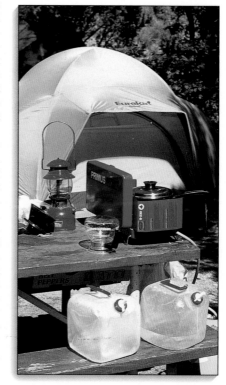

rado Plateau underwent a period of violent geologic activity that caused it to break and weather along faults, such as the Hurricane, into distinctive plateaus. Seismic activity along this southern spur of the **Wasatch Range** is ongoing. In 1992, a powerful earthquake centered in St George caused a large slide in Springdale, still visible along Highway 9. Zion is riddled with fractures in the soft rocks, which, combined with water erosion, account for the unusual U shape of its canyons and the great spalling arches (locally called "bridges") in its sheer walls.

The Virgin River bore down in its course as the land rose, scouring soft rock and bearing away sediments, which ended up in Lake Mead far to the south. The Colorado and its tributaries have removed strata from this portion of the uplifted Colorado Plateau at differing rates, giving the canyon country a colorful, stepped look, referred to as the Grand Staircase. This can best be seen looking north over the Arizona Strip from the Kaibab Plateau, south of Zion.

The reds and pinks (and, occasionally, yellows and browns) found in the rocks at Zion generally result from iron within the rock, which has been washed through by percolating ground water. Dark streaking, as on the **Altar of Sacrifice**, occurs when water falling over sheer precipices washes down minerals from vegetation or caprock. Weathering of organic material on rock faces also causes shiny "desert varnish," perhaps the most dramatic of all rock coatings in the Southwest.

Most visitors arrive in Zion via the South Entrance. The park has only two campgrounds (just inside the park), in addition to the rustic, log-framed **Zion Lodge**, which was built in the 1920s by the now-defunct Utah Parks Company to accommodate well-heeled park visitors. The lodge is on the Register of Historic Places. With its ice-cream fountain, pleasant gift shop, manicured lawns and shady trees, it's a good spot to take a breather as you tour Zion Canyon. Just don't expect to spend the night without reservations; bookings must usually be

Waterfall and pools in Subway Grotto.

secured a year in advance. Instead, expect to bed down in nearby Springdale or east of the park along Highway 89, at **Mount Carmel** or **Kanab**. Zion's attractive visitor center is just within the park boundary, overlooked by the huge bulk of the **West Temple** and **Towers of the Virgin**. Frequent ranger talks, interpretive exhibits and a well-stocked bookstore make this an excellent place to plan your trip.

Seeing the park: Many people choose to drive or bicycle through Zion via the **Zion-Mount Carmel Highway** (Highway 9), which proceeds eastward, following a tributary of the Virgin River. The road passes beneath a huge alcove known as the **Great Arch of Zion**, then climbs in zigzag fashion through the canyon until it enters the 1-mile (1½-km) long **Zion-Mount Carmel Tunnel**, built in 1930 to shorten the route between Zion and Bryce Canyon and Grand Canyon national parks. (There are strictly enforced size restrictions on vehicles using the tunnel. Check with the park in advance.) On the other side

of the tunnel, the road passes alongside marvelously eroded Navajo slickrock formations, which are exactly what they look like: "petrified" sand dunes. The most distinctive of these is the spectacular **Checkerboard Mesa**, a huge, creamy giant with crosshatched surfaces caused by horizontal cross-bedding in the dunes and later deepening of vertical fractures by water erosion.

The turnoff for Zion Canyon itself is a short way up from the visitor center. The scenic drive parallels the tree-lined banks of the Virgin River and dead-ends beneath the amphitheater of the **Temple of Sinawava** and the popular **Riverside Walk**. Within this short drive are the **Court of the Patriarchs**, **Cable Mountain** and the **Great White Throne**, as well as shady hiking trails, where you are surrounded by dripping rocks and colorful hanging plants. From here, you can set out on longer hikes that take you into the high country, or simply dream away the day deep in the canyon paddling in the river shallows.

The first white man to see Zion Can-

Cooling off after a long hike.

yon was probably Nephi Johnson, a Mormon missionary and translator. In 1858, he was guided as far as Oak Creek by a Paiute, who refused to venture farther into the canyon. Shortly thereafter, the canyon became home to the Heaps, Isaac Behunin, and other 19th-century Mormon colonists who farmed the flood plains, raised livestock and cut timber in the high country. These hardworking farmers were not particularly given to eloquence, but until floods, sickness and poor crops caused them to group into larger settlements, they were satisfied enough with their new home.

Joseph Black, who lived in Springdale but frequently explored the upper reaches of Zion Canyon, gave such shining accounts of the place that it was dubbed "Joseph's Glory." Isaac Behunin apparently named the canyon Zion, a title that caught on with his religious brethren (although after a particularly uncomfortable trip to Zion, the Mormon leader Brigham Young is said to have remarked grumpily that it was definitely "not Zion"). An enterprising

young man, David Flanigan, also left his mark. As a teenager, he conceived of building a cable from the mountain summit to the canyon to transport lumber. At the turn of the century, Flanigan realized his dream. **Cable Mountain** commemorates his achievement.

Most of Zion's landmarks owe their fanciful names to an imaginative Methodist minister called Frederick Vining Fisher and his two companions. On a 1916 trip, they gave the Three Patriarchs, the Great White Throne, Angels Landing, and the Organ their evocative monikers. Other names, such as the Temple of Sinawava, Mount Kinesava, Parunuweap Canyon (and the park's official 1909 name: Mukuntuweap National Monument), are Paiute in origin, although these gentle and peaceful nomads only occasionally entered Zion. Prehistoric Anasazi apparently had no such qualms: they grew corn and built granaries in Zion. A small vessel for storing grain can still be seen near Weeping Rock.

Three short hiking trails – **Weeping Rock** (½ mile/1 km), **Emerald Pools** (2 miles/3 km) and Riverside Walk (2 miles/3 km) – meander through sheltered side canyons populated by singleleaf ash, manzanita, cliff rose and Gambel oak. Here, contact between porous Navajo Sandstone and impervious Kayenta river sandstones and shales below it has created seeping rocks, known as springlines, which are home to delightful "hanging gardens" of soft mosses, ferns, monkeyflowers and columbines, as well as the park's unique Zion snail. Another leitmotif of the park is sacred datura, or Zion lily, a poisonous, white-trumpeted flower that opens at night along waysides.

Other trails, most of them found close to Zion Lodge, lead to famous landmarks, such as the Court of the Patriarchs (100 yds/91 m), **Angels Landing** (5 miles/8 km) and **Hidden Canyon** (2 miles/3 km, between Cable Mountain and the Great White Throne). Eight-mile (13-km) **Observation Point Trail** skirts the base of Cable Mountain before climbing through woodlands, offering stunning views of the Great White

Climbing the walls in Zion Canyon.

186

Throne, Cable Mountain, the West Rim, Angels Landing and Zion Canyon.

Wildlife and white water: Four different life zones are to be found in the 3,666–8,726-ft (1,117–2,660-m) elevations at Zion, encompassing desert, riparian, woodland and coniferous forest. In the low, dry areas of the canyons, heavy-fruited prickly-pear cactus is found alongside desert residents, such as whip-tailed and desert spiny lizards, slow-moving chuckwallas and, occasionally, western rattlesnakes.

The river is a perfect refuge in 100°F (38°C) summer heat. Throngs of Fremont cottonwoods, box elders, willows and velvet ash crowd its banks, sharing the location with bank beavers, gnat-catchers and insects, as well as footsore hikers. The high country supports ponderosa pine, Rocky Mountain juniper and sagebrush, as well as oak, Douglas fir, quaking aspen and numerous wild-flowers. At twilight, you may glimpse a coyote, mule deer or bighorn sheep, the latter a recent return resident to Zion after years of persecution. Mountain lions, bobcats, badgers, foxes and weasels lead very private lives here and are rarely encountered. Your companions throughout much of the park will be sociable little ground squirrels, camp-robbing ringtail cats, and noisy ravens and pinyon jays, whose chatter usually drowns out the more melodic canyon wren and other songbirds.

During the summer rainy season, the full impact of water on rock is evident. Torrents of water pour off vertical rock faces in magnificent waterfalls, and the swollen Virgin River speeds noisily over and around boulders.

In spring, when snowmelt is greatest, or during summer rainstorms, don't even think of wading the 16-mile (26-km) **Narrows Trail**, which follows the Virgin River through a slot canyon 2,000 ft (610 m) high and, in places, only 20 ft (6 m) wide. Err on the side of caution during unpredictable weather. Flash floods funnel through the canyon at the speed of a runaway train, destroying everything in their path. Plan to make the trip in dry summer months, and read

A sheer canyon wall dwarfs a passing hiker.

warning signs before starting out. This is one expedition where you should be prepared to stay wet for hours in a place the sun rarely reaches. Be sure that you consult with rangers before attempting this hike.

If you have enough time and are fit, you may want to do an overnight backpacking trip along the strenuous, one-way 13-mile (21-km) **West Rim Trail**, which links Zion Canyon with **Lava Point** through breathtaking mountainous country. Extend the trip by taking **Wildcat Canyon Trail** into the beautifully carved **Finger Canyons** of the **Kolob** area. You can also drive to **Kolob Canyons**, proceeding west on Highway 9, then north to Exit 40 on Interstate 15.

Check in at **Kolob Canyons Visitor Center** before taking the 5-mile (8-km) scenic drive through the folded and eroded vermilion-colored cliffs. A lot of people miss visiting the Kolob Canyons because of its distance from the main park, but you should try not to. There are some fascinating hikes in this section, including a strenuous, 14-mile

(23-km) round-trip to **Kolob Arch**, which, at 310 ft (94 m) wide, is one of the world's longest natural spans.

Pipe Spring: If you decide to base yourself in Springdale for a few days, consider exploring southern Utah's scenic byways and back roads. One such unpaved road links Rockville and Highway 59 on the Arizona Strip, near the ghost town of **Grafton**, which was inundated by a great flood in 1861–62, and abandoned. Many Rockville residents, descendants of the original settlers, still look after the town and farm adjoining fields. Grafton was used as the backdrop for a scene in *Butch Cassidy and the Sundance Kid*. Its little cemetery is particularly poignant.

When you reach Highway 59, drive east for about 30 minutes to **Pipe Spring National Monument**, one of those small but fascinating units that abound in the park system but often get overlooked. Prehistoric Anasazi, Kaibab Paiutes (whose reservation surrounds Pipe Spring) and early western settlers were all attracted to this spot because of the natural springs that come bubbling up the Sevier Fault in the **Vermilion Cliffs**.

Pipe Spring is essentially a fortified ranch built by the Mormons in 1870 to accommodate the church's burgeoning cattle herds. The "fort" and its outlying cabins, corrals, pens and ponds have been preserved very much as they were in their heyday, when Anson Winsor and his wife constructed the two modest stone houses that were dubbed Winsor Castle (a punning reference to Winsor's British roots). Pipe Spring served as a base for Major John Wesley Powell, the Colorado River explorer, during his survey of the region in the 1870s.

Many descendants of the original Paiute and Anglo settlers still live in the area and maintain a strong attachment to Pipe Spring. The Paiutes operate a small campground next to the park, and a cafeteria offers western fare to hungry travelers. The monument is open year-round, and both guided and self-guided tours are available. Return to Zion via Kanab and Highway 89, entering the park through the East Entrance to gain a different perspective.

Left, bobcats are nocturnal hunters. **Right**, strong fall colors in Zion Canyon.

GREAT BASIN

In 1843–44, the intrepid western explorer John Charles Fremont labeled a map of the Great Basin, "contents unknown, but believed to be filled with rivers and lakes which have no connection to the sea." Fremont's pronouncement told the basic hydrologic truth of the Great Basin: its streams and rivers do not flow into the ocean. Instead, water runs off the mountains into the many valleys, sits in salty playas and mud flats, and eventually evaporates into the air or soaks into the ground.

The **Great Basin** is the 210,000 sq. miles (543,900 sq. km) of country between the Wasatch Mountains in Utah and the Sierra Nevada in California. It is mostly high, cold desert of grassland and sagebrush. Endless valleys stretch to the horizon. Blue mountains float up from the valleys, one after another in harmonic succession.

Of his overland journey across the Great Basin, journalist Horace Greeley wrote in 1859 that the vegetation he was seeing was "the same eternal sage-brush and grease-wood, which I am tired of mentioning, but which together or separately, cover two-thirds of all the vast region between the Rocky Mountains and the Sierra Nevada."

Greeley obviously missed what is now **Great Basin National Park**. For it is much more than eternal sagebrush. With the **Snake Range** at its heart, the park is, as the name indicates, a classic example of Great Basin landscape. The Snake Range is filled with unexpected surprises. These cool, green mountains are terrestrial islands separated by oceans of sagebrush desert. The contrasts they exhibit, both biologically and physically, are striking. Eight thousand feet (2,440 m) of vertical relief soar from the valley floor to the summit of **Wheeler Peak**, the second highest point in Nevada. Visitors can go from hot desert to alpine tundra in a few miles. They can also go underground. Beneath the mountain lies **Lehman Caves**, carved out of the earth by ground water over millions of years and now "decorated" with fascinating limestone formations.

Lehman Caves: Absalom Lehman failed to find his fortune in the California Gold Rush, so he came to the Snake Range in eastern Nevada and settled along a creek to try his hand at ranching. One day in 1885, as one story tells it, Absalom was tracking his cows when he discovered a cave only 2 miles (3 km) from his ranch.

Lehman explored and developed the cave which bears his name, and people came from near and far, scrambling, stooping and crawling by candlelight to see its strange wonders. Things were going so well in the cave business that Lehman sold his ranch in 1891, but he died only five weeks later.

Lehman Caves became a national monument in 1922 and was included in 1986 in the newly created Great Basin National Park. After stopping at the visitor center, you can take the guided tour of Lehman Caves (actually only one cave, despite the plural) on a fairly short paved trail. In the cave, you will

Preceding pages: an ancient bristlecone pine. **Left,** ascending Wheeler Peak. **Right,** a storm brews over the Snake Range.

see the magical creations made by limestone and water: fanciful stalactites and stalagmites and other unusual features, such as the jointed shields. You may also see a bat, flea, cricket or pseudoscorpion. Dress warmly, for the temperature inside is a cool 50°F (10°C).

Peak experience: Interesting though it is, Lehman Caves is one small part of Great Basin National Park. Emerging from underground, you can drive from sagebrush desert to alpine tundra in less than an hour. High alpine lakes, bristlecone pine forests, beaver ponds, a limestone arch and even a glacier are a few of the delights that await those who are willing to walk even a short distance.

In the extreme elevation change from valley to mountaintop, the park contains seven communities, or zones, of plants and animals. Travelers can glimpse a good portion of this incredible biological diversity by driving or walking part of the 12-mile (19-km) **Wheeler Peak Scenic Drive**.

Starting at the visitor center, you find yourself amid sagebrush, prickly-pear cactus and juniper trees. Heading up the road you enter another zone: pinyon pine and curlleaf mountain mahogany. Though considered a shrub in most places, mountain mahoganies here reach tree size. The dense, hard wood was at one time harvested for firewood and for charcoal to stoke smelters. Not a true mahogany, it is instead a member of the rose family. The edges of the leaves curl under, a feature that helps the plant conserve water during dry times. The seeds are lovely feathery plumes.

Growing with mountain mahogany at this 6,000–7,000-ft (1,830–2,134-m) elevation is the singleleaf pinyon pine. The tree's cones hold delicious, oily nuts that have served as a staple food of Native Americans in the Great Basin for a very long time. The nut harvest is still a cherished ritual in early autumn. For 19th-century explorer John Charles Fremont, staring into the face of a Great Basin winter, the bag of pinyons an elderly Indian man sold him helped save him from starvation. Pinyon nuts are also a staple for pinyon jays, Clark's

Bald eagle feather.

nutcrackers, rock squirrels and mice.

From the dwarf pinyon woodland you enter the cool aspen forest. Hugging the ground beneath the quaking aspens is a red-stemmed shrub called manzanita. It's a pioneer, one of the first plants to colonize burned or disturbed land. Among the manzanita grows the sharp-leaved Oregon grape or barberry, sporting yellow flowers which later become edible blue fruits.

As you go even higher, stately, loden evergreens – Douglas fir, white fir and Engelmann spruce – begin to appear. Here too you encounter limber pine and bristlecone pine, forming a community that one botanist calls the "quintessential Great Basin forest."

Wheeler Peak trails: The scenic drive ends at an elevation of 10,000 ft (3,000 m). The air here is crisp and filled with piney fragrance. By now, you've probably dug out a jacket, and maybe a hat and gloves. From a nearby parking area, several trails lead to alpine lakes, a bristlecone grove, the glacier, or the top of Wheeler Peak. These trails are mostly

Lexington Arch.

free of snow and passable by early June. (A forewarning: snow can fall all year round on Wheeler Peak, so be ready for any kind of weather.)

In 1885 William Eimbeck, of the US Coast and Geodetic Survey, wrote: "A region more unfavorable for the formation of glaciers could scarcely be found." In fact, there *is* a glacier, and it's found on 13,063-ft (4,000-m) Wheeler Peak.

The glacier is tucked into a cirque on the northeast side of Wheeler Peak. It is a remnant of the Ice Age, when the entire Great Basin was colder and wetter, and the Snake Range was covered with alpine glaciers. Ten to fifteen thousand years ago, the valleys here were filled with lakes comparable in size to the US's Great Lakes. Big mammals lumbered across the land, occasionally holing up in caves. Although the huge lakes and megafauna are long gone, the isolated mountains of Great Basin National Park still harbor Ice-Age holdovers – bristlecone pines, alpine lakes and tundra plants among them.

The walk to the bristlecone grove is a

4-mile (6-km) round-trip, with only a 400-ft (122-m) gain in elevation. Even so, the wise person initially takes it slowly at this altitude. The air is thin, and if you have just come from lower elevations, the altitude, combined with exercise, may cause headaches or shortness of breath.

But the destination is worth the effort. Simply to be among these, the oldest living trees on earth, is a moving experience. Their gnarled, polished bodies evidence their great age and the harsh climate they have endured. Some elders still standing in the Wheeler Peak grove have lived at least 3,000 years. One, called Prometheus, was a record holder. Ironically, Prometheus was cut down so the annual growth rings in the wood could be counted to learn its age; the tree turned out to be 4,900 years old. The impressive longevity of bristlecones is probably due to resins that somehow help preserve the trees.

For a full view of the Wheeler Peak glacier, continue on the trail another mile from the bristlecone grove. Or, as

you head back from the grove to the parking lot, you may detour onto a loop to visit **Teresa Lake** and her nearby sister, **Stella**. These clear lakes are set like sapphires at the feet of the steep mountain peaks. In summer, waves dance across their surfaces in a light afternoon breeze, and their green grassy shores are dotted with glossy golden buttercups and white phlox.

On another day, you may wish to undertake the more demanding hike to the summit of Wheeler Peak: a 3,000-ft (914-m) ascent, 5 miles (8 km) up and 5 miles back. The well-traveled trail heads toward Stella Lake but then branches off toward the peak. Climbing gently at first, the path passes through a forest of limber pines full of squawking Clark's nutcrackers. The wind has pruned the exposed trees and left them stunted. At the treeline, the trail steepens and crosses rockier terrain.

The rubble of pinkish-gray rock clattering underfoot is a quartzite, a nearly pure quartz sandstone changed by great heat and pressure into harder, metamorphic rock. The quartzite originated as the beaches and continental shelves of extensive oceans that covered this part of the country 600 million years ago.

Arriving suddenly on top of Wheeler Peak, you see before you a scene of unearthly beauty. To the west, there is a vertiginous drop-off. Elegant fans of alluvium – talus, scree and gravel – sweep down and bury the base of the mountains. Immediately to the east is a 1,500-ft (457-m) vertical wall, the cirque that contains the glacier. **Baker**, **Pyramid** and **Washington** peaks jut up from the southern end of the Snake Range. And in all directions, more mountains interrupt the valleys, like battleships plowing through the sea.

By midday in summer, black thunderclouds are likely to gather over the mountains. If they have reached Wheeler Peak, you will want to take a quick look and hustle back down, for you do not want to be standing unprotected at such a high altitude with lightning anywhere nearby.

On a July night in 1869, Lieutenant George Montague Wheeler climbed the peak. By the light of the moon, he took

Setting up camp.

a barometric reading and determined his elevation to be 13,000 ft (3,962 m) (soon corrected to a more precise 13,063 ft/3,982 m). Lieutenant Wheeler was head of a major 19th-century Army survey of the West, and the Great Basin was part of his territory. With him was state geologist A.V. White, who named the peak (previously known as Union, Lincoln and Jeff Davis) for Wheeler.

You might also want to hike from **Wheeler Peak Campground** down to **Upper Lehman Creek Campground**. This gentle 4-mile (6-km) walk along Lehman Creek introduces the diversity of the park in reverse – from aspen forest past those huge mountain mahoganies and back down to sagebrush, following a lovely running stream all the way.

Backcountry sites: Great Basin was made for exploration on unpaved, backcountry roads. Most roads can be negotiated in two-wheel-drive passenger vehicles, but inquire locally to be sure. You can hike 5 miles (8 km) or so up **Baker** or **Snake** creeks to alpine lakes, or make a longer loop between the two. Your only company may be a few cows, allowed to graze as part of the agreement that established the park. Along the way are signs of the mountains' mining history – an old cabin and equipment. A 30-mile (48-km) drive south and a mile walk up a creekbed takes you to **Lexington Arch**, the largest limestone arch in the country.

Winter offers an entirely different experience. The road up Wheeler Peak is open as far as Upper Lehman Campground. From there, you can explore on snowshoes or skis.

One of the most attractive aspects of Great Basin National Park is its remote, undeveloped state. Accessible from US Highway 6/50, the park isn't near any major town or interstate. The tiny town of **Baker**, 5 miles (8 km) east of the park entrance, has a cafe and motel but few other services. **Ely**, Nevada, 60 miles (97 km) west, is the nearest town with full services. The great distances between gas stations make it advisable to fill the fuel tank at every opportunity.

Looking up at Wheeler Peak.

PETRIFIED FOREST

If it weren't for the signposts along Interstate 40, it would be easy to drive past **Petrified Forest National Park** in northeastern Arizona. For miles, your constant companion is an arid, high desert of scrub and short grasses, crumbling pastel hills, dry washes, distant mesas and dancing cloud shadows – a place of lingering silences and subtle beauty that inspires daydreams, as mile after mile ticks by on the freeway.

But don't imagine that these expansive vistas are empty. Far from it. Just beyond the anonymity of the cross-country highway, only slightly hidden from view, lies a compelling landscape filled to bursting with the fossilized remains of ancient plants and animals, the world's largest and most spectacular cache of colorful petrified wood, and the scattered artifacts of people who lived here for close to 8,000 years – all of them protected within the 147 sq. miles (381 sq. km) of the park.

It sits on either side of the highway, east of **Holbrook**, Arizona. Plan on eating and spending the night in Holbrook; no basic lodging or campgrounds are to be found in the park. If you are coming from the west, turn onto Highway 180 at Holbrook and enter from the south entrance (this area contains the greatest concentration of petrified logs). Drivers from the east should exit Interstate 40 and approach the park through the north entrance (where the best views of the **Painted Desert** and important Anasazi ruins and rock art are found).

Rainbow rocks: Visitor centers at either end of the park provide information, wilderness camping permits, exhibits, gifts and refreshments. But the **Painted Desert Visitor Center** (near Interstate 40) is the best bet. It offers a 17-minute film and a wide range of interpretive activities. About 1½ miles (3 km) from the visitor center, the restored 1924 **Painted Desert Inn** is an official National Historic Landmark.

The only designated trails in the park are short strolls through petrified wood

in the southern portion, although you may hike cross-country if you're adequately prepared with a gallon of water per person per day, food, a map, good footwear and a sense of adventure. It's very exposed here, with summer temperatures soaring near 100°F (38°C), possible thunderstorms, and cold winter winds. Always bring protective clothing and watch out for changes in weather that could be hazardous. Camping is allowed with a free permit in the **Painted Desert Wilderness** north of the interstate highway and in the **Rainbow Forest Wilderness** at the park's southern end. Wilderness camping rules apply.

A 27-mile (43-km) paved scenic drive gives you a good overview of the park. Beginning in the north, the road loops past the **Kachina**, **Chinde** and other viewpoints that guide the eye directly into the Painted Desert Wilderness, across Navajo reservation land, to the far-off Hopi Buttes. The screed hillsides, gullied flats and dark mesas of the Painted Desert are constantly shifting in hue, from charcoal gray to sage green to

taupe to pale rose to blood red; the colors are particularly intense after a summer thunderstorm. The rock that is responsible for this rainbow palette is the Chinle Formation, whose sands, silts and clays make up some of the softest and most easily eroded rocks in the Southwest. It's amazing to think that weathering has stripped away thousands of feet of overlying rocks to create this spare landscape.

The Chinle Formation was laid down more than 225 million years ago on a flat plain braided by shallow streams that meandered through the low-lying area. Gradually, several thousand feet of sediment accumulated. The Chinle Formation constantly fascinates geologists, preserving as it does Triassic-era fossils, petrified wood and abundant materials that give it its distinctive coloration, as well as large amounts of uranium – which provoked a new "gold rush" throughout the Southwest in the 1940s and 1950s.

After about 6 miles (10 km), the scenic road goes over the freeway, crosses the Santa Fe Railroad tracks, and passes **Puerco Indian Ruin**, a 75-room, 14th-century Anasazi village that has been partially excavated. The **Puerco River**, which roughly follows the railroad, was an important lifeline for Anasazi residents and seems to have supported them longer than other water sources in the Four Corners region. This ruin is one of 600 prehistoric sites in the park, which include scatterings of artifacts, pit houses and masonry pueblos, spanning a period of 8,000 years. Puerco Pueblo was occupied from AD 1100–1200 and from AD 1300–1400. It may have been abandoned during the 13th century when a long-lasting drought occurred throughout the Southwest.

The Anasazi wrested a living from this stark environment by their sheer adaptability. They knew exactly which desert plants to gather for food and clothing, which soils would yield good clay for pots and minerals for paints, how to use every part of a jackrabbit or deer, and the best way to irrigate small plots of squash, corn and beans to en-

Quartz crystals replace wood cells.

sure good crops. They lived on a cultural frontier, between the Mogollon to the south and other branches of the Anasazi farther north, and probably traded petrified wood for shells, food, pottery and other items. It's not clear why the Anasazi moved on around AD 1400, but they may have joined the Hopi villages to the north or Zuni Pueblo farther east. After they left, the Navajo moved into the region. Their enormous reservation adjoins the park.

Rock art: Just past the pueblo is **Newspaper Rock**, a sandstone cliff that was once used as a place of inscription by the Anasazi. The Anasazi valued creativity greatly, which is evidenced in early baskets and later in decorated pots, as well as crafted implements found wherever the people settled. No one has yet deciphered the exact meaning of the rock art they left behind, although this area of archaeology is beginning to turn up interesting results. On Newspaper Rock are pecked numerous sheep, lizards, geometric shapes and eerily anthropomorphic forms, faint echoes of a culture at whose daily concerns we can only guess. Telescopes at the overlook allow visitors to get a closer look at the fascinating images.

At this halfway point, the surrounding country has been carved by wind and water erosion into a rocky badlands of mesas, conical hills and bald hummocks colored by iron (red), manganese (black and purple) and other minerals. They sport names like the **Teepees**, the **Haystacks** and **Blue Mesa**, but no names seem adequate to describe nature's handiwork in this hot, dry location. A 3-mile (5-km) spur road reaches into Blue Mesa, where erosion has left petrified logs balanced precariously on pedestals of soft clay.

The southern portion of the park is strewn with large quantities of petrified wood, which are concentrated in the aptly named **Jasper** and **Crystal** forests. These stone logs are the preserved remains of 200-ft (61-m) conifers, known as *Araucarioxylon*, that grew on the banks of shallow streams and swamps 225 million years ago. When

Rock fan;
Puerco
Indian Ruin.

they toppled, they were washed into the flood plain, forming great logjams in the shallow rivers. Silty water and mineral-laden volcanic ash covered them, cutting off oxygen and delaying decay; silica gradually seeped into the cells of the trees, hardening into colorful quartz crystals. In some cases, the cell walls were completely dissolved and replaced by jasper, amethyst and smoky quartz. The Anasazi certainly appreciated the beauty of the stone logs, fashioning them into tools and even building with them. **Agate House** (near Long Logs) is surely one of the most unusual Anasazi dwellings in the Southwest. Its sturdy petrified-wood walls are a testament to the utilitarian beauty that was the Anasazi hallmark.

The petrified forest lay largely intact for centuries, until the United States acquired much of the Southwest through a treaty with Mexico in 1848. Three years later, United States Army Surveyor Lorenzo Sitgreaves and fellow officers were sent to chart the new territory, which they found largely unimpressive, save for gemstones they pried from petrified wood. Word spread quickly, and tourism grew in the late 19th century. Hordes of travelers and traders boarded trains and came west to obtain petrified wood for their collections. In no time at all, boxcars of petrified logs were shipped back east for sale, and the Southwest was in danger of losing one of its most remarkable natural assets.

But not everyone was intent on making off with buried treasure. By 1895, a small but vocal group of local residents began to lobby for protection. Petrified Forest National Monument was created in 1906, expanded several times, and redesignated a national park in 1962.

And yet, petrified wood is still disappearing, at the rate of some 12 tons (11 metric tons) a year. Visitor after visitor leaves with "just one little piece," all of which adds up to a continual loss for the park and for future generations. One rule: buy your petrified wood in the gift shop, and leave this national park intact.

Right, fossilized logs, the Blue Mesa area.

THE SONORAN DESERT

The desert must seem an alien place to anyone not used to it – eyeball-scorching, empty moonscapes devoid of water. But in fact, it is a complex ecosystem, full of living things, each one playing a vital role in maintaining the health of this extraordinary environment.

To truly appreciate the desert, wrote Wallace Stegner, "You have to get over the color green; you have to quit associating beauty with gardens and lawns; you have to get used to an inhuman scale; you have to understand geological time."

The desert timetable, with its different seasons and nocturnal emphasis, is different from most others, but no less specific. Give yourself time here, and the unusual rhythms of this place start to have their own logic, and its stubborn character may even become alluring. Once embarked upon, it is a love affair that for many people lasts a lifetime.

Southern Arizona sits in the upper half of the Sonoran Desert, which extends southward from the Phoenix Basin into Mexico. Two national monuments – **Saguaro** and **Organ Pipe Cactus** – highlight the Sonoran Desert's unique biological and geological attributes. A third, **Chiricahua National Monument**, rises 7,000 ft (2,134 m) on the desert's eastern edge. All three are within driving distance of Tucson, Arizona, which makes a good base for your explorations.

Saguaro: The two units of **Saguaro National Monument** are just a stone's throw from Tucson, bellied up to the **Tucson** and **Rincon** mountains to the west and east of the city, respectively. The star of this park is the symbol of the Sonoran Desert itself: the many-armed giant cactus known as the saguaro (sa-*wah*-ro). The east-side **Rincon Mountain Unit** was set aside in 1933 to highlight a giant forest of mature saguaros. The **Tucson Mountain Unit**, added in 1961 for research purposes, contains stands of younger saguaros. Both units have excellent scenic drives and a variety of long and short hiking trails that wind among the saguaros.

These gesticulating, green sentries, which march in formation up and down Sonoran slopes, seem as timeless as the desert. Indeed, they may live for more than 150 years, given warm exposure and sufficient rain. Blessed with a shallow but extensive root network, saguaros suck up moisture into barrel-like torsos supported by woody ribs. During a torrential storm, this cactus will swell like an accordion, storing as much as 200 gallons (757 liters) of water for the coming year in gelatinous tissues. (Mature saguaros can weigh several tons.)

The spines of the saguaro and other cacti are specially adapted to deal with temperatures that range between the low 100s (F) (around 38°C) in summer and below freezing in winter. Spines protect them from unwelcome intruders, trap cool air, provide shade, and, along with the cacti's waxy coating, offer protection from dehydration. Unlike plants with leaves, the saguaro photosynthesizes food from water and sunlight along its arms and trunk, the latter often reaching 35–40 ft (11–12 m) in height.

Young saguaros establish themselves best on bajadas – slopes of rock washed down from desert mountains. This is particularly obvious along the 6-mile (10-km) **Bajada Loop Drive** through the Tucson Mountain Unit, 15 miles (24 km) west of Tucson. Here, on the dark slopes of these jagged, volcanic peaks, "nurse" trees, such as mesquite and olive-trunked palo verde, protect saguaro seedlings beneath delicate branches.

Slightly older saguaros form stands here, evenly spaced for optimal survival. In the spring, these cacti sprout glorious white blossoms with heavy pollen centers – a show that rivals that of the wildflowers. More importantly, the creamy blooms attract visiting Mexican long-nosed bats, which pollinate the cactus with their wings as they sup nectar. Come back in late summer to see the result: ruby-colored fruits that, for centuries, have been harvested and made into syrup and jelly by desert-dwelling Tohono O'odham Indians. The ancestors of the Tohono O'odham – the

Hohokam – wandered great distances throughout the desert and left petroglyphs on dark volcanic rocks. These can still be seen in places such as the **Signal Hill** picnic area.

The Rincon Unit is more diverse, with hiking trails that take you from low desert scrub into woodland and eventually to high-country forest, as the elevation varies from 2,600–8,666 ft (792–2,641 m). Eight-mile (13-km) **Cactus Forest Drive** passes through a forest of saguaro old-age pensioners. Here, dying saguaros have been hollowed out by gilded flicker and Gila woodpeckers for nests. Later, screech owls, elf owls and cactus wrens will commandeer the cool burrows.

Don't expect to see many creatures in the day; most are nocturnal, waiting for cooler temperatures to exit their burrows and hiding places. You may surprise the hare-like jackrabbit, a colorful collared lizard, or perhaps one of the hawks nesting in the saguaro's upstretched arms. Go hiking in the early morning or in the evening if you hope to encounter twilight hunters such as kit foxes, coyotes or pig-like javelinas. If you don't have a lot of time, stop in at the delightful **Arizona-Sonora Desert Museum**, south of the Tucson Mountain Unit, for an excellent introduction to Sonoran Desert natural history through living exhibits.

Organ Pipe Cactus: Camp overnight in the campground adjoining the Tucson Mountain Unit, then continue southwest toward the ever-questioning town of Why. As you head south, the kingdom of the saguaro is joined by that of another many-armed cactus, the organ pipe, which is associated with the 516 sq. miles (1,336 sq. km) of Sonoran Desert protected as **Organ Pipe Cactus National Monument**. This park encompasses an area of low mountain ranges, broad plains and sere salt flats – a juxtaposition of habitats that is home to wildlife of such diversity that the monument was named an International Biosphere Reserve in 1976. Here, the organ pipe cactus and other unusual desert denizens usually found on the **Saguaros; Mount Ajo.**

Mexican side of the border have unknowingly become United States immigrants in a place where nature, not people, makes the rules. Two long scenic drives take you through the park's different habitats, beginning at the **visitor center**. A campground and the **Desert View** and **Victoria Mine trails** are also to be found here.

The **Ajo Mountains** in the park's eastern section receive the most rainfall, meaning that a spin along the 21-mile (34-km) **Ajo Mountain Drive** is one of the most pleasant outings in the park. Organ pipe cacti eagerly gulp in sunlight on mountain bajadas and favor south-facing exposures where frost cannot reach them. In spring, the pipes of the cactus sport showy flowers, which open as soon as temperatures drop in the evening. In springtime, when rainfall is adequate, the ground is covered with colorful hordes of lupines, golden poppies, pink owl's clover and other wildflower extroverts.

In addition to the organ pipe, 28 sharp-spined cacti, including teddybear cholla, prickly pear and saguaro, are found here – many of them participating in a seasonal round of "you scratch my back, I'll scratch yours" with birds, bats, plants and trees that help the cacti reproduce in return for food and shelter. The canyons offer some respite from heat and aridity, providing places where juniper, rosewood, agave and jojoba trees and animal residents can take refuge. It is here that the Tohono O'odham and their ancestors also retreated from desert extremes, camping in the shade of trees and harvesting the desert bounty.

The western section of the park, in the **Lower Colorado Desert** zone, is one of the least hospitable areas for residents and visitors alike. You get a strong flavor of the place by taking the 53-mile (85-km) **Puerto Blanco Drive**, which skirts the **Puerto Blanco Mountains**. Creosote and bursage populate 80 percent of the sandy valleys, gradually changing to a mixture of scrub and palo verde on nearby volcanic slopes. The florescent-lit landscape shimmers harshly under 105°F (41°C) summer

Lightning in the night sky.

heat, and sensible desert dwellers like bighorn sheep, coyotes, kangaroo rats, desert tortoises, snakes and high-flying hawks give it a wide berth in the daytime, waiting for the evening to refill empty bellies.

Even more hostile is the salt valley along the Mexican border, where saline soil offers prospects for saltbush but little else. Drive north along the spur road to the **Senita Basin** and an exotic community of Mexican elephant trees, senita cactus and limberbush appear alongside organ pipe cactus, protected in the lee of two mountain ranges. Signs of ranching and mining can be seen along the border with Mexico, but the area within the park is gradually recovering from man-made intrusions.

Remember: proceed with caution during summer, a time of soaring temperatures and torrential rainfall. Even if you are driving, take along a few high-carbohydrate snacks and at least a gallon of water per person per day. Always wear a hat and consider purchasing good-quality sunglasses for eye protection.

Chiricahua: By now, you may be ready to escape from the heat for a while in one of the small mountain ranges that rise enticingly from the desert floor. The rugged **Chiricahua Mountains**, east of Tucson, make a particularly fine destination. Here, a fascinating combination of strange rock formations, unusual wildlife and human history is packed into the 17 sq. miles (44 sq. km) that make up **Chiricahua National Monument**.

Like other borderland parks, Chiricahua is home to a cosmopolitan mix of Mexican-American flora and fauna, which inhabit the protected corridor provided by these tall and well-watered mountains. But Chiricahua is more than just a haven for exotics; it is also home to a truly bizarre collection of carved-rock features that have been created here by erosion. It was to preserve these strange phenomena that the park was set aside in 1924.

Hundreds of balanced rocks, spires, pinnacles, columns and other sculpted stones form deep ranks in the northwest section of the Chiricahuas. But unlike many other sculpted Southwestern landscapes, these are not sedimentary rocks; they are made of grayish volcanic tuff (fused ash) which spewed from nearby **Turkey Creek Caldera** 25 million years ago, forming a 2,000-ft (610-m) plateau. Future geologic activity pushed up the Chiricahuas and left behind horizontal and vertical faults. **Duck on a Rock, Totem Pole, Sea Captain, Punch and Judy** and other whimsically named features gradually took shape as wind, water and ice went to work on areas of weakness.

For an overview, take the 8-mile (13-km), winding **Bonita Canyon Drive**, which gradually climbs from the visitor center (5,400 ft/1,646 m) to **Massai Point Overlook** (6,870 ft/2,094 m) through pinyon, juniper and oak woodland. From Massai Point, you can look down into the eroded badlands and out across the crest of the Chiricahuas to **Cochise Head** beyond the park boundary. On the way back, stop and hike the 3-mile (5-km) round-trip to the fire lookout on **Sugarloaf Mountain**, at 7,365 ft (2,245 m) the park's highest peak. From

Organ Pipe Cactus National Monument.

Massai Point, a number of maintained, intersecting trails wind down deep into the canyons to the **Heart of Rocks**, where the most fascinating rock sculptures are found. One good loop trail takes you through **Echo Canyon** (4-mile/6-km round-trip), dropping 450 ft (137 m) into the stone galleries. Another way in is to hike the **Rhyolite Canyon Trail** (2 miles/4 km) east from the visitor center, a pleasant walk through a cool, riparian habitat.

These eroded uplands are the reason that wildlife of such an unusual variety coexists here. In the moister canyons, you will find Southwestern trees such as dwarf oak, alligator juniper and Arizona cypress alongside rare Mexican Chihuahua and Apache pine. The high mountainsides are even more lush, supporting Douglas fir, aspen and ponderosa pine, which, in turn, attract browsing white-tailed deer. What a contrast with the surrounding desert environment, where aridity has hardened the competition. Most noticeable is the number of exotic birds crossing into the park from across the border: sulphur-bellied flycatchers and Mexican chickadees are frequent visitors. Bring your binoculars; this is birding heaven.

A pleasant, short hike begins at the **visitor center** and wanders through an open meadow environment, ending at the campground (2-mile/3-km round-trip). Turn west, though, and the trail leads to **Faraway Ranch** in Bonita Canyon, the home of the Erickson family for nearly 90 years. The Ericksons moved here two years after the treaty that ended the all-out war between the United States Army and the Chiricahua Apaches, to whom these mountains were a much-loved home. The Apaches, led by Cochise and later by Geronimo, held out for years in a valiant attempt to retain their land. By 1886, however, a treaty had been signed, and the Apaches were imprisoned and eventually forced to accept reservation living. They are gone but not forgotten. If you're interested in learning more, pay a visit to nearby **Fort Bowie National Historic Site**, a ruined fort from the late 1800s.

Chiricahua
National
Monument.

GUADALUPE MOUNTAINS AND CARLSBAD CAVERNS

There aren't many places in America where you can explore both the outside and inside of what was once a 400-mile (644-km) long barrier reef lying below an ancient shallow sea. But at the neighboring Guadalupe Mountains and Carlsbad Caverns national parks, on the southern New Mexico–Texas border, this is indeed possible, for climatic change, geologic activity and the elements have uncovered a limestone reef formation of startling beauty, long buried in the past, which today offers a respite from the heat of the surrounding desert and a glimpse of a natural world usually hidden from view.

Guadalupe Mountains National Park: Just a couple of hours from El Paso, Texas, the towering ramparts of the 50-mile (80-km) long **Guadalupe Mountains** rise up abruptly between the broken plains of southern New Mexico and the searing Chihuahuan Desert, which extends south into Mexico. US Highway 62/180 passes through the natural divide of **Guadalupe Pass**, below the jutting headland of **El Capitan** and its neighbor, **Guadalupe Peak**, which at 8,749-ft (2,667-m) is the tallest mountain in Texas. The sheer limestone walls seem expressionless, shimmering in the summer heat, but don't be fooled by appearances: enter this rocky wilderness from any one of 80 miles (130 km) of hiking trails connecting the desert, interior canyons and high mountain slopes, and a protected sanctuary teeming with wildlife opens up.

The best way to explore the backcountry is from a base at **Pine Springs Campground** (5,700 ft/1,737 m elevation) next to the visitor center and take the long, strenuous **Guadalupe Peak**, **El Capitan** and **Tejas** trails from the **Pine Springs Trailhead**. About 4 miles (6 km) from Pine Springs, the Tejas Trail intersects the **Bowl Trail**, which loops through a high-country, relict conifer forest 2,500 ft (762 m) above the desert floor. Shy bobcats, bears and mountain lions are found at higher elevations, but you are most likely to encounter mule deer and elk, which are abundant here. Plan to camp out in one of several primitive backcountry campgrounds. The 12-mile (19-km) Tejas Trail connects Pine Springs with **Dog Canyon**, clear on the other side of the mountains. Dog Canyon has a ranger station and a campground and may be reached only on foot or via the 70-mile (113-km) road that skirts the back of the Guadalupe Mountains just south of Carlsbad. It's a long way but well worth the extra mileage.

Guadalupe Mountains is mostly designated wilderness, and wilderness rules are strictly enforced. Everything packed in must be packed out. Remember, too, that with no modifying influences, deserts tend to be very hot or very cold, depending on the time of year. Take along a hat, water, very sturdy hiking boots and layered clothing. Also note that there are no food or gasoline services in the park, so visitors are advised

Preceding pages: claret cup cactus and cholla skeleton in the Guadalupe Mountains. Left, tarantula on limestone, Carlsbad Caverns. Right, Guadalupe Peak.

to bring what they'll need and fill their gas tanks before departing.

A backcountry trip into the mountains takes planning and stamina, but there are several more moderate day hikes at the lower elevations. Get help in planning your visit from knowledgeable park rangers at the tourist-friendly visitor center, and don't miss one of the excellent evening campfire talks about desert wildlife (some of the subjects of the talks may join you for the show). Cooler morning and evening temperatures enliven the desert, and coyotes and crickets sing a nightly serenade that lulls the senses hypnotically. Emblematic of the desert are water-saving species such as lechuguilla, prickly pear and sotol, which dot the foothills.

Some beautifully marked reptiles, such as collared lizards and mostly harmless snakes, live here, but you will need to be quick to see them in daytime, when they shelter from the heat beneath rocks or burrow into the ground. Equally furtive are large-eared jackrabbits and smaller cottontail rabbits, which dash out suddenly from cover, only to disappear again instantly.

Just on the other side of the **visitor center** are the ruins of a horse-changing station of the **Butterfield Stage Line**, which carried the mail cross-country in the mid- to late 1800s. A little farther north, the whitewashed **Frijole Ranch**, a pioneer home, is open to visitors. From here, the 2-mile (3-km) **Manzanita** and **Smith Springs Loop Trail** makes a pleasant day hike. The white settlers who moved into the area when it became US territory in 1849 were subject to attack by Mescalero Apaches, whose detailed knowledge of these desert mountains made them worthy opponents. By 1880, though, the Mescalero Apaches had been subdued and removed from their homelands to a nearby reservation, where today they pursue ranching.

The 7-mile (11-km), round-trip **McKittrick Canyon Trail** is easily the most popular day hike in Guadalupe Mountains. It starts at the **McKittrick Canyon Visitor Center**, just off High-

A rare glimpse of a bobcat.

way 62/180 to the northeast of Pine Springs. The canyon is famous for the brilliant fall colors of its Texas madrone, bigtooth maple, oak, ash and walnut trees, which cluster along the only perennial stream in the park. The sweet songs of canyon wrens and tanagers echo musically here; quieter, though, are stealthy bobcats and mountain lions which pad after mule deer and elk at dawn. More common are small rodents and reptiles, which make their home in lower elevations.

Also beginning at McKittrick Canyon is the 8-mile (13-km), round-trip **Permian Reef Geology Trail**, a long day hike that offers an excellent introduction to the park's geology. The steep trail takes you through a cross section of the Permian Reef, which was formed by the limey secretions of calcareous algae, sponges and other marine organisms that lived in the shallow Permian Sea 250 million years ago. When the sea evaporated, potash, gypsum, salt and other sediments entombed the reef, until a period of geologic uplift and subse-

quent erosion again exposed the formation 10 to 12 million years ago. The Guadalupes continue to be sculpted today by the dissolving action of rainwater made acidic by carbon dioxide and organic matter in the soil. Crystalline calcite deposits have formed pale, marble-like travertine or flowstone around seeps and in streambeds – a taste of the treasures that lie below the surface at nearby Carlsbad Caverns.

The Permian Reef shales contain large amounts of oil, and it was oil exploration in the 1920s that indirectly led to the establishment of the park in 1972. Wallace Pratt, a gifted petroleum geologist who fell in love with **McKittrick Canyon** and made his home there, donated 5,000 acres (2,023 hectares) of the canyon to the United States government. Pratt's 1931 stone lodge sits a couple of miles up McKittrick Canyon. Farther up, you'll find the remains of J.C. Hunter's ranching operation. Both Pratt and Hunter were instrumental in the creation of the park.

Other earlier ranches in the area did

A ranger leads a nature walk.

not fare well, however. South of the park, dwarfed by Guadalupe Peak, sit the lonely, boarded-up remains of the **Williams Ranch**, 9 miles (14 km) down bone-shaking, unpaved road. The house was built in 1908 by Robert Belcher, who had deluded himself that his new wife would be impressed by this new home. Appalled by the location, she spent one day and one night at the cabin before leaving him. Other small-time ranchers followed; no one stayed long. Today, the cabin is a curiously Western reminder of the folly of human ambition in the face of overwhelming odds.

Carlsbad Caverns: The scorching summer heat can be overwhelming, and there is no better way to cool down fast than to visit the world-famous **Carlsbad Caverns**, 35 miles (56 km) north of Guadalupe Mountains National Park, off Highway 62/180. Carlsbad is as much about ballyhoo as Guadalupe Mountains is about silence, but you should not miss either of them.

Visitors to Carlsbad Caverns may hike the area along 50 miles (80 km) of backcountry trails or else take a 10-mile (16-km) scenic loop drive through the Guadalupes, but the principal attractions of this national park are the huge, fantastically shaped stalactites, stalagmites and other precipitated limestone forms that crowd the surfaces of a large underground cave system deep below the Guadalupe Mountains.

Depending on how much time you have, you can descend on foot through the decorated rooms of Carlsbad Cavern on the mile-long **Natural Entrance Route** or make a speedy drop by elevator directly into the 750-ft- (230-m) deep **Big Room**, where the most splendid of these underground features occur. You can view the **Kings Palace**, **Queens Chamber** and **Papoose Room** by guided tour only (check at the information desk for times), where the action of acidic rainwater percolating through the Permian Reef Formation has hollowed out great chambers in the pale rock. Farther along, at the **Green Lake Room**, calcite "lily pads" sit in clear water, and the constant dripping sound

Wary mule deer are alert to danger.

is a reminder of what has created this curious place. Some scientists now theorize that fresh water, mixed with hydrogen-sulfide gas seeping into the reef from the oil-rich basin to the south, produced sulfuric acid and accelerated corrosion of the limestone.

The features in Carlsbad Cavern, just one of 80 caves currently known to exist in the park, are nearly half a million years old and may have begun forming when the climate was wetter and cooler. Carlsbad's odd decorations result from carbon dioxide loss from water droplets and evaporation inside the caves, which leave behind calcite crystals. These deposits gradually build into a variety of strange forms: translucent flowstone and rimstone dams around slow-moving pools, delicate curtains of icicle-like "soda straws," waving helictites growing in all directions, enormous stalagmites growing up from the floor, and gravity-defying stalactites hanging from the ceilings. Great columns are created when stalactites and stalagmites join, providing a counterpoint to fragile arago-

Time to pay up.

nite formations, which are composed of a different crystalline structure. Park rangers are stationed throughout the cavern and give talks at the **Top of the Cross**, in the spectacular Big Room.

Caves of even more marvelous proportions, such as **Lechuguilla Cave** and others, are being found here constantly. If you have time, you may want to sign up to visit undeveloped **Slaughter Canyon Cave**, which provides a truer caving experience for the physically fit. Carlsbad is also known for another natural phenomenon of great interest: bats. More than 300,000 Mexican free-tailed bats raise their young in the **Bat Cave** passage during spring and summer, exiting in a long black cloud at dusk and returning at dawn, where their re-entry into the cave is marked by a strange whistling sound as they fold their wings and plummet into the darkness. You can watch this mesmerizing daily summer ritual from an amphitheater seating area.

Although Indians are known to have used these caves as far back as 12,000 years ago, it was an Anglo cowboy, Jim

White, who, among others, popularized the caves in the early 1920s. White noticed bat droppings, or guano, which make fine fertilizer, at the cave entrance and ventured inside, stumbling by accident on something that turned out to be much more intriguing. Over the next two decades, White gave unofficial tours of the cavern, unceremoniously dropping visitors into the caves in a guano bucket for a fee. He was a logical choice for chief ranger when the cave was given national monument status in 1923 (Carlsbad eventually became a national park in 1930).

Contrary to popular belief, the garish cluster of tourist facilities at the cave entrance known as White's City was not named after Jim White. Don't be put off by the rampant commercialism you'll find here. You can always stay in Carlsbad (20 miles/32 km farther north) or camp in the Guadalupes. Like the Grand Canyon, Carlsbad Caverns is an unmissable sight – a spectacle of nature that makes human creations look gaudy.

While you are in southern New Mexico, pay a visit to **White Sands National Monument**, 15 miles (24 km) southwest of Alamogordo. The glaring white dunes, some 60 ft (18 m) high, are formed from gypsum sediments that wash down from the **San Andres** and **Sacramento** mountains on either side and accumulate in lakes in the **Tularosa Basin**. In time, these deposits dry into fine grains that are scooped up by winds and blown into undulating dunes. The dunes are home to several kinds of specially adapted mice and lizards, which adopt a white camouflage to survive; as well as hardy plants like four-wing saltbush and iodinebush that can tolerate the alkaline conditions.

You can hike **Big Dune Trail** through the larger dunes, and a primitive campground is available with a free permit from the **visitor center**. This area is best known, of course, for the **White Sands Missile Range**, where the first atomic bomb was tested in 1945. A visit to "Ground Zero" and the museum is educational, though sobering.

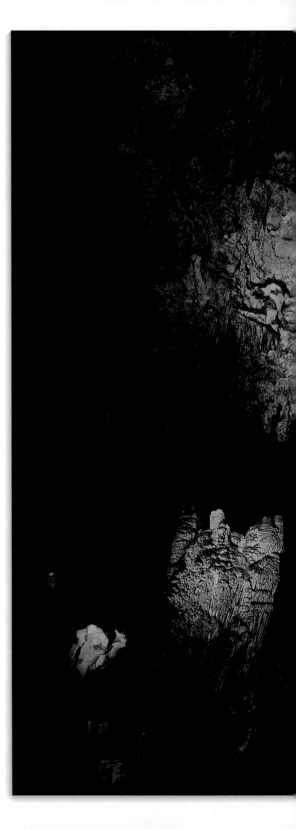

Right, limestone shapes, Carlsbad Caverns.

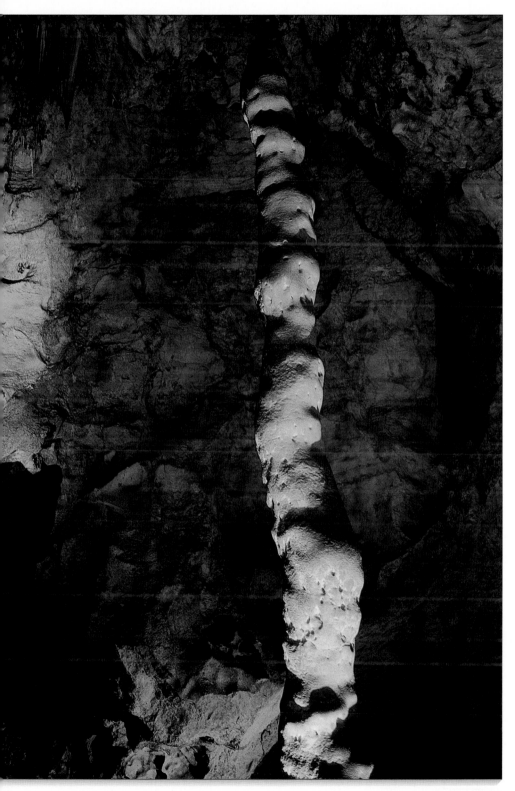

BIG BEND

Despoblado. The empty land. So the Spanish conquistadores named the almost uninhabited territory that borders the Rio Grande in what is now west Texas. Today, we know it as the Big Bend country. It's a dramatic land of contrasts where island-like mountains and deeply etched canyons break up a vast expanse of the Chihuahuan Desert. Named for the great looping curve the Rio Grande makes on its journey to the Gulf of Mexico, **Big Bend National Park** is still the *despoblado* – forbidding yet beautiful, an "empty land" that is abounding with life.

For most of its history, Big Bend was regarded as an in-between place, a crossing rather than a destination, far from the reach of law and order. Before the arrival of white settlers, Comanche and Apache Indians used its mountain hide-outs to raid villages in northern Mexico. And even as late as the 1920s, Mexican bandits stole across the border to raid isolated ranches on the American side. Miners and ranchers began trickling into the region in the late 1880s, but most didn't stay long. By the dust bowl days of the 1930s, the mines had played out and the rangelands were devastated by drought and overgrazing. The federal government acquired much of these damaged lands, and in 1944 more than 700,000 acres (283,280 hectares) were designated as Big Bend National Park.

This is a stark and unforgiving land, broken by lone buttes and naked peaks. Cactus, ocotillo and greasewood provide sparse cover in the lowlands; agave and lechuguilla rise like daggers from the desert floor. At the center of the park, the **Chisos Mountains**, southernmost in the continental United States, climb to more than 7,800 ft (2,377 m), an oasis of cool breezes and shady woodlands in the torrid Chihuahuan Desert. To the south, the Rio Grande, one of the great rivers of the American West, courses through the spectacular gorges of Boquillas and Santa Elena canyons, with walls up to 1,500 ft (457 m).

Although it may appear inhospitable to the first-time visitor, Big Bend is among the most biologically diverse sites in the national park system and has been named a United Nations Biosphere Reserve. It's particularly known as a paradise for birds. More bird species – some 434 (half the species in North America) – have been sighted in Big Bend than in any other national park. The endangered peregrine falcon can still be seen here, as can gray hawks, zone-tailed hawks and black hawks, rarely spotted north of the park. There are also about 52 species of warblers and, in summer, a variety of humming-birds, including a few species like the Lucifer's hummingbird, seldom seen elsewhere in the United States. And of course, there's the more common roadrunner, which you may see chasing after lizards or grasshoppers.

At dusk, some 19 species of bats swoop through the air, hunting insects. Evening is also the best time to catch sight of the shy Carmen Mountains white-tailed deer, a rare subspecies usually found in

Preceding pages: in the saddle at sunset. Left, the Rio Grande winds through the Sierra del Carmen. Right, porcupine with spiny quills.

mountain haunts around the Basin. The larger and more common mule deer can be found in the desert surrounding the Chisos Mountains, and a few fleet-footed pronghorn still roam the flatlands, particularly around upper **Tornillo Creek**. The pig-like javelina, or peccary, is also fairly common. Extremely nearsighted and not a pig at all, it relies on scent to detect intruders, and can often be seen blithely munching prickly pear.

Javelina and deer feed one of the most elusive predators of the West – mountain lions, or panthers, which have made a strong comeback after decades in which there were no controls on hunting them. They are rarely encountered, but it's not unusual to see their tracks. The park's other large predators, coyotes and bobcats, are also rather shy, although it's not uncommon to hear the coyote's haunting night-time howl.

If this is your first time in Big Bend, start your tour at the **visitor center** at **Panther Junction** in the very heart of the park. From the north, enter on Highway 385 through **Persimmon Gap**, a

pass through the Santiago Mountains once used by Comanche Indians to run stolen livestock north from Mexico. About 7 miles (11 km) past the entrance station, a dirt road leads east to **Dagger Flat**, where giant dagger yucca – laden with large white flowers during the springtime bloom – can be seen in their northernmost range. A bit farther south, another turnoff leads to a fossil bone exhibit where ancient mammals once roamed, some 50 million years ago.

You can enter from the more scenic west side, too, following Highway 118 through the old mining town of **Study Butte**. Just past the entrance gate, the road passes over a landscape of baked tawny bluffs and dry washes sparsely covered with desert shrub and ocotillo. To the north looms **Maverick Mountain**, a dome of intruded magma (molten rock) now exposed by erosion. To the east, the Chisos Mountains – the park's focal point and most popular destination – rise like rusty battlements.

When you're finished at the visitor center, strike out for **the Basin**. The road starts about 3 miles (5 km) west of Panther Junction and climbs through Green Gulch into the heart of the Chisos Mountains, a cool (sometimes frigid) island of timbered ridges and rugged peaks. As you drive upward, past the jagged profile of **Pulliam Ridge** (to the right) and **Lost Mine Peak** (to the left), desert scrub gives way to a belt of grassland and then scattered savanna-like forest. The road crests at **Panther Pass**, breaches an outer wall of peaks and then makes a winding descent into the Basin – an open, mountain-rimmed valley scattered with a relict woodland of Arizona cypress, Douglas fir, quaking aspen, ponderosa pine and bigtooth maple, many at the southern limit of their range.

Once damaged by overgrazing, the Basin has made a strong recovery. Lush grasses have returned to the valley floor and mountain slopes, interspersed with thorny patches of cactus. Wildlife is recovering, too. After decades of absence, a breeding population of black bears is now re-established, having recently returned to the park from Mexico. Two other casualties of the ranching

Prickly pear cactus blooms near the Rio Grande.

228

period – the desert bighorn sheep and the Mexican wolf – haven't been quite so lucky. Several attempts to introduce bighorn sheep have failed, although there are now some flocks grazing in nearby mountains. But Big Bend may yet prove to be one of the most promising areas in the Southwest for the reintroduction of Mexican wolves.

The road dead-ends at a collection of visitor facilities at the foot of 7,550-ft (2,286 m) **Casa Grande Peak**, where you'll find a campground, lodge, restaurant and store as well as a network of trails. For first-time visitors, **Boulder Meadow Trail** is an easy 3-mile (5-km) round-trip through pinyon-juniper woodland to a beautiful meadow. Those who have plenty of time and energy can press on to the sweeping vistas at 7,100-ft (2,164-m) **Pinnacle Pass**, and then either make the strenuous journey to the top of 7,825-ft (2,385-m) **Emory Peak**, highest in the park, or continue to **Boot Spring** in densely forested Boot Canyon, the summer home of the rare Colima warbler.

Another good introduction to the Basin is the 5-mile (8-km) round-trip to **the Window**, a V-shaped notch, or pour-off, on the Basin's west side, with gorgeous views of Casa Grande Peak and surrounding mountains. The trail follows a dry creek lined with maples, oaks and Texas madrone, making for a pleasant and shady stroll. Carmen Mountains white-tailed deer are often seen along this trail. For experienced backpackers, there is a 33-mile (53-km) circuit of the rim and mountain flanks that makes an excellent three-day journey.

Ross Maxwell Scenic Drive: From the visitor center at Panther Junction, it's a short ride east on Highway 118 to the **Ross Maxwell Scenic Drive**, which makes a 30-mile (48-km) trip past some of the park's most dramatic geologic formations to Santa Elena Canyon. Heading south from Santa Elena Junction along the foot of **Burro Mesa**, you quickly come to the **Sam Nail Ranch**, built in 1916, where a windmill, water tank and the remains of an old adobe ranch house make a pleasant stop to

A clearing snowstorm in the high country.

bird-watch or picnic. Continuing south, Casa Grande Peak comes into view framed by the gunsight notch of the Window.

Farther on, near the southern end of Burro Mesa, three dikes radiate from the Chisos Mountains. These long rock walls were formed by molten lava which was squeezed into a narrow fault. The softer overlying rock gradually eroded, leaving behind freestanding walls of volcanic rock. In some cases the dikes eroded into fanciful shapes, like **Mule Ears Peaks**, which can be viewed from the overlook a few miles farther south. Watch for **Sotol Vista** too, where you'll be treated to glorious views into Mexico. A bit farther, a spur road veers right to **Burro Mesa**, where you can take a short hike up the dry wash for a first-hand look at desert geology.

Just beyond the Mule Ears Overlook, the road passes through a narrow canyon of white ash, spewed from a volcano about 35 million years ago. Within the bed of ash, near **Cerro Castellan**, are what look like petrified trees; they are really "lava necks," upright tubes of molten rock that have hardened into bizarre shapes.

At **Castolon** you can stop for refreshments and a stroll around the historic army garrison, manned between 1914 and 1918 to protect settlers from Mexican bandits and now used as a trading post and ranger station. **Cottonwood Campground**, your best bet for a campsite during the crowded spring season, occupies a shady spot on the Rio Grande just beyond the old village.

From Castolon the Scenic Drive parallels the **Rio Grande** for about 8 miles (13 km) before coming to a dead end at **Santa Elena Canyon**. A short trail leads into the canyon where 1,500-ft (457-m) limestone cliffs tower over the muddy river. When you're ready, you can either double back to Santa Elena Junction or loop through the backcountry on a 13-mile (21-km) dirt road to the park entrance at Maverick.

Rio Grande Village: The 24-mile (39-km) drive from Panther Junction to Rio Grande Village passes around the east-

Rocknettle and Torrey yucca in the Chisos Mountains.

ern flank of the Chisos Mountains to the cottonwood-shaded Rio Grande. A dirt road heading west just before Dugout Wells leads 9 miles (14 km) to **Glenn Spring**, an abandoned village that was the site of a bandit raid in 1916. **Dugout Wells**, another developed spring and old ranch headquarters, is a shady place, ideal for a picnic or a walk along the self-guiding nature trail.

As you descend the long hill toward the Rio Grande, the rugged limestone cliffs of the imposing **Sierra Del Carmen** come into sight across the border in Mexico. Much of the Sierra Del Carmen is part of a proposed sister park that may unite Big Bend and its Mexican counterpart in an international reserve.

About 3 miles (5 km) from Rio Grande Village, another dirt road takes off to the south leading to the now abandoned site of **Hot Springs**, a former health spa and trading post. A stone building still stands on the spot. A short hike takes you to natural hot springs that bubble out of the ground on the banks of the Rio Grande.

Cottonwood trees fringe the river near **Rio Grande Village**, the largest development in the park, offering camping facilities, supplies, gasoline, laundry and showers. Bird-watching is particularly good in this area, which is a meeting place for river species such as the beautiful vermilion flycatcher, and desert species such as the animated roadrunner. If you would like to visit the Mexican village of Boquillas, there is usually a nearby ferryman to row you across the river. **Boquillas Canyon Overlook** is at the end of the road and features marvelous views of the canyon.

The Rio Grande borders the park for 118 miles (190 km); another 127 miles (204 km) below the park, an area known as the "lower canyons", are managed by the Park Service, too. Outfitters provide equipment and offer float trips lasting from a day to a week or more, but the most popular is the one-day float through Santa Elena Canyon. The trip covers a few sections of white water as well as long stretches of calmer water. For more information about float trips, get in touch with Big Bend headquarters.

Eroded rock formations are hidden in a remote canyon.

THE ANCIENT ONES

Stand at the overlook of **Cliff Palace** in Mesa Verde. Imagine it at night-time, the windows glowing with the warm light of fires within the small rooms.

Once upon a time, ordinary people lived in this "palace." They cooked simple food over the fires and warmed themselves around the hearths on long winter nights. They mended sandals, polished pottery, and ground corn, while elders told stories to the young ones.

The prehistoric residents of **Mesa Verde National Park** are called the Anasazi, a name conferred on them by 20th-century Anglo archaeologists. We really don't know what the people called themselves, or what language they spoke, for theirs was a time before written history. What we do know is that for nearly 1,500 years, from before the 1st century AD until the 15th century, the Anasazi inhabited the **Four Corners** region where Utah, Arizona, New Mexico and Colorado meet. The concentration of national parks in the four-state region preserves the country's most impressive prehistoric sites.

For a closer view of the lives of Anasazi of Mesa Verde, you can take the 2-mile (3-km) trail from the **Chapin Mesa Museum** to **Spruce Tree House**. Here you can stoop through the small doorways, see the soot-blackened ceilings, and feel the cool trickle of the spring that was their lifeblood.

Sacred space: Initially, the Anasazi did not build cliff dwellings but simply dug pits into the rocky ground and covered them with sticks and mud. Examples of these early pithouses can be seen along a self-guiding walk along **Ruins Road**. As time went on, the Anasazi began to lay up courses of stone block into above-ground pueblos of interconnected living and storage rooms. Often two stories high, pueblos usually arced around a more elaborate central pithouse, called a kiva.

Kivas evolved from the basic pithouse plan and became special places to the Anasazi. Men gathered in kivas to weave, and all the villagers crowded into them to take part in ceremonies. The existence and uses of prehistoric kivas are inferred from kivas found in modern-day Southwestern pueblos. Spruce Tree House alone has eight round kivas, and others are found at nearly every Anasazi community.

The Anasazi made a living among the mesas and canyons by hunting, gathering and farming. They stalked mule deer and rabbit, gathered the fibers of the yucca plant for woven baskets and sandals, and cultivated small fields and gardens. With only stone or wood hoes and clever water collection systems, they successfully grew crops in this dry environment for millennia.

Corn, which came from Mexico, was the earliest and most important domesticated crop, along with squash. Beans were added later, possibly with the advent of pottery around AD 500. Plain gray, corrugated jars and bowls served for everyday cooking and storage. A finer pottery painted with black designs on white became a hallmark of the

Preceding pages: moonrise over Wupatki. **Left,** Canyon de Chelly in winter. **Right,** ancient pictograph.

Anasazi; the finest black-and-white wares were sometimes traded to others.

Although Mesa Verde is often considered the crown jewel of Anasazi culture, it is by no means the only site. In fact, its famous cliff dwellings were not built until the 13th century, almost the end of Anasazi occupation in the region north of the San Juan River.

Fifty miles (80 km) west of Mesa Verde, on the Colorado-Utah border, is **Hovenweep National Monument**. Here, also in the 13th century, the Anasazi built elegant towers which rise organically from the bedrock. Six clusters of multi-story towers are located at the heads of canyons. They may have been built for food storage, defense, ceremonies or skywatching. No one really knows. Hovenweep is a quiet, out-of-the-way spot, accessible only by dirt roads.

Some Mesa Verde people went south to what is now **Aztec National Monument** on the Animas River in northern New Mexico. Aztec features a large, fully excavated pueblo called **West Ruin**

and a finely restored great kiva. Great kivas, larger versions of the standard village kiva, were host to people from many surrounding communities during social and religious events.

Chaco Canyon lies 60 miles (97 km) south of Aztec, and a visit here means a jolting 20-mile (32-km) drive over dirt roads. But Chaco is a mecca because it was a center of Anasazi culture at its peak. Between 900 and 1115, the Anasazi invested considerable effort in building nine "great houses" in the Chaco Canyon area. One is **Pueblo Bonito**, a five-story, 800-room, D-shaped pueblo of superb masonry. Pueblo Bonito and several other great houses can be toured along the main road through **Chaco Culture National Historical Park**. Nearby is **Casa Rinconada**, a great kiva that is 63 ft (19 m) in diameter.

The Anasazi also designed and built a road system that radiates from Chaco in all directions and connects with outlying prehistoric villages. Lacking the wheel, the Anasazi must have had an

Stronghold House, Hovenweep National Monument.

important reason to engineer such a system. Because Chaco was a major regional center, the roads may have brought people in for trade, ceremonies or business affairs. After this outpouring of labor, though, Chacoans packed up and left, mysteriously, by the end of the 12th century.

From Chaco, we head to **Canyon de Chelly National Monument** in eastern Arizona, where the Anasazi built many dwellings in the alcoves of the soaring sandstone walls. The rock walls were also canvases for Anasazi artwork; hundreds of panels in Canyon de Chelly testify to their long occupation here.

White House Ruin is the only site in Canyon de Chelly accessible without a Park Service or Navajo guide. The self-guiding trail leads down from **White House Overlook** on the **South Rim Drive**. In summer, the hike is best done in the cool of the morning. White House Ruin is fenced off now and cannot be entered, but it can be viewed closely after a hike down the 1-mile (1½-km) trail and crossing of Chinle Wash.

Canyon de Chelly is part of the Navajo Nation. Navajo farmers still live in the canyon in summer and on the rims in winter, and they control access into the canyon. Navajo guides can be hired for jeep, hiking and horseback trips to view **Antelope**, **Standing Cow** and other sites. Some sites can be seen from viewpoints along the South Rim Drive, which follows Canyon de Chelly proper; and the **North Rim Drive**, which follows **Canyon del Muerto**, a major tributary. Inquire at the park **visitor center** for information about the sites.

To the northeast across the Navajo Reservation, past the town of Kayenta, Arizona, is **Navajo National Monument**. From the visitor center, a half-mile walk on the **Sandal Trail** ends at an overlook of **Betatakin**. In this home in a cave lived the Kayenta Anasazi, the third major branch, from 1250 to 1300. During the summer, rangers lead tours down into Betatakin.

Though a small preserve, Navajo National Monument also contains the largest ruin in Arizona: **Keet Seel**. It's a

An uninvited guest.

180-room pueblo dating to the late 13th century. An 8-mile (13-km) hike or horseback ride will get you there (open from Memorial Day to Labor Day, by advance reservation).

Chaco, Mesa Verde, Canyon de Chelly – all were deserted by the Anasazi when the first Anglo-Europeans came upon these places in the mid-1500s. The Anasazi did not simply disappear. Rather, as happened repeatedly throughout their reign in the Southwest, they moved on. Drought may have been a driving force, or changes in social and trade networks may have been a factor. Many pueblo people today say it was prophesied that they should keep moving until they reached their final destinations – which today are the Hopi Mesas in Arizona and Zuni, and villages on the upper Rio Grande in New Mexico.

Bandelier National Monument in northern New Mexico was one of these late stopping places. Here the Anasazi planted fields along Frijoles Creek and built dwellings in cavities in the cliffs. From the visitor center, the mile-long **Ruins Trail** forms a loop which follows the creek and gives access to some of the ruins. Unexcavated sites can be seen on longer excursions into Bandelier's 23,000-acre (9,300-hectare) backcountry wilderness. Ask at the **visitor center** about trails and permits, which are required for overnight trips.

The Sinagua: The Sinagua were close neighbors and contemporaries of the Anasazi. Walnut Canyon, Wupatki and Sunset Crater national monuments near Flagstaff in northern Arizona contain remains of the people "without water." Harold Sellers Colton, founder of the Museum of Northern Arizona, named the culture, based on finds in the cinder hills around Flagstaff.

By AD 600, the Sinagua were living in "earth lodges" at the edges of large grassy valleys, called parks, in the ponderosa pine and pinyon-juniper forests of northern Arizona. The eruption of Sunset Crater in 1064 forced them to flee. But as the earth settled down, the Sinagua discovered that the volcanic cinders held moisture and made good

Lightning strikes at Lomaki Ruin.

farmland. Combined with a period of favorable rainfall, these conditions brought them back to begin farming again. The Sinagua also began to build pueblos, similar but not as elaborate as those of their Anasazi neighbors.

To see some of their pueblos, drive the 17-mile (27-km) road north from Sunset Crater to **Wupatki National Monument**. The **Wupatki Pueblo** near the **visitor center** is the largest and most popular. Here there is also a ball court, a feature introduced by the Hohokam of the southern deserts, and a prehistoric amphitheater. Hopi Indians of the Bear Clan say they stopped at Wupatki for a time, building a village and growing corn. But the old men told the people that the land was too rich, and that they had to move on before they became too comfortable.

Side trips to **Lomaki** and **Wukoki** pueblos are well worth the time. The **San Francisco Peaks**, the highest mountains in Arizona, form a magnificent backdrop to these lovely structures.

Tucked into the terraced limestone cliffs of **Walnut Canyon** east of Flagstaff are small Sinagua dwellings. Between 1125 and 1250, the Sinagua grew corn, beans and squash on the canyon rim and took advantage of the diverse plant life – walnut trees and grapes along the stream, cacti and wolfberry on the rocky hillsides, and pinyon pine and juniper on the mesa tops. The quarter-mile (½ km) **Island Trail** leads part of the way into Walnut Canyon and provides intimate views of many of the rooms.

A southern contingent of Sinagua lived in the **Verde Valley** south of Flagstaff, their golden years dating from 1300 to 1400. The warmer, lower valley was a transition area between the northland and the deserts. Adapting gradually to this different environment, the southern Sinaguans appeared in many ways unlike their northern cousins. In the words of archaeologist Christian Downum: "There were, evidently, many ways to be Sinagua."

Because of their intermediate location, the southern Sinaguans served as

Bicycle touring at Wupatki.

middlemen in a brisk trade for salt, cotton, argillite, parrots and shells. What were first called forts in Sinagua country have more recently been reinterpreted as possible large storage structures for trade goods. The Sinagua were also expert weavers and skilled jewelers.

Montezuma Castle National Monument, just off Interstate 17 near Cottonwood, preserves two multi-story cliff dwellings built by the Sinagua just before the year 1000. A short trail along sycamore-lined **Beaver Creek** leads from the **visitor center** to a view of the castle from below; the ruin itself is off-limits. Nearby **Montezuma Well** is a natural limestone sink fed by artesian springs, which drew prehistoric farmers who practiced irrigation. By the 14th century, the "well" supported a community of 150 to 200 residents.

Tuzigoot National Monument, about 30 miles (48 km) west near the town of **Clarkdale**, furnishes a striking comparison to Montezuma Castle. Tuzigoot is a sprawling pueblo perched on an open ridge, with rooms spilling randomly down the hillside. The settlement takes in a full view of the **Verde River**, whose flood plain provided prime farmland. The pueblo was added to over time, and at its peak it was home to perhaps 225 souls. Tuzigoot and Montezuma Castle were finally abandoned by the Sinaguan people around 1425. Some of them may have joined the Yavapai who were moving in from the west, while many others resettled at big villages on Anderson Mesa south and east of Flagstaff.

The Hohokam: The Sonoran Desert, land of saguaro cactus and palo verde trees, was home to the Hohokam Indians. The Hohokam had a superb ability to survive in this dry, hot desert that receives on average only about 7–10 inches (18–25 cms) of rain a year.

The Hohokam people built their houses in pits; several pithouses together made a rancheria. They never congregated in great numbers, as did their Anasazi contemporaries. Their favored building material was caliche, a calcium-rich, rock-hard substance of the

White House Ruins, Canyon de Chelly.

240

valley floors. Mixed with water, caliche turns to a mud that can be daubed over a stick foundation.

The Hohokam were master irrigators. With backbreaking labor, they constructed and maintained a system of dams, headgates and canals that reached many miles into the surrounding desert. The valleys of two major Southwest rivers, the Gila and the Salt, were their heartland. And though the Hohokam are most often viewed as a riverine society, their traces have more recently been found in the rocky slopes of the foothills around Tucson, where they cultivated wild plants such as agave. The Hohokam also manufactured extraordinary buff and orange pottery and excellent stone and shell goods.

Around AD 700–900, the Hohokam built elliptical, walled arenas where ball games were played. Another, more enigmatic structure, was the platform mound. These multi-storied buildings atop a flat mound were frequently walled, and within the walls was an entire village. Platform mounds may have been residences of the elite priests.

Casa Grande National Monument south of Phoenix is the only national park area now open to the public that is devoted to Hohokam culture. Preserved here is a Hohokam ball court. Rising in solitude nearby is the **Casa Grande**, or Big House. This four-story, 11-room structure was built during the early 14th century and roofed in modern times to protect the mud walls.

In the walls are portholes, whose edges are struck by the sun's rays on the summer solstice. This has led some to suggest that Casa Grande may have been home to priests or chiefs responsible for announcing celestial events that signaled planting and harvest times. Whatever its purpose, Casa Grande was built in the waning days of the Hohokam. By 1350–1400, the people were gone. Their descendants may be the Pima and Tohono O'odham Indians who live in southern Arizona today.

The Salado: On the higher reaches of the Salt River in central Arizona a different culture had emerged by 1150.

Casa Rinconada, Chaco Culture National Historical Park.

These people were called the Salado. Some think they were newcomers to the region; others believe they were essentially Hohokam who had adapted to the more rugged Tonto Basin.

Tonto National Monument is the only national park that protects Salado remains. Within the monument, a pair of pueblos, **Upper Ruin** and **Lower Ruin**, are tucked into caves high in the side of a cliff overlooking **Lake Roosevelt**. From the visitor center, a rather steep trail leads to the larger Upper Ruin.

Though they show traits of several surrounding cultures, the Salado are distinguished as makers of a pottery known as polychrome. This gorgeous red, black and cream-colored ceramic was commonly formed into large water jars and bowls. The Salado also wove exquisite cotton textiles and knew how to live off the desert's bounty. Prickly pear, mesquite, agave, rabbit and deer fed them well.

They also farmed, and by 1200 they had settled into villages along the **Salt River** and were irrigating fields. When the valley became too crowded, the people moved higher into the hills and built the two pueblos at **Tonto**.

For nearly three centuries, the Salado thrived in the Tonto Basin. They outlasted the Hohokam and Anasazi, but just barely. The Salado too moved on, perhaps driven out by climate change, salty fields or outside invaders, leaving the ruins at Tonto silent for 600 years.

The Mogollon: There was nothing at all flashy about the Mogollon (pronounced *muggy-own*) people. They were farmers, but they clung to a strong hunting tradition. Before the end of the 10th century, they made mostly plain brown pottery and lived in crude pithouses. After the turn of the century they started to build Anasazi-style pueblos and to make black-and-white pottery. Called Mimbres, this pottery is some of the most beautiful produced by any prehistoric Southwestern peoples.

The huge territory of the Mogollon included the rolling hills, mountains and river valleys of the upper Gila and Black rivers in southwest New Mexico and central Arizona. The small, remote **Gila Cliff Dwellings National Monument** in southern New Mexico is the sole site devoted to the Mogollon in the park system. North out of Silver City, Highway 15 winds for 44 miles (71 km) through the mountains, providing heart-stopping views of the rugged canyons of the upper Gila River.

At the national monument, you may stop first at the **visitor center**, then drive the short distance up the West Fork of the Gila. From there, a mile loop trail leads up **Cliff Dweller Canyon** and into the dwellings 180 ft (55 m) up the canyon wall. Cliff dwellings were not as characteristic of the Mogollon as they were of other Southwest cultures, because the Mogollon tended to build in the open, leaving little of their architecture for us to see.

Built between 1270 and 1290, Gila Cliff Dwellings represent almost the last of the Mogollon people. From there, they probably moved to central Arizona, where they eventually merged with other cultures.

Left, Cliff Palace, Mesa Verde National Park. **Right**, Anasazi kiva, an ancient ceremonial chamber.

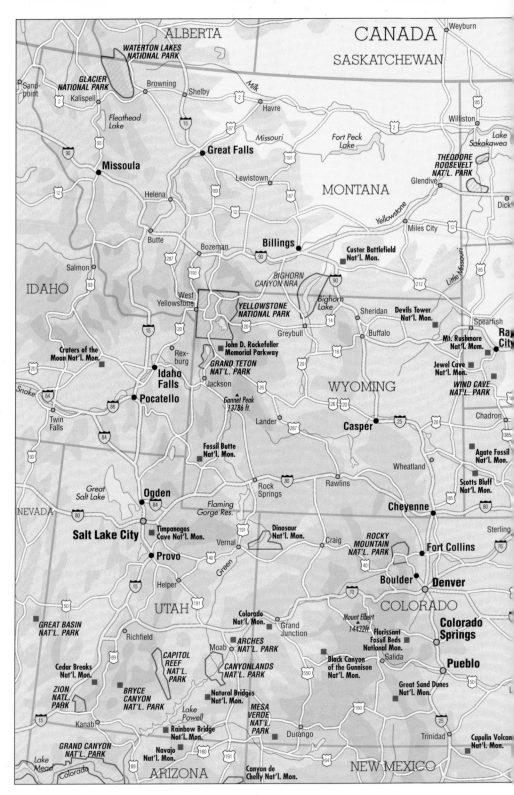

ALBERTA

CANADA

SASKATCHEWAN

Weyburn

WATERTON LAKES
NATIONAL PARK

Browning Shelby
Milk

GLACIER
NATIONAL PARK

Sandpoint

2 Kalispell

Fleathead
Lake

93 90

Missoula

12

Havre

15

87

Missouri

Great Falls

Helena

89

Butte

287

Bozeman

191

MONTANA

Lewistown

Fort Peck
Lake

87

Yellowstone

2

Williston

Lake
Sakakawea

85

THEODORE
ROOSEVELT
NAT'L. PARK

Glendive

Dick

Miles City 12

Billings

90

Salmon

93

IDAHO

West
Yellowstone

15

20

Craters of the
Moon Nat'l. Mon.

20

Snake

84

86

Twin
Falls

84

93

Rexburg

Idaho
Falls

Pocatello

Custer Battlefield
Nat'l. Mon.

BIGHORN
CANYON NRA

YELLOWSTONE
NATIONAL PARK

20

Greybull

John D. Rockefeller
Memorial Parkway

GRAND TETON
NAT'L. PARK

Jackson

26

Gannet Peak
13786 ft.

Fossil Butte
Nat'l. Mon.

Bighorn
Lake

14

Sheridan

16

Buffalo

212

Little Missouri

85

Devils Tower
Nat'l. Mon.

Spearfish

Mt. Rushmore
Nat'l. Mem.

Ra
City

Jewel Cave
Nat'l. Mon.

WIND CAVE
NAT'L. PARK

WYOMING

26 20

Lander

287

Casper

25

20

Chadron

385

Agate Fossil
Nat'l. Mon.

Great
Salt Lake

NEVADA

Ogden

84

Salt Lake City

80

Timpanogos
Cave Nat'l. Mon.

Flaming
Gorge Res.

Provo

191

Vernal

40

Green

Helper

15

50

UTAH

191

89

Richfield

Cedar Breaks
Nat'l. Mon.

ZION
NATL.
PARK

15

Kanab

GRAND CANYON
NAT'L. PARK

Lake
Mead

Colorado

ARIZONA

GREAT BASIN
NAT'L. PARK

CAPITOL
REEF
NAT'L.
PARK

BRYCE
CANYON
NAT'L. PARK

Lake
Powell

Navajo
Nat'l. Mon.

89

Colorado
Nat'l. Mon.

Moab

ARCHES
NAT'L. PARK

CANYONLANDS
NAT'L. PARK

550

Natural Bridges
Nat'l. Mon.

Rainbow Bridge
Nat'l. Mon.

160

MESA
VERDE
NAT'L.
PARK

Durango

Canyon de
Chelly Nat'l. Mon.

191

64

Rock
Springs

80

Rawlins

Wheatland

Scotts Bluff
Nat'l. Mon.

85

Cheyenne

80

Sterling

ROCKY
MOUNTAIN
NAT'L. PARK

Craig

Dinosaur
Nat'l. Mon.

Fort Collins

76

40

Boulder

Denver

70

COLORADO

Grand
Junction

Mount Elbert
14432ft

Florissant
Fossil Beds
National Mon.

Salida

Black Canyon
of the Gunnison
Nat'l. Mon.

Colorado
Springs

Pueblo

Great Sand Dunes
Nat'l. Mon.

25

50

160

Trinidad

Capulin Volcan
Nat'l. Mon.

NEW MEXICO

244

THE ROCKY MOUNTAINS

They are known as the backbone of the world. The Rocky Mountains are a crooked spine of peaks and ridges that were thrust skyward more than 50 million years ago and now run through the country's mid-section. In Rocky Mountain and Glacier national parks, the mountains were shaped by great sheets of ice, grinding, gouging and fracturing the bedrock into serrated peaks, bowl-like cirques, "hanging valleys" and enormous mounds of morainal debris.

At Yellowstone, the nation's first national park, an ancient volcanic blast tore open a massive crater where hot springs, geysers and fumaroles continue to steam and spurt. Immediately to the south, the Teton Range towers grandly over Jackson Hole, a chain of shimmering lakes at its feet.

To the east of the Rockies, a mountainous outlier known as the Black Hills rises from the plains like an island of granite. At their base, the limestone passages of Wind Cave honeycomb the earth beneath prairie and ponderosa forest. In the Dakota badlands, the plains have been carved by rushing water into a moonscape of gullies, canyons, ravines and "tables" shared by prairie dogs, bison, pronghorn and soaring hawks and eagles.

Together, these parks form some of the richest wilderness in the United States, with dense coniferous forests, shady rivers, dazzling wildflower meadows and extensive swaths of alpine tundra. Hikers can explore hundreds of miles of backcountry trails into the realms of mountain goats, bighorn sheep, mountain lions, bobcats, grizzly bears and wolves. Even motorists are likely to see a variety of large mammals, including bison, elk, mule deer and pronghorn, not to mention smaller species such as chipmunks, squirrels and marmots and a wide variety of bird life.

YELLOWSTONE

It is perhaps the world's most famous natural preserve. And yet, despite its renown and its rank as the first national park ever created, Yellowstone is capable of surprising even those who know it well, to say nothing of those who visit for the first time.

Most visitors have in mind at least one destination: **Old Faithful Geyser**. Beyond that, they may expect to see some wildlife, have a picnic under the pines, or enjoy a meadow of wildflowers. But what they find is so much more. Beyond Old Faithful are more than 10,000 other thermal features, including even bigger geysers and several that are more faithful – that is, they erupt at more regular intervals than their celebrated cousin.

The park's 2.2 million acres (829,600 hectares) support approximately 20,000 elk, 3,500 bison and hundreds of deer, along with moose, bighorn sheep, mountain goats, pronghorn antelope, black bears, grizzly bears, coyotes, trumpeter swans, Canada geese, sandhill cranes, white pelicans, cutthroat trout and others. After the long anticipated reintroduction of wolves, the park will represent the entire panoply of Rocky Mountain wildlife. Yellowstone contains snow-covered mountain peaks, several magnificent high-altitude lakes, numerous rivers and streams renowned for trout fishing, a brightly colored canyon that nearly dwarfs two major waterfalls, one of the most significant volcanic calderas in the world, and layer upon layer of buried petrified forest. None of this came easy. Yellowstone has a history of staggering geologic violence, and it remains one of the most geologically active places on earth.

The lay of the land: Most of Yellowstone occupies a high plateau averaging between 7,000 ft (2,134 m) and 8,000 ft (2,438 m) in elevation, ringed by mountains that rise several thousand feet higher. In the northwest, the **Gallatin Range** is capped by **Mount Holmes** and **Electric Peak**, both rising over 10,000 ft (3,000 m). On the northeast

stands the **Beartooth Plateau**, a massive Precambrian block where Montana's highest mountain, 12,799-ft (3,900-m) **Granite Peak**, rises a few miles outside the park. Yellowstone's eastern boundary follows the crest of the **Absaroka Range**, a line of rubbly snow-covered volcanic summits that include **Eagle Peak**, which at 11,358 ft (3,460 m) is the highest point in the park. Lofty terrain continues along the south on **Big Game Ridge** and the wind-swept **Pitchstone Plateau**, while the **Madison Plateau** holds up the park's southwest corner.

Winding circuitously across the park's southern third, the **Continental Divide** separates waters flowing toward the Pacific Ocean from streams heading to the Atlantic. Waters from Yellowstone and the surrounding area find their way into many famous rivers, including the Missouri, the Snake, the Big Horn and the Yellowstone itself. These rivers and their tributaries – the Wind, Sweetwater, Popo Agie, Madison, Gallatin, Clark's Fork, Shoshone and many others – re-

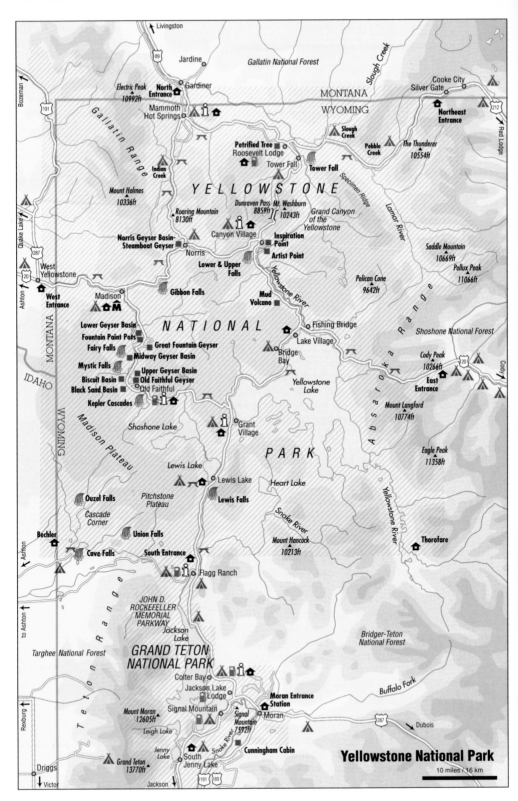

Yellowstone National Park

Livingston
Jardine
89
Gallatin National Forest
Slough Creek
MONTANA
WYOMING
Cooke City
Silver Gate
212
Red Lodge
Electric Peak 10992ft
North Entrance
Gardiner
Northeast Entrance
Mammoth Hot Springs
Bozeman
191
Gallatin Range
Indian Creek
Petrified Tree
Roosevelt Lodge
Tower Fall
Slough Creek
Pebble Creek
The Thunderer 10554ft
Mount Holmes 10336ft
Tower Fall
YELLOWSTONE
Specimen Ridge
Roaring Mountain 8130ft
Dunraven Pass 8859ft
Mt. Washburn 10243ft
Grand Canyon of the Yellowstone
Saddle Mountain 10669ft
Canyon Village
Pollux Peak 11066ft
Norris Geyser Basin-Steamboat Geyser
Inspiration Point
Artist Point
Lamar River
Quake Lake
287
West Yellowstone
20
Norris
Lower & Upper Falls
Yellowstone River
Pelican Cone 9642ft
Absaroka Range
Shoshone National Forest
West Entrance
Madison
Gibbon Falls
NATIONAL
Mud Volcano
Fishing Bridge
Cody Peak 10266ft
20
Cody
Ashton
MONTANA
IDAHO
M
Lower Geyser Basin
Fountain Paint Pots
Fairy Falls
Great Fountain Geyser
Midway Geyser Basin
Lake Village
Bridge Bay
East Entrance
WYOMING
Madison Plateau
Mystic Falls
Biscuit Basin
Black Sand Basin
Upper Geyser Basin
Old Faithful Geyser
Old Faithful
Yellowstone Lake
Mount Langford 10774ft
Kepler Cascades
Shoshone Lake
Grant Village
PARK
Eagle Peak 11358ft
Lewis Lake
Heart Lake
Ouzel Falls
Lewis Lake
Pitchstone Plateau
Lewis Falls
Snake River
Yellowstone River
Cascade Corner
Union Falls
Mount Hancock 10213ft
Thorofare
Bechler
Ashton
Cave Falls
South Entrance
Flagg Ranch
JOHN D. ROCKEFELLER MEMORIAL PARKWAY
Bridger-Teton National Forest
Jackson Lake
to Ashton
Targhee National Forest
Teton Range
GRAND TETON NATIONAL PARK
Colter Bay
Jackson Lake Lodge
Moran Entrance Station
Buffalo Fork
Rexburg
Signal Mountain
Mount Moran 12605ft
Moran
287
Dubois
Leigh Lake
Signal Mountain 7592ft
Snake River
Cunningham Cabin
Driggs
Jenny Lake
South Jenny Lake
Grand Teton 13770ft
Victor
Jackson
191
89

10 miles / 16 km

Yellowstone National Park

verberate through the history of westward exploration and settlement.

Congress established Yellowstone as the world's first national park in 1872. It was an act of foresight brought about largely because of the park's amazing collection of geysers and hot springs, unmatched anywhere else. For years mountain men and other travelers had told stories of strange doings in the area, so strange that they were disbelieved by most who heard them. Lakes of boiling mud? Gushers of hot water shooting 200 ft (61 m) or more in the air? These could only be tall tales from the imaginations of men who had spent too much time alone in the wilderness.

The stories turned out to be true, and Yellowstone's thermal features are no less wonderful today than they were more than 120 years ago. In the meantime the park has acquired new significance for other values: wildlife and wilderness. When America was young, the country was rich in wildlife and pristine landscapes. The national occupation was the subduing of wilderness, not its preservation. Forests were being cut down, marshes drained, animals slaughtered. In 1872, millions of bison still darkened the Great Plains. Who would have guessed that within 30 years Yellowstone would become a refuge for the last surviving wild bison in America? Or that, nearing the end of the 20th century, people from around the world would come here simply to see wild animals in a natural setting? Or that, thanks in large part to recovery efforts carried out in Yellowstone, a few remnant herds of bison would survive?

In recent years it has become evident that the park, for all its size, is nowhere near big enough to provide safe haven for many of its creatures. As it happens, Yellowstone is only the heart of a much larger area called the Greater Yellowstone Ecosystem. It shows up clearly from satellite photos, an expanse of high, mostly-forested land, punctuated by mountains and bounded on all sides by semiarid plains – a region defined by climate and geography, not by administrative decree.

The region is under siege. Chopped into a variety of jurisdictions, sliced by roads and other developments, its best winter range occupied by cattle ranches and towns, the integrity of the ecosystem – that is, its ability to sustain the species that live here – has been compromised. Yellowstone by itself is not large enough for the bison, who, when snow lies deep in the high country, migrate out of the park to their ancient wintering grounds and into a conflict with ranchers. The same geographic concerns hold true for any creatures that move with the seasons, or for those that range over large areas, like coyotes and grizzlies. They all need more space than any one administrative unit can provide. It is toward a coordinated policy throughout the region that conservation efforts are now focused.

The big bang: The Yellowstone landscape was built by a series of volcanoes. Beginning around 50 million years ago, eruptions along the eastern edge of the plateau gave rise to the **Absaroka Range** and continued through cycles of activity for another 20 million years. The

Yellowstone's Grand Canyon from Inspiration Point.

following period of relative quiet was marked by such events as the uplift of the **Teton Range**, which began some 10 million years ago and continues to this day. Volcanic activity picked up again some 2 or 3 million years ago.

One event surpasses all – the great Yellowstone volcano, which erupted roughly 600,000 years ago in a cataclysmic explosion. Its scale is difficult to imagine but some idea can be gained by comparing it with the 1883 eruption of Krakatoa, the South Pacific volcano. According to accounts at the time, the Krakatoa explosion was heard more than 1,000 miles (1,610 km) away; its dust rose so high and in such quantities that it colored the atmosphere around the world for three years, causing what viewers as far away as London called Krakatoa sunsets. It was an enormous event, yet the Yellowstone explosion was far greater, perhaps 100 times larger. Were it to happen again in the near future (geologists say it could happen any time), the eruption would be history's worst catastrophe by a considerable margin.

After the eruption, the center of Yellowstone was a smoking crater, or caldera, 28 by 47 miles (45 by 76 km) wide and several thousand feet deep. Subsequent nonexplosive eruptions filled in parts of the caldera and obscured its once-distinct walls. Glaciers further altered its shape when ice covered the Rocky Mountains during the Pleistocene. But not all has disappeared. Yellowstone Lake occupies the bulk of the old caldera. The rim itself forms the south slope of Mount Washburn and is traversed by the road near Dunraven Pass to the village of Canyon.

As a footnote to the story, geologists tell us that the eruption was not a singular event. Two others of comparable violence occurred in the region 1.3 million and 2 million years ago. In fact, going back some 17 million years, a series of eruptions have made their way across southern Idaho. Moving west to east in a broad curve, the eruptions created the current Snake River Plain – in effect a geologic burn path that ends, for now, in Yellowstone. The eruptions have all been caused by the same "hot spot," an upwelling of molten material beneath the earth's crust. The hot spot has not moved; rather, the continent has drifted across it like a sheet of steel over a cutting torch. Currently, the torch burns beneath Yellowstone's many geysers and hot springs.

Seeing the park: Many of Yellowstone's thermal features are centered along the **Firehole River**, which rises on the Continental Divide above Old Faithful. The river begins much like any mountain stream, its cold clear water tumbling over rhyolite cascades. But once it hits the geyser basins, it becomes a steaming beauty that never freezes, even on the coldest winter nights.

In its short course (it ends at Madison Junction, just 16 miles/26 km north of Old Faithful) the Firehole passes through three concentrations of geysers, called the **Upper**, **Midway** and **Lower geyser basins**. All are worth seeing, but no one should visit Yellowstone without spending a day in the Upper Geyser Basin. Besides Old Faithful (which is faithful only in its unpredictability: it is neither

Travertine terraces at Mammoth Hot Springs.

hourly nor regular), there are several other major geysers that erupt frequently, including **Castle**, **Grand**, **Beehive**, **Riverside** and **Daisy**. In the same area, geysers like **Giant**, **Giantess**, **Fan** and **Mortar** erupt irregularly but with spectacular results. Dozens of smaller geysers spout and steam on all sides, in the company of hot pools large and small. A network of boardwalks and trails make for easy walking

If one plans it right, by stopping at the **visitor center** for a list of predicted eruption times, one can catch most of the eruptions in a period of several hours. Early morning is a particularly rewarding time to be out, as is late on a moonlit night. Don't leave the basin without a visit to the historic **Old Faithful Inn**, a magnificent log structure built during the winter of 1903–04 from local lodgepole pines on a massive base of rhyolite.

Noteworthy farther down the Firehole is **Grand Prismatic Spring**, more than 300 ft (91 m) across and brilliantly colored. Its neighbor, **Excelsior Geyser**, last erupted in 1983. Apparently the force of its 300-ft (91-m) eruptions was too much for its plumbing, and it became a simple hot pool – but a most impressive one. A boardwalk leading through dense clouds of steam allows you to get a closer look.

On the **Firehole Lake Loop Drive**, **Great Fountain Geyser** performs in a manner that lives up to its name, while at **Fountain Paint Pots** several large boiling mud cauldrons simmer like immense kettles of viscous sauce. Farther north lies **Norris Geyser Basin**, the hottest ground in the park. Among its features is **Steamboat**, the world's largest active geyser, capable of climbing 400 ft (122 m) with a thunderous roar. Seeing such an event, however, is a matter of pure luck; years may pass between eruptions. Quite a few smaller geysers, notably **Echinus**, **Veteran**, **Little Whirligig** and **Minute**, erupt frequently or even continuously, making the basin a noisy, active place.

The park's third major thermal area, **Mammoth Hot Springs**, overlooks old **Fort Yellowstone**, a collection of fine

Firehole River flows through a geyser basin.

stone buildings built in the years when the United States Army was in charge of the park. Civilian management, lacking funds and poorly organized, had failed to protect the park adequately. In 1888 the Army was appointed to what surely stands as one of its most unusual missions. Arresting poachers, guiding tourists, patrolling roads and trails, the soldiers stayed until 1916 when the newly created National Parks Service took over park management.

There are no geysers at Mammoth. Instead, hundreds of hot springs varying from trickles to small rivers build gleaming white terraces, tier upon tier, brightly painted by bacteria and minerals. The basic material being deposited is calcium carbonate, or travertine, derived from limestone; in the geyser basins, deposits are a different substance – silicon dioxide, or geyserite. The springs are constantly changing, shifting their vents from one location to another. That change happens quickly is evidenced by stands of trees swallowed up by fresh travertine deposits while nearby, young vegetation thrives in places recently abandoned by scalding waters.

Lakes and rivers: Those interested in seeing thermal features under completely natural conditions should know that thousands of hot springs are scattered throughout backcountry areas of the park. **Heart Lake** and **Shoshone Lake** both have attractive thermal areas on their shores. The whole southwest corner of the park, called the **Bechler Region**, is known both for waterfalls and isolated hot springs.

Closer to the road, hikers willing to walk a short distance can find springs and fumaroles (steam vents), in the hills surrounding any geyser basin. Be careful when approaching backcountry thermal ground; it can give way and scald incautious feet, or worse. Also remember that these features are fragile; footprints can last for years. A good rule of thumb is to stay on ground that supports vegetation, a sign that underlying temperatures are not too hot, and stay on marked trails whenever possible.

Other centers of interest include

Stevenson Island trees on Yellowstone Lake.

Yellowstone Lake, one of the largest high-altitude lakes in the world. Roughly 20 by 14 miles (32 by 23 km), with 110 miles (177 km) of shoreline, it is filled with clear, icy water. At its deepest point, 390 ft (120 m), temperatures are a constant 42°F (6°C). Yet not even the lake is free of thermal influence. Scattered across the bottom are numerous hot springs and several underwater geysers. These are generally invisible from the surface, but some are strong enough to keep patches of the lake free of ice in the winter.

Yellowstone Lake can be a dangerous place for the unprepared. When a summer storm moves through, the most inviting, mirror-smooth surface can fast become a seething mass of whitecaps. Nonetheless, boating is popular, the fishing is good, and stony beaches offer miles of pleasant walking. The area around **Bridge Bay** is particularly inviting for shore activities. Also worth a visit is the **Lake Hotel**, recently restored to its turn-of-the-century beauty. Its lounging areas provide excellent views of the lake and the Absaroka Mountains.

On the north shore, the **Yellowstone River** leaves the lake and slides beneath **Fishing Bridge** – once a famous place for catching native cutthroat trout, now (since fishing is prohibited here) a superb place for watching fish in their natural setting.

A short distance north lies the **Grand Canyon of the Yellowstone River**. Here the green water explodes into white froth as it tips over the edges of two great falls into a 1,200-ft (366-m) deep gorge between brilliant multicolored walls. The canyon is basically a river-eroded geyser basin. The hot acidic water of numerous hot springs in the canyon have altered the volcanic rocks here, coloring and weakening them, making them vulnerable to rapid erosion. Since the glaciers melted a little more than 10,000 years ago geologists estimate that the river has deepened the canyon by about 50 ft (15 m).

The northern part of Yellowstone stands distinct from the rest. Lower, warmer and drier than the interior, characterized by sagebrush and open valleys, it is an important wintering ground for large animals – and for sightseers. The road from Gardiner, Montana, to the northeast entrance is the only park road kept plowed in winter.

It is a pity that most visitors never get more than a few hundred yards from their vehicles. So much of experiencing Yellowstone requires contact with the wild world, and this means going some distance – even if not very far – away from vehicles and pavement. Good day hikes include any of the thermal areas. Even the Upper Geyser Basin, subject to midday madness, can be quite deserted at 7am, and this is probably its most beautiful time.

In the north, strong hikers can visit the petrified trees of **Specimen Ridge**, or hike up one of the other bare mountain slopes in the **Lamar Valley**. From **Dunraven Pass**, a moderate trail up **Mount Washburn** to a fire lookout offers a tremendous panoramic view. In the Grand Canyon area, easy shaded paths follow both rims. On the shore of

Surveying the backcountry.

WOLVES OF YELLOWSTONE

The wolves are coming. After an absence of 60 years, they're returning to Yellowstone National Park.

Once upon a time, they were tracked down and killed by the tens of thousands by bounty hunters equipped with an arsenal of traps, guns and poison. And this with the sanction of the federal government, until by the late 1930s the last of Yellowstone's *Canis lupus* – gray wolves – was silenced. It took decades before the biologists who had encouraged this kind of thing realized the mistake they had made.

Now, the United States Fish and Wildlife Service is working up a strategy to reintroduce wolves to Yellowstone. Artificial restoration is to begin in the Lamar Valley with the establishment of a single breeding pair. And if all goes well, the pair will form the nucleus of the first pack. Although pack sizes can vary, the initial goal is to sustain 10 packs with 10 wolves in each.

Removing an apex predator like the wolf has thrown the entire ecosystem out of

balance. For example, with fewer predators, Yellowstone's elk herd has swelled, which has led to serious overgrazing. It's believed that restoring wolves will not only decrease the elk population but also drive many elk out of the park during the winter, when overgrazing is at its worst.

Wolves have already colonized Glacier National Park and the surrounding ecosystem. And there are indications that wolves are getting a foothold in North Cascades National Park and the adjoining wilderness areas. Scattered sightings are tantalizing proof that nomadic individuals are roaming Yellowstone, too. But there is a big difference, biologists say, between lone wolves and packs. And that's one reason why artificial introduction is being used to complement natural colonization.

Not everyone is happy about the return of wolves. A coalition of ranchers and politicians has tried to throw up roadblocks until the government guarantees that wolves who prey upon cattle or sheep can be shot on sight. The gray wolf is currently listed as an endangered species in the West and is subject to strict protection. Many environmentalists agree that animals who continually prey on livestock should be destroyed, but they are unwilling to give ranchers the authority to kill wolves on their own discretion. Some conservation groups are trying to come up with innovative alternatives. Defenders of Wildlife, for example, has offered ranchers a "bounty" of several thousand dollars if they allow a wolf bitch to den and give birth to pups on their property.

Recently, wildlife photographer Michael H. Francis recalled an outing in Yellowstone when he was watching animals gather in a far-off meadow at dusk. Suddenly, the crisp winter night was pierced by an unexpected howl. It was clearly a wolf, and Francis said that he felt chills run down his spine, not from fear but from excitement. He understands that wolves are a natural part of Yellowstone, and that their re-introduction will help restore balance to the ecosystem. And he's not alone in that. Many opinion polls show that Americans favor reintroducing the wolf. After centuries of unjustly demonizing these creatures, we at last seem ready to embrace them as a valuable component of the food chain and an enduring symbol of the wilderness. ■

Canis lupus, the gray wolf.

Yellowstone Lake, a morning beach stroll reveals pelicans, gulls, jumping cutthroat trout and evaporating mists. From here, you can head to the east entrance, where a steep but rewarding unmarked trail leads to the summit of **Avalanche Peak**.

The great fire: Over much of Yellowstone, dead trees remind visitors of the fires of 1988, a historic event that touched about a third of the park, in some areas opening vistas and dramatically changing the appearance of the landscape. The biggest conflagration to affect the Northern Rockies in 50 years, the fires burned 793,880 acres (321,272 hectares), or 36 percent of the total area of the park (although less than half of that total represents fire-killed forest). Over the course of the summer, about 25,000 firefighters worked in Yellowstone, while dozens of helicopters and more than 100 fire trucks were deployed to protect developed areas. The total cost ran over $120 million, making this the biggest and most expensive firefighting operation in history.

On hot windy days during that unforgettable summer, big fires ran as far as 12½ miles (20 km) in a day. Winds gusting over 60 mph (97 kph) threw embers 1–2 miles (2–3 km) ahead of the fire front, triggering yet more blazes. Fires jumped highways, rivers and even the Grand Canyon of the Yellowstone River, not to mention fire lines cleared through the forest to the width of five bulldozer blades.

Yet not one major feature was destroyed. The geysers, waterfalls, herds of wildlife – even the forest – are still here. Many places show no impact at all. Side by side, burned areas and non-burned areas provide an intriguing study in the causes and effects of fire in wild places. Yellowstone has witnessed far greater natural events than any fire.

Bighorn Canyon: East of Yellowstone lies the big, dry and dusty **Bighorn Basin**, where oil pumps oscillate above cattle ranches, and irrigated sugar-beet farms grow green on the edge of vast badlands. The basin reminds us that despite forested, snow-topped mountains, western America is predominantly an arid region in which, as the old song puts it, "the skies are not cloudy all day." Places that have abundant water are exceptionally striking, attracting groups of wildlife and people.

One such place is **Bighorn Canyon National Recreation Area**, which was once a deep cottonwood-lined gorge carved into native limestone by the muddy **Bighorn River**. In 1967, the **Yellowtail Dam** converted the river into a winding reservoir 71 miles (114 km) long. The dam and most of the reservoir is in Montana, but road access to the spectacular central section is through Wyoming.

Just outside the town of Lovell, the **Bighorn Canyon Visitor Center** offers exhibits and information, including a three-dimensional model of the region that provides a good orientation. From here, the paved access road heads north, following the canyon rim past numerous scenic points, ending at a campground and boat launch called **Barry's Landing** on **Bighorn Lake**.

Along the way, the road traverses a

Bison graze near burned trees.

rugged bench separating the sharp escarpment of the **Pryor Mountains** from the vertical depths of the canyon. Several viewpoints provide glimpses into the tawny- and terracotta-colored gorge. Among plants and animals, only desert dwellers thrive at this end of the canyon. In places, vegetation thins out to almost nothing. Scraggly junipers and mountain mahogany pepper the hills, while cottonwood trees line the draws. Sharp-pointed yucca and prickly pear are like little interpretive signs saying "It's dry here." How true: **Horseshoe Bend**, near the head of the canyon, receives an average of only 6 inches (15 cms) of rainfall a year.

The river's namesake, bighorn sheep, can sometimes be seen in cliffy areas near the road. Watch for the ewes and lambs that remain at lower elevations throughout the year. The rams climb into the neighboring Pryor Mountains for the summer and are less often seen. Watch also for peregrine falcons. Young birds have been released here as part of a regional attempt to re-establish the formerly vanished population.

Part-way to Barry's Landing, the road passes through the **Pryor Mountain Wild Horse Range**, a 46,800-acre (18,939-hectare) area administered for the protection of wild horses. The herd numbers around 120 animals. Every few years a roundup is held, and the surplus population is taken away for adoption.

How long these horses have lived in this rugged strip of land between the Pryor Mountains and the canyon is uncertain. Some people believe they have been here since the 1700s, when Spanish horses were first introduced to the area. Indeed, they do resemble the horses of the conquistadores. If this is true, these animals are a direct link to one of the most important events in the history of the American West. Their arrival gave birth to the great horse cultures of the buffalo plains. Where people had once moved and hunted only on foot, horses brought mobility, power and an entirely new way of life.

Left, forest at Grand Prismatic Spring.

GRAND TETON

If any range in America serves as a model for how mountains should look, it's the Tetons. Without warning, these superb peaks rise suddenly from a flat plain for a giddy 7,000 ft (2,134 m). From base to summit, the angle of slope is the same: unrelentingly steep. Anchoring the range, which extends across northwestern Wyoming just south of Yellowstone, is a trio of granite spires – **Grand Teton**, **Middle Teton** and **South Teton** – flanked by peaks hardly less spectacular, including **Mount Owen**, **Mount Teewinot** and **Mount Moran**. These are quintessential mountains, rising to sharp, almost delicate points while at the same time retaining a sense of massive strength. The rock is hard, clean and the color of steel. Snowfields and glaciers perch on what appear from a distance to be vertical cliffs. Up close, they look even steeper.

Glacial lakes strung like watery gems adorn the base of the mountains. Each one – Jackson, Jenny, Leigh, Bradley, String and Taggart – is filled with icy snowmelt and trout. Beyond the lakes spread the flat reaches of **Jackson Hole**, a valley rimmed by mountains, carpeted by sagebrush and punctuated by neatly spaced groves of aspens, cottonwoods and conifers. Pronghorn antelope, bison and mule deer favor these flats, while large numbers of elk stage a spectacular show during the autumn rutting season. The **Snake River**, having grown to size in Yellowstone Park, meanders through Jackson Hole in no evident hurry to leave the Tetons. On either side of the river, willow flats and ponds provide habitat for a variety of wildlife, including beavers, moose, coyotes, trumpeter swans, osprey, bald eagles, sandhill cranes and many others.

The quintessential mountains: Although the Teton Range consists of very old, very hard rock, these mountains are relatively young, among the youngest in the Rockies. About 9 or 10 million years ago, two blocks of the earth's crust began to shift along a fault line,

one tilting up while the other went down. The western block became the mountains while the eastern block swung downward, forming the valley. The movement has not stopped, and so far, displacement has totaled some 30,000 ft (9,144 m). In the process, the valley block has sunk roughly four times as far as the mountain block has risen. Because rock has eroded from the mountain summits and debris has filled the valley, we see only part of the great escarpment, impressive as that may be.

On their western slope, facing Idaho, the Tetons present a different aspect. The high peaks rise with the same craggy fierceness, but the valleys approaching them are longer and the surrounding country is less steep. Because the range dips in that direction, the slopes are less abrupt and softened by foothills. Seen from this side, it is easier (but only a little) to understand why early French trappers named them *Les Trois Tétons* ("The Three Breasts").

In its 485 sq. miles (1,256 sq. km), **Grand Teton National Park** includes

Preceding pages: a tranquil moment. **Left**, black bear, *Ursus americanus*. **Right**, elk in winter.

most of Jackson Hole, some of the hills to the east, **Jackson Lake**, and the Teton Range to its crest *(see map, page 258)*. Looking from the east, you might assume that the crest (defined as the divider of watersheds) follows the line of high peaks, but in fact it runs behind them, and all the snow melting from "The Grand" flows eastward into Jackson Hole.

In 1929, when the park was established, it included only the peaks and a few of the morainal lakes at their base. Political wrangling and strong local opposition continued to prevent any enlargement until 1943, when President Franklin D. Roosevelt declared parts of Jackson Hole a national monument and made it possible for the nation to accept a gift of some 33,000 acres (13,355 hectares) of private land from the Rockefeller family. In 1950, Congress joined the monument to the park, essentially forming the single national park we see today.

Like Yellowstone to the north, Grand Teton is one part of a larger wild region.

National forests, wilderness areas and wildlife refuges crowd in on all sides. Notable among them is the **National Elk Refuge**, a 24,700-acre (10,000-hectare) reserve set aside to replace historic wintering grounds that once stretched more than a hundred miles south, to Pinedale, Wyoming, and beyond. Much of that land is now used for cattle ranching or taken up by private homes. In winter, 7,000 to 10,000 elk migrate into the refuge from the surrounding high country. As the snows melt in spring, the herds return to their summer range.

Also worth knowing about is the **John D. Rockefeller Memorial Parkway**, a strip of land between Yellowstone and Grand Teton national parks. Although officially national forest land, this small area is managed by the Parks Services. It has many of the same values as the adjacent national parks, and therefore it deserves the same protection.

Touring Grand Teton, visitors have a choice of two main roads. US 89 goes from Jackson to Moran, where it meets US 287 from Dubois, before continuing north to Yellowstone. Most of this route follows the flat, sage-covered terraces above the Snake River, affording superb views of the Tetons. This road is usually chosen by people in a hurry, which is not to say you can't drive it slowly. Numerous pullouts allow for stopping. Look for antelope and coyote along the way and, in the fall, elk. If you visit on an early-autumn morning or evening, be sure to walk away from the car for a little distance and listen for bull elk bugling challenges to each other. This eerie, passionate sound, coupled with the crisp, sharp bite of autumn air, is one of the Rockies' most powerful and lasting experiences.

The option to Highway 89 is the **Teton Park Road**, which begins at **Moose Junction**, where there is a **visitor center** and park headquarters – a good orientation stop. From Moose, the road runs north along the base of the mountains, past **Jenny Lake** and part of Jackson Lake to a junction with US 89 and 287. Along the way, it provides access to many of the park's alpine trailheads and the glacial lakes at the base of the moun-

The Teton range reflected in the Snake River.

tains. It should be traversed slowly, with frequent stops. A speed of 35 mph (56 kmh) seems none too slow, as each turn brings into sight another classic view.

For many, Jenny Lake is the heart of the park. It is certainly the main focus of attention and, crowds notwithstanding, one glimpse of the surrounding country explains why. There are two access points: the **South Jenny Lake Area** is a complex of parking lots and visitor services. A few miles north, the **Jenny Lake Road** leads to **String Lake** and various trailheads before skirting the shore of Jenny Lake itself. The section along the shore is one-way for vehicles, two-way for bicycles.

High-country hikes: Grand Teton is a gawking park, the sort of place where you'll want to sit and stare at the shining mountains rising so improbably from the plain. Gawking is a worthwhile activity here. It deserves serious effort. Yet eventually many visitors itch to hit the trails, to get *into* that amazing scenery; and once they get away from the roads, they discover the true essence of the park. Choices are many, from trails that follow the valley bottom past morainal lakes with mountains soaring from their opposite shores, to others that strike off among the high peaks. And you don't have to be a mountaineer to get up high. As grand a landscape as this one is, it is remarkably accessible.

Most of the mountain hiking in the Tetons is in several main valleys, called canyons because of their precipitous sides. The most popular is **Cascade Canyon**, reached by an inexpensive boat ride across Jenny Lake. In geologic terms, this is a hanging valley, meaning that it was not carved as deeply by glaciers as the main valley, and is now marked by a steep drop at its lower end. The trail climbs steeply up this drop for a half-mile (1 km) to **Hidden Falls**, a lovely bridal-veil cascade. A short distance on, the trail emerges from the forest at **Inspiration Point**, giving fine views across the lake to the **Gros Ventre Range**, which forms the eastern horizon. Most hikers turn around at this point, yet those who go even a short distance farther up Cascade Canyon find

their efforts well rewarded. From open areas you can see the dividing line on the canyon wall between smooth glaciated rock and the more angular, broken surface that was never reached by the ice. About three hours of hiking will take you to the back side of the central Teton group, where the trail forks.

Heading south on the **Teton Crest Trail**, it is possible to circle the peaks by way of spectacular **Alaska Basin**, which is actually part of the **Jedediah Smith Wilderness Area**, and return to Jackson Hole by way of **Death Canyon**. The entire circuit is a two- or three-day trip, but either canyon is a good choice for day hiking; simply go up until you feel like turning around.

Easy lakeshore trails include the ever-popular circuit of Jenny Lake, which can be shortened by riding part way on the boat. Another trail parallels String Lake and wanders along the east shore of **Leigh Lake**, with spectacular views of Mount Moran and Leigh Canyon. This is also a prime canoeing lake, easily reached by canoe from String Lake

Hidden Falls tumbling through Cascade Canyon.

and requiring one short portage. No motors are permitted, and with Mount Moran rising precipitously from the water's edge, this is a spectacular and peaceful place. Nowhere else in the park can one get so quickly and easily into a wilderness setting.

South of Jenny Lake, **Bradley** and **Taggart** lakes lie cupped in forested basins with high peaks exposed above them. Getting to either lake involves an interesting walk of several miles through an area burned by a forest fire in 1985.

The wild north: Other highlights in the center of the park include **Signal Mountain**, which rises like a grandstand in the middle of Jackson Hole. A paved drive leads to the summit and the best panoramic view of the area. If you can take your eyes off the mountains, you may find your attention drawn to the glittering surface of Jackson Lake, a natural lake enlarged by a 39-ft (12-m) high dam and filled with snowmelt from the mountains. Of course the biggest supplier of water is the Snake River, pouring southward out of Yellowstone National Park. Although the road parallels the shoreline for some miles, a boat is clearly the best tool for exploring the lake and its surroundings – and is practically the only way of getting into the northern end of the Tetons, the very wild, seldom visited chain of peaks rising on the west side of the lake.

This is country for serious hikers only. Getting through it requires following the routes of elk and moose up steep slopes of loose rock and through willow tangles along stream bottoms. Inevitably, game trails vanish into impenetrable thickets, leaving no option but a blind search for another path. For all this effort, the reward is a feeling of being truly remote, in country rarely traveled by any but the native wildlife.

Less heroic walkers interested in exploring the lakeshore area will find pleasant, well-maintained and largely flat trails in the area of **Colter Bay**. While there, be sure to check out the superb collection in the **Indian Arts Museum** in the **Colter Bay Visitor Center**.

A less crowded section of the park lies

Aspens ablaze with autumn color.

266

south of Moose, along the partly paved **Moose-Wilson Road**. The drive is scenic in a low-key way – a good place to see wildlife and the starting point for hikers headed for Death Canyon, **Phelps Lake** and **Granite Canyon**. On the opposite side of the valley, another road goes to the Gros Ventre Campground, the town of Kelly, and Slide Lake.

Located just outside the park, **Slide Lake** was created by the Gros Ventre Slide, in June, 1925. A cowboy named Huff was herding cattle down the valley when he noticed the mountain sliding toward him, trees, rocks and all. He lost several cattle but managed to get out without losing his life. Behind him, the slide built a dam 225 ft (70 m) high, impounding the Gros Ventre River and creating a large new lake. It took two years for the lake to breach the dam; when it did, a wall of water swept down the canyon, taking the town of Kelly with it, killing six people, and doing widespread damage downstream along the Snake River.

During the summer months, the Snake provides good floating through the park and into the **Snake River Canyon** about 20 miles (32 km) south of Jackson. Because the park section lacks rapids, it can be run in rowboats, canoes and inflatable rafts. Yet the river is deceptively tricky, its channel braided and in many places blocked by deadfall. The current is always fast, especially during spring runoff, resulting in conditions that can be dangerous for inexperienced boaters.

On the other hand, there are few better ways to see the park than by floating silently past towering cottonwoods while the Tetons come in and out of view. There is always some wildlife to be seen, including moose, elk and bison. Among common birds are herons, swans, Canada geese and mergansers; ospreys and bald eagles nest in treetops along the riverbanks and are often seen with fish in their talons. Speaking of fish, the river offers cutthroat trout fishing that can be good at lower water levels. Guided trips are available from several local companies.

Antelope Flats at the foot of the Teton Range.

GLACIER

High in the mountains of northwestern Montana, **Glacier National Park** ranges over a broad, heartbreakingly beautiful landscape of sharp-edged peaks, deep evergreen forests and large, pristine lakes. Its plunging waterfalls, radiant wildflower meadows and swirling turquoise streams have left millions of visitors slack-jawed with admiration since the 1890s. The naturalist John Muir called it "the best care-killing country on the continent." And Ernie Pyle, the war correspondent who saw a bit of the world in his time, said he "wouldn't trade one square mile of Glacier for all the other parks put together."

Celebrated not only for the beauty of its land but also for its abundant wildlife and excellent network of hiking trails, Glacier lies at the center of a sprawling territory of protected lands. Huge national forests extend to the west and south of the park, embracing wild and scenic river corridors and immense wilderness areas. To the north lies Canada's **Waterton Lakes National Park** and more forest preserves. Much of the land to the east of both parks belongs to various bands of the Blackfeet tribe, which controlled this portion of the Great Plains until the late 19th century.

Natural history: Throughout this incredible spread of primitive country roam some of North America's most impressive and beautiful animals. Mountain goats scamper among the park's highest pinnacles and cliffs. Bighorn sheep graze in the meadows at timberline, never far from the protection of steep boulder fields and scree slopes. Grizzly bears wander the high country basins, digging up ground squirrels and munching on roots, sedges, grasses and berries. And a colony of gray wolves has recently returned to the park after an absence of more than 40 years. Glacier also abounds with animals common throughout the Rockies – elk, moose, deer, black bear and mountain lion.

Scan the flanks of any mountain in the park and you will soon see that it is composed of layer upon layer of sedimentary rock. These layers are the pages of Glacier's early geologic history, and their story reaches back approximately 1.6 billion years to a time when this portion of Montana was flat.

Mud, sand and silt which washed out onto this plain for several hundred million years, accumulated to depths of 3–5 miles (5–13 km) and turned to stone – much of it very colorful; vivid red and blue-green mudstone are the most notable deposits. The rock layers preserved ripple marks, mud cracks and even impressions made by raindrops that fell more than a billion years ago. (You can pass your hand over some of these ripple marks beside St Mary Lake.)

Collision course: This thick sheet of strata remained buried until just 70 million years ago, then rose through the surface as the earth's crustal plates collided along the western edge of North America. Like a fender bender in slow motion, the western portion of the continent crumpled, gradually elevating chains of mountains.

Here, though, the strata did not simply rise in place. It broke away in pieces and slid more than 35 miles (56 km) eastward before coming to rest in what are now Glacier and Waterton parks. The mountains that rise abruptly on the east side of the parks represent the leading edge of that colossal slab.

For tens of millions of years, erosion carried away the upper layers until all that remained were the oldest tiers of rock. Then came the great Ice Ages. At least three times in the past 200,000 years, enormous glaciers formed in the upper ramparts of the mountains and plowed their way down to the plains and river valleys. These great masses of ice sometimes exceeded depths of 2,000 ft (610 m), and their effects can be seen at every turn. The steep, semicircular walls and flat floors of the park's spacious valleys trace the outlines of the largest glaciers. Huge mounds of morainal debris confine the park's big lakes. There are knife-edged ridges, horn-shaped peaks, cirques and hanging valleys.

All were created in one way or another by glaciers, but not by the 50 or so

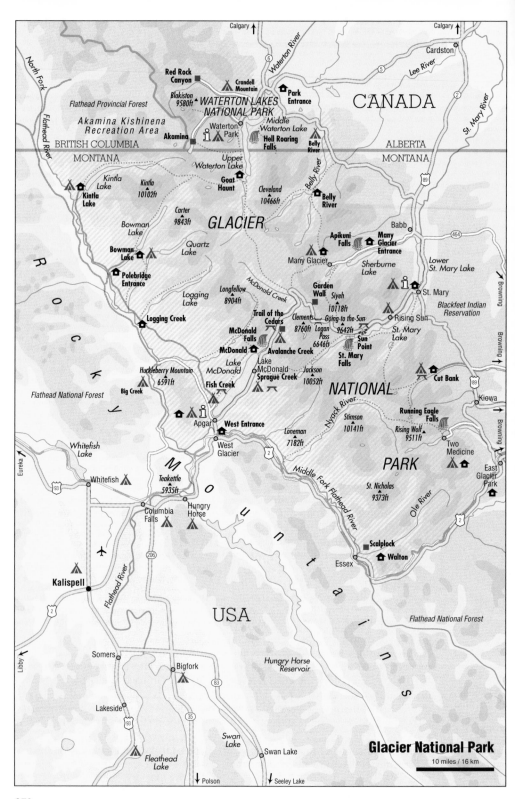

Glacier National Park

10 miles / 16 km

relative dwarfs that nibble away at the peaks today. The last of the titanic glaciers that shaped the park melted away about 6,000 years ago. By that time, people had been living in and around Glacier for at least 2,500 years.

Native peoples: They probably came from the northeast corner of Asia, walking over the land bridge that formed in the Bering Strait during the Ice Ages. They fished the lakes and rivers along the eastern slopes of the mountains and hunted bison, elk, bighorn sheep and deer. Some of them moved to the west side of the park about 1,000 years ago, venturing east just a few times a year to hunt bison. These were probably the ancestors of the Kootenai, Flathead and Kalispel tribes.

Meanwhile, the powerful Blackfeet confederation expanded south from the North Saskatchewan River and began to dominate the entire eastern half of what is now Glacier and Waterton. Superb horsemen, the Blackfeet became the most powerful military force on the northwestern plains. By the end of the 19th century, though, the Blackfeet were laid low by smallpox epidemics and illicit alcohol, byproducts of the westward expansion of Anglo civilization. Eventually they were confined to a reservation that included the eastern half of what is now Glacier. But when miners found traces of minerals in the mountains, the tribe sold that portion to the United States government.

Boomtowns sprouted in the St Mary and Many Glacier valleys, and in Waterton, roughnecks drilled for oil. Meanwhile, conservationists in the United States and Canada were trying to convince their respective governments to preserve the lands as national parks. The mining claims soon played out, and objections to creating the parks were dropped. Waterton was set aside in 1895, and Glacier was designated in 1910.

Sensing that the region could rival the Alps as a destination resort, owners of the Great Northern Railway built a series of Swiss-style lodges and backcountry chalets with a network of horse trails and roads. Many of the buildings have been torn down, but three of the grand old lodges still put up guests: the **Glacier Park Hotel** in East Glacier; the **Many Glacier Hotel** in the heart of the park; and, in Waterton, the **Prince of Wales Hotel**.

The Glacier Park Hotel was built in 1912–13 on a frame of massive, unpeeled logs cut from cedar and Douglas fir trees 500 to 800 years old. The largest of these posts and beams stand in the hotel's three-story central lobby and support the roofs of the hotel's verandas.

The Many Glacier Hotel was erected in 1914–15 on the shores of **Swift-current Lake**, directly across the water from some of the park's most spectacular mountain scenery. Like the Glacier Park Hotel, it boasts a rustic central lobby built with large timbers and native stone.

A bit more formal and graceful than its American counterparts, the seven-story Prince of Wales Hotel stands on a spit of land extending between **Upper** and **Middle Waterton** lakes. Never visited by its namesake, the hotel offers a smashing, and wind-free, view of Waterton's mountains. During construc-

East Glacier Lodge.

tion in 1927, a fierce blast of Waterton's famous wind shifted the hotel's timber frame a full 8 inches (20 cm). The building hasn't been square since.

In the years since it became a national park, Glacier has changed a bit. Several major fires have swept through its forests. Populations of animals, particularly predators, have fluctuated wildly. Even the glaciers have shrunk. Roads teem with automobiles and motor homes. Roadside campgrounds fill by early afternoon, and backcountry travelers have to reserve spots to pitch their tents. By and large, however, Glacier appears pretty much the same today as it did in the early years.

You will find wetlands throughout the park, which are thick with marsh grasses, cattails, reeds and a cornucopia of insects, fish, amphibians, waterfowl and semiaquatic mammals such as beaver, muskrat and mink. These wetlands also attract osprey and some large mammals, including moose.

Arms of prairie grass stretch into many of the eastern valleys, and grasslands appear as isolated pockets in the forests of the west side. The meadows support elk and deer as well as many types of small rodents, which attract predators such as wolves, mountain lions, hawks, owls, coyotes and badgers.

Groves of aspen, cottonwood and other deciduous trees shade the edges of meadows and give way at higher elevations to evergreens, which are better adapted to the shorter growing season. The middle slopes of the park's mountains consist mainly of lodgepole, spruce and fir. However, warm Pacific air masses stall out on Glacier's western slopes and drop enough moisture to support stands of cedar and hemlock.

Among the small valleys and basins that dot Glacier's high country, forests of Engelmann spruce, whitebark pine and sub-alpine fir grow alongside sprawling meadows carpeted with wildflowers, sedges and grasses. Thickets of berry bushes crowd the avalanche slopes. Known as the sub-alpine zone, this niche is home to grizzly bears, bighorn sheep, wolverines, marmots, wea-

A grizzly bear takes it easy.

sels, ground squirrels and, far up in the highest reaches, mountain goats.

Finally, along the crest of the mountains, the trees give out almost entirely. Those that survive here hug the ground and seek cover from the wind by twisting and bending around rocks. A thin layer of grasses, sedges and wildflowers also manages to eke out a supremely fragile existence, but few animals besides mountain goats and pikas (tiny hares) spend much time here.

Going to the sun: Most visits to Glacier start with a trip over **Logan Pass** on **Going-to-the-Sun Road**. Aptly named, this amazing strip of switchbacked pavement climbs over the spine of the park's mountains and connects two of its most spectacular valleys. You can start the trip from either side of the park, but it is perhaps best to begin from the east-side village of **St Mary** in the morning, with the sun at your back.

The road skirts the shore of **St Mary Lake,** a 10-mile (16-km) body of crystal-clear water that occupies an enormous depression gouged out by one of the huge valley glaciers thousands of years ago. At the head end of the lake, **Sun Point** offers a smashing view of the lower valley and the surrounding peaks.

Soon you plunge into deep forest and begin the long climb to Logan Pass. A roadside exhibit identifies **Jackson Glacier**, one of the few active glaciers visible from the road. It has shrunk by 75 percent during the past 150 years.

Logan Pass (6,646 ft /2,026 m), was formed by two glaciers gnawing away on either side of the ridge. Eventually, they chewed clear through the intervening rock and created this relatively low spot along the **Continental Divide**. It is a stunning place. Valley walls plunge from sight, and row upon row of summits reach off in all directions. Jagged peaks loom directly overhead. Waterfalls spill over cliffs just a hundred yards from the visitor center parking lot, and broad meadows of wildflowers spread at your feet.

Park naturalists offer two guided walks from Logan (between mid-June and Labor Day). One passes through the wildflower meadows above the visitor center to **Hidden Lake Overlook**, on the rim of a spectacular cirque of peaks towering over a beautiful lake. The other hike follows the **Highline Trail** across cliffs and avalanche slopes to grassy meadows overlooking **McDonald Valley**. Chances of seeing mountain goats are good on both hikes.

From Logan Pass, the road slants down the side of the **Garden Wall**, a knife-edged ridge that runs north through the heart of Glacier's most popular backcountry areas. A 1967 fire cleared much of the wall, opening the slope to various types of shrubs, including berry bushes, which attract bears in late summer and autumn.

On the valley floor, you follow **McDonald Creek**, a lovely watercourse that curls through the ancient cedar and hemlock forest of the park's warmer, moister west side. At **Red Rock Point**, the creek zigzags between tilting blocks of vermilion mudstone and whirls into a deep turquoise pool. A bit farther along, **Trail of the Cedars** loops through a cathedral stand of ancient cedar, hem-

Dense growth of devils club on Trail of the Cedars.

lock and cottonwood trees. The mossy forest floor, the banks of ferns, the sunlight slanting through the mist – all lend an air of the primordial to the grove.

Before long, you find yourself along the shores of **Lake McDonald**, the largest body of water in the park. Lined with cedar trees and warm enough to swim in during late summer, the lake has many colorful pebble beaches that offer sweeping vistas of the mountains. Going-to-the-Sun Road stops just beyond the west end of Lake McDonald, and offers a fine overview of the park.

Back on the park's east side, the **Many Glacier** area lies in a striking, high-country basin carved out by glaciers, ringed by mountains and dotted with chains of small lakes. It is the hub of a large trail network offering everything from an afternoon's stroll to week-long treks, and it is an excellent area for spotting bears, bighorn sheep and mountain goats. The road ends at **Swiftcurrent Lake**, where you'll find the Many Glacier Hotel. The railroad stalled the dismantling of a sawmill across the lake

until 1925, when the director of the Parks Service lost patience. In the most spectacular interpretive event in the park's history, he had crews place dynamite charges, then invited hotel guests out on the veranda to watch him blow up the offending structure.

Like Going-to-the-Sun Road, Many Glacier attracts throngs of visitors. You'll find a much quieter and only slightly less impressive glacial basin at **Two Medicine Lake**, between East Glacier and St Mary. The area got its name from a tradition of two Blackfeet tribes, who held their annual sun dance in adjacent medicine lodges.

Across the border: Waterton Lakes National Park is just a seventh the size of Glacier, but well worth the visit into Canada. You may need a driver's license, visa or a passport to cross the border; check before you leave home. The park embraces three beautiful and very different valleys and, like Glacier, its mountains rise abruptly from the Great Plains. Waterton enjoys a rich and varied climate in which moist Pacific air battles with frigid arctic weather. This turbulent mix kicks up high winds, drops plenty of rain and snow and accounts in part for the tremendous variety of plants that thrive here – 1,300 species all told.

Squeezed between two rows of mountains, **Upper Waterton Lake** occupies a long, narrow trough at the head end of the park's main valley. The **Prince of Wales Hotel** (*see pages 273–4*) commands a fabulous view of the surrounding peaks, the town of Waterton and the narrow waters of the lake, which extends south across the international border into Glacier. Excursion boats cruise to **Goat Haunt**, in Glacier. There, naturalists lead hikes into the **Kootenai Lakes**, a common hangout for moose.

Red Rock Canyon Parkway follows Blakiston Creek up the floor of another of the park's valleys, ending at a gorge cut through red mudstone by turquoise water. **Akamina Parkway** follows a chasm into Waterton's third valley, climbs through the park's highest forests, and dead-ends at **Cameron Lake**, a small alpine lake ringed with cliffs.

A young hoary marmot.

ROUGHING IT

Wherever you hike and camp in the West, a few commonsense rules will help keep you safe. First, do your homework. Check weather and road conditions, and obtain the required permits. If possible, hike with a partner. And tell someone where you're going and when you'll return, and stick to it.

Before you head into a new area, think through your situation. Do you have the proper clothing? A hat, sweater, jacket, sturdy footwear? How about a lightweight pullover with a hood? What begins as a cloudless summer morning can end with a pelting thunderstorm. Is water readily available? If not, carry a little more than you think you'll need. The rule of thumb is a gallon a day per person, more if you're hiking in extreme conditions. Gulp down at least a quart at the start of a hike, and don't forget to drink the rest once you're on the trail. Even if you're not perspiring or feeling thirsty, your body needs water. Don't wait until you've become dehydrated. Don't trust springs or rivers, either. Giardia is found throughout the West and can cause severe cramps and diarrhea.

Hiking burns up energy, so take high-carbohydrate snacks to munch along the way. Gatorade powder is helpful, too, and has perked up many a wilting hiker. In terms of equipment, start from the ground up and take care of your feet first. Lightweight, nylon hiking boots require little break-in time and are relatively affordable.

A light pair of polypropylene liner socks with a heavier sock on top is the best protection against blisters. The liner wicks moisture away from your feet and helps prevent soreness. When blisters do show up, catch them early. Stop when you feel "hot spots" forming and patch the sore spot with a square inch of moleskin. You'll find it in most drugstores.

Many parks have designated campsites, even in the backcountry. Sometimes, however, you have to camp "at large." Wherever you bed down, remember the "low impact-no impact ethic." Don't break branches to hang your food, and don't dig up rocks under your sleeping bag. The old-fashioned campfire you've been dreaming of is history;

Outdoor living.

the fire ring would scar the land for years. As for a hot meal or coffee, spend a few bucks and get yourself a backpack stove.

When nature calls, dig a cathole about 6 inches (15 cms) deep and at least 100 ft (31 m) from water. Many people think it's disgusting to pack your used toilet paper, but in some places it's required, so do it. Back on the trail, keep a watch for animals. Never approach or feed wild animals, not even the "cute" ones. In bear country, remember that clean camps help prevent encounters. Hang food as high as possible at least 100 yards (91 m) from camp. Watch scents from deodorants, colognes and anything else that might tickle a bear's nose.

In the desert, snakes and scorpions hide under ledges during the day. Even if you don't see them, they're probably nearby. If you're bitten by a snake, don't panic. Most poisonous snakebites hurt like the dickens but are not fatal. Get to a doctor immediately. At the end of the day, don't unstuff your sleeping bag until you're ready to get in. Scorpions and other crawly things sometimes get in and, when you come to lie down, they'll let you know it's occupied. ∎

THE DAKOTAS

The Great Plains are a land of liberating and, some would say, terrifying space. Endless miles of grasslands sprawl beneath a pale-blue dome. The earth stretches in every direction as flat and featureless as a tide of forgetting.

"Outsiders have considered this prairie place barren, desolate, monotonous, a land of more nothing than almost any other place you might name," writes William Least Heat-Moon. For those who know them well, however, these plains can form a land of subtle enchantment. Take a good look and you'll find that sky and grass can produce fascinating variations and that the prairie – seemingly endless – is punctuated with landforms of extraordinary ruggedness and beauty.

The high plains of North and South Dakota are such a place. Here, in the semi-arid country west of the Missouri River, the rolling prairie abruptly gives way to the Badlands and the Black Hills. Three national parks – **Wind Cave**, **Badlands** and **Theodore Roosevelt** – highlight the natural and cultural features of these extraordinary places. Wind Cave and Badlands are separated by about 100 miles (160 km) and are within easy driving distance of Rapid City, South Dakota, which is on the eastern edge of the Black Hills. Theodore Roosevelt National Park is near Dickinson, North Dakota, and is a full day's drive from Rapid City.

Cave of the Winds: Two worlds are preserved at **Wind Cave National Park**. On the surface, this 28,292-acre (11,450-hectare) park is a sanctuary of rolling grasslands and ponderosa forest snuggled against the foot of South Dakota's fabled Black Hills. Below ground, it's a hidden world of dark and silent passages honeycombed through an ancient bed of limestone.

People who think of caves as cold, damp holes in the ground suitable only for bats and hibernating bears will find Wind Cave surprisingly hospitable. It's a relatively dry cave, the temperature hovers around 53°F (12°C) year-round, and with the exception of a few errant bats, mice and insects, it is virtually lifeless. With more than 75 miles (121 km) of explored passages, it's the third longest cave in the United States and one of the most complex "maze caves" in the world.

Formation of this subterranean labyrinth began about 50 million years ago. Water, made acidic by carbon dioxide in the air and soil, began trickling through the limestone, widening the joints and cracks that were created during the uplift of the Black Hills. When the water table dropped, it left behind a tortuous network of caverns and crawlways that are still largely unexplored. Air-volume studies indicate that only about 5 percent of the cave has been mapped.

The cave's most conspicuous feature is the wind that streams in and out of its narrow mouth, sometimes as fast as 70 miles per hour (113 kph), equalizing air pressure on either side of the surface. The Lakota Indians were the first to take notice of the mysterious winds. Accord-

Preceding pages: Norbeck Pass, White River Badlands. **Left**, someone to watch over you, Mount Rushmore. **Right**, three young prairie dogs.

ing to Lakota mythology, the Cave of the Winds is a sacred place where bison, pronghorn and other creatures emerged from the underworld.

Probably the first white men to discover the cave were the Bingham brothers, Jesse and Tom, who stumbled across the entrance in 1881. Attracted by a whistling noise, one of them peered into the narrow mouth and was amazed when the wind blew his hat off. He was even more amazed when, on a return trip with friends, he held his hat over the blowhole and it was sucked into the cave.

Systematic exploration didn't start until nine years later, when 17-year-old Alvin McDonald began a short but remarkable career as the self-appointed "Permanent Guide of Wind Cave." Alvin's father brought the family to the cave in 1890, and together with John Stabler, they created the Wonderful Wind Cave Improvement Company, hoping to attract tourists from nearby Hot Springs. Although several family members were involved in the project, Alvin was the most committed, record-ing his adventures in a diary that is still on display at the **visitor center**. With nothing but a candle, a hammer and a ball of twine to mark his path, Alvin logged more than 1,000 hours of exploration. Visitors can still see the letters Z.U.Q. that he burned into the cave walls, although nobody knows exactly what they mean.

What Alvin discovered was a cave of remarkable beauty and complexity. Among his most significant finds was the abundance of boxwork, a mineral formation made of crisscrossing calcite fins found almost exclusively in Wind Cave. In some places, the fins are no more than a few centimeters long, giving the appearance of an intricate crystal web embedded in a limestone matrix. Elsewhere, the fins protrude as much as 10 or 12 inches (25 or 30 cms), creating spectacular crystal "crates." Alvin also came across an abundance of other delicate formations such as popcorn, frostwork, and branching, antler-like helictites, all created by the gradual accretion of calcite crystals in seeping

A calcite formation known as boxwork inside Wind Cave.

water. He found gypsum needles as fine as hair and patches of hard, diamond-shaped crystals known as dogtooth spar.

Unfortunately, Alvin didn't live long enough to see Wind Cave get the attention it deserved. He died of typhoid fever when only 20 years old. But, like Alvin, people who know the cave best confess a deep affection for it. "There's definitely a spiritual attachment," says Bill Rodgers, a former ranger. "I know, when I allow myself to, I feel a real love for the cave. And maybe that's what Alvin felt too." Ten years after Alvin's death, following several long and bitter ownership disputes, the federal government took possession of the cave. It was designated a national park in 1903.

Going underground: All cave tours start at the visitor center, where you'll find books, maps, a cafeteria (summer only) and a schedule of nature walks, campfire talks and other special events. The 45-minute **Garden of Eden** tour is offered year-round and introduces visitors to the cave's human and natural history on a short paved trail. Longer tours are offered during the summer season; they last between one and two hours and require varying levels of fitness. The **Candlelight Tour** (reservations required) is particularly interesting. It recreates cave exploration back in Alvin's day when visitors saw "Wonderful Wind Cave" by the dim light of makeshift lanterns. The tour lasts about two hours and covers a few patches of rough terrain.

For a more intimate look at the cave, the park also offers longer **exploration tours** (reservations required) in which small groups are suited up in caving gear and taken off-trail. The tours last three to four hours and are very strenuous. There's lots of crawling and climbing, so expect to get good and dirty.

But the cave is only half the story here. The park is also a wildlife sanctuary, an ecological crossroads where the Great Plains meet the mountains. The park encompasses a transitional zone between high-country ponderosa forest and the surrounding sea of mixed-grass prairie. Here, where the solitary Black

Bald eagles migrate seasonally through the Dakotas.

Hills rise from the plains, eastern and western species overlap. Ponderosa pine, reaching its eastern boundary, shares the park with American elm, at its westernmost range. The western wood pewee and pinyon jay share the skies with the eastern bluebird and phoebe.

Starting at the park's northern boundary, Highway 87 winds through a forest of ramrod-straight ponderosa pines that finger into swells of grassland fringed here and there by deciduous trees that grow along creeks and ravines. Bison, pronghorn and mule deer often graze near the road, and there are several roadside prairie-dog towns where you can watch these highly social rodents pop in and out of their complex network of tunnels. You may even see a coyote scouting nearby for an early-morning or evening meal. Elk and mule deer find day-time cover in the woods, but venture into the grasslands to graze in the evening. If you visit in early fall, listen for the haunting bugle of bull elk establishing territory during the yearly rut.

About 2 miles (3 km) from the park

boundary, you'll find sweeping vistas at **Rankin Ridge Trail**, a steep mile-long loop along the edge of a forested ridge. At the top, a fire tower affords views of the Black Hills scrawled against the horizon and, to the south, **Buffalo Gap**, a natural corridor into the high country once used by bison, Indian hunters and mountain men like Jedediah Smith.

For a closer look at the backcountry, you can pick up the **Centennial Trail** about 4 miles (6 km) farther south on Highway 87. The trail follows **Beaver Creek** into a lovely shaded canyon for about 2 miles (3 km) and then heads north into wooded hills and rolling meadows. You can loop back to the parking area on **Lookout Point Trail** for a 3-mile (5-km) round-trip or hook up with **Highland Creek** or **Sanctuary** trails for longer and more strenuous backpacking trips.

For hikers competent with a compass and topographical map, cross-country travel is permitted throughout the park. Remember to steer clear of prairie-dog towns, and never try to feed the animals. Give bison a wide berth, too. They look placid and slow-moving but have been known to charge hikers who get too close. A free permit is required for overnight stays in the backcountry.

Back in the car, Highway 87 winds through the high country toward Highway 385. The first right off 385 takes you past **Elk Mountain Campground**, where a short self-guiding trail loops through the surrounding woods and prairie. Back on the highway, Highway 385 dips into **Bison Flats**, where the great beasts can often be seen grazing, wallowing in the dust or nourishing themselves at a nearby mineral lick.

Seekers of solitude may prefer the two gravel roads – **NPS 5** and **6** – that cross the park's less-traveled eastern flank. Especially lovely is **Boland Ridge Trail**, off NPS 6, which strikes out on a 3-mile (5-km) journey up and over the sage-colored ridge into a prairie world where lone bison munch on grassy hillsides, golden eagles glide on columns of air, and the wind whispers incessantly through a scattering of pines.

Wind Cave makes a convenient jump-

Seal of approval.

ing-off point for sites throughout the Black Hills. **Custer State Park** adjoins the park's northern boundary and offers hiking trails, lakes, a wildlife road and entree into some of the most stunning sections of the Black Hills. The dramatic **Iron Mountain Road** leads through tunnels and over picturesque bridges to **Mount Rushmore National Memorial**, where sculptor Gutzon Borglum blasted his colossal presidential portraits out of the granite mountainside. Work on the project began in 1927 and was still unfinished when Borglum died in 1941. His studio can be visited, and the nightly lighting ceremony makes a dramatic impression.

If you're in the mood for more underground adventures, **Jewel Cave National Monument** – named after the layer of calcite crystals that adorn its walls – is about 35 miles (56 km) west of Wind Cave. **Devils Tower National Monument**, an 865-ft (264-m) column of volcanic rock near Sundance, Wyoming, and a popular rock-climbing site, is a three-hour drive from Wind Cave.

Badlands National Park: About 60 air-miles (97 km) east of Wind Cave, the prairie takes on a completely different aspect. This is the Badlands, an immensely rugged country of furrowed cliffs, gnarled spires and deep, branching ravines that were torn from the plains of South Dakota by a half-million years of soil erosion.

In the early 19th century, French fur traders called the area *les mauvaises terres à traverser* – "the bad lands to cross" – because of the maze of twisting canyons that blocked their passage to the White River basin. Many years later, American surveyors compared the fantastic landscape to the remains of "some ancient city in ruins." John Evans, a government geologist dispatched to Dakota Territory in 1849, likened the area to a "magnificent city of the dead, where the labor and genius of forgotten nations had left… a multitude of monuments of art and skill." He marveled at the well-defined layers of rock that striped the canyon walls, and, like many explorers before him, was fascinated by

Devils Tower.

the "ponderous character" and "strange physiognomy" of the ancient creatures whose bones lay exposed on the eroded earth.

First-time visitors may very well agree with Evans's initial impression: this is indeed a city of the dead, as stark and barren as any ancient ruin. The effect is especially chilling in the light of the midday sun, when short shadows exaggerate the landscape's fractured lines and give the Badlands a threatening, almost sinister look. Ridges twist like crooked spines; grass-capped buttes or "tables" rise to dizzying heights; turkey vultures hang on the wind; and, here and there, the bones of long-dead creatures poke through crumbling earth.

But in the evenings, when the light softens, the air of desolation begins to lift, and the Badlands become a different place, warmer, more inviting. As the sun goes down, delicate shadows creep along broken ridges, softening folds and crevices that look severe in full daylight. The long rays bring out the deep bruise-colors that stripe the cliffs, and

where the sun's full glare reflects only gray and white, the more forgiving light of evening shows shades of red, umber and burning violet.

The evening also brings a rush of life. Eagles circle overhead scanning for a final meal. Chipmunks dash between the shadows. Bighorn sheep clamber to higher ground. Out on the prairie, owls, bobcats, coyotes and prairie rattlers begin their nocturnal hunt.

Scenic drive: Entering the park from the northeast, Highway 240 passes the **Big Badlands Overlook**, your first grand view of the country's ravaged landscape, and then descends through the **Badlands Wall**, a 100-mile (160-km) long barrier between the upper prairie and the jumbled landscape below. The road bottoms out near the **Ben Reifel Visitor Center**, where exhibits, maps, and books – as well as rangers – will help acquaint you with the park; be sure to inquire about ranger-guided nature walks and other special programs held at the nearby **Cedar Pass Campground** and elsewhere. The road continues along the base of the Badlands Wall for a short stretch and then makes a winding ascent toward the **Journey to Wounded Knee Overlook**.

Here the cliffs face northwest over **Bigfoot Pass** with nothing but broken land between you and the horizon. Dusk is particularly dramatic. The sun sets as it must have on the first day of creation, over an unfinished world still imperfectly shaped. The pass is named after Chief Bigfoot, who led a band of Minniconjou Sioux through the Badlands in the winter of 1890 in order to escape United States troops. The Indians were captured and brought to a place called **Wounded Knee** about 50 miles (80 km) south, where the infamous massacre of more than 200 of Bigfoot's people took place.

From Bigfoot Pass, the road climbs to the upper prairie over arid grasslands where homesteaders worked "starvation claims" during the land boom after 1910. This final stretch of paved road is particularly spectacular, with wide-open views of jagged peaks, sheer-sided buttes and chromatic, low-lying humps laid

A young red fox peeks out its den.

bare by more than a half-million years of wind and water. The **Rainbow**, **Pinnacles** and **Seabed Jungle** overlooks are especially stunning.

If time and weather permit, continue on an unpaved road along the edge of the **Sage Creek Wilderness Area**. The road passes a prairie-dog town, and bison, pronghorn and mule deer can often be seen grazing nearby. There are no marked trails, but hikers can strike out cross-country from the **Sage Creek Campground**. Motorists should follow the **Sage Creek Rim Road** to Highway 44 and then turn left toward the Ben Reifel Visitor Center, making a 90-mile (145 km) loop.

For a closer look at the backcountry, try the maintained trails in the eastern end of the park. The most challenging is the **Notch Trail**, which leads to a chink in the cliffs overlooking the Badlands' southern border. In order to get there, you have to walk a ¾-mile (1-km) trail across rugged terrain. At the end, a 40-ft (12-m) ladder leads up a canyon face. The trail continues along the edge of a cliff toward the viewing area. From here, the Badlands seem to melt into the White River basin, where rain and countless rills and rivulets wash them away. The jagged peaks gradually grow smaller and less defined, until there is nothing left but bluffs and hollows stretching to the horizon like the folds of a rumpled blanket.

Two other short, easy trails start at this parking area, too. The **Door Trail** makes a short round-trip into a moonscape of branching canyons and gullies. The ¼-mile (400 m) **Window Trail** leads to a fenced viewing area overlooking a dramatic mudstone canyon.

Farther down the road, the short but steep **Cliff Shelf Nature Trail** circles a depression created by a massive slump of the cliff above. The hollow collects water, creating an oasis of plant and animal life in the stark Badlands Wall. A short drive brings you to the **Fossil Exhibit Trail**, which makes a flat ¼-mile (400 m) loop. Replicas of fossils are displayed under plastic domes; most are ancient mammals dating from the

Badlands near the Little Missouri River, Theodore Roosevelt National Park.

Oligocene Period, around 23–30 million years ago.

For longer hikes, try the **Castle Trail**; the trailhead is directly across the road. It's a fairly easy 5-mile (8-km), one-way walk through prairie and mud flats past eroding mudstone castles, and flat-topped rain pillars. You can lengthen the hike by sidetracking onto the **Medicine Root Trail** or the extremely steep but short **Saddle Pass Trail**.

Sheep Mountain Table: The balance of beauty and desolation is nowhere more precarious or powerful than at Sheep Mountain Table, a high plateau on **Pine Ridge Indian Reservation** overlooking a labyrinth of barren canyons. A rutted dirt road (impassable when wet) veers off County Road 589 and crosses white alkali flats to the hill. Squat, mushroom-shaped formations stand like guardians on either side of the road.

At the top, the table is broad and flat and surprisingly lush. A thick growth of prairie grass, prickly-pear cactus and yucca blankets the ground, and scattered groves of juniper stand near the

edge. This is one of the least-traveled parts of the Badlands, and the best place to go if you're looking for solitude. Head to the very end of the table, where unmarked trails lead to stark panoramas of interlocking cliffs and canyons. It wasn't always so quiet out here. During World War II, ranchers were forced to relocate when the military used the area as a gunnery range. Apparently, a few bombs went astray. According to a roadside display, one old settler was interrupted during breakfast when "an errant shell crashed through her roof, her bed, and the bedroom floor."

To the south of Sheep Mountain Table is a vast undeveloped area of prairie and tablelands known as the **Stronghold Unit**. The main attraction here is **Stronghold Table**, a slender finger of high ground where Lakota Ghost Dancers gathered in December 1890. Hungry, desperate, impoverished by war and reservation life, they came to the Stronghold to dance, "die" and dream of a new world washed clean of white men. The only way to the Stronghold is a gravel road about 7 miles (11 km) off County Road 589, and then you must hike or drive another 2 miles (3 km) or so until you reach the "narrows," the eroding land-bridge that connects the table with the "mainland." You can get directions and ask about road conditions at the **White River Visitor Center**, open only in summer.

The plateau itself is flat and featureless. There are no signs or monuments to mark the spot, just a lonely swath of prairie grass and cactus. Sitting on the cliffs is like dangling your feet over the edge of the world – only an occasional meadowlark and a few semi-wild horses to keep you company. At times, the only thing that stirs is the wind, coursing like a restless spirit through the canyons and ravines. Its ceaseless whispering is a slender defense against the powers of silence, but it does remind you that, despite the stark surroundings, this is not "a city of the dead."

Theodore Roosevelt National Park: In 1883, a young New Yorker headed west to hunt bison in North Dakota. During his two-week stay he became absorbed

Bison now roam in several Dakota parks.

with the cattle industry and, being well-off financially, invested some of his money in the Maltese Cross Ranch.

He was Theodore Roosevelt, and he returned the following year to set up his own operation, the Elkhorn Ranch, on the banks of the Little Missouri River. Alas, it was a short-lived affair. The range was exhausted by overgrazing and couldn't sustain the herds through the severe winter of 1886–87.

Roosevelt's herd was virtually wiped out, like those of most other ranchers on the northern plains, and the Elkhorn went under. Nevertheless, the brief time spent "among the barren, fantastic and grimly picturesque deserts of the so-called Bad Lands" left a deep impression on this future president and his conception of conservation – the need to protect natural resources.

Today, much of the land that TR knew and loved is protected in the three units of **Theodore Roosevelt National Park**: the 72-sq. mile (187-sq. km) **South Unit** immediately off Interstate 94 at Medora, the 38-sq. mile (98-sq. km) **North Unit**,

and the undeveloped site of the erst-while **Elkhorn Ranch**.

Union Army General Alfred Sully, who conducted campaigns against the Plains Indians, described the North Dakota Badlands in 1864 as "Hell with the fires out." It is a harsh and inhospitable land, broken into countless ridges, coulees and fluted bluffs. Water has shaped the landscape. Pelting summer rains collect in rivulets and ravines, cutting through layers of sediment laid down by ancient seas, swamps and volcanoes. The runoff carries debris to the **Little Missouri River**, which moves in lazy bows along a wide flood plain.

But there's a softer side, too. Laid bare by erosion, the slump-shouldered hills are brightened by patches of brick-red "scoria" (*see page 291*) bluish bentonite clay and thin veins of lignite coal. On cooler, moister, north-facing slopes, dense stands of juniper and ash provide cover from the sun, as do groves of cottonwood trees along the Little Missouri. Elsewhere, the park is home to rolling mixed-grass prairie, rabbit-

Snow patterns near the Badlands Wall.

brush, prickly-pear cactus, spiky yucca and thick patches of aromatic sage.

The park sustains bison, wild horses, prairie dogs, mule deer, white-tailed deer, elk, pronghorn and a variety of predators – coyotes, bobcats, badgers and rattlesnakes. Songs of meadowlarks, sparrows, and towhees carry through woodlands and prairies. Golden eagles ride air currents overhead; bald eagles migrate through in autumn.

The South Unit: A leisurely driving tour of either unit takes about a half-day and features breathtaking views of multihued gullies, coulees and canyons and, more often than not, a close-up look at wandering bison, pronghorn and prairie dogs. Starting in the South Unit, the **Medora Visitor Center** has modest exhibits on natural history as well as a collection of artifacts left behind by TR during his ranching days. The tiny **Maltese Cross Cabin**, occupied by Roosevelt during his first stab at ranching life, is restored with period furnishings.

The first leg of the 36-mile (58-km) **Scenic Loop Drive** takes you to the **Medora Overlook**, with a grand view of the tiny western town founded by the Marquis de Mores, a French aristocrat who came to the Badlands in 1883 intending to establish a cattle empire. The marquis built his home, the **Chateau de Mores**, on a bluff overlooking the town, which he named after his wife.

Back on the road, you pass the first of several prairie-dog towns then get your first good look at the Badlands from **Skyline Vista**. The road winds down to the **River Woodland Overlook** for a closer look at the dense grove of cottonwoods crowding the Little Missouri River, which is surrounded by tawny bluffs peppered with stands of juniper. A little farther on, the **Cottonwood Campground** occupies a relaxing and shady spot along the river.

Turning right at the intersection, the next 10 miles (16 km) twist through bluffs and valleys into the ravaged heart of the badlands, with glorious, sweeping vistas at the **North Dakota Badlands**, **Buck Hill** (requires a short steep walk) and **Boicourt** overlooks. Two

<u>**Left**</u>, tiger swallowtail butterflies. <u>**Right**</u>, evening primrose.

self-guiding nature trails do a fine job of introducing visitors to the park's varied ecology. The **Ridgeline Trail** is about a ½ mile (800 m) long and quite steep in places. The **Coal Vein Trail** is about a mile (1½ km) long and is also rather steep. A coal seam burned here from 1951–77, baking overlying clay into the reddish brick-like substance known locally, but incorrectly, as scoria.

The trail loops through shady stands of juniper, along a canyon rim, and across patches of prairie grass before returning to the parking lot. Have you noticed that signposts and tree trunks look worn around the edges? Bison walk these trails, too, and often use trees and posts to scratch themselves.

The Scenic Loop Drive comes to a visual crescendo at **Wind Canyon Trail**, a short but steep climb along the rim of a dramatic side-canyon of the Little Missouri River. The view is glorious. It's a short drive past another prairie-dog town to historic **Peaceful Valley Ranch**, where horseback riding is available between May and October. You'll also find several trailheads on this final stretch of the Scenic Loop.

Ambitious hikers can try the 16-mile (26-km) **Petrified Forest Loop Trail** into the heart of the South Unit's wilderness area, where they'll find the largest and most plentiful samples of petrified wood; a cutoff on the **Lone Tree Spring Loop Trail** along Knutson Creek covers much of the same ground.

To the east, the **Paddock Creek Trail** is a one-way, 11-mile (18-km) hike across the Scenic Loop and into the stunning **Painted Canyon** area, where the park maintains a small herd of wild horses. Backpackers can make it a round-trip on the **Talkington Trail**, which loops back toward the trailhead. The **Jones Creek Trail** is shorter but no less interesting – perfect for a leisurely day hike. It cuts a 4-mile (6-km), one-way path through the grassy folds of Jones Creek valley, occasionally skirting the edge of a deep ravine. Although there are a few gradual slopes, most of the trail is flat and grassy.

The North Unit: The North Unit is even

Wind Cave National Park.

farther off the beaten path and offers wonderful seclusion during the off-season. The 14-mile (23-km) **Scenic Drive** runs roughly parallel to the Little Missouri for the first 5 miles (8 km) or so. Just beyond the visitor center, you may see a few head of Texas longhorns, maintained by the park as a reminder of the area's ranching history. At the **Slump Block Pullout** you'll get an explanation of "slumping" – the way an entire block of earth slides down a hillside, keeping its sedimentary layers intact and giving the hills a characteristic slope-shouldered profile.

There's another geologic curiosity at the **Cannonball Concretions Pullout**, where hard sandstone spheres eroded away from softer deposits. From the river bottom, the road winds to the plateau above, passing overlooks and pullouts with gorgeous views of the river, prairie and rugged canyons. Views from the **River Bend** and **Oxbow** overlooks are particularly spectacular.

Two self-guiding nature trails – the **Squaw Creek Nature Trail** and the

Caprock Coulee Nature Trail – are fairly short and easy. Leaflets available at the trailheads explain the complex relationship between water, fire, earth, plants and animals that make up Badlands ecology. If you're feeling ambitious, you can continue on the **Upper Caprock Coulee Trail** for a 4-mile (6-km) loop. The trail makes a gradual 400-ft (122-m) ascent through the Badlands, alternating between the hotter, drier north-facing slopes and the ash and juniper groves of the wetter south-facing slopes. It tops out on the prairie, offering magnificent views of the Badlands, then crosses the Scenic Drive onto a steep, deeply eroded bentonite cliff. (Be careful, bentonite clay is extremely slippery, even when dry.)

The trail follows a ridgeline overlooking the Little Missouri, crosses the **River Bend Overlook**, and then descends through grasslands and juniper groves to the parking area.

For longer hikes, the 16-mile (26-km) **Achenbach Trail** heads up and over the **Achenbach Hills**, crosses the Little Missouri (ask rangers about river crossing conditions), and then rises steeply to the magnificent **Oxbow Overlook** before returning to Squaw Creek Campground along the river bottom. Eleven-mile (18-km) **Buckhorn Trail** loops around the eastern portion of the park, with long stretches on Squaw Creek to the upper prairie and then back into the Badlands to the river bottom.

Adventurous travelers may also want to consider a trip to the undeveloped site of TR's **Elkhorn Ranch**, about 20 miles (32 km) from the South Unit along a dirt road. Be sure to ask a ranger about road and river crossing conditions before striking out. For those who prefer floating to walking, the Little Missouri winds gracefully through all three units. The 120-mile (193-km) trip takes about three days and is usually best in April and May. The park is open year-round, but snowfall, usually between October and March, can limit travel. Weather changes quickly in the Badlands, and nights can be chilly even in summer. Be prepared for some foul weather, high winds and extreme temperatures.

Left, coyote pups raise a howl. **Right**, "the bad lands to cross."

ROCKY MOUNTAIN

When Pope John Paul II journeyed to Denver in 1993, he asked to see **Rocky Mountain National Park**. The pontiff's hiking outfit was a bit unusual (His Holiness wore a white cassock, gold pallium and sneakers with matching gold shoelaces), but the visit confirmed what lovers of the park already knew: Rocky Mountain can truly be considered a religious experience.

Like John Paul, millions of pilgrims have thrilled at this sea of mountain peaks since the park was created in 1915. Many of the peaks within Rocky Mountain's 414 sq. miles (1,072 sq. km) soar over 12,000 ft (3,658 m). "There are higher peaks elsewhere," author Freeman Tilden wrote in 1951. "But for a sheer sense of towering density, of closely packed mountaintops, I know of nothing like this."

The majestic Rockies are the offspring of geologic events that stirred at the bottom of an inland sea more than 135 million years ago, when powerful forces buckled and uplifted the earth's crust. The mountain range we see today is actually the third to rise here. The ancestral Rockies rose twice and were eroded away, only to be thrust skyward again about 50 million years ago. Glaciers finished the job. The great shields of ice gouged out deep valleys, chiseled the bedrock into jagged pinnacles and smooth granite outcroppings, and left a string of bowl-like depressions – now lakes or cirques – in their wake.

By the time Zebulon Pike set eyes on the Rockies in 1807, Indians had been venturing into the high country for at least 7,000 years. Later, mounted hunters of the Ute, Arapaho, Cheyenne and Shoshone tribes tracked deer and buffalo in the foothills and bighorn sheep on the alpine slopes. Late in the 19th century, a flood of trappers, miners and ranchers tried to tap the mountains' natural wealth. Mining camps such as Lulu City sprang up overnight and disappeared just as quickly. Hunting campaigns drove grizzly bears, wolves, elk and bison to the brink of extinction. Among the pioneers was a different breed, too – people like Enos Mills, who mined peace and rejuvenation from the mountains and made a living sharing them with others. Hailed as the "John Muir of the Rockies," Mills hatched the idea for the park and spent years rallying support and lobbying Congress, which finally gave its consent in 1915. These days, most of the 3 million people who come here each year are backpackers, birders, rock climbers, naturalists, or just anyone who wants to spend a day or two in some of the most beautiful country in the American West.

Estes Park to Grand Lake: The **Trail Ridge Road**, the park's main thoroughfare, is perhaps the most scenic drive in North America. Open seasonally from mid-May until the first heavy snowstorms blanket the interior in October, it features well over a dozen spectacular overlooks and exposes visitors to a large expanse of alpine tundra, one of the rarest ecosystems in the lower 48 states.

Starting at the **visitor center** in **Estes**

Preceding pages: camping in the San Juan Mountains. **Left**, dead wood on Nymph Lake. **Right**, biking is allowed on paved roads only.

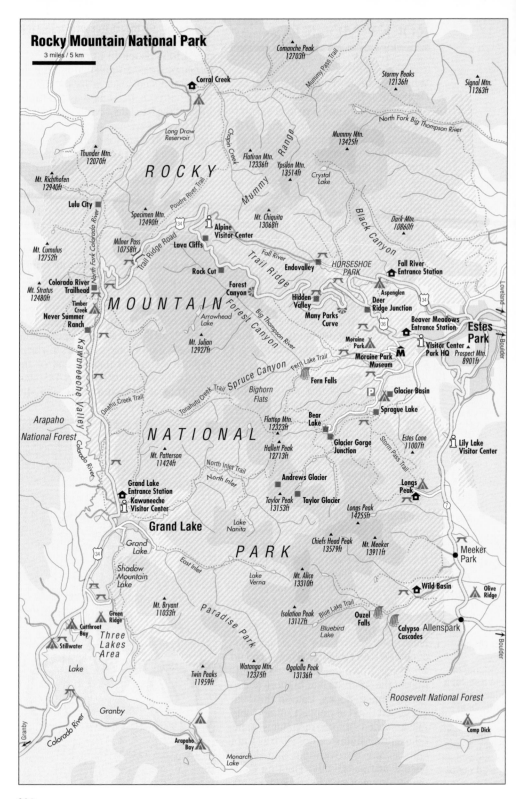

Rocky Mountain National Park

3 miles / 5 km

Comanche Peak 12703ft

Stormy Peaks 12136ft

Signal Mtn. 11263ft

Corral Creek

Mummy Pass Trail

North Fork Big Thompson River

Long Draw Reservoir

Mummy Mtn. 13425ft

Thunder Mtn. 12070ft

R O C K Y

Mt. Richthofen 12940ft

Flatiron Mtn. 12336ft

Ypsilon Mtn. 13514ft

Crystal Lake

Dark Mtn. 10860ft

Lulu City

Specimen Mtn. 12490ft

Mt. Chiquita 13068ft

Black Canyon

Mt. Cumulus 12752ft

Milner Pass 10758ft

Alpine Visitor Center

Lava Cliffs

Fall River

Endovalley

HORSESHOE PARK

Fall River Entrance Station

Colorado River Trailhead

Mt. Stratus 12480ft

Rock Cut

Forest Canyon

Aspenglen

Deer Ridge Junction

Timber Creek

Never Summer Ranch

M O U N T A I N

Arrowhead Lake

Hidden Valley

Many Parks Curve

Beaver Meadows Entrance Station

Estes Park

Mt. Julian 12927ft

Big Thompson River

Moraine Park

Visitor Center Park HQ

Prospect Mtn. 8901ft

Kawuneeche Valley

Spruce Canyon

Fern Lake Trail

Moraine Park Museum

Tonahutu Creek Trail

Onahu Creek Trail

Fern Falls

Glacier Basin

Arapaho National Forest

N A T I O N A L

Bighorn Flats

Sprague Lake

Colorado River

Mt. Patterson 11424ft

Flattop Mtn. 12323ft

Bear Lake

Estes Cone 11007ft

Lily Lake Visitor Center

North Inlet Trail

Hallett Peak 12713ft

Glacier Gorge Junction

Storm Pass Trail

North Inlet

Grand Lake Entrance Station

Kawuneeche Visitor Center

Andrews Glacier

Taylor Peak 13153ft

Taylor Glacier

Longs Peak

Grand Lake

Lake Nanita

Longs Peak 14255ft

P A R K

Chiefs Head Peak 13579ft

Mt. Meeker 13911ft

Meeker Park

Grand Lake

East Inlet

Lake Verna

Mt. Alice 13310ft

Wild Basin

Olive Ridge

Shadow Mountain Lake

Green Ridge

Mt. Bryant 11033ft

Paradise Park

Isolation Peak 13117ft

Blue Lake Trail

Bluebird Lake

Ouzel Falls

Calypso Cascades

Allenspark

Cutthroat Bay

Three Lakes Area

Stillwater

Lake

Twin Peaks 11959ft

Watanga Mtn. 12375ft

Ogalalla Peak 13136ft

Roosevelt National Forest

Granby

Colorado River

Arapaho Bay

Monarch Lake

Camp Dick

Granby

Boulder

Loveland

Park, Highway 36 climbs gently through foothills scattered with ponderosa pine and sagebrush. At **Deer Ridge Junction**, Trail Ridge Road veers left and makes an abrupt ascent along **Hidden Valley Creek**, dammed in several places by beavers who usually emerge from their lodges in the early evening. The creek is also home to rare greenback cutthroat trout; a roadside exhibit explains the fish's recovery.

Just beyond, the overlook at **Many Parks Curve** perches over deep valleys cut by Pleistocene glaciers more than 13,000 years ago. (Several small glaciers remain in Rocky Mountain, most straddling the eastern edge of the Continental Divide in the park's central area.) Overhead, a red-tailed hawk or golden eagle may be scanning the "parks," or meadows, for an opportunity to snatch a small rodent or even a marmot sunning itself on a rock.

Trail Ridge Road passes through stands of fir and Engelmann spruce common in the sub-alpine zone and then, beyond the stunning overlook at **Forest Canyon**, enters alpine tundra. One of the highest overland routes on the continent, Trail Ridge Road stays above treeline for 11 miles (18 km), cresting at 12,183 ft (3,713 m) near **Lava Cliffs**.

Alpine tundra: A treeless, windblown realm, alpine tundra exists only in the highest reaches of the Rockies, North Cascades and Sierra Nevada. For a closer look, walk the self-guiding **Tundra Nature Trail** near **Rock Cut**.

As you walk the trail, look closely for camouflaged ptarmigan, a member of the grouse family whose plumage changes from snowy white in winter to mottled brown in summer. You may also spy a water pipit foraging for insects, tiny pikas, or pudgy yellow-bellied marmots scampering across a talus slope, or perhaps bighorn sheep, elk or mule deer grazing warily in a distant meadow.

Be sure to bring along a jacket. The temperature here can be 20°F (–7°C) cooler than at Estes Park. Remember, too, that you are more than 4,000 ft (1,220 m) higher. The air is thin and it's not uncommon for lowlanders to feel short of breath, lightheaded or nauseated.

Only the hardiest plants can survive in these arctic-like conditions. Stunted by wind and cold, gnarled whitebark pine hugs the ground; although no larger than bushes, some are as much as 200 or 300 years old. Silver-dollar-sized patches of lichen – actually an alga and fungus that grow symbiotically – can be centuries old as well. A bouquet of wildflowers – including yellow snow buttercups, lupines, shooting stars, daisies and blue Colorado columbines, among others – send a blush through the meadows in late June and often last until the first snowfall of autumn.

For more information about alpine tundra ecology, stop at the **Alpine Visitor Center**, a short drive from the Tundra Nature Trail. And remember, this is an extremely fragile environment; it's imperative to stay on the trails at all times. Trampling delicate tundra plants can cause damage that takes decades, if not centuries, to repair.

Trail Ridge Road dips about 1,000 ft (305 m) in 4 miles (6 km) and then, at

Calypso orchids thrive in secluded wooded settings.

Milner Pass, crosses the **Continental Divide**, which runs diagonally through the park from west to east. A raindrop that falls on the western side of the Divide flows toward the Pacific Ocean; water on the eastern side runs toward the Atlantic. Known as the "backbone of America," the Divide also has a profound effect on climate. Trapped behind mountain peaks, clouds blowing in from the Pacific dump rain and snow on the western slopes, supplying the headwaters of the **Colorado River**.

Half as much moisture falls east of the Divide, and incessant, drying winds tend to rob the land of what little water it manages to capture. Naturally, there's a difference in vegetation and wildlife as well. The lush riparian environment of the western side sustains moose, river otter, Colorado River trout and a profusion of conifers. The more arid, eastern landscape is home to the Abert's squirrel, endangered greenback cutthroat trout, the ponderosa pine, prickly pear and wood lily.

From Milner Pass, the road zigzags

several dizzying miles and then heads south toward the **Colorado River Trailhead**, where you can start a moderate 2-mile (3-km) hike to the tumbled-down cabin of Joe Shipler, a miner who tried his luck here in the 1870s. About 2 miles (3 km) farther north, a few old shacks are all that remain of **Lulu City**, where hundreds of prospectors, hearing stories of gold and silver strikes, came to make their fortunes in the early 1880s. The trail follows the North Fork of the Colorado River, which here is hardly more than a trickle. Believe it or not, this is the beginning of one of the mightiest rivers in the West – the same rushing waters that flow through the Grand Canyon several hundred miles away.

About 2 miles (3 km) farther south, a short trail leads to the **Never Summer Ranch**, a dude ranch founded in the 1920s and now operated as a "living history" exhibit, with guides in period costume. The final stretch of Trail Ridge Road descends into **Kawuneeche Valley** to the **Kawuneeche Visitor Center**. Coniferous forests grow thick here, and the Colorado River is fringed with aspens and willows that explode with autumn colors. Moose and elk are a common sight and the bird-watching, especially for neotropical songbirds such as warblers, thrushes and finches, is generally excellent.

For a more intimate experience of the western slope, seasoned backpackers can make a leisurely two-day, 17-mile (27-km) round-trip on the **Tonahutu Trail** between the **Green Mountain** trailhead and **Haynach Lake**, or a 15-mile (24-km) round-trip on the **North Inlet Trail** between **Grand Lake** and **North Inlet Falls**.

Horseshoe Park: There's plenty to see and do beyond Trail Ridge Road. If time allows, plan a side trip to **Horsehoe Park**, a popular area for wildlife-watching northeast of Estes Park. From the **visitor center**, take Highway 36 into the park, then turn right at the junction with Highway 34 to **Sheep Lake**, where naturally-occurring mineral licks attract bands of bighorn sheep. The **Old Fall River Road**, a one-way unpaved lane open only in summer, starts at **Endovalley**

Bear Lake reflection.

and makes a 9-mile (14-km) climb, much of it above the treeline, to the Alpine Visitor Center. Notice the rocky debris scattered along the road; it was deposited by a dam break in 1982 that sent a flood of mud, rocks and water downslope as far as Estes Park.

Bighorn sheep are frequently seen in this area. About 200 bighorns graze on the lush meadows and rocky slopes around Horseshoe Park. During the winter breeding season, males vie for dominance, using their massive corkscrew horns in dramatic head-butting contests. The report can be heard echoing through the mountains.

Elk, or wapiti, are frequently spotted here, too, never far from the forest edge. Overhunted in the early 1900s, the animals descend from the Yellowstone herd. Few sounds are more haunting than the mournful bugling of bull elk during the autumn rut. The call resonates across glens and valleys and is meant to ward off competitors. Bulls will sometimes go head to head too, jousting with their sharp antlers.

Clean living.

Another option is to explore **Moraine Park** and **Bear Lake Road**, which leads into one of the most picturesque and heavily used regions of the park. The area is laced with interconnecting trails, and it's possible to spend a day or more hiking from one mountain lake to another and experiencing a variety of life zones. Hikers can spend the morning wandering among tree-ringed glens and turquoise lakes and then make a push toward the Continental Divide, where glaciers and snowfields send meltwater cascading down the eastern slope.

You can get your bearings at the **Moraine Park Museum**, where exhibits and a short interpretive trail explain the area's cultural and natural history, and then strike out on any number of possible tours.

A short drive to the **Cub Lake Trailhead** puts you in a good spot to explore Moraine Park or to make a gentle 4-mile (6-km) climb to **Cub Lake**, **Fern Falls** and **Fern Lake**; an extension trail makes a steep connection to the stark shoreline of **Odessa Lake**. Farther south, a free

summer shuttle bus runs from **Glacier Basin** to the end of Bear Lake Road. An easy nature trail around **Sprague Lake** (wheelchair-accessible) makes a pleasant stroll through a storybook mountain setting. Farther down, a steep 4-mile (6-km) round-trip takes hikers up to and around the forested shore of **Bierstadt Lake**. You'll find tougher hikes at **Glacier Gorge Junction**, which has branches that go to the foot of **Andrews** and **Taylor** glaciers via **Loch Vale** as well as a 5-mile (8-km) scramble through Glacier Gorge to frigid **Black Lake**, well above the treeline.

The most traveled and possibly the most beautiful route is the short trail from **Bear Lake** to **Dream Lake**, which is cupped in a magnificent high-country basin with the snow-dusted summits of **Flattop Mountain** and **Hallett Peak** rising grandly from behind.

Longs Peak and Wild Basin: Farther south, an ascent of **Longs Peak** is a challenge even to the most ambitious and physically fit hikers. At 14,255 ft (4,345 m), **Longs Peak** towers over the

eastern side of the park; its flat summit and nearby **Chasm Lake** are considered by many to be the most magical destination in the park. And although technical equipment isn't necessary to make the climb, it's a mistake to underestimate just how arduous the 16-mile (26-km) round-trip, taking from 12 to 15 hours, can be.

Hikers should be prepared for high winds, biting cold, and a fair amount of hand-and-foot scrambling. It's essential to start the hike well before daybreak in order to avoid dangerous afternoon lightning storms; many hikers stay at nearby **Longs Peak Campground** the night before. Greenhorns can inquire at the **Colorado Mountain School** in Estes Park about climbing lessons and guide services.

Finally, if you really want to escape the crowds, try the **Wild Basin** region, off Route 7 just south of Longs Peak. Cut off from the rest of the park by a crescent of surrounding mountains, this isolated pocket of mountain lakes and exuberant waterfalls is still recovering in places from a 1978 forest fire. In the early days, a park official tried promoting Rocky Mountain by dressing a woman, dubbed Eve, in animal skins and letting her wander around Wild Basin, much to the delight of reporters looking for a tantalizing story.

Hikers can spend a leisurely afternoon on the moderate, 3-mile (5-km) trail leading to **Calypso Cascades** and **Ouzel Falls**, named after the tiny riverfaring bird that John Muir found so enchanting. The trail branches a bit farther on, following a string of lakes into the highlands.

If you get tired of using your own two feet, **Glacier Creek Stables**, located at Moraine Park and Sprague Lake, offer guided horseback riding. Snow usually closes Trail Ridge Road between mid-October and late June, but opportunities for cross-country skiing and snowshoeing are abundant. Permits are required for overnight backcountry trips in all seasons, and camping is allowed in designated areas only. There are no hotels in the park, but five campgrounds offer spaces for both tents and RVs.

Left, mountain lions are powerful predators. Right, heading for the slopes.

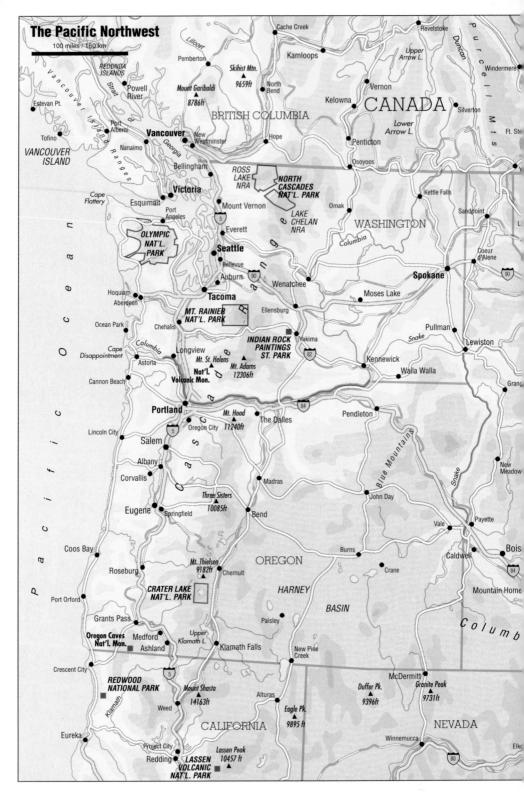

The Pacific Northwest

100 miles / 160 km

CANADA

BRITISH COLUMBIA

REDONDA ISLANDS

VANCOUVER ISLAND

Pacific Ocean

Cache Creek
Revelstoke
Purcell Mts.
Duncan
Lillooet
Pemberton
Kamloops
Upper Arrow L.
Windermere
Skihist Mtn. 9659ft ▲
North Bend
Mount Garibaldi 8786ft ▲
Vernon
Kelowna
Silverton
Ft. Ste
Estevan Pt.
Powell River
Lower Arrow L.
Tofino
Port Alberni
Nanaimo
Vancouver
New Westminster
Hope
Penticton
Georgia
Bellingham
Osoyoos
Kettle Falls
Sandpoint
Cape Flattery
Victoria
Esquimalt
Port Angeles
Mount Vernon
ROSS LAKE NRA
NORTH CASCADES NAT'L. PARK
LAKE CHELAN NRA
Omak
WASHINGTON
L
Everett
Coeur d'Alene
OLYMPIC NAT'L. PARK
Columbia
90
Seattle
Bellevue
Auburn
90
Wenatchee
Spokane
Hoquiam
Aberdeen
Tacoma
Moses Lake
Ocean Park
MT. RAINIER NAT'L. PARK
Ellensburg
Pullman
Chehalis
Cascade Range
Snake
Lewiston
Cape Disappointment
Columbia
Longview
INDIAN ROCK PAINTINGS ST. PARK
Yakima
82
Astoria
Mt. St. Helens ▲
Nat'l. Volcanic Mon.
Mt. Adams 12306ft ▲
Kennewick
Walla Walla
Cannon Beach
Granc
Lincoln City
Portland
5
Oregon City
Mt. Hood 11240ft ▲
The Dalles
84
Pendleton
Salem
Albany
Blue Mountains
New Meadow
Corvallis
Madras
Snake
Three Sisters 10085ft ▲
John Day
Eugene
Springfield
Bend
Payette
Vale
Bois
Coos Bay
Burns
Caldwell
84
Roseburg
Mt. Thielsen 9182ft ▲
Chemult
OREGON
Crane
Port Orford
CRATER LAKE NAT'L. PARK
HARNEY
Mountain Home
Grants Pass
BASIN
Paisley
Columb
Oregon Caves Nat'l. Mon.
Medford
Ashland
Upper Klamath L.
Klamath Falls
New Pine Creek
McDermitt
Crescent City
5
Duffer Pk. 9396ft ▲
Granite Peak 9731ft ▲
REDWOOD NATIONAL PARK
Klamath
Mount Shasta 14163ft ▲
Alturas
Eagle Pk. 9895 ft ▲
NEVADA
Eureka
Weed
CALIFORNIA
Winnemucca
Elk
Project City
Lassen Peak 10457 ft ▲
80
Redding
LASSEN VOLCANIC NAT'L. PARK

PACIFIC NORTHWEST

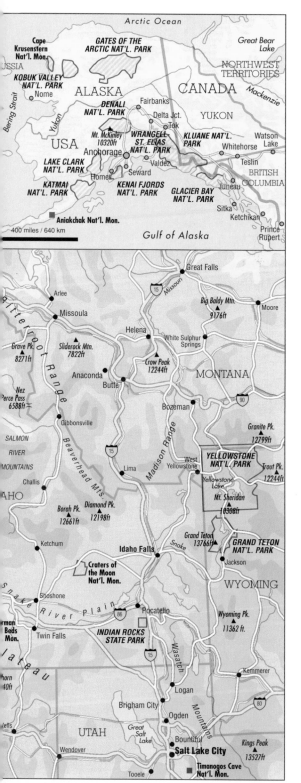

The Pacific Northwest sustains a riotous profusion of life. For sheer biomass, its old-growth forests are virtually unsurpassed in the American West.

The Cascade Range runs along the region's western flank, catching moisture that blows in from the Pacific Ocean and casting a long rain shadow over the eastern plateau. Evidence of the range's volcanic origins is everywhere. In Oregon, the caldera of a dormant volcano cups the enchanting blue waters of Crater Lake, the deepest in the country. To the north, the great mass of Washington's Mount Rainier rises like a titan, its peak crowned with more than 25 glaciers, its shoulders draped with dazzling wildflower meadows and deep-green ancient forests.

In North Cascades National Park, a jumble of craggy volcanic peaks, lovely waterfalls and sparkling lakes are surrounded by a remote mountain wilderness where mountain goats, black bears, mountain lions, lynx, eagles and hawks range freely.

To the west, the snow-dusted peaks of the Olympic Mountains seem to float above the wild, wave-battered Pacific Coast, where bald eagles soar over waters inhabited by seals, sea otters and migrating gray whales. Lush temperate rain forest cloaks Olympic's western slope, where annual rainfall in excess of 120 inches (305 cms) nourishes an emerald cathedral of Douglas fir, Sitka spruce, western red cedar, and thick growths of mosses and ferns.

Far to the north, Alaska contains 54 million acres (22 million hectares) of National Parks Service land. From the frigid peak of Mount McKinley, the highest in North America, to the vast tundra of Gates of the Arctic and Kobuk Valley, Alaska's parks can be described only in superlatives.

OLYMPIC

It was in 1788 that Captain John Meares gave them their name. Awestruck by the snowcapped pinnacles that loom over the rugged Washington coast, he dubbed the tallest peak Mount Olympus, "home of the gods." Today, **Mount Olympus** stands at the center of **Olympic National Park**, a 922,000-acre (373,120-hectare) sanctuary of glacier-clad mountains, lush temperate rain forest, and miles of wild shoreline. It is such an exemplary reservoir of ecological diversity that the United Nations has designated Olympic a World Heritage site and International Biosphere Reserve.

Alpine fossils: Believe it or not, the sawtooth summits that crown the Olympic Mountains were once at the bottom of the Pacific Ocean. Scratch away the mantle of snow and ice, and you'll find fossils of ancient sea creatures entombed in alpine rock. About 30 million years ago, as the Pacific plate collided with North America, the upper layers of the ocean floor were planed off and thrust upward, creating the jigsaw of basalt and sedimentary rocks that are now the Olympic Mountains.

Glaciers finished the job. They carved out their signature U-shaped valleys, fracturing and polishing bare rock, scooping out lakebeds, and transporting boulders, or erratics, miles from their origin. Glaciers also bulldozed Puget Sound and the Straight of Juan de Fuca, isolating the Olympic Peninsula from inland species. The result is several evolutionary detours – the so-called "endemic 16" – species such as the Olympic pocket gopher, Olympic Mazama marmot, Crescenti trout and Flett's violet that are found only on the peninsula.

Glaciers remain atop the Olympic Mountains, fed by moist Pacific breezes that dump about 200 inches (500 cms) of precipitation on the crest each year. It's not uncommon to have 20 overcast days per month on the west side of the park, or several weeks of nearly constant drizzle. Thirteen major rivers drain the high country, including the Queets

and Hoh rivers, which cascade down mountainsides toward the Pacific. Oddly, only miles to the east, on the opposite side of the mountains, parts of the park are among the driest spots on the West Coast. Nevertheless, a traveler's best friend is a rain jacket and an extra pair of dry shoes.

Olympic contains one of the largest tracts of roadless land in the United States. Highway 101 wraps around three sides of the park, and spoke roads give limited access to the interior. If you've never been here before, the best place to start is the **Olympic Park Visitor Center and Museum** in Port Angeles (on the north side of the park), where exhibits, maps, books and rangers will help organize your journey. From here, you can drive a counterclockwise circuit that takes you to the mountains, the rain forest, and then to the coast.

The mountains: After stopping at the visitor center, head directly to **Hurricane Ridge**, the highest point you can reach by car. Steep and winding, the road climbs nearly 5,000 ft (1,524 m) in 17 miles (27 km), giving you a good sense of just how abruptly the mountains rise from the sea. Pull out binoculars at the **Hurricane Ridge Visitor Center** for a close-up look at the park's mightiest, glacier-saddled peaks. At nearly 7,000 ft (2,134 m), **Mount Carrie** and her ringlet of glaciers dominate the foreground, while 7,965-ft (2,428-m) Mount Olympus, clothed in the pearly-white robe of **Blue Glacier**, rises from behind. Seven glaciers hang from Olympus; its massive shoulders have been draped in ice for thousands of years, and almost every storm that blows in from the Pacific drops a fresh payload of snow, sometimes as much as 200 inches (500 cms) a year. Heavy snowfalls often keep the steep gravel road from Hurricane Ridge to 6,450-ft (1,966 m) **Obstruction Peak** closed until early July, but intrepid motorists will find the trip worth their time and patience.

The **Elwha River Trail**, which follows the stream for a few dozen miles through the Elwha Valley at the foot of Mount Olympus, is downright magical in solitude and beauty. The route links

Preceding pages: sea stars on the Washington coast. Left, Olympic Mountain portrait.

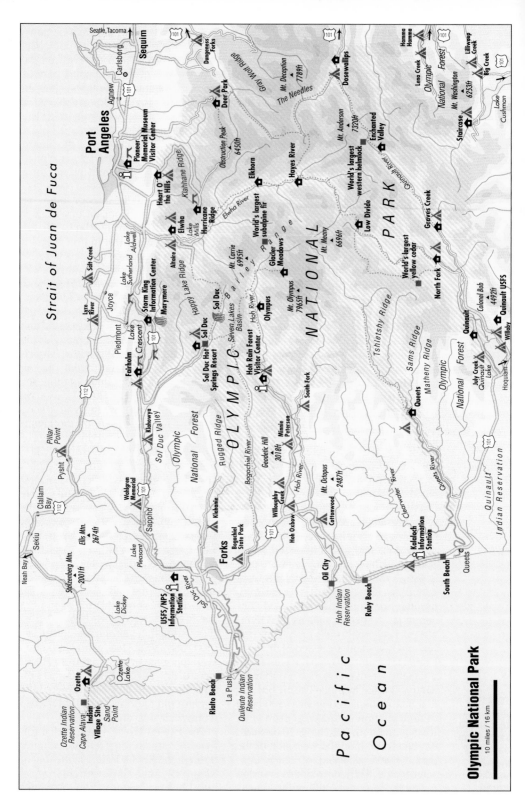

Strait of Juan de Fuca

Seattle, Tacoma
Sequim
Carlsborg
Agnew
101
Dungeness Forks

Port Angeles

Pioneer Memorial Museum Visitor Center

Heart O' the Hills
Klahhane Ridge
Elwha
Lake Mills
Hurricane Ridge
Altaire

Gray Wolf Ridge
Mt. Deception 7789ft
The Needles
Obstruction Peak 6450ft
Deer Park
Elkhorn
Hayes River
Mt. Anderson 7320ft

Dosewallips
Hamma Hamma
Lena Creek
Lillwaup Creek
Big Creek
101

Olympic National Forest
Mt. Washington 6253ft
Staircase
Lake Cushman

Enchanted Valley
World's largest western hemlock

Quinault River

Range
Mt. Carrie 6995ft
Bailey
Glacier Meadows
World's largest subalpine fir

Low Divide
Mt. Meany 6696ft

Graves Creek

Salt Creek
Lyre River
Lake Crescent
Lake Sutherland
Lake Aldwell
Piedmont
Joyce
Storm King Information Center
Marymere
Fairholm

Happy Lake Ridge
Sol Duc Ridge
Sol Duc
Sol Duc Hot Springs Resort

Seven Lakes Basin
Mt. Carrie
Hoh River
Olympus
Mt. Olympus 7965ft

OLYMPIC

NATIONAL

PARK

World's largest yellow cedar
North Fork
Colonel Bob 4492ft
Quinault USFS
Quinault
Willaby
July Creek
Lake Quinault
Hoquiam

Tshletshy Ridge
Sams Ridge
Matheny Ridge
Olympic National Forest

112
Pillar Point
Pysht
Klahowya

Sol Duc Valley
Olympic National Forest
Rugged Ridge

Hoh Rain Forest Visitor Center
Bogachiel River
Geodetic Hill 3018ft
Minnie Peterson
South Fork

Queets

Queets River
Clearwater River
Quinault Indian Reservation

Clallam Bay
Sekiu
Neah Bay
Stolzenberg Mtn. 2001ft
Ellis Mtn. 2674ft

Lake Pleasant
Sappho
Wahlgren Memorial
Klahonie

Bogachiel State Park
Willoughby Creek
Cottonwood
Hoh Oxbow
Mt. Octopus 2487ft

Forks

Lake Dickey
USFS/NPS Information Station
Sol Duc River

Oil City
Hoh River
Hoh Indian Reservation

Kalaloch Information Station

Ozette Indian Reservation
Cape Alava
Sand Point
Ozette
Ozette Lake
Indian Village Site

Rialto Beach
La Push
Quileute Indian Reservation

Ruby Beach
South Beach
Queets

Pacific

Ocean

Olympic National Park

10 miles / 16 km

summer ranger stations at Elkhorn, Hayes River and Low Divide, then connects with the **North Fork Trailhead** on the southern end of the park. In 1889, James Christie led an expedition along this route and emerged at **Quinault Lake** – six months later.

From Hurricane Ridge, you can backtrack through the **Heart O'the Hills Entrance** and then continue west on Highway 101 to the shores of **Lake Crescent**, a moody, misty tarn that was scooped out by glaciers about 10,000 years ago. Set near an ancient landslide that divided the lake in two, the **Storm King Information Center** is a great place to catch a sunset or to watch storm clouds gather above the coast. A short walk on the **Marymere Falls Trail** leads to a lovely 90-ft (27-m) cascade, just one of dozens that gush over mountain ridges throughout the park. For a refreshing break, consider stopping for lunch at the historic **Lake Crescent Lodge**, snuggled against the lakeshore at the base of **Mount Storm King**.

Continue on the highway along the southern shore of Lake Crescent and then turn left about 2 miles (3 km) past Fairholm toward **Sol Duc**. Notice that the trees are getting bigger. This is the western front of the Olympic Range, one of the rainiest spots in the country.

The road passes the rustic **Sol Duc Hot Springs Resort**, which was built in 1911 and still caters to travelers who want to soak away their aches and pains after a long day of hiking. Indian legend tells of a confrontation between two "lightning fish" who shed tears into the springs after doing battle with each other, giving the water healing qualities.

At the height of the spring runoff, cataracts such as **Sol Duc Falls** tumble with a roar. Located about a mile from the end of the road, the falls are a watery gateway to the hard-scrabble **Seven Lakes Basin Trail**, which makes a 17½-mile (28-km) loop at the headwaters of the Sol Duc and Bogachiel rivers, an area of mostly sub-alpine forest, meadows and deep-blue lakes that is particularly rich in wildlife.

The rain forest: Rejoin Highway 101 and make the long drive to Hoh Road

and the **Hoh Rain Forest Visitor Center**. Olympic National Park protects the world's largest temperate rain forest – one of only three in the entire world. As a park botanist put it, this is as close as a higher-latitude forest gets to becoming a jungle. The perpetual mist and showers, together with a deep layer of decaying organic matter, produce trees of truly gargantuan size, including a western hemlock that measures 22 ft (7 m) in diameter and a sub-alpine fir that is 21 ft (6 m) around. In all, there are 10 trees in the western half of the park which hold records for being the biggest of their kind.

Two short interpretive trails start near the Hoh Visitor Center, the **Spruce Nature Trail** and the **Hall of Mosses Trail**. Here, a leafy canopy of western hemlock, bigleaf maple, Sitka spruce and red cedar cast an emerald twilight of shade and sunbeams. A veil of moss and vine epiphytes hangs from the trees like ragged curtains, with the occasional flash of nuthatches, bluebirds, finches, warblers or hummingbirds flitting between

Great horned owlet.

the branches. Licorice and sword ferns, spike moss and a host of large mushrooms soak up water from the forest floor, and fallen trees, called nurse logs, provide a fertile spot for seedlings to sprout. The endangered spotted owl makes its home here, and black bear, black-tailed deer and Roosevelt elk are occasionally seen feeding in the underbrush. During the autumn rut, you may hear the distinct bugling of bull elk challenging their competitors.

Those who want to penetrate deeper into the forest can hike all or part of the one-way 17-mile (27-km) **Hoh River Trail** to **Glacier Meadows**, the staging ground for most climbs of Mount Olympus. (The ascent can be hazardous; only good climbers should attempt it.) Fishing is excellent in the Hoh River and the other watercourses that tumble toward the ocean. Licenses are not required for trout, but a state punchcard is needed for salmon and steelhead.

To explore even more remote parts of the forest, consider taking the long drive to the **Queets** or **Quinault** districts in

the southwestern corner of the park. About 80 miles (130 km) from the Hoh Rain Forest Visitor Center, the Queets Campground is the jumping-off point for either a moderate 3-mile (5-km) loop trail through the rain forest or a much more demanding one-way 18-mile (30-km) backpacking trip along the Queets River. The Quinault district offers three short hikes – the half-mile **Quinault Rain Forest Nature Walk**, the 1-mile (1½-km) loop at **Graves Creek**, and a 3-mile (5-km) stretch of the **Enchanted Valley Trail** from the Graves Creek Ranger Station to the canyon at Pony Bridge. Several other, more challenging, trails follow Graves Creek, the North Fork of the Quinault River and Skyline Ridge into the park's mountainous interior.

The coast: Set apart both physically and spiritually from the main body of the park, Olympic's 57-mile (92-km) coastline occupies a narrow strip of land that is constantly pummeled by surf and wind and blessed with an abundance of fascinating marine life.

There are more than 600 miles (966 km) of backcountry trails in Olympic, but nothing quite compares to hiking on the beach. Veiled in mist, a scattering of rock arches, "sea stacks" and tiny islands gives the coast a dreamy, otherworldly quality. (The islets are critical breeding sites for seabirds and seals. Most are national wildlife refuges and strictly off-limits to visitors.)

Harbor seals haul out on the rocks; bald eagles prowl the skies and nest in the forest fringe; seagulls drop clams onto the rocky beach and then swoop down for a meal; otters float on their backs in kelp beds, using stones to crack shellfish; raccoons, skunks and an occasional black bear wander toward the water looking for a meal; sandpipers and black oyster-catchers patrol the beach; California gray whales swim near shore during their spring and winter migrations; and hikers can spend hours examining the crabs, sea anemones, snails, sea urchins, barnacles, mussels, starfish and other creatures that inhabit the crowded world of tide pools.

Highway 101 leads directly to the

Sulfur bracket fungus in the Hoh Rain Forest.

southern beaches (**Ruby Beach** to **South Beach**), which tend to be busy during the summer months. Rangers at the **Kalaloch Information Station** lead free summer nature hikes that are well worth joining. If you intend to explore on your own, be sure to pick up a tide table, crucial to planning a safe hike. In-coming tides can trap hikers between headlands, leaving them stranded on the rocks for hours, or worse. Be wary of floating logs, too. An unexpected wave can send them hurtling toward the beach, crushing anything that gets in the way, including you.

To the north of **Rialto Beach**, hikers can explore miles of wild forest and coastline. Long spur roads from Highway 101 lead to **Oil City** (unpaved) and **La Push**, where you can pick up a connecting 17-mile (27-km) trail that weaves in and out of beach and forest. Farther north, you can follow a long road off Highway 112 to **Ozette**. Stop at the **ranger station** for information, and then follow the glorious **Cape Alava Trail** 3 miles (5 km) across a patch of coastal forest to **Cape Alava**, the westernmost point in the continental United States. To make a loop, walk south along the beach for another 3 miles (5 km) to **Sand Point**, and then return to the ranger station on 3-mile (5-km) **Sand Point Trail**. Campgrounds are located along the coast at Kalaloch, Mora and Ozette. Here, as elsewhere, backcountry camping permits (issued free) are required.

Even at this wild coastal outpost, the modern world has a way of intruding. All sorts of debris are washed ashore, interspersed with kelp fronds and stranded jellyfish. Occasionally, glass bulbs from Japanese fishing nets are tossed onto the beach; park rangers say they take about a year to cross the ocean. Olympic is truly a vast and wild sanctuary, but it remains vulnerable to the outside world. To appreciate the value of this undisturbed ecosystem, you need only look at the huge swaths of clear-cut timber just beyond Olympic's perimeter. It makes the national park seem all the more precious.

Tiny islets, or sea stacks, dot the Olympic coast.

NORTH CASCADES

North Cascades National Park is often overlooked by travelers. A relative newcomer to the Parks System (it was established in 1968), North Cascades is tucked away in the northwestern corner of Washington state. Those who do get to see it, however, can only gape in wonder. "Nowhere do the mountain masses and peaks present such strange, fantastic, dauntless and startling outlines as here," declared Henry Custer after surveying the region for the government in 1859.

North Cascades has razor-edged summits, massive blue glaciers and primeval forests. Its towering, snow-draped peaks are routinely compared to the Swiss Alps; its long, deep lakes are said to resemble Norwegian fjords; and its broad expanse of alpine tundra is ecologically akin to conditions in the Arctic. In the mid-19th century, explorers found the terrain so rugged they considered it impenetrable, giving the peaks names such as **Mount Challenger**, **Mount Fury**, **Mount Terror** and **Mount Despair**.

Though laced with a well-maintained network of hiking trails, North Cascades remains a remote mountain wilderness that is best known by the mountain goats who wander its highest peaks, and by the black bears and mountain lions who range across dense forests and sub-alpine meadows.

Beyond park boundaries, there is an expanse of protected wildlands – including the **Pasayten**, **Mount Baker**, **Noisy-Diobsud** and **Glacier Peak wilderness areas** – that ensure solitude for creatures requiring vast open spaces and for backpackers who want to immerse themselves in wilderness. Nature seems to be responding to the protection. Grizzly bears and gray wolves, both severely reduced by bounty hunters 60 years ago, have recently been sighted in the park. Efforts are also being made by private organizations to increase protection across the Canadian border in order to create an international reserve embrac-ing much of the surrounding ecosystem.

Geologic history: The region owes its ruggedness to a tumultuous geologic past. Scientists speculate that about 100 million years ago mountainous Pacific islands rafted into North America, rumpling the land like an accordion and sending great wads of magma coursing to the surface. The collision set off a long and turbulent period of faulting, tilting, folding and volcanic eruptions that jumbled the bedrock. The snow-capped peaks we see today were not the first to pierce the sky. Several mountain ranges were thrust upward and then gradually broken down. The present range didn't begin to rise until about 6 million years ago, and some volcanic cones such as 10,775-ft (3,284-m) Mount Baker are geologic youngsters, no more than 4 million years old.

The latest chapter in North Cascades' geologic story was written by the great jacket of ice that retreated north about 10,000 years ago, shearing mountaintops into aretes and dagger-like horns, gouging out bowl-shaped basins, depositing

Preceding pages: after the climb. **Left**, elk skull. **Right**, more than 1,500 plant species grow in the ancient forest.

mounds of debris, and widening valleys. More than 300 glaciers remain in the park, more than half of the glaciers in the lower 48 states. Some advance or retreat several inches per year, grinding the underlaying rock into a glacial "flour" that washes into waterways like the Skagit River, turning them a lovely shade of turquoise.

True to its name, the park contains hundreds of cascades, fed by storms that blow in from the Pacific, dumping more than 100 inches (254 cms) of precipitation per year on the western slope. Blocked by mountain peaks, few storm clouds reach the eastern side, which receives scarcely one-fifth of the precipitation that falls on the west.

North Cascades is actually three parks managed under one administrative roof. The **Ross Lake National Recreation Area** divides the national park into two units – north and south – and the **Lake Chelan National Recreation Area** forms a southern appendage. There's only one main road into the park complex: the **North Cascades Highway** (State Route 20), dubbed "the most scenic mountain drive in Washington." Visitors can stop at overlooks and trailheads directly on the highway as well as take boating tours of the park's three largest lakes – **Diablo Lake**, **Ross Lake** and **Lake Chelan**.

Getting oriented: As you approach the park, you'll notice that the highway follows the magnificent **Skagit River**, a favorite wintering spot for bald eagles who gorge on salmon. About 10 miles (16 km) from the park boundary, you'll reach **Newhalem**, one of the villages created by Seattle City Light in the 1920s to house workers who built the three dams that stand farther upstream – the **Gorge**, **Diablo** and **Ross**. Today, a third of Seattle's energy needs are drawn from the Skagit's glacier-driven waters.

Turn right toward the **North Cascades Visitor Center**, where you can pick up maps and books, take in the exhibits, and inquire about weather conditions, hiking, camping, nature walks and tours offered by Seattle City Light. On your way back to the highway, stop

A party of climbers at Ptarmigan Traverse.

at the **Newhalem Creek Campground**, where two short interpretive trails – the **To Know a Tree Trail** and the **Trail of the Cedars** – introduce hikers to a variety of local trees, including lodgepole pine, Douglas fir, western red cedar, yew and western hemlock, some of them several hundred years old. The trees account for only a small portion of more than 1,500 plant species that flourish in the park's cool, damp forest.

Back on the highway, stop at **Gorge Creek Falls**, one of hundreds of cataracts that tumble down the mountains, and then continue to the little town of **Diablo** across the Diablo Dam, where you can catch a Seattle City Light tour (reservations recommended), learn about the early days of hydropower at the **Davis Museum**, or limber up on one of the trails. For hikers in top physical condition, a strenuous 10-mile (16-km) round-trip on **Sourdough Mountain Trail** leads to a gorgeous panorama of lakes, glaciers and surrounding peaks. A more moderate alternative is a tugboat ride to **Ross Dam** and then a fairly easy 4-mile (6-km) hike along **Diablo Lake Trail** back to your car.

Beyond Diablo, the highway dips south toward **Colonial Creek Campground**, where the short but steep **Thunder Woods Nature Trail** takes you on a 1-mile (1½-km) loop into the realm of giant cedars. For a longer hike, try a portion of 19-mile (31-km) **Thunder Creek Trail**, which passes through a densely forested valley beneath **Neve**, **Klawatti** and **Boston** glaciers before climbing toward 6,063-ft (1,848-m) **Park Creek Pass**.

If arduous hiking isn't your cup of tea, drive to the **Diablo Lake Overlook** for a stunning view of some of the places you might have gone to see up close. A reflection of Sourdough Mountain shimmers on the lake, and the glacier-carved pinnacles of **Colonial Peak** and **Ruby Mountain**, both over 7,000 ft (2,134 m), rise to the south. Before reaching the park boundary you will pass a short interpretive boardwalk at the **Happy Crest Forest Walk** and, just beyond, the **Ross Lake Overlook**, where you'll

A mountain lion prowls the high country.

get a heavenly view of the park's largest lake and where, on spring and fall nights, you may be lucky enough to hear a loon's eerie yodel echo off the water.

Ross Lake: To explore the northern reaches of the park, base yourself at the "floating cabins" of rustic **Ross Lake Resort** (reservations required well in advance), reached only by hiking trails from Diablo or Ross Dam. Here, you can rent canoes, kayaks or motorboats, or hire a water taxi, to one of several camping areas or trailheads. Backpackers can pick up **Big Beaver Trail**, which traces the lakeshore for about 2½ miles (4 km) before veering into Big Beaver Creek valley, where river otter, beavers, black-tailed deer and other wildlife are often sighted amid one of the most extensive stands of gigantic, ancient, western red cedar.

The trail toils over 3,619-ft (1,103-m) **Beaver Pass** and then intersects **Little Beaver** and **Brush Creek** trails at the toes of the **Picket Range**, which shoulder the park's largest glaciers. From here, backpackers can choose either to return the way they came, to make the difficult 11-mile (18-km) trek to **Ross Lake**, or to continue exploring the park's wild northwestern corner.

Stehekin Valley: The southern area of the park (including **Lake Chelan National Recreation Area**) is equally remote. The only road access is bumpy, gravelly **Cascade River Road**, which makes a winding 30-mile (48-km) climb from Marblemount toward **Cascade Pass**. From here, you can pick up the **Cascade Pass Trail**, reportedly used more than 180 years ago by Alexander Ross, the first white man to explore the region. Beginners may want to think twice before attempting the pass; it's steep, rugged and often besieged by wind and biting cold. But those who make the effort will be rewarded with gorgeous views of **Johannesburg Mountain**, **Boston Peak**, **Sahale Mountain**, **Boston Glacier** and **Doubtful Lake**, not to mention hardy stands of krummholz, whitebark pine and a riotous blend of wildflowers.

A steep side trail leads about 4 miles (6 km) past 15 waterfalls to **Horseshoe Basin**, where you can poke around the abandoned **Black Warrior Mine**. Be extremely careful. Old structures and mine shafts can be dangerous. Tread lightly and stay on the trails throughout the area; alpine meadows are fragile and have been damaged by careless hikers.

The Cascade Pass Trail eventually loops down to **Cottonwood Campground**, where you can catch a bus on a bumpy old mining road that follows the **Stehekin River** to Lake Chelan's isolated but busy north shore. Make reservations in advance, and note that bus route and schedule are subject to change. The ride takes about two hours.

There are stops at several backcountry campgrounds where you can pick up a short segment of the **Pacific Crest Trail**, which snakes along the Cascade Range from the Canadian border on its way to Mexico.

An easier way into the Stehekin Valley is either by floatplane or by boat from the lower end of Lake Chelan. Board at the little town of **Chelan** on Highway 97. Ferries run year-round,

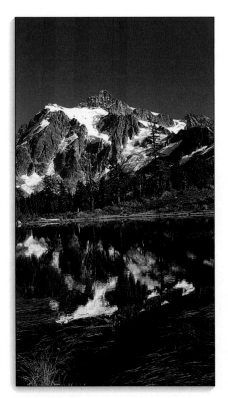

Twin peaks in a mountain lake.

weather permitting. The ride, which can take as much as four hours, passes through a glacier-gouged trench surrounded by forest-clad mountains. Enlarged by the Chelan Dam, **Lake Chelan** is one of the deepest freshwater lakes in the country, with a depth of about 1,500 ft (457 m).

As the boat approaches the docks at **Stehekin Landing**, you begin to see why this region is called the "Wilderness Alps of the Stehekin." Tourists have been finding refuge in this remote pocket of natural beauty since the late 1800s, when the first hotel was built. Modest accommodations (reservations recommended well in advance) as well as campgrounds, stores and a restaurant are available at **Stehekin**, which is operated by some of the 70 permanent residents. You can visit the historic **Buckner Homestead** for a revealing illustration of the hardships and pleasures of life in the wilderness.

Rangers at the **Golden West Visitor Center** can help decide which hiking trails are best for you. The short **Imus Creek Nature Trail** is a good introduction to the variety of plants you're likely to see in the valley. A longer walk on **Lakeshore Trail** heads south from the visitor center and features lovely views of Lake Chelan. Farther afield, you can take the bus to High Bridge for a moderate 5-mile (8-km) round-trip to **Agnes Gorge**, or, for an extremely tough workout, you can make the 6,000-ft (1,829-m) climb up 8-mile (13-km) **MacGregor Mountain Trail**. For something a bit more relaxing, consider strolling up the road a few miles for a picnic at 312-ft (95-m) **Rainbow Falls** on the eastern edge of the valley.

The shuttle bus runs from mid-May to mid-October. The park is open year-round, but heavy snowfall closes the highway as early as mid-October, leaving the park interior sealed off until late spring. Campgrounds are located throughout the park complex. Tent and RV sites are available on a first-come, first-served basis. Most sites are closed in winter, and free permits are required for overnight stays in the backcountry.

Moonrise over the North Cascades.

MOUNT RAINIER

On a clear day, you can see **Mount Rainier** from 100 miles (160 km) away. Its peak towers 14,411 ft (4,392 m) into the sky, making it the highest in the Cascade Range and the fifth highest in the contiguous United States. Its glacial crown shines in the sun like a studded pearl. Even cloaked in mist, its presence is commanding, a nearly perfect volcanic cone, standing among the clouds in majestic solitude.

Rainier's volcanic fires have been dim for more than a century, but its allure is as bright as ever. "If in the making of the West, Nature had what we call parks in mind – places for rest, inspiration and prayers – this Rainier region must surely be one of them. Of all the fire mountains which, like beacons, once blazed along the Pacific Coast, Mount Rainier is the noblest." That is high praise indeed, coming as it does from John Muir, the spiritual father of environmentalism.

The great mountain: The Indians who summered on Rainier's slopes called it *Tahoma*, "The Great Mountain." They shared the meadows, forests and alpine crags with a bounty of wildlife, including Roosevelt elk, black-tailed deer, mountain goats, black bears, porcupines and whistling picas. Today, much of the same land is contained within the 378 sq. miles (980 sq. km) of **Mount Rainier National Park**. It is a sanctuary of forests, waterfalls, lakes, snowfields and wildflower meadows that sustain nearly a thousand species of plants and animals.

A giant among mountains, Rainier is nonetheless a geologic infant. Less than a million years old, it is a classic example of volcanic development. Thousands of lava flows have increased the height and mass of the cone, the last occurrence about 150 years ago. And geologists say that Rainier isn't finished yet. It's quite likely that lava will flow again in the next century or two. And if the explosion of nearby Mount Saint Helens is any indication, the results could be devastating.

Fire and ice: Meanwhile, ice continues to break down what fire has already built up. Rainier is mantled with 27 glaciers, the largest and most active on any mountain in the lower 48 states. From above, they look like a frozen flower, a sunburst, with fingers of ice radiating down the slopes in every direction. Buried under more than 50 ft (15 m) of snow annually, the great frozen rivers can move as much as a foot per day, depositing boulders and debris in morainal mounds and grinding bedrock into powder.

Touring the park requires at least a full day. To get properly acquainted, you should plan on two or three days or more, preferably during the week in order to beat the crowds that pour out of Seattle and Tacoma on summer weekends. Entering the park from the west, you are immediately swept away by Rainier's grandeur. Route 706 between the Nisqually Entrance and Paradise truly deserves its reputation as one of America's most breathtaking drives. With views of the mountain and the

Preceding pages: Mount Rainier's snowcapped summit. **Left**, wildflowers enlivens an alpine meadow. **Right**, the Nisqually River flows below Christine Falls Bridge.

glistening mass of **Nisqually Glacier** crowding your windshield, the road passes through a cathedral of aged Douglas fir, western hemlock and red cedar, climbing 3,400 ft (1,036 m) in 18 miles (29 km). According to one park ranger, the rapid elevation change, which can literally take the breath away from lowlanders, "is the same as traveling from Seattle to the Arctic Circle in a straight line."

Make your first stop at the **Longmire Museum** 6 miles (10 km) from the entrance, where you can get a lesson in local history. Longmire is the oldest settlement in the park and is named after James Longmire, who opened the Mineral Spring Resort here in the early 1880s. The village is now occupied by the **National Park Inn**, a rustic, 25-room hotel that is open year-round.

The nearby **Hiker Information Center** is the best place to inquire about weather, road and trail conditions and obtain backcountry permits for overnight hikes along the park's 300 miles (483 km) of trails. A short jaunt on the

Trail of the Shadows will help acquaint you with the park's fragile meadow ecology; the walk passes the mineral springs that James Longmire promoted as a wonder cure in the late 19th century and a pioneer cabin built by his son. Longmire also makes a good starting point for backpacking trips on all or part of the **Wonderland Trail**, which makes an epic 93-mile (150-km) loop around Mount Rainier. Hailed as one of the premier trails in the National Parks System, it makes a rugged up-and-down passage through a variety of animal and plant communities, skirting glaciers, meadows, lakes and rivers over the course of a two-week hike.

From Longmire, the road continues along the **Nisqually River**, winding and switchbacking up the grade past **Christine Falls**, just one of several cascades in this area that send glacial runoff plunging down the mountain. You may notice that in places the water runs green; it's tinted with the powdery residue of glacier-ground bedrock. To the south you'll begin to see the jagged

A lynx pounces on a snowshoe hare.

peaks of the **Tatoosh Range**, a small mountain spur that outdates Rainier by about 30 million years. Keep your eyes peeled for **Ricksecker Point Road**, a short loop about 6 miles (10 km) from Longmire where you'll be treated to dazzling views of Nisqually Glacier clinging to Rainier's southern face. The icy juggernaut is slipping in your direction, but don't worry. In May 1970, Nisqually made one of the swiftest advances ever recorded – 29 inches (74 cms) in a single day.

Life in Paradise: As the road climbs into alpine meadows filled with a stunning array of wildflowers, you'll begin to understand why Martha Longmire, upon first seeing the area in 1885, proclaimed: "This must be what Paradise is like!" **Paradise** is crosshatched with trails that are perfect for an afternoon or a full day of hiking. If you plan on staying longer, consider making reservations (as much as a year in advance) at the historic **Paradise Inn**, a rustic gem built of local cedar in 1917. Stop briefly at the **Henry M. Jackson Memorial Visitor Center** (open from May to mid-October, depending on the weather) to see exhibits on natural history, buy books and maps, and check on the schedule of ranger-guided nature walks.

If you want to start with an easy hike, the self-guiding **Nisqually Vista Trail** makes a 1-mile (1½-km) loop past glorious splashes of Indian paintbrush, shooting star, mountain daisy, monkeyflower and dozens of other wildflowers that follow the retreating melt line up the slope, sometimes popping right through the snow. The 1½-mile (2-km) **Alta Vista Trail** is also quite manageable, meandering through summer wildflowers to a view of Rainier's explosive southern neighbor, **Mount Saint Helens**, some 45 miles (72 km) away. For a tougher hike, the **Skyline Trail** makes a 5-mile (8-km) loop to 6,800-ft (2,073-m) **Panorama Point**, where you'll enjoy spectacular views of Nisqually Glacier with the Cascade Range trailing off into the southeast. The 5-mile (8-km) **Lakes Trail** leads to **Reflection** and **Louise** lakes, placid tarns that, on still days, reflect Rainier as well as any mirror.

Wherever you hike in this area, be sure to tread lightly. Alpine plants are easily damaged by careless feet, so stay on designated trails at all times.

Paradise is also a staging area for most attempts on Mount Rainier's summit. The first well-documented ascent was completed by Hazard Stevens and P.B. Van Trump in 1870, although curious Indians may have done it earlier. John Muir made the climb in 1888, and **Camp Muir**, a climber's outpost, is named in his honor.

These days, about 3,000 climbers reach the summit every year. The 18-mile (29-km), two-day trek is extremely strenuous and potentially life-threatening. More than 50 people have died on Mount Rainier; many were unprepared for the physical hardships and extreme weather, or were simply inexperienced. If you would like to make the climb, the Parks Service strongly recommends contacting **Rainier Mountaineering**, a climbing school and outfitting service based in Paradise.

Sunrise: From the **Jackson Visitor**

A climber contemplates Rainier's grandeur.

Center, the road loops around Paradise Valley and then runs past Reflection Lake along the base of the Tatoosh Range, which cradles the glistening waters of **Bench** and **Snow** lakes at its feet. Here, as elsewhere, the fishing is nothing to write home about. The park doesn't stock its lakes, and the native trout offer pretty slim pickings.

The road enters the sheer, glacier-carved walls of **Stevens Canyon**. At the end, a short nature trail leads to the **Box Canyon** gorge, a narrow slot about 100 ft (30 m) deep sliced out of the rock by the **Muddy Fork of the Cowlitz River**. About 10 miles (16 km) farther, a second nature trail, the **Grove of the Patriarchs**, loops beneath a canopy of ancient cedar, hemlock and fir, some as much as 1,000 years old. Turn left at the Stevens Canyon Entrance and swing north on Highway 123 beneath **Shriner** (which has a steep trail leading to a fire tower), **Double** and **Buell** peaks. Continue north on Highway 410 at **Cayuse Pass** and then take the first left toward the **White River Entrance** on a wind-ing mountain road that quickly climbs above the timberline. Notice the stunted growths of whitebark pine. Although only a few feet tall, they may be centuries old. Again, it's imperative to tread lightly here. A few missteps can cause damage that takes years to heal.

At an elevation of 6,400 ft (1,951 m), the **Sunrise Visitor Center** (open from early July to mid-September, weather permitting) offers a breathtaking entree to lush wildflower meadows and an intimate look at Rainier's ice cap. The closest is **Emmons Glacier**, the largest in the contiguous United States. Take an easy walk on **Emmons Vista Trail** for the best views. The **Sourdough Mountain Trail** is about 1½ miles (2 km) long and steep in places, but a wonderful introduction to the plant life on the drier side of the mountain. Hardier hikers can climb into alpine tundra on the 7-mile (11-km) **Burroughs Mountain Trail**. If snow remains, only hikers experienced with an ice axe and crampons should attempt the slippery slopes. Check trail conditions before leaving the visitor center.

Finally, if you really want to get off the beaten path, consider the **Carbon River** region in the park's far northwestern corner. Take Highway 165 about 17 miles (27 km) from the town of Wilkeson and then, upon entering the park, a 6-mile (10-km) unpaved road leading to **Ipsut Creek Campground**. This is where you can start lengthy day hikes into a rare hinterland of temperate rain forest, or take overnight trips to **Mowich**, **Eunice** or **James** lakes or to the foot of **Carbon Glacier**. Here, high above the craggy **Goat Island Rocks**, is the headwall of a glacial cirque known as **Willis Wall** that attracts legions of rock climbers.

About 5,000 years ago, an event known as the Osceola Mudflow swept a 70-ft (21-m) deep wall of debris many miles beyond the park's northern boundary. The scar can still be seen. A similar mudflow devastated Kautz Creek, near the Nisqually Entrance, in 1947 – a powerful reminder that even in the absence of volcanic activity, the forces of nature are still at work at Mount Rainier.

Left, the White River courses below Rainier's glacier-clad slopes.

THE BATTLE FOR ANCIENT FORESTS

How do we use something and yet manage, somehow, to preserve it at the same time? That is the big question at the heart of a fierce battle being waged over the Pacific Northwest's old-growth forest.

The battle pits loggers against environmentalists, and there seems to be little middle ground. At the center of the controversy is an unlikely culprit, the diminutive Northern spotted owl, which was declared a threatened species in 1990. Biologists say that the reason for the bird's decline is the loss of habitat. The owl requires the type of multi-layered canopy and diverse ecology found only in ancient forests – pristine woods that have never been cut, with trees 200 or 300 years old or more.

Most environmentalists argue that there is more at stake than a single bird. As they see it, the owl is an "indicator species" whose threatened status signals the destruction of the entire ecosystem. In fact, only about 10 percent of old-growth forest remains in the lower 48 states, much of it on federally held land. And while national parks and wilderness areas are protected from logging, national forests are not. In 1991, a federal judge restricted most timber sales in the Northwest's national forests until the Forest Service, the timber industry and environmentalists could come up with a plan to protect the owl.

For loggers, the ban meant major job losses. Jobs in the timber industry had been on the decline throughout the 1980s owing largely to automation and a trend toward processing logs overseas rather than at local mills. Logging towns were hard hit. Unemployment approached double digits, and a variety of social ills – including suicide, teen pregnancy, runaway children and spouse abuse – were on the rise. Loggers weren't simply losing jobs but an entire way of life. And their frustration was plain to see in the slogans that began popping up on T-shirts and bumper stickers: "Save a logger – kill an owl. I love spotted owls...fried. If it's hooting, I'm shooting."

In 1993, after a so-called Timber Summit in Portland, Oregon, a compromise plan was unveiled that has temporarily cooled the rhetoric on both sides but is wholly satisfactory to neither. The policy reduces the sale of old-growth timber to less than one-third the amount sold in the 1980s and establishes protection zones around critical watersheds and stands of ancient forest. It also provides a $1.2 billion package to help logging communities make the transition to a more diversified economy.

The measure will no doubt cost both jobs and precious acres of old-growth forest. But for the time being, both sides are trying to get the most out of the compromise and are preparing themselves for future confrontations. In northern California, for example, environmentalists are trying to prevent a timber company from cutting a privately-owned forest of old-growth redwoods. Efforts are also being made to restrict timber sales from Alaska's vast Tongass National Forest. Even old growth in the eastern states is coming under scrutiny. In the end, industry, government and environmentalists will have to devise ever more innovative plans to preserve the health of both the environment and the economy. ∎

Rallying to support the old-growth forests.

CRATER LAKE

Crater Lake has been called "the bluest lake on earth" and "the shimmering jewel of the Cascades." It's a picture of nature in repose, a lake so round, so blue, so perfectly tranquil that it seems unearthly. Its waters are cupped like a chalice offered to the sky. Stars reflect on its surface like a thousand torches.

How odd, then, that such an enchanting place, such flawless composure, is the byproduct of a violent explosion. It occurred some 7,700 years ago when **Mount Mazama** erupted and collapsed. The event was catastrophic, filling nearby canyons with hundreds of feet of ash and sending debris as far downwind as Alberta, Canada. The 1980 eruption of Mount Saint Helens pales by comparison.

Underworld spirits: According to a Klamath Indian legend, Mazama's demise was caused by a fierce battle between Llao and Skell, the spirits of the underworld and sky. Spurned by a human woman, Llao rushed to the peak of Mount Mazama and rained fire on her people in punishment. Skell took pity on the humans and, after an earthshaking confrontation, drove Llao back into the bowels of the volcano and buried him under a torrent of rock and flame.

Geologists tell a similar story in a slightly more dispassionate way. Like other volcanic peaks in the Cascade Range, they say, Mazama is the product of a tectonic process known as subduction that causes the ocean floor to be forced under the North American plate. As the ocean bedrock is driven deeper into the earth, it's transformed by heat and pressure into molten magma which, in some cases, wells up to the surface in great gushes of mountain-building, or mountain-destroying, lava and ash. The eruption probably lasted only a few days, but so much magma was ejected from reservoirs beneath Mount Mazama that its walls buckled inward, leaving a gaping maw.

Heavy snow and rain blowing in from the Pacific Ocean took about 800 years to fill the caldera, which, at a depth of 1,932 ft (589 m), now contains the deepest freshwater lake in the United States. A few small eruptions have followed the collapse, and several warm springs continue to flow far below the lake's surface. But in recent years, Mazama has remained relatively quiet. Not dead, geologists warn, just sleeping.

Today, Crater Lake sits at the bull's-eye of Oregon's only national park, created in 1902 at the urging of William Gladstone Steel. An indefatigible campaigner, Steel became enchanted by the lake as a schoolboy after reading about it in a newspaper that was wrapped around his lunch. Thanks to William Steel's enthusiasm, the lake is circled by a lovely 33-mile (53-km) road known as **Rim Drive**, which is punctuated by more than two dozen scenic overlooks and several trailheads.

Taking Rim Drive at a leisurely pace, with time set aside for a picnic and a few hikes, requires a full day, although determined motorists can make the circuit in just a few hours. **Rim Village**, on the

Preceding pages: painting near Mount Hood. **Left**, blasted by snow. **Right**, mountain lions occasionally pass through the Crater Lake region.

southwest side of the caldera, is the center of tourist activity. Stop first at the **visitor center** for a selection of books and maps, and to inquire about free campfire talks and ranger-led nature walks, and then take a quick stroll to the **Sinnott Memorial Overlook**, where sweeping views will help you get a feel for the lay of the land.

The caldera is ringed with a thick blanket of conifers that drop to the water's edge and envelop the mountain in every direction but north, where the ash-smothered **Pumice Desert** remains stark and treeless. A few of Mazama's sister peaks, including **Mount Scott** and **Union Peak**, flank the caldera, and 9,182-feet (2,800-m) **Mount Thieleon** towers to the north.

Driving north from the visitor center, high above the lake's surface, you'll encounter several landmarks. The first, **Discovery Point**, is believed to be the spot where, in 1853, the first white men – a group of prospectors searching for the fabled "Lost Cabin" gold mine – set eyes on the lake, which they promptly

named Deep Blue Lake. About 2 miles (3 km) up the road, a second peak, the 8,025-feet (2,446 m) **Watchman**, towers over the caldera. A short, steep trail leads to a fire tower atop the peak, affording the best views on the western shore. With binoculars in hand, you'll see scores of soaring birds in summer and autumn, such as falcons, hawks and, if you're lucky, bald or golden eagles.

Almost directly north, **Hillman Peak** is one of Mazama's ancient volcanoes, now sheared in half by the mountain's collapse. Farther along the caldera wall, a formation known as the **Devil's Backbone** – a wall, or dike, of volcanic rock – juts into the water. Beyond that, **Llao Rock** is an ancient lava flow that hangs from the rim. Keep your eyes open for protected peregrine falcons who build aeries in the cracks and overhangs.

The most prominent landmark on this stretch of the rim is **Wizard Island**, a cone-shaped "volcano within a volcano." It rises more than 700 ft (213 m) above water level like a wizard's cap.

A western tiger swallowtail on a penstemon blossom.

The **Wizard Island Overlook** offers the best view. If time allows, you can also catch a tour boat to the island from **Cleetwood Cove** on the northeast lakeshore. The mile-long trail from **Cleetwood Cove Overlook** to the boat landing is extremely steep. While it may seem like an easy walk on the way down, the hike up is another matter. If you are in poor health, or simply out of shape, you may not want to try it. Then again, it's not every day you can climb into the mouth of a volcano.

Boats to Wizard Island leave hourly from 10am to 4.30pm between late June and mid-September. A park naturalist leads the tour. Along the way, you may spot waterfalls cascading toward the lake, cormorants and gulls skimming the water, a bald eagle circling over the cliffs, or a variety of migratory waterfowl bobbing peacefully on the surface. On the island, the fairly strenuous **Wizard Island Summit Trail** leads about a mile to its crater, which stands at an elevation of 6,940 feet (2,115 m). Tree-ring dating suggests that the waterlocked cinder cone is certainly more than 4,000 years old.

Back on the road, the eastern side of the lake features three extraordinary viewpoints. The first, **Skell Head**, is an ancient volcanic formation that bulges toward the water. About 2½ miles (4 km) farther on, a steep, 2½-mile trail climbs to the summit of 8,926-ft (2,721-m) **Mount Scott**, the park's highest peak. The footpath makes a switchback ascent through dense stands of subalpine fir and scattered clusters of wildflowers before rising above the timberline, where bleached and gnarled whitebark pine manage to eke out an existence under brutal conditions. The trees may look no bigger than bushes but are often hundreds of years old.

Mount Scott is easily the finest visual perch in the park. Keep your eyes peeled for red-tailed hawks, golden eagles and other raptors who soar on the air currents that curl up the mountain like invisible waves.

Just beyond the Mount Scott trailhead, a spur road leads to **Cloudcap**, the high-

Bunches of rabbitbrush on the edge of the caldera.

est overlook on the rim, where you can get good views of **Phantom Ship**, an island of tough volcanic rock that pokes through the surface just offshore. For a closer look, stop at **Kerr Notch**, a classic U-shaped valley carved by glaciers well before Mazama's catastrophic eruption. If time allows, you can pick up the 7-mile (11-km) spur road that shoots out to the **Pinnacles**, spiky, fang-like formations – some 100 feet (30 m) tall or more – that have eroded out of a bed of volcanic ash.

Return to Rim Drive and turn left. The last leg of the journey takes you past **Videa Falls**, where you can picnic next to a stepped 100-ft (30-m) cascade. About 3 miles (5 km) farther on, the **Castle Crest Wildflower Trail** takes you on a half-mile stroll through a medley of blossoming flowers – lupines, shooting stars, paintbrushes, phlox, gilias and others – during the summer months. Interpretive signs point out the names of species that grow beneath the cool understory of old-growth fir and hemlock as well as those that prefer the sunny meadows. A variety of hummingbirds summer in this area, and you can often see or hear them zipping through the underbrush, busily collecting nectar.

Beyond the rim: The park doesn't end with Rim Drive. There are several areas outside the caldera perimeter that are well worth a visit. And it's here that you're most likely to catch a glimpse of the park's shy wildlife, including elk, black-tailed deer, pronghorn and black bear. About 2 miles south of park headquarters, for example, the **Godfrey Glen Trail** makes an easy 1½-mile (2-km) loop through a dense stand of fir and hemlock that grows at the edge of a weirdly eroded canyon of volcanic ash. Just a bit farther down the road, at the **Mazama Campground**, 2-mile (3-km) **Annie Creek Trail** enters yet another canyon carved out of ancient beds of ash which are now embroidered with wildflowers. For longer hikes, a segment of the **Pacific Crest Trail** runs the length of the park, swerving around the lake to the west and then flanking the stark, ash-covered Pumice Desert, reclining beneath Mount Thielsen just north of the park boundary. Several spur trails make interesting side trips along the way. It takes two to three days, possibly more, to cover the entire 33 miles (53 km), but short stretches are accessible from Highway 62 west of Annie Spring Station and the North Entrance Road.

Free permits are required for overnight backcountry trips and may be obtained at the visitor center. Snowfall usually closes all or part of Rim Road between mid-October and late June, but cross-country skiing or snowshoeing can provide a magical way of seeing the lake and surrounding countryside. Fishing for non-native kokanee salmon and rainbow trout (there are no native fish in Crater Lake) is allowed at Cleetwood Cove and Wizard Island. A park motel, the Mazama Motor Inn, is open from May to October. The lovely old **Crater Lake Lodge** is scheduled to reopen in the summer of 1995 after extensive renovations. Mazama Campground offers spaces for tents and RVs on a first-come, first-served basis.

Left, a bald eagle snatches a fish. **Right**, view of Wizard Island from Hillman Peak.

ALASKA'S NATIONAL PARKS

There it stands, thrusting mightily against the sky. At 20,320 ft (6,194 m) above sea level, **Mount McKinley** is the perfect symbol of Alaska. In a land of superlatives and extremes, this granite monolith is the 49th state's most dominating feature.

It is also the centerpiece of **Denali National Park and Preserve**. Towering above its Alaska Range neighbors, McKinley – also commonly known by its Athapaskan name Denali, "The High One" – is a wild, desolate world of ice, snow and extreme cold, much different from the semi-wilderness that most park visitors experience.

McKinley's great height, combined with its sub-arctic location, makes it one of the coldest mountains on the planet. And the peak is so massive, it creates its own weather systems; some storms have produced winds greater than 150 mph (240 kph). No wonder McKinley has earned a reputation as the ultimate challenge in North American mountaineering. But the great peak's magnetism also tugs on those who'll never climb its slopes. Denali is the most popular of Alaska's federal parklands. And the majority of visitors have two main goals: first, to see McKinley; second, to see Alaska's wildlife.

Unfortunately, the chances of seeing the continent's highest peak are not very good. McKinley is visible only one out of every three days between Memorial Day and Labor Day, Denali's main tourist season. Opportunities to view wildlife are much greater, however. Nearly everyone who travels into the 6-million-acre (2-million-hectare) park sees at least one of Alaska's "big four": grizzly bear, Dall sheep, moose or caribou. Wolves have also become increasingly visible in recent years.

Abundant wildlife: It's not by chance that Denali offers such wildlife riches. Situated 120 miles (193 km) south of Fairbanks and 240 miles (386 km) north of Anchorage, the park was established in 1917 to protect the region's large mammals, especially Dall sheep, from hunting. Because wildlife viewing is a key ingredient of most people's "Denali experience," and because most visitors don't leave the park's single 97-mile (156-km) gravel road, travel restrictions have been enacted to ensure that uncontrolled traffic doesn't drive wildlife from the road corridor.

The large majority who "explore" Denali via the road system use the park's free shuttle-bus service. Shuttle buses begin leaving **Riley Creek Visitor Access Center** in early morning and continue on a regular schedule through mid-afternoon. Suggested items to bring: food, drink and warm clothes, none of which is available beyond the park entrance. Mid-summer temperatures range between 40°F (4°C) and 85°F (29°C).

Those seeking guided tours may travel on buses operated by a park concessionaire. Drivers describe the park's wildlife, plants, geology and history on six- to seven-hour excursions (advance reservations recommended).

Beyond the road corridor are millions of acres of scenic wildlands. Backcountry explorers wishing to camp overnight must obtain a permit, issued at the visitor center. Denali's backcountry areas have been divided into 43 units; most have visitor quotas to prevent crowding. Wilderness travelers are cautioned that backcountry trips require careful planning and a knowledge of bears, minimum-impact camping, river crossings, route finding, and wildlife-viewing ethics.

The park also has six road-accessible campgrounds. In peak season, they fill quickly. Lodging is also available at the **Denali Park Hotel**, or outside the park at hotels and campgrounds along the Parks Highway.

Accessible by railroad, bus or private vehicle, Denali National Park is often filled to overflowing in July and August, and visitors who haven't made advance reservations should allow themselves at least two days to get a campsite or shuttle seat. Registration for shuttle-bus seats and campground sites can be made in person at the visitor center, or can be reserved in advance. For more

Preceding pages: a polar bear mother with yearling cubs. Left, horned puffin.

information on shuttle buses, camping permits, backcountry travel and naturalist programs, you should contact the park headquarters.

New discovery: Less than a decade ago, **Wrangell–St Elias National Park and Preserve** was an overlooked and undervalued mountain wilderness. Created in 1980, our nation's largest park – at 13 million acres (5 million hectares), the size of six Yellowstones – was also one of its least known. But some time in the late 1980s, Wrangell–St Elias was "discovered." And Kit Mullen, a park staffer from 1981 to 1992, guesses that this park abutting the Canadian border "will become the next Denali, in terms of visitor use. There's so much access, probably more than any other national park in Alaska; you've got two roads into the park and airstrips all over."

The northern entry is the 45-mile (72-km) long **Nabesna Road** (only the first 30 miles/48 km are fit for two-wheel-drive vehicles) which connects Alaska's highway system with the tiny mining community of Nabesna. But the principal avenue into Wrangell–St Elias is **McCarthy Road**. Sixty miles (97 km) long and also unpaved, it stretches from Chitina, at the park's boundary, to the gateway community of **McCarthy**. (To enter McCarthy, visitors must leave their vehicles and cross the Kennicott River on hand-pulled trams.)

The number of people funneled down McCarthy Road has grown exponentially in recent years, from 5,000 in 1988 to more than 20,000 in 1992. Overall park visitation has approached 50,000 – less than one-tenth of Denali's total, but a significant threefold jump from the early 1980s.

Only a small percentage of those who drive along McCarthy Road actually visit the park's awesome backcountry. Most are content to spend time in McCarthy – for decades a haven for Alaskan recluses, but now a tourist town – hike to the nearby **Kennicott** and **Root** Glaciers, or travel the 4½ miles (7 km) to the historic and now abandoned Kennicott copper-mining camp.

But the park's real treasures lie be-

Ice cave, Wrangell-St Elias National Park.

yond such roadside attractions, in a wild and magnificent alpine world that guide Bob Jacobs calls "North America's mountain kingdom."

It's a kingdom that includes four major mountain ranges and six of the continent's 10 highest peaks, including 18,008-ft (5,489-m) **Mount St Elias**. Here too is North America's largest sub-polar icefield, the **Bagley**, which feeds a system of gigantic glaciers; one of those, the **Malaspina**, is larger than Rhode Island. Rock walls rise thousands of feet above glacially carved canyons, like the **Chitistone** and **Nizina**. And rugged, remote coastline is bounded by tidewater glaciers and jagged peaks. The park's alpine superlatives, along with those of neighboring **Kluane National Park** in Canada, have prompted their combined designation as a World Heritage site.

There's a certain irony to the newfound interest in Wrangell–St Elias: much of what's been "discovered" by modern-day explorers was known to local residents centuries ago. One of the park's

best-known overland routes, the primitive and rugged **Goat Trail**, was traditionally used by Athapaskan people for hunting and trading.

Most of Wrangell-St Elias' natural wonders are inaccessible to those who remain along the road system. Air-taxi services provide transportation into the park and guide outfits offer river rafting, climbing and trekking opportunities. Increasingly popular are "flightseeing" tours out of McCarthy or communities that neighbor Wrangell–St Elias. There are accommodations at both McCarthy and Kennicott and a wilderness lodge is located in the backcountry, but park facilities are minimal.

Kenai Fjords: The third (and only other) federal parkland connected to Alaska's highway system is 580,000-acre (234,718-hectare) **Kenai Fjords National Park**, located on the Kenai Peninsula in south-central Alaska. As its name suggests, this unit is dominated by coastal fjords: long and steep-sided glacially carved valleys now filled with seawater, and accessible only by float-

An iceberg drifts through Kenai Fjords.

plane or boat. High above the rugged coastline is the 300-sq. mile (777- sq. km) **Harding Icefield**, whose eight tidewater glaciers calve icebergs into the fjords, creating thunderous booms audible 20 miles (32 km) away.

The best-known fjord is **Aialik Bay**, simply because it's the closest to the park's entryway, **Seward**. A favorite of sea kayakers, Aialik and neighboring **Harris Bay** are also visited daily by commercial tour boats, weather and seas permitting, during the summer. Only rarely explored, the park's outer fjords are ideally suited to wilderness travelers seeking solitude.

Though they barely touch the tip of the park's coastal wilderness, full-day boat tours nevertheless offer quite a show: calving glaciers, rugged scenery and abundant marine life. There are whales, porpoises, sea otters, sea lions, seals and thousands of seabirds.

Despite all of Kenai Fjord's coastal splendors, its chief attraction is an inland, road-accessible glacier about 130 miles (209 km) by road from Anchorage.

In 1993, about two-thirds of the park's 185,000 visitors traveled the 9-mile (14-km) gravel road (open to vehicles from late May to early October) to **Exit Glacier**. A gentle trail leads to the glacier's snout, while a steeper trail follows the glacier's edge and allows visitors to peer into caverns beneath the ice and hear its groaning movements.

Like most Alaska parks, Kenai Fjords has few visitor amenities but does feature a limited number of facilities both along the road system and in the backcountry. Headquarters is based in Seward (which also has full tourist accommodations) and a small walk-in campground is located near Exit Glacier. Four rustic public-use cabins – they must be reserved well in advance – are located at Aialik Bay, Holgate and North Arms and Delight Beach. A fifth cabin, for winter use only, is located near Exit Glacier. A variety of nature walks and interpretive programs are provided daily from the Memorial Day weekend to Labor Day.

Lake Clark: With abundant wildlife

Bleached elk bones...

344

and wilderness that seems to stretch forever, **Lake Clark National Park and Preserve** epitomizes wild Alaska. Indeed, this 4-million-acre (2-million-hectare) unit may be the quintessential Alaskan parkland. Within its boundaries lie two active volcanoes, including one that erupted in 1989. The cliffs along its rugged coastline serve as rookeries for multitudes of seabirds. Two major mountain systems, the **Aleutian** and **Alaska** ranges, join to form the **Chigmit** and **Neocola** mountains, whose pristine snowcapped peaks are mostly unclimbed.

The park also embraces a remarkably diverse mix of plant communities: from coastal rain forest to boreal forest typical of interior Alaska, and several varieties of tundra. Those ecosystems support more than 100 species of birds and nearly 40 species of mammals.

Several river and lake systems, including three designated wild rivers, offer world-class fishing. And Lake Clark's recreational opportunities appeal to a wide variety of user groups, from hunters and anglers to river runners, kayakers, hikers, mountaineers and wildlife enthusiasts.

Adding to the park's appeal is its close proximity to two population centers, Anchorage and the western Kenai Peninsula. Located on the western side of **Cook Inlet**, Lake Clark can easily be reached by air from several different communities: Anchorage, Kenai, Homer and Iliamna.

Here, then, is a national park with fantastic scenery, easy access and diverse recreational opportunities. Yet Lake Clark remains among Alaska's least appreciated national parks for a variety of reasons. First, it doesn't have a focus, like Katmai's bears, Denali's "High One" and wildlife viewing, or Kenai Fjords' Exit Glacier and coastal tours. Second, it's not accessible by road. Third, there's a lack of visitor facilities. Management's goal has been to keep development to a minimum; there's little apart from a field headquarters at Port Alsworth, a small community on the shores of 42-mile (68-km) long Lake Clark.

The Parks Service largely depends on the private sector to provide amenities. Several privately-owned wilderness lodges are located within, or near, Lake Clark, and more than three dozen guide services operate in the park. Those who explore the park on their own should be wholly self-sufficient and prepared for cool and often wet weather. Storms commonly delay backcountry flights, so it's best to have a flexible schedule.

Katmai: The ritual begins in early July, as thousands of bright, silvery sockeyes push upstream toward **Brooks Lake**. As they near their spawning grounds, the salmon face one final obstacle: 5-ft-(2-m) high **Brooks Falls**. It's not high enough to stop the fish, but it's enough to stall them.

Following the salmon to Brooks Falls is *Ursus arctos*, the brown bear. Coastal equivalents of grizzlies, brown bears are usually solitary animals. But here, in the presence of abundant salmon, they've learned to tolerate each other. As many as a dozen bears may gather at the falls in July, with 35 to 40 inhabiting

...**and mew gull feather.**

GRIZZLY BEARS

Alaska is often called the last stronghold of North America's grizzly bears, and for good reason: this is where *Ursus horribilis* has been given its last, best chance to survive. And thrive. Tens of thousands of grizzlies once roamed the lower 48 states. Now there are less than 1,000, distributed in isolated groups in Montana, Wyoming, Idaho and Washington.

In Alaska, meanwhile, the population of grizzlies and their coastal counterparts, brown bears, is estimated to be about 31,000. Powerful carnivores equipped to kill other large mammals, grizzlies deserve our respect. When surprised or threatened, they'll do whatever it takes to protect themselves. That may mean fleeing. Or attacking.

Bear attacks on humans are, in fact, quite rare. Yet grizzlies have been inaccurately portrayed as marauding and unpredictable killers. "We've been raised with an ingrained fear of bears that's out of proportion to reality," says an Alaska biologist, Mike McDonald. "We've been taught that if you see a bear, you're gonna get eaten."

Several precautions can be taken to minimize the chances of an unwanted encounter. Whenever possible, walk in open country, during daylight hours. When passing through forested areas or thick brush, make noise. Sing, talk loudly, clap your hands. Keep alert and look for signs of bears: fresh tracks, bear scat, claw marks on trees, matted vegetation or animal carcasses. And leave the family dog at home. Traveling in groups is recommended: no grizzly bear assault has ever been reported on a group of six or more people. Cook all meals away from tents, and hang food out of reach. After fishing, change clothes before entering your tent, and store the fish away from camp.

Garbage should be put in airtight containers and packed out. When establishing camp, stay away from trails and berry patches. And avoid areas where scavengers have gathered, or which smell rotten. A bear's food cache may be nearby.

If a bear is encountered, talk to it. But don't yell. "That might be interpreted as aggression," McDonald says. "For heaven's sake, don't growl." And don't run. In most instances, that's the worst thing you can do, because it will almost certainly trigger a bear's predatory instincts. When dealing with a sow and cubs, avoid getting between mother and young. As a general rule, bigger is better with bears. With two or more people, stand side by side, or stretch out a piece of clothing.

In forested areas, it may help to climb a tree. But know that young grizzlies can climb, and even adults can pull their way quite high. Learn to recognize when a bear is stressed. Warning signs include yawning, salivation, huffing, growling, flattened ears, stiff-legged walk, swatting vegetation or jaw popping. Many threatening displays end with a bear walking away. And even when a bear charges, most times it's a bluff. But if a grizzly does make contact, the best thing to do is play dead. Lie on your stomach, or curl into a ball, with hands behind the neck. And remain passive. The only time when playing dead isn't appropriate is when a bear shows predatory, stalking behavior. If you're certain you're being treated as prey, never play dead. But, fortunately, such occurrences are exceedingly rare. ■

Ursus horribilis, the grizzly bear.

the 1½-mile (2-km) long Brooks River drainage. The bears, in turn, attract humans. When bears are fishing, people can be found at the Brooks Falls viewing platform from dawn to dusk.

Located in 4-million-acre (2-million-hectare) **Katmai National Park and Preserve** 300 miles (483 km) southwest of Anchorage, Brooks Falls and nearby **Brooks Camp** have become one of Alaska's fastest-growing visitor destinations, thanks to increasingly abundant and easy-to-see bears. But only in the last decade has Katmai become renowned for its bears. For most of its existence, Katmai's primary appeals have been sportfishing and the **Valley of Ten Thousand Smokes**, formed in 1912 by a giant volcanic eruption.

The 1912 blast caused the collapse of Mount Katmai, devastated the surrounding landscape and created thousands of steaming fumaroles (only a few active vents remain). Scientific expeditions to the area led to the creation of Katmai National Monument in 1918; the monument, in turn, was enlarged and elevated to park status in 1980.

Katmai received little attention until entrepreneur Ray Petersen established five remote fishing camps within the unit during the 1940s. The largest was Brooks, where clients fished for rainbows and salmon and visited the valley.

Now, as then, Brooks Camp is Katmai's premier attraction. But bears, not fishing or volcanic devastation, are what lure most people. The majority fly in, using plane services based in **King Salmon**. Those who stay overnight use the park campgrounds or **Brooks Lodge** cabins. Reservations are essential for either. But a large and growing number of visitors are day-trippers who stay for only a few hours.

Beyond Brooks is the "unseen" Katmai: vast untrammeled wilderness that includes a multitude of destinations, from the Valley of Ten Thousand Smokes (daily bus tours offer sightseers a glimpse of the barren landscape) to glacier-covered mountains, the **Alagnak Wild River** and rugged fjord-like coastal areas. A Parks Service brochure, *Traveling the Katmai Backcountry*, is

available upon request. For more information about the park, call headquarters in King Salmon.

Glacier Bay: Much has changed since John Muir found an "icy wilderness unspeakably pure and sublime" during his 1879 visit to Glacier Bay. **Grand Pacific Glacier**, which carved the bay, has receded 20 miles (32 km). Cruise ships and tour boats annually bring more than 100,000 visitors. The bay, its glaciers, wildlife and surrounding landforms are now protected by 3-million-acre (1-million-hectare) **Glacier Bay National Park and Preserve**.

Yet for all its changes, Glacier Bay remains an icy wilderness still largely unspoiled and, by most standards, remote. Sixty miles (96 km) northwest of Juneau in Alaska's Panhandle, the park can be reached only by boat or plane. And except for a short stretch of road and limited facilities (including visitor center, campground, trail system, lodge and restaurant) at **Bartlett Cove**, Glacier Bay is undeveloped. It is, in essence, a backcountry "marine park" with

Mule deer buck.

a glacial landscape which is best explored by boat.

Sixty-two miles (100 km) long and surrounded by a horseshoe rim of mountains, Glacier Bay is best known for its 17 tidewater glaciers and whale watching. In summer, the bay is frequented by orcas, minkes and humpbacks. Porpoises, sea otters, sea lions, harbor seals and seabirds also populate its waters, while bears, wolves, moose and mountain goats inhabit its shores. The landscape also shows the stages of plant succession left by a retreating glacier: lush coastal forests give way to fields of willow and alder, soft shrubby mats and finally bare rock and blue ice.

The bay has about a dozen inlets or arms to explore – one reason it's considered a kayakers' paradise. But most visitors explore Glacier Bay in the comfort of cruise ships or charter boats, which make daily sightseeing trips. Reservations are advised.

Beyond Glacier Bay itself, the park encompasses miles and miles of rugged, rarely visited outer coastline. Inland are huge icefields, dozens of glaciers, legions of unnamed and unclimbed mountains and a portion of the spectacular **Alsek River**, born in neighboring British Columbia.

The best time to explore Glacier Bay is mid-May through mid-September, but visitors should come prepared for rainy, cool weather even in summer. Besides Bartlett Cove's facilities (*see page 347*), a variety of services are available at nearby **Gustavus**, which is just a 30-minute flight from Juneau.

Gates of the Arctic: In 1929, while exploring the North Fork of the Koyukuk River in Alaska's Brooks Range, wilderness advocate Robert Marshall encountered "a precipitous pair of mountains, one on each side" of the stream. The eastern peak Marshall named **Boreal Mountain**; its western neighbor he christened **Frigid Crags**. Together, they became the Gates of the Arctic.

A half-century later, in 1980, Boreal Mountain, Frigid Crags and several million acres of arctic landscape were forever protected in **Gates of the Arctic**

Dall sheep, Denali National Park.

National Park and Preserve. Four times larger than Yellowstone, Gates of the Arctic girdles the central **Brooks Range**, the Rocky Mountains' northernmost extension. Billed as America's "ultimate wilderness," the 8-million-acre (3-million-hectare) unit lies entirely above the Arctic Circle and has some of the continent's wildest, most fragile, ecosystems. Its forests, alder thickets and tundra are home to 36 species of mammals, including grizzly and black bears, wolves, moose, Dall sheep, caribou and wolverines.

Capping the range are wave upon wave of mountain ridges and jagged peaks – most of them nameless – that seem to stretch forever. The mountains are dissected by expansive U-shaped valleys that magnify the sense of wide-open spaces. Among the streams knifing through the park are six officially designated "wild rivers."

Chief visitor attractions include "the Gates," 8,510-ft (2,594-m) **Mount Igikpak**, **Walker Lake** and a group of towering granite spires called the **Arrigetch Peaks**. The spires were named by the Nunamuit Eskimos (Inuit), whose legends say the Creator placed his glove on the land as a reminder of his presence. The fingers of that glove are the Arrigetch, which means "fingers of the hand upright, or extended."

Since park managers are required to preserve Gates of the Arctic's primitive wildness, no maintained trails or other visitor facilities have been developed within its boundaries. The only easy access is by plane, though it's also possible to enter by boat, or walk in from the **Dalton Highway**, which roughly parallels the park's eastern edge. Most visitors fly into the park from **Bettles**, which is the regional supply center and ranger station site.

Visitors are warned that they should be "fully competent in outdoor skills" and totally self-sufficient. Minimum-impact camping is urged to protect the fragile environment. The best time to visit is from June through August. Even then, be prepared for occasional freezing temperatures. A few wilderness

Eielson Visitor Center and Mount McKinley.

lodges/cabins located within or near the park offer some degree of arctic comfort, and several locally based outfitters conduct guided trips.

Kobuk Valley: It's one of the strangest sights anywhere in America: sand dunes in arctic Alaska. Surrounded by more typical boreal forest, the 25-sq. mile (65-sq. km) **Great Kobuk Sand Dunes** are the provocative centerpiece of **Kobuk Valley National Park**.

At 2 million acres (1 million hectares), Kobuk Valley is one of Alaska's smallest national parks and almost certainly its least known. Centered around the Kobuk River Valley in northwest Alaska, it's accessible by either boat or air. Most visitors begin their trips in **Kotzebue**, an Eskimo village 75 miles (120 km) to the east.

Summer temperatures may exceed 90°F (32°C) in the ever-shifting dunes, made of ancient glacial sand carried to the Kobuk Valley by wind and water. They're most easily reached at their northern end, where they come closest to the **Kobuk River**. (Also within the park are two smaller dunes, the **Little Kobuk** and **Hunt River**.)

The Kobuk is the region's major travel corridor, for both humans and caribou. Its valley is an important fall and winter range for the Western Arctic caribou herd; the animals can be seen crossing the Kobuk River from late August through October, during their annual migration. Caribou are an important food source for the region's native residents, who have lived along the Kobuk for at least 12,000 years. Eskimos still hunt caribou at a well-known archaeological site called **Onion Portage**.

Bordering the Kobuk Valley on the north and south are the **Baird** and **Waring** mountains, respectively. Born in the Baird Mountains, the **Salmon River** flows through the park's eastern region; a wild and scenic river, it's popular with river floaters.

As at Gates of the Arctic, park facilities are minimal and visitors must be self-sufficient. For more details, contact the park headquarters in Kotzebue.

<u>**Right**</u>, humpback whale, Glacier Bay.

350

TRAVEL TIPS

Getting Acquainted

Time Zones

The continental US is divided into four time zones. From east to west, later to earlier, they are Eastern, Central, Mountain and Pacific, each separated by one hour. Most of Alaska is situated in the Alaska Time Zone, an hour earlier than the Pacific Coast. Hawaii is in the Hawaii Time Zone, which is two hours earlier than the Pacific Coast. Thus, when it is 8pm Greenwich Mean Time it is 3pm in New York City, 2pm in Chicago, 1pm in Denver, 12pm in Los Angeles, 11am in Anchorage and 10am in Honolulu.

National parks situated in the different time zones include:

Mountain Time Zone: Arches, Badlands, Bryce Canyon, Canyonlands, Capitol Reef, Carlsbad Caverns, Glacier, Grand Canyon, Grand Teton, Guadalupe Mountains, Mesa Verde, Rocky Mountain, Theodore Roosevelt, Wind Cave, Yellowstone and Zion.

Pacific Time Zone: Crater Lake, Death Valley, Joshua Tree, Lassen Volcanic, Mount Rainier, North Cascades, Olympic, Redwood, Sequoia-Kings Canyon, Yosemite.

Alaska Time Zone: Denali, Gates of the Arctic, Glacier Bay, Katmai, Kenai Fjords, Kobuk Valley, Lake Clark and Wrangell-St Elias.

Hawaii Time Zone: Haleakala and Hawaii Volcanoes.

In spring, many states move the clock ahead one hour for daylight savings. In fall, the clock is moved back one hour to return to standard time.

Climate

Climate in the national parks varies dramatically by region, season and elevation. Bad weather, including violent rain, snow, lightning or dust storms, can kick up unexpectedly. A change in elevation can cause temperatures to fall or rise by more than 20°F (7°C). It

may be warm and sunny in low-lying areas but frigid in the mountains. In some parks, daytime temperatures can top 90°F (32°C) and then plummet below freezing during the night. Similarly, a day may start clear and sunny but end with cold, drenching rain. Snowfall may close roads in some mountain parks as much as nine months a year. Flash floods may temporarily close roads in desert areas and can make hiking in canyons and other low-lying areas dangerous.

It is imperative to call the parks in advance for up-to-date weather, road and trail conditions. For specific weather information, *see* the separate park listings.

Best Time to Visit

The parks – especially the popular mountain parks – tend to be crowded in summer. Traffic jams, inadequate parking and crowded facilities are common at Grand Canyon, Yellowstone, Yosemite, Mount Rainier and many other parks during the peak of the season. To beat the rush, consider visiting in late spring or early fall. The weather may not be quite as balmy, there may even be snow on the ground, but it's worthwhile to see the parks without the crowds. Weekends are the busiest times, so try to visit on weekdays. Some park roads and most trails may be closed in winter, but snowshoeing, cross-country skiing and other winter activities are often permitted and give visitors a unique perspective on the parks.

In desert parks such as Death Valley, Joshua Tree, Organ Pipe Cactus, Saguaro, Carlsbad Caverns, Guadalupe Mountains and Big Bend, fall, spring and winter are the busy seasons. With summer temperatures in excess of 100°F (38°C), it is too hot to do much sightseeing or hiking.

Planning the Trip

Clothing

Weather can change unpredictably in any season, so be prepared for just about anything. The best plan is to dress in layers that can be pulled off or put on as conditions dictate. Bringing rain gear is always a good idea.

If you plan on hiking any distance, consider investing in a sturdy pair of hiking boots. Properly broken in, they will save painful blisters and protect your feet from bumpy trails, jagged rocks, cacti, thorns and other hazards. Two pairs of socks – a polypropylene inner and a heavy outer – will also help keep your feet dry and comfortable.

Day hikers should also consider bringing a small waistpack (or, in American parlance, "fanny pack") to carry essentials. A checklist of necessary items includes a compass, map, guidebook, flashlight, sunglasses, pocket knife, lighter, candle, water bottle, high-energy food, water-purification tablets, first-aid kit, hat, sweater and rain gear. A high-SPF sunblock is a good idea, too, even if the day starts out cloudy. The sun can be merciless, especially in desert areas where there is little shade.

Electrical Adapters

Standard American electric current is 110 volts. An adapter is necessary for European appliances, which run on 220–240 volts.

Film

A variety of 35mm, 110 and cartridge films are available in most grocery stores, pharmacies and convenience stores. Concessionaires in most of the larger parks carry film, although many smaller parks or parks without concessionaires do not, and the film you buy may be more expensive than if you purchased it elsewhere. Call ahead to be sure. If you need professional-quality photographic equipment or film, consult the local telephone directory for the nearest camera shop. If you don't have a camera, consider the relatively inexpensive disposable cameras that are now available at many supermarkets, pharmacies and convenience stores.

Maps

Free maps of the national parks are available from the National Park Service regional offices or directly from the parks themselves (see listings for telephone numbers and addresses). Free city, state and regional maps as well as up-to-date road conditions and other valuable services are also available to members of the Automobile Association of America. If you plan on driving any distance, the service is well worth the price of membership. Free maps may also be available from state tourism bureaus (see listings).

High-quality topographical maps of the national parks and other natural areas are available from **Trails Illustrated**, PO Box 3610, Evergreen, CO 80439, tel: 800-962-1643 or tel: 303-670-3457. Topographical maps are also available from the **US Geological Survey**, PO Box 25286, Denver Federal Center, Denver, CO 80225, tel: 303-236-7477.

Entry Regulations

Passports & Visas

A passport, a visitor's visa and evidence of intent to leave the US after your visit are required for entry into the US by most foreign nationals. Visitors from the United Kingdom and several other countries (including but not limited to Japan, Germany, Italy, France, Switzerland, Sweden and the Netherlands) staying less than 90 days may not need a visa if they meet certain requirements. All other foreign nationals must obtain a visa from the US consulate or embassy in their country. An international vaccination certificate may also be required depending on your country of origin.

Exceptions are Canadians entering from the western hemisphere, Mexi-

cans with border passes, and British residents of Bermuda and Canada. Normally, these travelers do not need a visa or passport, although it's best to confirm visa requirements before leaving your home country.

Once admitted to the US, you may visit Canada or Mexico for up to 30 days and re-enter the US without a new visa. If you lose your visa or passport, arrange to get a new one at your country's nearest consulate or embassy. For additional information, contact the US consulate or embassy in your country or the US State Department in Washington, DC, tel: 202-663-1225.

Customs

All people entering the US must go through Customs. Be prepared to have your luggage inspected and keep the following guidelines in mind:

1. There is no limit to the amount of money you can bring into the US. If the amount exceeds $10,000 (in cash and other negotiable instruments), however, you must file a special report with customs.

2. Any objects brought for personal use may enter duty-free.

3. Adults may enter with a maximum of 200 cigarettes or 50 cigars or 2 kilograms of tobacco and/or 1 liter of alcohol duty-free.

4. Gifts valued at less than $400 can enter duty-free.

5. Agricultural products, meat and animals are subject to complex restrictions; to avoid delays, leave these at home unless absolutely necessary.

6. Illicit drugs and drug paraphernalia are strictly prohibited. If you must bring narcotic or habit-forming medicines for health reasons, be sure that all products are properly identified, carry only the quantity you will need while traveling, and have either a prescription or a letter from your doctor.

For additional information, contact US Customs, 1301 Constitution Ave NW, Washington, DC 20229, tel: 202-927-6724.

Extensions of Stay

Visas are usually granted for six months. If you wish to remain in the country longer than six months, you

must apply for an extension of stay at the **US Immigration and Naturalization Service**, 2401 E St, Washington, DC 20520, tel: 202-514-4330.

Money Matters

Credit Cards and ATMs: Major credit cards are widely accepted at shops, restaurants, hotels and gas stations, although not all cards are accepted by every vendor. To be safe, try to carry at least two kinds. Major credit cards include American Express, Visa, MasterCard, Access, Carte Blanche, Discover and Diners Club. Some credit cards may also be used to withdraw cash from automatic teller machines (ATMs) located in most larger towns and cities. Out-of-town ATM cards may also work. Check with your bank or credit card company for the names of the systems your card will operate.

Money may be sent or received by wire at any **Western Union** office (tel: 800-325-6000) or **American Express Money Gram** office (tel: 800-543-4080).

American Currency & Exchange

American money is based on the decimal system. The basic unit, a dollar ($1), is equal to 100 cents. There are four basic coins, each worth less than a dollar. A penny is worth 1 cent (1¢). A nickel is worth 5 cents (5¢). A dime is worth 10 cents (10¢). And a quarter is worth 25 cents (25¢).

In addition, there are several denominations of paper money. They are: $1, $5, $10, $20, $50, $100 and, rarely, $2. Each bill is the same color, size and shape; be sure to check the dollar amount on the face of the bill.

It's advisable to arrive with at least $100 in cash (in small bills) to pay for ground transportation and other incidentals. It's always a good idea to carry internationally recognized traveler's checks rather than cash. Traveler's checks are usually accepted by retailers in lieu of cash. They can also be exchanged for cash at most banks. Bring your passport with you to the bank. Major credit cards are also a big help and will be necessary if you want to rent a car.

Foreign currency is rarely accepted

in the US. You can exchange currency at major big-city banks, hotels, international airports and currency-exchange offices.

Holiday closings vary from park to park. In most cases, park facilities are open every day except Christmas. They may be closed on Thanksgiving and New Year's Day, too. Generally speaking, wild areas never close.

Outside the parks, all government offices, banks and post offices are closed on public holidays. Public transportation usually runs less frequently on these days.

January 1:	New Year's Day
January 15:	Martin Luther King, Jr's Birthday
Third Monday in February:	Presidents' Day
Last Monday in May:	Memorial Day
July 4:	Independence Day
First Monday in September:	Labor Day
Second Monday in October:	Columbus Day
November 11:	Veterans Day
Fourth Thursday in November:	Thanksgiving Day
December 25:	Christmas Day

Getting There

Generally speaking, there is very little public transportation to or within the national parks. In order to see them conveniently, you must either travel by car or join a private bus tour.

By Air

If driving directly to the parks is impractical because of distance, the next best way to get there is to fly to a nearby city and rent a car. The major hubs closest to the western parks are:

Rocky Mountains: Billings-Logan, Missoula, Great Falls, Bozeman, Denver-Stapleton, Salt Lake City.

Inquire about connections to air terminals at Rapid City, South Dakota; Jackson Hole and Yellowstone, Wyoming; and Kalispell and Glacier Park, Montana.

Northwest: Portland, Seattle-Tacoma, Spokane.

Inquire about connections to air terminals at Medford, Oregon, and Port Angeles, Washington.

California: San Diego, Los Angeles, San Jose, Oakland, San Francisco.

Inquire about connections to air terminals at Palm Springs, Crescent City, Fresno, Vidalia and Merced, California.

Southwest: Albuquerque, Las Vegas-McCarran, Phoenix Sky Harbor, Tucson, El Paso, Salt Lake City.

Inquire about connections to air terminals at Moab, Bryce Canyon, St George and Cedar City, Utah; Flagstaff, Page and Grand Canyon, Arizona; Grand Junction, Colorado; and Cavern City, New Mexico.

By Train

Amtrak offers more than 500 destinations across the US, but it services only one national park directly. The Empire Builder between Chicago and Seattle stops seasonally at Glacier National Park. Other lines make stops near several parks where you can rent a car or arrange another mode of transportation. Generally speaking, the trains are comfortable and reliable, with lounges, restaurants, snack bars and, in some cases, movies and live entertainment.

Amtrak's **Southwest Chief** runs from Chicago to Los Angeles, with stops near park areas at Albuquerque and Gallup, New Mexico; Winslow, Flagstaff (Amtrak Thruway bus service to Grand Canyon) and Kingman, Arizona; and Barstow, California.

The **Sunset Limited** runs from Miami to Los Angeles, with stops near park areas at Alpine and El Paso, Texas; Deming, New Mexico; and Tucson and Phoenix (Amtrak Thruway bus service to Grand Canyon), Arizona.

The **California Zephyr** runs from Chicago to San Francisco, with stops near park areas at Denver and Grand Junction, Colorado; Thompson and Salt Lake City, Utah; Reno, Nevada; and Sacramento, California.

The **Pioneer** runs from Chicago to Seattle, with stops near parks at Denver, Colorado; Ogden, Utah; Pocatello, Idaho; and Tacoma, Washington.

The **Empire Builder** also runs from Chicago to Seattle, with stops near park areas at Williston, North Dakota;

Glacier Park, Montana; and Seattle, Washington.

The **Desert Wind** runs from Chicago to Los Angeles, with stops near park areas at Denver and Grand Junction, Colorado; Thompson and Salt Lake City, Utah; Las Vegas, Nevada; and Barstow, California.

The **Coast Starlight** runs from Seattle to Los Angeles, with stops near park areas at Tacoma, Washington; Klamath Falls, Oregon; Redding and Sacramento, California.

The **San Joaquins** line of the **California Corridor** runs from Oakland to Bakersfield, with stops near park areas at Merced (Amtrak Thruway bus service to Yosemite) and Fresno, California.

Be sure to ask about two- or three-stopover discounts, senior citizen and children's discounts, and Amtrak's special national parks vacation package. Tel: 800-USA-RAIL or your local Amtrack representative for detailed scheduling information.

By Bus

One of the least expensive ways to travel in America is by bus. The biggest national bus company is Greyhound (tel: 800-231-2222). The company routinely offers discounts such as a $99 go-anywhere fare and a $1 ticket for moms on Mother's Day. Call the Greyhound office nearest you for information on special rates and package tours. However, Greyhound generally does not service national parks. A car rental or other mode of transportation will be necessary from the major hubs.

By Car

Driving is by far the most flexible and convenient way of traveling to the national parks. Major roads are well-maintained, although backcountry roads in or near the parks may be unpaved. If you plan on driving into remote areas or will be encountering heavy snow, mud or severe weather, it's a good idea to use a four-wheel-drive vehicle with high chassis clearance and carry chains.

Your greatest asset as a driver is a good road map. These can be obtained from state tourism offices, gas stations, supermarkets and convenience stores. Although roads are maintained even in remote areas, it is advisable to listen to local radio stations and to check with highway officials or park rangers for the latest information on weather and road conditions, especially if you plan on leaving paved roads.

Driving conditions vary dramatically depending on elevation. During fall, winter and early spring, your car should be equipped with snow tires or chains, a small collapsible shovel, and an ice scraper. Also, be prepared for the extra time required to drive along winding, narrow mountain roads.

If you plan to drive in desert areas, carry extra water – at least 1 gallon (4 liters) per person per day. It's a good idea to take along some food, too. Flash floods may occur during the rainy season, from early summer to fall. Stay out of arroyos, washes and drainage areas.

Service stations can be few and far between in remote areas. Not every town will have one, and many close early. Check your gas gauge often. It's always better to have more fuel than you think you will need.

A word of caution: If your car breaks down on a back road, do not attempt to strike out on foot, even with water. A car is easier to spot than a person and gives shelter from the elements. Sit tight and wait to be found.

Finally, if you intend to do a lot of driving, it's a good idea to join the **American Automobile Association**. The AAA offers emergency road service, maps, insurance, bail bond protection and other services (AAA, 1000 AAA Drive, Heathrow, FL 32746, tel: 407-444-4300).

Car Rentals

National car rental agencies are located at all airports, cities and large towns. In most places, you must be at least 21 years old (25 in some states) to rent a car, and you must have a valid driver's license and at least one major credit card. Foreign drivers must have an international driver's license. Be sure that you are properly insured for both collision and personal liability. Insurance may not be included in the base rental fee. Additional cost varies depending on the car and the type of coverage, but usually ranges between $10 and $20 per day. You may already

be covered by your own auto insurance or credit card company, so be sure to check with them first.

It is also a good idea to inquire about an unlimited mileage package. If not, you may be charged an extra 10¢–25¢ or more per mile over a given limit. Rental fees vary depending on time of year, how far in advance you book your rental, and if you travel on weekdays or weekends. Be sure to inquire about discounts or benefits for which you may be eligible, including corporate, credit card or frequent-flyer programs.

Alamo: 800-327-9633
American International: 800-669-7312
Avis: 800-331-1212
Budget: 800-527-0700
Dollar: 800-800-4000
Enterprise: 800-325-8007
Hertz: 800-654-3131
National: 800-227-7368
Thrifty: 800-331-4200.

RV Rentals

No special license is necessary to operate a motor home (or recreational vehicle – RV for short), but they aren't cheap. When you add up the cost of rental fees, insurance, gas and campsites, you may find that renting a car and staying in motels or camping is less expensive. Keep in mind, too, that RVs are large and slow and may be difficult to handle on narrow mountain roads. If parking space is tight, driving an RV may be extremely inconvenient. Access to some park roads may be limited – call the parks in advance for details. For additional information about RV rentals, call the **Recreational Vehicle Rental Association**, tel: 800-336-0355.

Hitchhiking

Hitchhiking is illegal in many places and ill-advised everywhere. It's an inefficient and dangerous method of travel. In a word, don't do it!

Special Facilities

Traveling with Children

Children love the parks, but it is important to take precautions. First, take everything you need. Some parks are quite remote and supplies may be limited. If you need baby formula, special foods, diapers or medication, carry them with you. It's also a good idea to bring a general first-aid kit for minor scrapes and bruises. Games, books and crayons help kids pass time in the car. Carrying snacks and drinks in a day pack will come in handy when kids (or adults) get hungry and there are no restaurants or campsites nearby.

Inquire about campfire talks, guided nature tours and special children's programs. Rangers do a fine job of interpreting the natural and cultural features of the parks and kids usually find these presentations fascinating.

The parks can be dangerous. Children need close supervision. Ask a ranger if a specific trail or region is suitable for children. Are there steep slopes, cliffs, river crossings, other hazards? Is the trail too strenuous for a child? Are there special precautions in regard to wildlife?

Avoid dehydration by having children drink plenty of water before and during a hike, even if they don't seem particularly thirsty. Put a wide-brimmed hat and high-SPF (at least 30 SPF) on children to protect them from the sun. Don't push children beyond their limits. Rest often, provide plenty of snacks, and allow for extra napping.

Give yourself plenty of time. Remember, kids don't travel at the same pace as adults. They're a lot less interested in traveling from point A to point B than in exploring their immediate surroundings. What you find fascinating (a rare species of bird), they may find boring. And what they think is "really cool" (a bunch of ants in the parking lot), you may find totally uninteresting.

Disabled Travelers

The Park Service makes an effort to accommodate travelers with disabilities. Although accessibility varies from park to park, it's not unusual for visitor centers, exhibits, some campsites and short nature trails to be wheelchair-accessible. Braille and tape recordings may also be available in some parks. For information on handicapped accessibility, contact the parks directly (*see* listings) and ask for the accessibility coordinator.

Visitors with a permanent handicap can obtain a Golden Access Passport at any park. The passport entitles the holder and his or her party (so long as they ride in the same car) to free entry as well as a 50 percent discount on park facilities, tours and other services, except those offered by independent concessionaires.

For general information on travel for the handicapped, contact the **Moss Rehabilitation Hospital Travel Information Service**, 1200 West Tabor Road, Philadelphia, PA 19141, tel: 215-456-9600, TDD 215-456-9602, or **The Information Center for Individuals with Disabilities**, 27–43 Wormwood St, Boston, MA 02210, tel: 617-727-5540.

Good resources for handicapped travelers are *Access America Guides to the National Parks*, Northern Cartographic, Inc., PO Box 133 Burlington, VT 05402; *Access National Parks: A Guide for Handicapped Visitors*, Superintendent of Documents, US Government Printing Office, Washington, DC 20402.

Practical Tips

Weights & Measures

Despite efforts to convert to metric, the US still uses the Imperial System of weights and measures.

1 inch	=	2.54 centimeters
1 foot	=	30.48 centimeters
1 yard	=	0.9144 meter
1 mile	=	1.609 kilometers
1 pint	=	0.473 liter
1 quart	=	0.946 liter
1 ounce	=	28.4 grams
1 pound	=	0.453 kilogram
1 acre	=	0.405 hectare
1 sq. mile	=	259 hectares
1 centimeter	=	0.394 inch
1 meter	=	39.37 inches
1 kilometer	=	0.621 mile

1 liter	=	1.057 quarts
1 gram	=	0.035 ounce
1 kilogram	=	2.205 pounds
1 hectare	=	2.471 acres
1 sq. km	=	0.386 sq. mile

Security & Crime

Don't be lulled into complacency by the beautiful surroundings. Crime is on the rise in the highly-used national parks, but a few common-sense precautions will help keep you safe. For starters, don't carry large sums of cash or wear flashy or expensive jewelry. Keep them locked in your trunk or in a hotel safe. Lock unattended cars and keep your belongings in the trunk. If possible, travel with a companion.

If you are a witness to or victim of a crime, or need to report an emergency situation of any kind, immediately contact the nearest ranger or call park headquarters.

Firearms may not be carried into national parks unless they are completely broken down, unloaded and encased. They must be kept in your car and out of sight. Hunting is prohibited at all but a few special times and areas. Unless hunting is explicitly allowed by the park superintendent, assume that it is forbidden. Poaching is a federal offense and is severely punished by fines and/or prison.

Fishing may be allowed in some areas depending on the site and the season. Permits and state licenses may be required. Inquire in advance at park headquarters.

Backcountry permits are required in many parks. Speak with park rangers before heading into the backcountry.

A few parks have restrictions on carrying and/or drinking alcohol. Contact the park in advance if you intend on bringing alcohol. State and local liquor laws apply.

Business Hours

Standard business hours are 9am–5pm, Monday–Friday. Many banks open a little earlier, usually 8–8.30am, and nearly all close by 3pm (Friday at 6pm). A few have Saturday morning hours. Most stores keep weekend hours and may stay open late one or more nights a week.

Hours at park facilities vary from site to site and season to season. During peak months, park facilities tend to stay open from 8.30am–6pm, seven days a week. Hours may be limited during the off-season. Holiday closings, if any, may include Thanksgiving, Christmas and New Year's Day.

Tipping

As elsewhere, service industry personnel (but not National Park Service employees) who work in and around the parks depend on tips for a large part of their income. With few exceptions, tipping is left to your discretion; gratuities are not automatically added to the bill. In most cases, 15–20 percent is the going rate for tipping waiters, taxi drivers, and barbers. Porters and bellmen usually get about 75¢–$1 per bag, but never less than $1 total.

Media

Books and Magazines

The parks offer a variety of free flyers, brochures and maps. Additional books can be purchased at visitor centers or by contacting the parks' cooperating associations (*see* separate listings).

The following magazines often feature articles about the national parks, natural history, environmental issues and outdoor recreation:

Arizona Highways, 2039 West Lewis St, Phoenix, AZ 85009, tel: 602-258-6641.

Audubon, 700 Broadway, New York, NY 10003, tel: 800-274-4201.

Backpacker, Rodale Press, Inc., 33 E Minor St, Emmaus, PA 18098, tel: 800-666-3434.

National Geographic & ***National Geographic Traveler***, 1145 17th St NW, Washington, DC 20036, Tel: 800-638-4077.

National Parks, 1776 Massachusetts Ave NW, Suite 200, Washington, DC 20036, tel: 202-223-6722.

National Wildlife, 8925 Leesburg Pike, Vienna, VA 22184, tel: 800-432-6564.

Natural History, American Museum of Natural History, Central Park West at 79th Street, New York, NY 10024, tel: 800-234-5252.

Outside, 400 Market St, Santa Fe, NM 87501, tel: 800-678-1131.
Sierra, 730 Polk St, San Francisco, CA 94109, tel: 415-923-5653.

Postal Services

Even the most remote towns are served by the US Postal Service. Smaller post offices tend to be limited to business hours (9am–5pm, Monday–Friday), although central, big-city branches may have extended weekday and weekend hours.

Stamps are sold at post offices, and some convenience stores, service stations, hotels and transportation terminals, usually in vending machines.

For reasonably quick delivery at a modest price, ask for first-class or priority mail. Second- and third-class mail is cheaper and slower. For expedited deliveries, often overnight, try **US Express Mail** or one of several international courier services: **Federal Express** (tel: 800-238-5355), **DHL** (tel: 800-345-2727), **United Parcel Service** (tel: 800-272-4877) or other local services listed in the telephone directory.

Telephone, Telegram, Telex and Fax

Public telephones are located at many highway rest areas, service stations, convenience stores, bars, motels and restaurants. The quickest way to get assistance is to dial 0 for the operator; or if you need to find a number, call information, tel: 555-1212. Local calls can be dialed directly. Rates vary for long-distance calls, but they can also be dialed directly with the proper area and country code. If you don't know the codes, call information or dial 0 and ask for the international operator.

Make use of toll-free numbers (area code 800) whenever possible. For directory assistance on toll-free numbers, dial 800-555-1212. For personal calls, take advantage of lower long-distance rates on weekends and after 5pm on weekdays.

To dial other countries (Canada follows the US system), first dial the international access code 011, then the country code. If using a US phone credit card, dial the company's access number below, then 01, then the country code. Sprint, tel: 10333; AT&T, tel: 10288.

Country codes:

Australia	61
Austria	43
Belgium	32
Brazil	55
Costa Rica	506
Denmark	45
France	33
Germany	49
Greece	30
Hong Kong	852
Israel	972
Italy	39
Japan	81
Korea	82
Netherlands	31
New Zealand	64
Nigeria	234
Norway	47
Singapore	65
South Africa	27
Spain	34
Sweden	46
Switzerland	41
United Kingdom	44

Western Union (tel: 800-325-6000) can arrange telegram, mailgram and telex transmissions. Check the local phone directory or call information for local offices. Fax machines are available at most hotels and even some motels. Printers, copy shops, stationers and office-supply shops may also have them, as well as some convenience stores.

Embassies

Australia: 1601 Massachusetts Ave NW, Washington, DC 20036, tel: 202-797-3000.
Belgium: 3330 Garfield St NW, Washington, DC 20008, tel: 202-333-6900.
Canada: 501 Pennsylvania Ave NW, Washington, DC 20001, tel: 202-682-1740.
Denmark: 3200 Whitehaven St NW, Washington, DC 20008, tel: 202-234-4300.
France: 4101 Reservoir Road NW, Washington, DC 20007, tel: 202-944-6000.
Germany: 4645 Reservoir Road NW, Washington, DC 20007, tel: 202-298-4000.
Great Britain: 3100 Massachusetts Ave NW, Washington, DC 20008, tel: 202-462-1340.
Greece: 2221 Massachusetts Ave NW, Washington, DC 20008, tel: 202-667-3168
India: 2536 Massachusetts Ave NW, Washington, DC 20008, tel: 202-939-7000.
Israel: 3514 International Drive NW, Washington, DC 20008, tel: 202-364-5500.
Italy: 1601 Fuller St NW, Washington, DC 20009, tel: 202-328-5500.
Japan: 2520 Massachusetts Ave NW, Washington, DC 20008, tel: 202-939-6700.
Mexico: 1911 Pennsylvania Ave NW, Washington, DC 20006, tel: 202-728-1600.
Netherlands: 4200 Wisconsin Ave NW, Washington, DC 20016, tel: 202-244-5300.
New Zealand: 37 Observatory Circle NW, Washington, DC 20008, tel: 202-328-4800.
Norway: 2720 34th St NW, Washington, DC 20008, tel: 202-333-6000.
Portugal: 2125 Kalorama Road NW, Washington, DC 20008, tel: 202-328-8610.
Singapore: 3501 International Place NW, Washington, DC 20008, tel: 202-537-3100.
South Korea: 2600 Virginia Ave NW, Washington, DC 20037, tel: 202-939-5600.
Spain: 2375 Pennsylvania Ave NW, Washington, DC 20037, tel: 202-452-0100.
Taiwan: 4201 Wisconsin Ave NW, Washington, DC 20016, tel: 202-895-1800.

Special Tours & Tour Guides

The following organizations offer a variety of park tours. Some feature horseback riding, backpacking, field seminars, bird trips, skiing, river running, photography and other special activities:
American Wilderness Experience, PO Box 1486, Boulder, CO 80306, tel: 800-444-0099.
Canyonlands Field Institute, PO Box 68, Moab, UT 84532, tel: 801-259-7750.

Gray Line Worldwide Association, 13760 Noel Road, Dallas, TX 75240, tel: 800-243-8353

National Audubon Society, 613 Riversville Road, Greenwich, CT 06831, tel: 203-869-2017.

National Wildlife Federation, 8925 Leesburg Pike, Vienna, VA 22184, tel: 800-432-6564.

North Cascades Institute, 2105 Highway 20, Sedro Woolley, WA 98284, tel: 206-856-5700.

Olympic Park Institute, 111 Barnes, Port Angeles, WA 98363, tel: 800-775-3720

Sierra Club, 730 Polk St, San Francisco, CA 94109, tel: 415-776-2211.

Yellowstone Institute, PO Box 117, Yellowstone National Park, WY 82190, tel: 307-344-2294.

Yosemite Association, PO Box 230, El Portal, CA 95318, tel: 209-379-2646.

Useful Addresses

State Tourism Offices

See listings under *National Parks* for regional tourism offices or chambers of commerce.

Alaska Tourism, PO Box 110801, Juneau, AK 99811-0801, tel: 907-465-2010.

American Samoa Office of Tourism, PO Box 1147, Pago Pago, American Samoa 96799, tel: 684-699-9280.

Arizona Office of Tourism, 1100 W Washington St, Phoenix, AZ 85007, tel: 800-842-8257 or tel: 602-542-8687.

California Tourism, 801 K St, Suite 1600, Sacramento, CA 95814, tel: 800-462-2543 or tel: 912-322-2881.

Colorado Tourism Board, 1625 Broadway, Suite 1700, Denver, CO 80202, tel: 800-265-6723 or tel: 719-592-1939.

Hawaii Convention and Visitors Bureau, 2270 Kalakaua Ave, Suite 801, Honolulu, HI 96815, tel: 808-924-0266.

Idaho Travel Council, 700 W State St, Boise, ID 83720, tel: 800-635-7820 or tel: 208-334-2470.

Kansas Travel and Tourism, 700 SW Harrison, Suite 1300, Topeka, KS 66603-3712, tel: 800-252-6727 or tel: 913-296-2009.

Travel Montana, Department of Commerce, 1424 9th Ave, Helena, MT 59620, tel: 800-541-1447 or tel: 406-444-2654.

Nebraska Travel and Tourism, 700 S 16th, Lincoln, NE 68509, tel: 800-228-4307 or tel: 402-471-2998.

Nevada Tourism, Capital Complex, Carson City, NV 89710, tel: 800-237-0774 or tel: 702-687-4322.

New Mexico Tourism, Lamy Building, 491 Old Santa Fe Trail, Santa Fe, NM 87503, tel: 800-545-2040 or tel: 505-827-7400.

North Dakota Parks and Tourism, Liberty Memorial Building, State Capitol Grounds, 604 E Blvd, Bismark, ND 58505, tel: 800-435-5663 or tel: 701-224-2525.

Oregon Tourism Division, Economic Development Department, 775 Summer St NE, Salem, OR 97310, tel: 800-547-7842 or tel: 503-373-1276.

South Dakota Department of Tourism, 711 Wells Ave, Pierre, SD 57501, tel: 605-773-3301.

Texas Tourism, PO Box 12728, Austin, TX 78711, tel: 800-888-8839 or tel: 512-462-9191.

Utah Travel Council, Council Hall, Capitol Hill, Salt Lake City, UT 84114, tel: 800-200-1160 or tel: 801-538-1030.

Washington Tourism, PO Box 42500, Olympia, WA 98504-2500, tel: 800-544-1800 or tel: 206-586-2088.

Wyoming Division of Tourism, I-25 at College Drive, Cheyenne, WY 82002, tel: 800-225-5996 or tel: 307-777-7777.

Hiking and Camping

Environmental Ethics

The old saw is good advice: "Take nothing but pictures, leave nothing but footprints." The goal of low-impact/no-impact backpacking is to leave the area in the same condition as you found it, if not better. If you're camping in the backcountry, don't break branches, level the ground or alter the landscape in any way. Make fires in designated places only. Otherwise, use a portable stove. When nature calls, dig a hole 6 inches (15 cm) deep and at least 100 ft (31 meters) from water, campsites and trails. Pack out all trash, including toilet paper.

Hiking Plan

Avoid solitary hiking. The best situation is to hike with at least two other partners. If one person is injured, one member of the party can seek help while the other two remain behind. If you must hike alone, be sure to tell someone your intended route and time of return. Backcountry hiking may require a permit. Ask a ranger before setting out.

Camping Reservations

Most tent and RV sites in the national parks are available on a first-come, first-served basis. Arrive as early as possible to reserve a campsite. Camp grounds fill early during the busy summer season (spring, fall and winter in the desert parks). A limited number of campsites in the most popular parks can be reserved in advance (*see* park listings section). Fees are usually charged for campsites. Backcountry permits may be required for wilderness hiking and camping.

Wildlife

Never approach wild animals. Don't try to feed or touch them, not even the "cute" ones like chipmunks, squirrels and prairie dogs (they may carry diseases). Some animals, such as bison, may seem placid and slow-moving but will charge if irritated. People who have tried to creep up on bison or moose in order to get a better photograph have been seriously injured. Buy a telephoto lens.

Store your food in airtight bags or containers, especially in bear country. Hang food at least 15 ft (5 meters) above the ground and several hundred yards from camp. If you've been fishing, change clothes before bedding down for the night. Be careful with deodorants, colognes, perfumes and anything else that a bear might think has an interesting odor.

Pets

Except for guide dogs for the blind, pets are generally prohibited from park facilities, trails, campgrounds and backcountry areas. Leashes are required elsewhere. Some parks offer kennels. Inquire in advance.

Entrance Fees & Park Passports

Many parks charge an entrance fee which entitles you to enter and exit as much as you like for one week. US citizens 62 years or older (with appropriate identification) may obtain a **Golden Age Passport** at any park; the passport entitles the holder to free admission and a 50 percent discount on camping fees and cave tours except those offered by independent concessionaires.

If you plan on visiting several parks, consider buying a **Golden Eagle Pass**. It can be obtained at any park that charges an entrance fee or by mail from park headquarters or regional offices. The pass entitles the holder to free admission to all parks for a year.

Permanently disabled travelers may obtain a free **Golden Access Passport**. It entitles the holder to free admission to any park and a 50 percent discount on cave tours and camping fees except those offered by private concessionaires.

Health & Safety

Most accidents and injuries are caused by inattentive or incautious behavior. You may be on vacation but your brain shouldn't be. Pay attention to where you are and what you are doing. Keep your eyes on the road when driving. If you want to gaze at the scenery, use an overlook or pullout. Better yet, get out of the car and walk. Don't take unnecessary chances on the trail. You have nothing to prove to yourself or your companions. Heed all posted warnings and, when in doubt, seek the advice of rangers.

Fitness & Altitude Sickness

Use common sense. Don't attempt trails that are too strenuous for your level of fitness. Ask rangers how long and steep the trail is before beginning. You may want to "warm up" on a shorter, less strenuous trail before starting a long hike.

Concentrate on what you're doing and where you're going. Even well-trod and well-marked trails can be dangerous. Be careful near cliffs, rocky slopes, ravines, rivers and other hazards. Don't attempt anything you're not comfortable with or anything that's beyond your level of skill.

Air is thinner at higher elevations. Unless properly acclimated, you may feel uncharacteristically winded. If you experience nausea, headache, vomiting, extreme fatigue, lightheadedness or shortness of breath, you may be suffering from altitude sickness. Although the symptoms may appear to be mild at first, they can develop into a serious illness. You should return to a lower elevation and try to acclimate gradually.

Water

It's always a good idea to carry a little more water than you think you'll need. The rule of thumb is 1 gallon (4 liters) a day per person, more in extreme conditions. Drink at least a quart at the start of a hike, and prevent dehydration by drinking at regular intervals while you're on the trail even if you don't feel particularly thirsty. Don't wait until you've become dehydrated before you start drinking!

All water taken from natural sources must be purified before drinking. *Giardia* is found in water (even crystal-clear water) throughout the West and can cause severe cramps and diarrhea. The most popular methods of purifying water are using a water-purification tablet, a water-purification filter (both available from camping supply stores) or by boiling water for at least 15 minutes.

Foot Care

Even if you plan to do only short day hikes, it's worthwhile investing in a sturdy pair of hiking shoes or boots. Consider buying them a half or full size larger then usual and be sure to break them in properly before arriving. A thin, inner polypropylene sock and a thick, outer sock will help keep your feet dry and comfortable. If blisters or sore spots develop, quickly cover them with moleskin, available at just about any pharmacy or camping supply store.

Sunburn

Protect yourself from the sun by using a high-SPF sunscreen and wearing a wide-brimmed hat and sunglasses, even if the day starts out cloudy. Avoid hiking during the midday hours.

Lyme Disease

Lyme disease is carried by tiny ticks no larger than a poppy seed. To protect yourself from ticks, wear long pants tucked into your socks and a long-sleeved shirt. Insect repellent will help, too. Check your body after hiking. If you find a tick, remove it carefully; don't try pulling it out, as the head will stay in. If you develop a rash (look for the classic bull's-eye pattern), run a fever or suffer other flu-like symptoms within several weeks, consult a physician immediately.

Frostbite & Hypothermia

Hypothermia – the potentially fatal loss of core body temperature – is preventable. First, dress appropriately. It's best to dress in layers so that you can take clothes off or on as required. The first layer should be made of fabrics that keeps moisture away from the skin such as silk, wool or synthetics. Avoid being both cold and wet. Bring along extra layers in case you get soaked. Keep your body well fueled and hydrated with food and water. Be prepared to turn back or seek shelter if weather turns bad. Keep in mind that it doesn't have to be freezing to get hypothermia.

The telltale signs of hypothermia are extreme shivering, loss of coordination and inability to reason (an outdoor writer calls these symptoms "the umbles," or stumbling, fumbling, mumbling). If a member of your party is hypothermic, set up camp and establish a stable, warm environment as quickly as possible. Put up a tent, build a fire or light a portable stove. Remove the victim's wet clothes and put him or her into a prewarmed sleeping bag. Try to reduce all heat loss from wind or moisture. If conscious, have the victim drink sweet, warm fluids. Remember, if one person is hypothermic, others may be too. Check all members of your party for symptoms of hypothermia.

Frostbite occurs when living tissue freezes. Symptoms include numbness, pain, blistering and whitening of skin. The most immediate remedy is to put frostbitten skin against warm skin. Simply holding your hands for several minutes over another person's frostbitten cheeks or nose, for example, may be sufficient. Otherwise, immerse frostbitten skin in warm (not hot) water. Refreezing will cause even more damage, so get the victim into a warm environment as quickly as possible. Again, if one person is frostbitten, others may be too. Check all members of your party for frostbite.

Swimming

Even the strongest swimmers can drown. Check with park rangers before swimming in any body of water. Strong currents and cold water can quickly overcome even an experienced swimmer. Wear a life vest when boating, and avoid hypothermia by staying out of frigid water.

National Park Service

The National Park Service is administered by the Department of the Interior. For general information about the parks, contact the **Office of Public Inquiries, National Park Service**, PO Box 37127, Washington, DC 20013; tel: 202-208-4747.

Information is also available from the appropriate regional offices:
Midwest Region, National Park Service, 1709 Jackson St, Omaha, NE 68102-2571, tel: 402-221-3471.
Rocky Mountain Region, National Park Service, 12795 Alameda Parkway, Lakewood, CO 80228, tel: 303-969-2000.
Southwest Region, National Park Service, PO Box 728, Santa Fe, NM 87504-0728, tel: 505-988-6016.
Western Region, National Park Service, 600 Harrison St, Suite 600, San

Francisco, CA 94107, tel: 415-744-3929.
Pacific Northwest Region, National Park Service, 909 First Ave, Seattle, WA 98104-1060, tel: 206-220-4013.
Alaska Region, National Park Service, 2525 Gambell St, Anchorage, AK 99503, tel: 907-257-2696.
National Trails System Branch, National Park Service, 1800 N Capitol St, Suite 490, Washington, DC 20013-7127, tel: 202-343-3780.

Other wilderness and public land areas are administered by:
Bureau of Land Management, Department of the Interior, 1849 C St NW, Washington, DC 20240, tel: 202-208-5717.
Fish and Wildlife Service, US Department of the Interior, 1849 C St NW, Washington, DC 20240, tel: 202-208-5634.
Forest Service, Department of Agriculture, 14th and Independence Ave SW, Agriculture Building, Washington, DC 20250, tel: 202-205-8333.

Accommodation

The price guide indicates approximate room/cabin rates:
* $50 or less
** $50–$100
*** $100–$150
**** $150+

CALIFORNIA & PACIFIC ISLANDS

AMERICAN SAMOA

THE NATIONAL PARK
OF AMERICAN SAMOA

c/o Pacific Area Office, PO Box 50165, Honolulu, HI 96850, tel: 684-699-9280 (Samoa Office of Tourism).
Access: Flights from Honolulu to Pago Pago on American Samoa's largest is-

land, Tutuila. Connecting flights from Pago Pago to smaller islands of Ofu and Aunu'u.
Seasons & Hours: The park is open year-round.
Entrance Fee: No.
Handicapped Access: No.
Activities: Wildlife-watching, backpacking, swimming, scuba diving.
Visitor Facilities: There are no facilities in the park. Information is available at the regional office in Honolulu and at American Samoa Office of Tourism, PO Box 1147, Pago Pago, American Samoa 96799, tel: 684-699- 9280.
Camping: None.
Permits & Licenses: Visitors must first get permission to enter the park. Contact regional park office or Samoa Office of Tourism.
Accommodations: None in the park. Lodging is available in Pago Pago. Contact American Samoa Office of Tourism, PO Box 1147, Pago Pago, American Samoa 96799, tel: 684-699-9280.
Food & Supplies: There is no food service or supplies in the park.
Weather: Expect hot, rainy, tropical weather year-round.
General Information: Established on 1988, the park's 9,000 acres (3,600 hectares) encompass pristine rain forest and coral reefs on three islands. The park is still being developed for travelers.

CALIFORNIA

CHANNEL ISLANDS NATIONAL PARK

1901 Spinnaker Drive, Ventura, CA 93001, tel: 805-658-5700.
Access: The islands can be reached by boat from park headquarters in Ventura. The authorized park concessionaire is Island Packers, 1867 Spinnaker Drive, Ventura, CA 93001, tel: 805-642-7688 or tel: 805-642-1393. For air transport, contact Channel Islands Aviation, 305 Durley Ave, Camarillo, CA 93010, tel: 805-987-1301. If possible, you should reserve well in advance. To visit Nature Conservancy lands on Santa Cruz, contact the Nature Conservancy, Santa Cruz Island Preserve, 213 Stearns Wharf, Santa Barbara, CA 93101, tel: 805-962-9111.
Seasons & Hours: Visitor center: daily 8am–5pm (extended hours in sum-

mer); closed Thanksgiving, Christmas and New Year's Day.

Entrance Fee: No, but concessionaire charges a fee for boat trips.

Handicapped Access: Visitor center.

Activities: Backpacking, camping, scuba diving, boating, wildlife-watching, interpretive programs.

Camping: Reservations and permits required.

Permits & Licenses: Free backcountry permits required. Private boaters may require a permit.

Accommodations: No lodging in park. Accommodations are available in Ventura. Contact Ventura Visitors & Convention Bureau, 89 C S California St, Ventura, CA 93001, tel: 800-333-2989.

Food & Supplies: Food and supplies are available in Ventura.

Weather: Summer is extremely dry, with temperatures usually 55°F–80°F (13°C–27°C). Winter temperatures usually 45°F–65°F (7°C–18°C). Expect windy conditions.

General Information: Backcountry users should carry all necessary food and water.

DEATH VALLEY NATIONAL PARK

Death Valley, CA 92328, tel: 619-786-2331.

Access: Death Valley is about 150 miles (241 km) from Las Vegas, Nevada. Follow I-95 north to Highway 373. Drive south to Death Valley Junction, then take Highway 190 into the park. If you're entering from California, enter the park on Highway 190 from the little town of Olancha or Highway 178 from Ridgecrest.

Seasons & Hours: The park is open daily year-round. The visitor center is open daily 8am–6pm, extended hours in winter.

Entrance Fee: Yes.

Handicapped Access: Visitor center, Salt Creek Nature Trail and some campsites.

Activities: Scenic drives, backpacking, camping, hiking, bicycling, wildlife-watching, interpretive programs, backcountry roads, golfing, riding.

Special Events: November: The Death Valley Encampment features special tours, presentations, art shows and other festivities.

March/April: Easter week is celebrated during the Spring Fling at Fur-

nace Creek Inn with Easter egg hunts, a parade and a golf tournament.

Camping: Some campsites may be reserved in advance; other sites are first-come, first-served. For reservations, contact Mistix, PO Box 85705, San Diego, CA 92186-5705, tel: 800-365-2267.

Permits & Licenses: Free backcountry permits are not required, but the park asks backcountry users to register at a nearby ranger station.

Accommodations: The Fred Harvey Company operates three lodges, ranging from a full-service resort to a modest motel:

*Furnace Creek Inn****.*

*Furnace Creek Ranch***.*

*Stovepipe Wells Village Motel***, PO Box 1, Death Valley, CA 92328, tel: 619-786-2361.

Make reservations well in advance. Additional lodging is available in Death Valley Junction, Trona and Beatty. Contact California Deserts Tourism Association, 37-115 Palm View Road, PO Box 364, Rancho Mirage, CA 92270, tel: 619-328-9256.

Food & Supplies: Restaurants and supplies are available in the park at Furnace Creek, Scotty's Castle and Stovepipe Wells.

Weather: Summer temperatures exceed 115°F (46°C) in the valley. Winter is milder, with snowfall in higher elevations. Flash floods can occur in any season.

General Information: Carry water for yourself and your car at all times. For people, carry at least a gallon (4 liters) per person per day. Do not underestimate the heat and aridity. Plan on visiting cooler, higher-elevation sites during summer. Flash floods are dangerous. Do not walk or drive in low-lying areas during or immediately after a rainstorm. Do not attempt to cross a flooded road. Abandoned mines are extremely dangerous. Contact rangers before entering.

DEVILS POSTPILE NATIONAL MONUMENT

PO Box 501, Mammoth Lakes, CA 93546, tel: 619-934-2289.

Access: The monument is about 13 miles (21 km) from Mammoth Lakes, California, along a winding narrow road. Follow Highway 395 south from Bridgeport or north from Bishop.

Seasons & Hours: The monument is open daily, mid-June–October. Call ahead to confirm opening.

Entrance Fee: No.

Handicapped Access: Visitor center.

Activities: Guided walks, hiking, camping, wildlife-watching, interpretive programs, fishing.

Camping: First-come, first-served.

Permits & Licenses: California fishing license.

Accommodations: None in the park. Lodging is available in Mammoth Lakes and Reds Meadow. Contact Mammoth Lakes Visitors Bureau, PO Box 48, Mammoth Lakes, CA 93546, tel: 800-367-6572.

Food & Supplies: None in the park. Restaurants and supplies are available in Mammoth Lakes and Reds Meadow.

Weather: The park is closed in winter. Expect cool nights and summer thunderstorms.

General Information: Located between Yosemite and Sequoia national parks, this 798-acre (333-hectare) park features dramatic basalt columns and a section of the John Muir Trail.

GOLDEN GATE NATIONAL RECREATION AREA

Fort Mason, Building 201, San Francisco, CA 94123, tel: 415-556-0560.

Access: The park is located at the headlands of the Golden Gate in San Francisco and Marin County. It can be easily reached by car from Highway 101 or by public transportation.

Seasons & Hours: Most facilities are open daily, 10am–5pm; closed Thanksgiving, Christmas and New Year's Day.

Entrance Fee: For select tours and facilities.

Handicapped Access: Visitor center, Muir Woods Nature Trail and Alcatraz tour.

Activities: Hiking, wildlife-watching, interpretive programs, tours of Alcatraz, museum and historic ships.

Camping: First-come, first-served.

Permits & Licenses: No.

Accommodations: None in the park. Additional lodging is available throughout the Bay Area. Contact San Francisco Convention & Visitors Bureau, 201 Third St, Suite 900, San Francisco, CA 94103, tel: 415-974-6900.

Food & Supplies: Food service is available at some facilities and throughout the surrounding area.

Weather: Cool, foggy and breezy. Bring a sweater or jacket even in summer. Expect rain in winter and spring.

General Information: This urban park includes beaches, coastal wildlands, hiking trails, Alcatraz Island, military sites and Fort Mason cultural center.

JOSHUA TREE NATIONAL PARK

74485 National Monument Drive, Twentynine Palms, CA 92277, tel: 619-367-7511.

Access: The park is about 140 miles (225 km) east of Los Angeles. To enter from the north, take I-10 east to Palm Springs, then Highway 62 to either Joshua Tree or Twentynine Palms. To enter from the south, take I-10 east to the Cottonwood entrance.

Seasons & Hours: The park is open daily year-round. The visitor centers are open daily 8am–5pm; closed Christmas.

Entrance Fee: Yes.

Handicapped Access: Visitor centers, Cap Rock and Twentynine Palms Oasis nature trails.

Activities: Scenic drives, backpacking, camping, hiking, bicycling, rock climbing, wildlife-watching, interpretive programs, backcountry roads.

Camping: Some campsites may be reserved in advance; other sites are first-come, first-served. For reservations, contact Mistix, PO Box 85705, San Diego, CA 92186-5705, tel: 800-365-2267.

Permits & Licenses: Self-registration at backcountry clipboards. Contact park for details.

Accommodations: None in the park. Accommodations are available in Twentynine Palms, Joshua Tree, Yucca Valley, Palm Springs and Indio. Contact California Deserts Tourism Association, 37-115 Palm View Road, PO Box 364, Rancho Mirage, CA 92270, tel: 619-328-9256.

Food & Supplies: Restaurants and supplies are available in Twentynine Palms, Joshua Tree, Yucca Valley, Palm Springs and Indio.

Weather: Summer temperatures exceed 100°F (38°C). Winter lows 35°F–45°F (2°C–7°C).

General Information: Carry water for yourself and your car during hottest months. For people, carry at least a gallon (4 liters) per person per day. Do not enter abandoned mine shafts; they are extremely dangerous.

LASSEN VOLCANIC NATIONAL PARK

PO Box 100, Mineral, CA 96063, tel: 916-595-4444.

Access: The park is 48 miles (77 km) east of Redding via Highway 44, 51 miles (82 km) east of Red Bluff via Highways 36 and 89.

Seasons & Hours: The park is open daily year-round. Sections of Lassen Park Road are usually closed by snow November–May. The visitor center is open daily 9am–5pm; closed October–May.

Entrance Fee: Yes.

Handicapped Access: Visitor center and select campsites.

Activities: Scenic drives, backpacking, camping, hiking, cross-country skiing, snowshoeing, boating, wildlife-watching, interpretive programs.

Camping: Campsites are available May–September on a first-come, first-served basis.

Permits & Licenses: Free backcountry camping permits required.

Accommodations: *Drakesbad Guest Ranch* (rustic lodge and cabins)***, call long-distance operator and ask for Drakesbad #2. Reservations required.

Additional lodging is available in Mineral, Chester, Redding and Red Bluff. Contact Shasta Cascade Wonderland Association, 14250 Holiday Road, Redding, CA 96003, tel: 916-275-5555.

Food & Supplies: Limited food service and supplies are available at Manzanita Lake Campground. Additional services at Mineral, Chester, Red Bluff and Redding.

Weather: Summer temperatures usually 40°F–80°F (4°C–27°C), colder in higher elevations. Winter temperatures usually 15°F–45°F (–9°C–7°C), with abundant snowfall.

General Information: Stay on marked trails near hot springs and other geothermal areas. The ground may be thin and easily broken, causing severe burns. Thin air makes hiking in the high country difficult for lowlanders. Check road and weather conditions before visiting.

LAVA BEDS NATIONAL MONUMENT

PO Box 867, Tulelake, CA 96134, tel: 916-667-2282.

Access: The monument is off Highway 139 about 30 miles (48 km) from Tulelake, California, and 60 miles (96 km) from Klamath Falls, Oregon.

Seasons & Hours: The park is open daily year-round. The visitor center is open 8am–5pm, extended hours in summer; closed on Thanksgiving and Christmas.

Entrance Fee: Yes.

Handicapped Access: Visitor center and select campsites.

Activities: Backpacking, camping, hiking, caving, wildlife-watching, interpretive programs.

Camping: First-come, first-served.

Permits & Licenses: No.

Accommodations: None in the park. Additional lodging available in Tulelake and Klamath Falls. Contact Shasta Cascade Wonderland Association, 114250 Holiday Road, Redding, CA 96003, tel: 916-275-5555.

Food & Supplies: None in the park. Services are available in Tulelake and Klamath Falls.

Weather: Summer temperatures usually 40°F–85°F (4°C–29°C). Winter temperatures usually 15°F–40°F (–9°C–4°C). Freezing temperatures and snow are possible at any time.

General Information: Located in northern California near the Oregon border, this 46,600-acre (18,858 hectare) park preserves a rugged volcanic landscape where Modoc Indians clashed with the US Army in 1872–73. Notify rangers before exploring backcountry caves or lava tubes.

MUIR WOODS NATIONAL MONUMENT

Mill Valley, CA 94941, tel: 415-388-2595.

Access: The monument is off Highway 1 about 20 miles (32 km) north of San Francisco.

Seasons & Hours: Daily 8am–sunset.

Entrance Fee: Yes.

Handicapped Access: Facilities and many trails are wheelchair-accessible.

Activities: Hiking, wildlife-watching.

Camping: No.

Permits & Licenses: No.

Accommodations: None in the park. Lodging is available throughout the Bay Area. Contact San Francisco Convention & Visitors Bureau, 201 Third St, Suite 900, San Francisco, CA 94103, tel: 415-974-6900.

Food & Supplies: Limited food service in the park. Additional services throughout the Bay Area.

Weather: Cool, foggy and breezy. Bring a sweater or jacket even in summer. Expect rain in winter and spring.

General Information: This small park features a virgin stand of coastal redwoods and several easy walking trails.

PINNACLES NATIONAL MONUMENT

Paicines, CA 95043, tel: 408-389-4485.

Access: The west district of the monument is located off Highway 101 about 12 miles (19 km) east of Soledad. The east district is about 35 miles (56 km) south of Hollister via Routes 25 and 146. There is no connecting road between the two districts.

Seasons & Hours: The monument is open daily year-round; visitor centers are open daily 9am–5pm.

Entrance Fee: Yes.

Handicapped Access: Visitor centers and some campsites.

Activities: Hiking, camping, interpretive programs, wildlife-watching.

Camping: First-come, first-served.

Permits & Licenses: No.

Accommodations: None in the park. Lodging is available in Soledad, Hollister and Salinas. Contact Salinas Area Chamber of Commerce, PO Box 1170, Salinas, CA 93902, tel: 408-424-7611.

Food & Supplies: None in the park. Services are available in Soledad, Hollister amd Salinas.

Weather: Summer temperatures can exceed 100°F (38°C). Spring and fall are mild.

General Information: This 16,265-acre (6,582-hectare) park features dramatic rock spires more than 1,000 ft (305 meters) tall. Rock climbing and caving should be attempted by experienced people only. Be sure to carry an adequate supply of water.

POINT REYES NATIONAL SEASHORE

Point Reyes, CA 94956, tel: 415-663-1092.

Access: The seashore is about 45 miles (72 km) north of San Francisco via Highway 1.

Seasons & Hours: The seashore is open daily year-round. The visitor center is open 9am–5pm, closed Christmas.

Entrance Fee: No.

Handicapped Access: Visitor centers and some trails are wheelchair-accessible.

Activities: Hiking, camping, biking, horseback riding, fishing, interpretive programs, wildlife-watching.

Camping: By permit, contact park headquarters.

Permits & Licenses: Camping permit is required.

Accommodations: *Point Reyes American Youth Hostel**, PO Box 247, Point Reyes Station, CA 94956, tel: 415-663-8811.

Additional lodging is available in Olema, Inverness, Novato, Petaluma. Contact Petaluma Area Chamber of Commerce, 799 Baywood Drive, Petaluma, CA 94954, tel: 707-762-2785.

Food & Supplies: There is a restaurant at Drakes Beach. Additional services available in Point Reyes Station, Olema, Inverness, Novato, Petaluma.

Weather: Cool, extremely foggy and windy conditions at the beaches even in summer. Expect heavy rain in winter and early spring.

General Information: The park features long beaches, rugged coastal wildlands, excellent trails, a wide variety of bird life and offshore marine life, including a large colony of sea lions.

REDWOOD NATIONAL PARK

1111 Second Street, Crescent City, CA 95531, tel: 707-464-6101.

Access: The park is about 40 miles (64 km) north of Eureka and about 20 miles (32 km) south of Crescent City via Highway 101.

Seasons & Hours: The park is open daily year-round. Information centers are open daily 8am–5pm, closed Christmas and New Year's Day.

Entrance Fee: State park picnic areas only.

Handicapped Access: Information centers, Tall Trees shuttle bus and select trails.

Activities: Scenic drives, backpacking, camping, hiking, fishing, boating, wildlife-watching, interpretive programs.

Permits & Licenses: California fishing license and free backcountry camping permits required.

Camping: Campsites are available by reservation May–August, first-come, first-served at other times. Contact Mistix, PO Box 85705, San Diego, CA 92186-5705, tel: 800-365-2267.

Accommodations: None in the park. Lodging is available in Crescent City, Klamath and Eureka. Contact the Eureka/Humboldt Convention and Visitors Bureau, 1034 2nd St, Eureka, CA 95501-0541, tel: 707-443-5097.

Food & Supplies: Food service and supplies are available in Crescent City, Requa, Orick, Klamath and Eureka.

Weather: Temperatures vary depending on location. On the coast, summer daytime temperatures range 55°F–70°F (12°C–21°C), winter temperatures 30°F–40°F (–1°C–4°C). Inland, summer highs reach 80°F–100°F (27°C–38°C), winter lows dip below freezing. Expect heavy rain and fog October–April.

General Information: Access to the Tall Trees Grove is limited; summer shuttle bus transports visitors down the rugged 7-mile (11-km) road to the trailhead. Otherwise, a limited number of private-vehicle permits are distributed on a first-come, first-served basis. Swimming can be extremely dangerous. Ocean water is cold, currents are strong, and no lifeguards are on duty.

SANTA MONICA MOUNTAINS NATIONAL RECREATION AREA

30401 Agoura Road, Agoura Hills, CA 91301, tel: 818-597-1036.

Access: The park borders Los Angeles and can be reached on Highways 101 and 1.

Seasons & Hours: The park is open daily year-round. The visitor center is open daily 8am–5pm.

Entrance Fee: No.

Handicapped Access: Visitor center.

Activities: Hiking, swimming, wildlife-watching, interpretive programs.

Permits & Licenses: California fishing license.

Camping: By reservation, contact headquarters.

Accommodations: Lodging is available throughout Los Angeles area. Contact Los Angeles Convention & Visitors Bureau, 633 W 5th St, Suite 6000, Los Angeles, CA 90071, tel: 800-228-2452.

Food & Supplies: Available along the Pacific Coast Highway (Highway 1).

Weather: Summer temperatures normally 65°F–105°F (18°C–41°C), winter temperatures 35°F–75°F (2°C–24°C).

SEQUOIA AND KINGS CANYON NATIONAL PARKS

Three Rivers, CA 93271, tel: 209-565-3134.

Access: The south entrance of Sequoia is 35 miles (56 km) from Visalia via Highway 198. The Grant Grove entrance of Kings Canyon is 55 miles (89 km) from Fresno via Highway 180.

Seasons & Hours: The park is open daily year-round. Sections of the Generals Highway and side roads within the park are closed by snow in winter; tel: 209-565-3351 for road and weather conditions.

Entrance Fee: Yes.

Handicapped Access: Visitor centers, paved trails in Grant Grove and Giant Forest, select campsites.

Activities: Scenic drives, backpacking, camping, hiking, rock climbing, mountain climbing, fishing, cross-country skiing, wildlife-watching, interpretive programs, backcountry roads.

Special Events: April: The Jazz Affair in Three Rivers brings music-lovers to a little town just outside the park.

May: Red Bud Festival in Three Rivers is a two-day arts and crafts fair.

December: Caroling and ecumenical Christmas service at the base of the General Grant tree, known as the nation's Christmas tree.

Camping: Some campsites may be reserved in advance; other sites are first-come, first-served. For reservations, contact Mistix, PO Box 85705, San Diego, CA 92186-5705, tel: 800-365-2267. Sites fill early in summer.

Permits & Licenses: Free backcountry camping permits required; make reservations well in advance. California fishing license.

Accommodations: Guest Services manages accommodations in the parks, ranging from cabins to comfortable lodges:

Bearpaw Meadow Camp (cabins)*.
Giant Forest Lodge***.
Cedar Grove Lodge***.
Grant Grove Lodge (cabins)**.
Stony Creek Lodge***, PO Box A-GF, Sequoia National Park, CA 93262, tel: 209-561-3314.

Additional accommodations are available in Three Rivers, Visalia and Fresno. Contact the Visalia Chamber of Commerce, 720 W Mineral King, Visalia, CA 93291, tel: 209-734-5876.

Food & Supplies: Restaurants and supplies are available in the park at Giant Forest, Cedar Grove, Grant Grove and Lodgepole; outside the park in Three Rivers, Visalia and Fresno.

Weather: Summer temperatures 50°F–95°F (10°C–35°C), colder in higher elevations. Winter temperatures 15°F–45°F (–9°C–72°C), with abundant snowfall.

General Information: Thin air makes hiking in the high country difficult for lowlanders. If possible, give yourself several days to adjust. Rivers are cold and swift; use caution when hiking near waterways. Check road and weather conditions before visiting in winter.

WHISKEYTOWN-SHASTA-TRINITY NATIONAL RECREATION AREA

PO Box 188, Whiskeytown, CA 96095, tel: 916-241-6584.

Access: The three units of this recreation area can be reached via Highways 5 and 299 from Redding.

Seasons & Hours: The recreation area is open daily year-round. The visitor center is open seasonally, hours vary.

Entrance Fee: No.

Handicapped Access: Visitor center.

Activities: Backpacking, camping, hiking, fishing, boating, wildlife-watching, swimming, water-skiing, horseback riding, interpretive programs.

Permits & Licenses: Free backcountry permits.

Camping: Some campsites can be reserved in advance by contacting Mistix, PO Box 85705, San Diego, CA 92186-5705, tel: 800-365-2267. Other campsites available on a first-come, first-served basis.

Accommodations: None in the park. Lodging is available in Redding. Contact Shasta Cascade Wonderland Association, 14250 Holiday Road, Redding, CA 96003, tel: 916-275-5555.

Food & Supplies: Limited food service at Oak Bottom and Brandy Creek in summer. Additional services available in Redding.

Weather: Summer temperatures 50°F–100°F (10°C–38°C), colder in higher elevations. Winter temperatures 20°F–50°F (–7°C–10°C).

General Information: The park features backcountry forest and a wide variety of water sports. The Whiskeytown unit is administered by the National Park Service. The other two units are administered by the National Forest Service.

YOSEMITE NATIONAL PARK

PO Box 577, Yosemite National Park, CA 95389, tel: 209-372-0200.

Access: The park is about 75 miles (121 km) northeast of Merced via Route 140, about 100 miles (161 km) east of Modesto via Routes 108/120, about 65 miles (105 km) north of Fresno via Route 41, and 125 miles (201 km) south of Carson City, Nevada, via Highway 395 and Route 120. Yosemite Sightseeing (tel: 209-443-5240) offers bus service from Fresno and Merced. Yosemite Via (tel: 209-722-0366) offers bus service from Merced.

Seasons & Hours: The park is open daily year-round. Visitor centers are open daily in summer 8am–5pm, extended hours in some locations, reduced hours in winter. Tuolumne Meadows Visitor Center is open summer only. Tioga Road, Tuolumne Grove and Glacier Point Road are closed by snow mid-November–late-May.

Entrance Fee: Yes.

Handicapped Access: Visitor centers, nature center, art center and select trails and campsites.

Activities: Scenic drives, bus tours, backpacking, camping, hiking, fishing, boating, horseback riding, biking, swimming, float trips, cross-country skiing, ice skating, snowshoeing, art workshops, wildlife-watching, interpretive programs. Call Yosemite Mountaineering School for rock and mountain climbing instruction and guide service, tel: 209-372-1244.

Special Events: Jan-Chefs' Holidays bring well-known chefs to the Ahwahnee Hotel for a gourmet banquet and demonstrations.

November–December: Vintners' Holidays, wine-tasting and seminars at the Ahwahnee.

December: Yosemite Pioneer Christmas recreates an old-fashioned yuletide at Pioneer Yosemite History Center.

Permits & Licenses: California fishing license and free backcountry camping permits required.

Camping: Some campsites may be reserved in advance; other sites are first-come, first-served. For reservations, contact Mistix, PO Box 85705, San Diego, CA 92186-5705, tel: 800-365-2267. Sites fill early in summer.

Accommodations: The Yosemite Concessions Services Corp., 5410 East Home Ave, Fresno, CA 93727, tel: 209-252-4848, manages accommodations in the park ranging from cabins to full-service, historic hotels:

*The Ahwahnee****.*
*Curry Village**.*
*High Sierra Camps**.*
Tuolumne Meadows Lodge.*
*Wawona Hotel**.*
White Wolf Lodge.*
*Yosemite Lodge**.*

Additional accommodations are available in Lee, Vining, Groveland, El Portal, Oakhurst and Mariposa. Contact Yosemite Visitors Bureau, 49074 Civic Circle, Oakhurst, CA 93644, tel: 209-683-4636.

Food & Supplies: Food service and supplies are available in the park at Yosemite Valley, Wawona, Tuolumne Meadows and White Wolf.

Weather: Temperatures vary depending on location. In the valley, summer temperatures usually 50°F–95°F (10°C–35°C), winter temperatures 20°F–50°F (–7°C–10°C). Summer temperatures are considerably cooler in the high country, 30°F–70°F (–1°C–21°C). Expect summer thunderstorms, and heavy snowfall November–May.

General Information: Free shuttle bus service is available year-round in Yosemite Valley. Guided tours are offered by Concessions Services Corp., tel: 209-252-4848.

Hawaii

Haleakala National Park

PO Box 369, Makawao, HI 96768, tel: 808-572-9306.

Access: The main entrance of the park is about 19 miles (31 km) from Pukalani via Routes 377 and 378. The coastal Kipahulu District is about 15 miles (24 km) from Hana via Route 31.

Seasons & Hours: The park is open daily year-round. Headquarters is open daily 7.30am–4pm. House of the Sun

Visitor Center is open sunrise–2pm.

Entrance Fee: Yes.

Handicapped Access: Visitor center and park headquarters

Activities: Scenic drives, camping, hiking, backpacking, wildlife-watching, swimming, interpretive programs.

Permits & Licenses: Permits required for backcountry camping in Haleakala crater.

Camping: Sites available on a first-come, first-served basis. Three cabins (accessible by foot) in crater are also available by reservation (call headquarters); three nights a month limit.

Accommodations: None in the park. Lodging is available in Hana and Pukalani. Contact Maui Chamber of Commerce, 26 N Puunene Ave, Kahului, HI 96732, tel: 808-871-7711.

Food & Supplies: None in the park. Food and supplies are available in Hana and Pukalani.

Weather: Weather varies considerably depending on elevation. At the summit, summers are comfortable with periods of cool, gusty, wet weather. The Kipahulu District near Hana is warmer and more moderate but subject to heavy rains.

General Information: Thin air at high elevations can make hiking difficult. Come prepared for sudden changes in weather. Rain at higher elevations can cause streams to rise suddenly. Do not swim during high water.

HAWAII VOLCANOES NATIONAL PARK

PO Box 52, Hawaii National Park, HI 96718, tel: 808-967-7184.

Access: The Kilauea Visitor Center is 29 miles (47 km) southwest of Hilo and 82 miles (132 km) southeast of Captain Cook via Route 11.

Seasons & Hours: The park is open daily year-round. The visitor center is open daily 8am–5pm.

Entrance Fee: Yes.

Handicapped Access: Visitor center, museum, several overlooks and nature trails.

Activities: Scenic drives, camping, hiking, backpacking, wildlife-watching, interpretive programs.

Permits & Licenses: Backcountry camping permits required in certain areas.

Camping: First-come, first-served.

Accommodations: *Volcano House****,*

PO Box 53, Hawaii Volcanoes National Park, HI 96718, tel: 808-967-7321.

Namakani Paio Cabins,* PO Box 53, Hawaii Volcanoes National Park, HI 96718, tel: 808-967-7321.

Additional lodging is available in Volcano Village and Hilo. Contact Hawaii Island Chamber of Commerce, 180 Kinoole St, Suite 118, Hilo, HI 96720, tel: 808-935-7178.

Food & Supplies: There is a restaurant at Volcano House. Additional food and supplies available in Volcano Village and Hilo.

Weather: Summer highs in the low 80°F (27°C). Winter temperatures occasionally dip into the low 40°F (4°C). Be prepared for daily rain.

General Information: Stay on marked trails. Hardened lava flows are easily broken. Consult rangers before approaching active lava flows. For eruption information, tel: 808-967-7977.

ARIZONA

CANYON DE CHELLY NATIONAL MONUMENT

PO Box 588, Chinle, AZ 86503, tel: 602-674-5436.

Access: The visitor center is 3 miles (5 km) from Route 191 in Chinle.

Seasons & Hours: The monument is open daily year-round. The visitor center is open 8am–5pm; closed Christmas.

Entrance Fee: No.

Handicapped Access: Visitor center and some overlooks on scenic drive.

Activities: Wildlife-watching, hiking, horseback riding, jeep tours, interpretive programs, scenic drive.

Special Events: September: Navajo Nation Fair celebrates Navajo life and culture with food, dancing, rodeo, arts and crafts at Chinle.

Visitor Facilities: Visitor center.

Camping: First-come, first-served.

Permits & Licenses: Backcountry travel and camping with authorized guides only.

Accommodations: *Thunderbird Lodge***, PO Box 548, Chinle, AZ 86503, tel: 602-674-5841.

Motels and hotels available outside the park in Chinle, Kayenta, Window Rock and Gallup. Contact Navajoland Tourism, PO Box 663, Window Rock, AZ 86515, tel: 602-871-6659.

Food & Supplies: Restaurant and limited supplies are available in the park. A supermarket is located in nearby Chinle.

Weather: Summer is hot and dry with highs in the 90°F (32°); winter is cold with occasional snow; temperatures commonly dip below freezing.

General Information: Situated within the Navajo Nation and occupied by several traditional Navajo families, Canyon de Chelly National Monument encompasses four canyons: Canyon de Chelly, Monument Canyon, Canyon del Muerto and Black Rock Canyon. The park also features dramatic Anasazi ruins, including White House Ruin, Antelope House and Mummy Cave. Respect the privacy of resident Navajos. Their hogans, corrals and fields are off-limits. Disturbing ruins in any fashion is strictly prohibited.

CHIRICAHUA NATIONAL MONUMENT

Dos Cabezas Route, Box 6500, Willcox, AZ 85643, tel: 602-824-3560.

Access: The monument is 36 miles (58 km) south of Willcox. From I-10, take Highway 186 to Highway 181 to park entrance.

Seasons & Hours: Open daily year-round. The visitor center is open 8am–5pm; closed Christmas.

Entrance Fee: Yes.

Handicapped Access: Visitor center, Faraway Ranch.

Activities: Interpretive programs, hiking, camping, scenic drive, wildlife-watching.

Visitor Facilities: Visitor center.

Camping: First-come, first-served.

Permits & Licenses: No.

Accommodations: None in the park; hotels and motels are available in Willcox, contact Willcox Chamber of Commerce, 1500 N Circle I Road, Willcox, AZ 85643, tel: 602-384-2272.

Food & Supplies: None in the park;

restaurants and stores are available in Willcox.

Weather: Summer temperatures usually 70°F–95°F (21°C–35°C), cooler at high elevations; thunderstorms are common in summer. Winter temperatures often dip below freezing with highs in the upper 40°F (4°C) and occasional snowfall.

CORONADO NATIONAL MEMORIAL

4101 E Montezuma Canyon Road, Hereford, AZ 85615, tel: 602-366-5515.

Access: The memorial is 20 miles (32 km) south of Sierra Vista or 25 miles (40 km) west of Bisbee via Route 92.

Seasons & Hours: The memorial is open year-round; the visitor center is open 8am–5pm; closed Thanksgiving and Christmas

Entrance Fee: No.

Handicapped Access: No.

Activities: Interpretive programs, hiking, scenic drive.

Visitor Facilities: Visitor center.

Camping: No.

Permits & Licenses: No.

Accommodations: None in the park. Accommodations are available in Bisbee and Sierra Vista. Contact Sierra Vista Convention & Visitor Bureau, 77 S Calle Portal, Suite 140A, Sierra Vista, AZ 85635, tel: 800-288-3861 or tel: 602-458-6940.

Food & Supplies: None in the park; restaurants and stores are available in Bisbee and Sierra Vista.

Weather: Summer temperatures usually 70°F–90°F (21°C–32°C), cooler at high elevations; thunderstorms are common in summer. Winter temperatures occasionally dip below freezing, with highs near 50°F (10°C).

General Information: The 4,750-acre (1,922-hectare) memorial on the US–Mexican border commemorates the exploratory journey of Francisco Vasquez de Coronado into the Southwest in 1540–42, as well as the nation's Hispanic heritage.

GLEN CANYON
NATIONAL RECREATION AREA

PO Box 1507, Page, AZ 86040, tel: 602-645-2471.

Access: The main entrance is in Page on Route 89 in north central Arizona.

Backcountry areas can be reached via Route 276 and 95 in southeast Utah.

Seasons & Hours: The park is open year-round. The visitor center is open 8am–5pm, with extended summer hours; closed Christmas and New Year's Day.

Entrance Fee: No.

Handicapped Access: Visitor center.

Activities: Backpacking, wildlife-watching, interpretive programs, guided tours of Glen Canyon Dam, boating, water-skiing, fishing.

Visitor Facilities: Visitor center and marinas.

Camping: First-come, first-served.

Permits & Licenses: Arizona and/or Utah fishing licenses.

Accommodations: Lodging is available in the park at Wahweap, Bullfrog, Hall's Crossing and Hite. Lodging is also available in Page. Make reservations well in advance. Contact Page-Lake Powell Chamber of Commerce, PO Box 727, Page, AZ 86040, tel: 602-645-2741.

Food & Supplies: Food and supplies are available at Wahweap, Bullfrog, Hall's Crossing and Hite; restaurants and stores are also available in Page.

Weather: Summer temperatures can exceed 100°F (38°C), with sudden, violent thunderstorms. Spring and fall are generally mild. Occasional snowfall in winter.

General Information: Houseboat and motorboat reservations can be made by calling ARA Lake Powell, tel: 800-528-6154. Rainbow Bridge National Monument with the world's largest natural bridge (280 ft/85 meters) high, may be reached by boat from Wahweap, Bullfrog or Halls Crossing.

GRAND CANYON NATIONAL PARK

PO Box 129, Grand Canyon, AZ 86023, tel: 602-638-7888.

Access: Grand Canyon Village and the South Rim Visitor Center are about 85 miles (137 km) from Flagstaff, Arizona, via Highway 180/64. Although only a few miles across the canyon, the North Rim is about 215 road-miles (346 km) from Grand Canyon Village. Take Route 64 east to Cameron, Highway 89/Alt. 89 north to Jacob Lake, and then Route 67 south to the North Rim. Visitors can also arrive by air at the Grand Canyon National Park Airport, just outside the park in Tusayan, or by rail from Williams, Arizona, on the Grand Canyon Railway.

Seasons & Hours: The South Rim is open year-round; the visitor center is open daily 8am–5pm. The North Rim is open May–October.

Entrance Fee: Yes.

Handicapped Access: South Rim Visitor Center and some shuttle buses. Contact park for Accessibility Guide.

Activities: Scenic drive, backpacking, wildlife-watching, river trips, mule packing, fishing.

Special Events: September: Grand Canyon Chamber Music Festival.

Visitor Facilities: Visitor centers, ranger stations, Tusayan Museum.

Camping: Campsites on North and South Rim usually fill by noon May–September; 7-day limit. Some sites can be reserved in advance by contacting Mistix, PO Box 85705, San Diego, CA 92186-5705, tel: 800-365-2267. RV sites are available on South Rim year-round at Trailer Village, tel: 602-638-2401 for reservations.

Permits & Licenses: Arizona fishing license. Free backcountry permits can be obtained by mail from Backcountry Reservations Office, PO Box 129, Grand Canyon, AZ 86023, tel: 602-638-7888. Reserve well in advance; popular trails can fill up early.

Accommodations: Several hotels and lodges are managed by Grand Canyon National Park Lodges, PO Box 699, Grand Canyon, AZ 86023, tel: 602-638-2401.

> Bright Angel Lodge & Cabins*.
> El Tovar Hotel****.
> Kachina Lodge**.
> Maswick Lodge**.
> Phantom Ranch**.
> Thunderbird Lodge***.
> Yavapai Lodge**.

North Rim: Grand Canyon Lodge***, TW Services, Inc, PO Box 400, Cedar City, UT 84721, tel: 801-586-7686.

For additional information, contact Grand Canyon Chamber of Commerce, PO Box 3007, Grand Canyon, AZ 86023, tel: 602-638-2901.

Food & Supplies: Restaurants and a variety of stores are located in the park at Grand Canyon Village, Desert View and the North Rim; outside the park at Tusayan, Cameron, Tuba City and Flagstaff.

Weather: Weather varies dramatically depending on location in the park.

South Rim: 50°F–85°F (10°C–29°C) in summer, 20°F–40°F (–6°C–4°C) in winter. **North Rim:** 40°F–75°F (4°C–24°C) in summer, 15°F–40°F (–9°C–4°C) in winter. **Inner canyon:** 75°F–115°F (24°C–46°C) in summer, 35°F–60°F (2°C–16°C) in winter. For weather updates, tel: 602-638-7888.

General Information: The inner canyon is subject to extreme heat in summer. Hikers should carry adequate food and water, at least a gallon (4 liters) per person per day.

ORGAN PIPE CACTUS NATIONAL MONUMENT

Route 1, Box 100, Ajo, AZ 85321, tel: 602-387-6849.

Access: The monument is located on Route 85 on the US–Mexican border about 140 miles (225 km) west of Tucson and 135 miles (217 km) southwest of Phoenix.

Seasons & Hours: The monument is open year-round; the visitor center is open daily 8am–5pm.

Entrance Fee: Yes.

Handicapped Access: Visitor center, a nature trail and some campsites.

Activities: Scenic drive, backpacking, hiking, wildlife-watching, interpretive programs.

Visitor Facilities: Visitor center and museum.

Camping: First-come, first-served.

Permits & Licenses: Free backcountry permits required.

Accommodations: None in the park. Lodging is available in Lukeville and Ajo. Contact Ajo District Chamber of Commerce, 321 Taladro, Ajo, AZ, 85321, tel: 602-387-7742.

Food & Supplies: Available in Lukeville, Why and Ajo.

Weather: Summer temperatures exceed 100°F (38°C); thunderstorms are common. Scenic roads may be impassable during or after heavy rain. Do not attempt to cross flooded areas. Winter temperatures are mild and comfortable, usually 40°F–60°F (4°C–126°C).

General Information: Carry adequate water in your car and on hikes. A gallon (4 liters) per person per day is the recommended amount. Contact park headquarters for information about crossing into Mexico.

PETRIFIED FOREST NATIONAL PARK

PO Box 2217, Petrified Forest, AZ 86028, tel: 602-524-6228

Access: The park is located on I-40 about 26 miles (42 km) east of Holbrook and 22 miles (35 km) west of Chambers.

Seasons & Hours: The park and visitor center are open daily 8am–5pm in winter. Extended hours in other seasons – call the park for exact times. Closed Christmas and New Year's Day.

Entrance Fee: Yes.

Handicapped Access: Visitor center and museum.

Activities: Scenic drive, backpacking, wildlife-watching, interpretive programs.

Visitor Facilities: Painted Desert Visitor Center, Rainbow Forest Museum.

Camping: No campgrounds in park.

Permits & Licenses: Free backcountry permits required.

Accommodations: Available in Holbrook, Chambers, Gallup and Winslow. Contact Holbrook-Petrified Forest Chamber of Commerce, 100 E Arizona St, Holbrook, AZ 86025, tel: 602-524-6558.

Food & Supplies: Meals are offered in the park at Painted Desert Oasis. Restaurants and supplies available in Holbrook, Chambers, Gallup and Winslow.

Weather: Summer days are hot (near 100°F/38°C) and sunny, with occasional thunderstorms. Winter temperatures can drop below freezing.

General Information: Carry adequate water on hikes. A gallon (4 liters) per person per day is recommended. Leave petrified wood and other objects where you find them. Removing any natural object or artifact from the park is a federal offense.

PIPE SPRING NATIONAL MONUMENT

HC 65, Box 5, Fredonia, AZ 86022, tel: 602-643-7105.

Access: The monument is 14 miles (23 km) west of Fredonia, Arizona, via Route 389 and 38 miles (61 km) southeast of Hurricane, Utah, via Route 59.

Seasons & Hours: The monument is open daily year-round. The visitor center is open daily 8am–4.30pm; closed Thanksgiving, Christmas and New Year's Day.

Entrance Fee: Yes.

Handicapped Access: Visitor center.
Activities: Self-guided and ranger-led tours.
Visitor Facilities: Visitor center.
Camping: No campgrounds in park.
Permits & Licenses: No.
Accommodations: No lodging in park. Accommodations are available in Kanab, Fredonia, Hurricane and St George. Contact Washington County Travel Bureau, 425 S 700 East, St George, UT 84770, tel: 800-869-6635.
Food & Supplies: There is a snack bar in the park. Additional food and supplies are available in Kanab, Fredonia, St George and Hurricane. Contact Fredonia Chamber of Commerce, 100 N Main St, Fredonia, AZ 86022, tel: 602-643-7241.
Weather: Summer days are hot and sunny (80°F–100°F/27°C–38°C), with occasional thunderstorms. Winter temperatures dip below freezing.

SAGUARO NATIONAL MONUMENT

3693 S Old Spanish Trail, Tucson, AZ 85730, tel: 602-296-8576.
Access: The Rincon Mountain Unit visitor center is on S Old Spanish Trail, about 2 miles (3 km) east of Tucson. The Tucson Mountain Unit information center is on Kinney Road, to the west of Tucson.
Seasons & Hours: Rincon Mountain Unit is open daily 7am–7pm in summer and 7am–6pm in winter. Tucson Mountain Unit is open daily 6am–sunset. The visitor centers are open daily 8am–5pm.
Entrance Fee: Yes, in Rincon Mountain Unit.
Handicapped Access: Visitor centers and a nature trail.
Activities: Scenic drive, backpacking, hiking, wildlife-watching, interpretive programs.
Visitor Facilities: Visitor center, information center.
Camping: Backcountry camping only.
Permits & Licenses: Free backcountry permits required.
Accommodations: No lodging in park. Accommodations are available in Tucson. Contact Tucson Convention & Visitors Bureau, 130 S Scott Ave, Tucson, AZ 85701, tel: 602-624-1817.
Food & Supplies: Food and supplies are available in Tucson.
Weather: Summer temperatures in

excess of 110°F (43°C) are not uncommon; occasional thunderstorms. Winter nights can dip below freezing.
General Information: Backcountry users should carry adequate water, a gallon (4 liters) per person per day. Sunscreen and hats are highly recommended.

NEVADA

GREAT BASIN NATIONAL PARK

Baker, NV 89311, tel: 702-234-7331.
Access: The park is about 67 miles (108 km) southeast of Ely in eastern Nevada via Highways 93, 50/6, 487 and 488.
Seasons & Hours: The park is open daily year-round. The visitor center is open daily 8am–5pm, extended hours in summer. The visitor center and cave are closed Thanksgiving, Christmas and New Year's Day. Sections of the park road and some trails may be closed by snow October–May.

Entrance Fee: For guided cave tours.
Handicapped Access: Visitor center, portion of cave and select campsites.
Activities: Camping, hiking, backpacking, cave tours, wildlife-watching, boating, fishing, cross-country skiing, snowshoeing, interpretive programs.
Permits & Licenses: Caving permits required for non-guided tours of any cave in park; voluntary registration for backcountry camping; Nevada fishing license.
Camping: First-come, first-served.
Accommodations: None in the park. Additional lodging is available in Ely and Baker. Contact the Great Basin Chamber of Commerce, PO Box 90, Baker, NV 89311, tel: 702-234-7302.
Food & Supplies: Limited food service near the visitor center. Additional services are available in Baker and Ely.
Weather: Summer temperatures usually 45°F–90°F (7°C–32°C), colder at higher elevations. Winters are cold, with heavy snow accumulation at higher elevations; temperatures usually 20°F–45°F (–7°C–7°C). Temperatures in the cave remain about 50°F (10°C) year-round.
General Information: Gas stations and other services are few and far between in this area. Keep your eye on the gas gauge and carry water. Consult with rangers and obtain a permit before

entering any cave in the park. Thin air at high elevations can make hiking difficult.

LAKE MEAD
NATIONAL RECREATION AREA

601 Nevada Highway, Boulder City, NV 89005, tel: 702-293-8907.
Access: The Alan Bible Visitor Center is 4 miles (6 km) northeast of Boulder City, Nevada, via Highway 93, about 25 miles (40 km) southeast of Las Vegas via Highway 95/93, and 76 miles (113 km) from Kingman, Arizona, via Highway 93.
Seasons & Hours: The recreation area is open daily year-round. The visitor center is open 8.30am–4.30pm; closed Thanksgiving, Christmas and New Year's Day.

Entrance Fee: No.
Handicapped Access: Visitor center, fishing pier and some campsites.
Activities: Camping, backpacking, horse back-riding, wildlife-watching, boating, water-skiing, fishing, swimming, interpretive programs.
Permits & Licenses: Arizona and/or Nevada fishing license.
Camping: First-come, first-served.
Accommodations: Several moderately priced motels are located in the park. Contact Seven Crown Resorts, tel: 800-752-9669.
  Additional lodging is available in Boulder City, Bullhead City, Henderson and Las Vegas. Contact Boulder City Chamber of Commerce, 1497 Nevada Highway, Boulder City, NV 89005, tel: 702-293-2034.
Food & Supplies: Food service and supplies are available in the park. Additional services available in Boulder City, Bullhead City, Henderson and Las Vegas.
Weather: Summer temperatures exceed 100°F (38°C). October–May are much more comfortable. Be prepared for sudden rainstorms and potential flash floods. The sunlight is intense. Bring sunscreen, sunglasses and a hat.
General Information: For houseboat and motorboat rentals and reservations, contact Seven Crown Resorts (tel: 800-752-9669) or Forever Resorts (tel: 800-255-5561).

New Mexico

Carlsbad Caverns National Park

3225 National Parks Highway, Carlsbad, NM 88220, tel: 505-785-2232.

Access: The park entrance is about 20 miles (32 km) southwest of Carlsbad, New Mexico, and 150 miles (241 km) east of El Paso, Texas, via Highway 180/62.

Seasons & Hours: The park is open daily year-round, except Christmas. The visitor center is open daily 8am–5.30pm, extended hours in summer.

Entrance Fee: Cave entrance.

Handicapped Access: Visitor center, bat flight amphitheater and portions of cavern.

Activities: Cave tours, camping, hiking, wildlife-watching, interpretive programs. Experienced cavers may arrange exploration of backcountry caves by contacting the Cave Resource Office, tel: 505-785-2232.

Seasonal Events: August: Bat aficionados gather for an early-morning Bat Flight Breakfast to watch the return of thousands of the winged mammals to their underground home.

Permits & Licenses: Free backcountry camping permits required.

Camping: Backcountry camping only.

Accommodations: None in the park. Accommodations are available in Whites City and Carlsbad. Contact the Carlsbad Chamber of Commerce, tel: 800-221-1224.

Food & Supplies: Food service and supplies are available in Whites City and Carlsbad.

Weather: Summer temperatures usually 60°F–95°F (16°C–35°C), winter temperatures 30°F–65°F (–1°C–18°C). Be prepared for high winds, sudden rainstorms and potential flash floods. Cave temperature is 56°F (13°C) year-round.

General Information: If you plan on hiking, carry sunscreen, sunglasses, a hat and adequate water (a gallon/4 liters per person per day). Contact park headquarters to make reservations for off-trail caving tour.

Star Route 4, Box 6500, Bloomfield, NM 87413, tel: 505-786-7014.

Access: The park is about 65 miles (107 km) north of Thoreau in northwest New Mexico via Routes 371 and 57. The last 20 miles (32 km) of Route 57 are unpaved and may be impassable in foul weather. From the north, the park is about 70 miles (113 km) from Bloomfield via Routes 44 and 57. The last 30 miles (48 km) of Route 57 are unpaved and may be impassable in foul weather.

Seasons & Hours: The park is open daily year-round. The ruins are open sunrise–sunset. The visitor center is open 8am–5pm, extended summer hours; closed Christmas and New Year's Day.

Entrance Fee: Yes.

Handicapped Access: Select campsites and some trails.

Activities: Camping, hiking, guided and self-guided tours, interpretive programs.

Permits & Licenses: No.

Camping: First-come, first-served.

Accommodations: None in the park. Accommodations are available in Bloomfield, Farmington and Gallup. Contact Farmington Chamber of Commerce, 203 W Main St, Suite 401, Farmington, NM 87401, tel: 800-448-1240; Gallup Chamber of Commerce, PO Box 600, Gallup, NM 87305, tel: 800-242-4282.

Food & Supplies: Limited food and supplies at Blanco and Nageezi Trading Posts. Additional services available in Crownpoint, Thoreau, Bloomfield and Farmington.

Weather: Summer temperatures usually 50°F–90°F (10°C–32°C) with occasional thunderstorms. Winter temperatures 10°F–40°F (–12°C–4°C) with occasional snow.

General Information: There are no food or supplies in the park; bring whatever you need and fill the gas tank before entering. Disturbing artifacts or other objects is strictly prohibited.

WHITE SANDS NATIONAL MONUMENT

PO Box 1086, Holloman Air Force Base, NM 88330, tel: 505-479-6124.

Access: The monument is 15 miles (24 km) southwest of Alamogordo via Highway 70 in southern New Mexico.

Seasons & Hours: The monument is open daily year-round. The visitor center is open daily 8am–4.30pm, extended hours in summer. Dunes Drive is open daily 7am–sunset, extended hours in summer; closed Christmas.

Entrance Fee: Yes.

Handicapped Access: Visitor center.

Activities: Backcountry camping, hiking, guided and self-guided tours, interpretive programs.

Permits & Licenses: Backcountry camping permit.

Camping: First-come, first-served.

Accommodations: None in the park. Accommodations are available in Alamogordo. Contact Alamogordo Chamber of Commerce, PO Box 518, Alamogordo, NM 88311, tel: 505-437-6120.

Food & Supplies: Limited food service at gift shop. Additional services available in Alamogordo.

Weather: Summer temperatures usually 60°F–100°F (16°C–38°C) with occasional thunderstorms. Winter temperatures 25°F–60°F (–4°C–16°C).

General Information: The monument preserves the dazzling white gypsum dunes (some as high as 60 ft/18 meters) that are scoured from the San Andres and Sacramento Mountains.

TEXAS

AMISTAD NATIONAL RECREATION AREA

HCR-3, Box 5J, Del Rio, TX 78840, tel: 210-775-7491.

Access: The recreation area is about 5 miles (8 km) northwest of Del Rio via Highway 90.

Seasons & Hours: The recreation area is open daily year-round. The information center is open Monday–Friday 8am–5pm; closed Thanksgiving, Christmas and New Year's Day.

Entrance Fee: No.

Handicapped Access: Park headquarters, amphitheaters and information center.

Activities: Camping, hiking, wildlife-watching, boating, water-skiing, fishing, swimming, interpretive programs.

Permits & Licenses: Texas and/or Mexican fishing licenses.

Camping: First-come, first-served.

Accommodations: None in the park. Lodging is available in Del Rio. Contact del Rio Chamber of Commerce, 1915 Ave F, Del Rio, TX 78840, tel: 210-775-3551.

Food and Supplies: Limited food service in the park. Additional services in Del Rio.

Weather: Summer temperatures usually 60°F–100°F (16°C–38°C), with occasional thunderstorms. Winter temperatures 30°F–65°F (–1°C–18°C).

General Information: The recreation area is centered around Lake Amistad Reservoir and features a variety of water sports, fishing and lakeshore camping.

BIG BEND NATIONAL PARK

Big Bend National Park, TX 79834, tel: 915-477-2251

Access: Panther Junction Visitor Center is about 106 miles (171 km) south of Alpine via Route 118 and about 137 miles (221 km) south of Fort Stockton via Highway 385.

Seasons & Hours: The park is open daily year-round. Panther Junction Visitor Center is open daily 8am–6pm. Rio Grande Village Visitor Center is open daily mid-November–mid-May, 8am–4pm.

Entrance Fee: Yes.

Handicapped Access: Visitor centers, some nature trails and campsites.

Activities: Scenic drive, camping, hiking, backpacking, wildlife-watching, float trips, interpretive programs.

Special Events: October: International Good Neighbor Day celebrates good will between the US and Mexico with food, music, dance and crafts at Rio Grande Village.

Permits & Licenses: Free backcountry camping permits required.

Camping: First-come, first-served.

Accommodations: In the park: *Chisos Mountain Lodge***, National Park Concessions, Basin Rural Station, Big Bend National Park, TX 79834, tel: 915-477-2291.

Additional services are available in Terlingua, Marathon and Alpine.

Food and Supplies: Limited food and supplies are available at Basin, Rio Grande Village, Castolon and Panther Junction. Additional services in Alpine, Study Butte, Lajitas and Marathon.

Weather: Temperatures vary depending on elevation. Summer temperatures 60°F–105°F (16°C–41°C), with

occasional thunderstorms. Winter temperatures 30°F–65°F (–1°C–18°C) with little snow.

General Information: The sun is intense. Bring sunscreen, sunglasses and a hat. Carry water in your car and on hikes (a gallon/4 liters per person per day). Gas stations are few and far between in this area. Keep your eye on the gas gauge and fill up the tank before starting long trips.

GUADALUPE MOUNTAINS NATIONAL PARK

HC 60, Box 400, Salt Flat, TX 79847, tel: 915-828-3251.

Access: The park is 55 miles (89 km) southwest of Carlsbad, New Mexico, via Highway 62/180 and 110 miles (117 km) east of El Paso via Highway 62/180.

Seasons & Hours: The park is open daily year-round. McKittrick Canyon area is closed just before dusk. Visitor centers are open 8am–4.30pm, extended hours in summer; closed Christmas.

Entrance Fee: No.

Handicapped Access: Visitor centers, a nature trail and select campsites.

Activities: Scenic drive, camping, hiking, backpacking, wildlife-watching, interpretive programs.

Permits & Licenses: Free backcountry camping permits required.

Camping: First-come, first-served.

Accommodations: None in the park. Lodging is available in Carlsbad, Whites City and Van Horn. Contact Van Horn Convention & Visitors Bureau, PO Box 488, Van Horn, TX 79855, tel: 915-283-2682.

Food and Supplies: There are no supplies in the park. Services are available in Carlsbad, Whites City and Van Horn.

Weather: Temperatures vary depending on elevation. Summer temperatures 60°F–95°F (16°C–35°C), cooler at higher elevations, with highs in excess of 100°F (38°C) and occasional thunderstorms; winter temperatures 25°F–65°F (–4°C–18°C) with occasional snowstorms. Be prepared for sudden changes of weather and high winds.

General Information: If you plan on hiking, carry sunscreen, sunglasses, a hat and adequate water (a gallon/4 lit-

ers per person per day). Gas stations are few and far between in this area. Keep your eye on the gas gauge and fill up the tank before starting long trips.

LAKE MEREDITH NATIONAL RECREATION AREA

PO Box 1460, Fritch, TX 79036, tel: 806-857-3151.

Access: Headquarters are located in Fritch, 38 miles (61 km) north of Amarillo.

Seasons & Hours: The recreation area is open daily year-round. Headquarters are open Monday–Friday, 8am–4.30pm; closed Christmas and New Year's Day.

Entrance Fee: No.

Handicapped Access: Headquarters and some campsites.

Activities: Camping, hiking, wildlife-watching, boating, water-skiing, fishing, swimming, interpretive programs.

Permits & Licenses: Texas fishing license.

Camping: First-come, first-served.

Accommodations: None in the park. Lodging is available in Fritch, Borger, Amarillo. Contact Amarillo Convention & Visitors Bureau, 1000 S Polk St, PO Drawer 9480, Amarillo, TX 79105, tel: 806-374-1497.

Food and Supplies: Limited food service in the park at the marina. Additional services in Fritch, Borger, Amarillo.

Weather: Summer temperatures usually 60°F–100°F (16°C–38°C), with occasional thunderstorms. Winters 15°F–60°F (–9°C–16°C); expect windy conditions.

General Information: Located in the Texas panhandle, this semi-developed recreation area offers a variety of water sports, fishing and camping.

PADRE ISLAND NATIONAL SEASHORE

9405 S Padre Island Drive, Corpus Christi, TX 78418-5597, tel: 512-937-2621.

Access: The national seashore is 2 miles (3 km) across the causeway from Corpus Christi via Park Road 22.

Seasons & Hours: The seashore is open daily year-round. The visitor center is open daily 9am–4.30pm, extended hours in summer; closed Christmas and New Year's Day.

Entrance Fee: Yes.

Handicapped Access: Visitor center and Bath House.
Activities: Camping, hiking, wildlife-watching, boating, fishing, swimming, interpretive programs.
Permits & Licenses: Texas fishing license.
Camping: First-come, first-served.
Accommodations: None in the park. Lodging is available in Corpus Christi. Contact Corpus Christi Area Convention & Visitors Bureau, 1201 N Shoreline, PO Box 2664, Corpus Christi, TX 78403, tel: 800-678-6232.
Food and Supplies: Limited food and supplies are available in the park. Additional services in Corpus Christi.
Weather: Summer temperatures usually 70°F–90°F (21°C–32°C) and humid. Winter is cool and windy with temperatures usually 50°F–60°F (10°C–16°C).
General Information: A 60-mile (97-km) barrier island on Texas' Gulf coast features unspoiled beaches, abundant marine life and a variety of water sports.

UTAH

ARCHES NATIONAL PARK

PO Box 907, Moab, UT 84532, tel: 801-259-8161.
Access: The visitor center is 5 miles (8 km) northwest of Moab via Highway 191.
Seasons & Hours: The park is open daily year-round. The visitor center is open daily 8am–4.30pm, extended hours in summer; closed Christmas.
Entrance Fee: Yes.
Handicapped Access: Visitor center, one campsite and Park Avenue Viewpoint.
Activities: Scenic drive, camping, hiking, backpacking, wildlife-watching, interpretive programs.
Permits & Licenses: Free backcountry camping permits required.
Camping: First-come, first-served.
Accommodations: None in the park. Lodging is available in Moab. Contact Utah's Canyonlands Region, PO Box 550-R9, Moab, UT 84532, tel: 800-635-6622 or tel: 801-259-8825.
Food and Supplies: No food service or supplies in the park. Services are available in Moab.
Weather: Summer temperatures usually 60°F–105°F (16°C–41°C) with sudden

thunderstorms; winter temperatures 15°F–45°F (–9°C–7°C) with occasional snow.
General Information: If you plan on hiking, carry sunscreen, sunglasses, a hat and adequate water (a gallon/4 liters per person per day). Unpaved roads may be impassable during or after rainstorms. Contact the park for road and weather conditions. Off-road biking is prohibited.

BRYCE CANYON NATIONAL PARK

Bryce Canyon, UT 84717, tel: 801-834-5322.
Access: The park is 80 miles (129 km) east of Cedar City via Routes 14, 89 and 12, and 26 miles (42 km) southeast of Panguitch via Routes 89 and 12.
Seasons & Hours: The park is open daily year-round. The visitor center is open 8am–4.30pm, extended hours in summer; closed Christmas, Thanksgiving and New Year's Day.
Entrance Fee: Yes.
Handicapped Access: Visitor center, some campsites and a section of Sunset–Sunrise Point Trail.
Activities: Scenic drive, camping, hiking, backpacking, horseback riding, wildlife-watching, interpretive programs.
Permits & Licenses: Free backcountry camping permits required.
Camping: First-come, first-served.
Accommodations: In the park: *Bryce Canyon Lodge*******, TW Services, PO Box 400, Cedar City, UT 84720, tel: 801-586-7686.
Additional lodging is available in Panguitch, Tropic, Cedar City and on highways leading to the park. Contact Washington County Travel Bureau, 425 S 700 East, St George, UT 84770, tel: 800-869-6635.
Food and Supplies: There is a restaurant at Bryce Canyon Lodge. Additional services available in Panguitch, Tropic, Cedar City and on highways leading to the park.
Weather: Summer temperatures usually 40°F–85°F (4°C–29°C) with sudden thunderstorms; winter temperatures usually 5°F–45°F (–15°C–7°C) with heavy snow at higher elevations.
General Information: If you plan on hiking, carry sunscreen, sunglasses, a hat and adequate water (a gallon/4 lit-

ers per person per day). Unpaved roads may be impassable during and immediately after rain or snowstorms. Contact the park for road and weather conditions. Off-road biking prohibited.

CANYONLANDS NATIONAL PARK

282 SW Resource Blvd, Moab, UT 84532, tel: 801-259-7164.
Access: The Island in the Sky District is 32 miles (52 km) from Moab via Highway 313 and Route 313. The Needles District is 80 miles (129 km) from Moab via Highway 313 and Route 211.
Seasons & Hours: The park is open daily year-round. Vistor centers are open 8am–4.30pm, extended hours in spring and fall; closed Christmas.
Entrance Fee: Yes.
Handicapped Access: Visitor centers, some campsites and some overlooks.
Activities: Scenic drive, camping, hiking, biking, float trips, backpacking, horseback riding, backroad driving, rock climbing, wildlife-watching, interpretive programs.
Permits & Licenses: Backcountry camping permits required.
Camping: First-come, first-served.
Accommodations: None in the park. Lodging is available in Moab, Green River and Monticello. Contact Utah's Canyonlands Region, PO Box 550-R9, Moab, UT 84532, tel: 800-635-6622.
Food and Supplies: No services in the park. Food and supplies are available in Moab, Green River and Monticello.
Weather: Summer temperatures usually 65°F–105°F (18°C–41°C) with sudden thunderstorms; winter temperatures usually 5°F–45°F (–15°C–7°C) with occasional snow.
General Information: If you plan on hiking, carry sunscreen, sunglasses, a hat and adequate water (a gallon/4 liters per person per day). Carry water in your car. Unpaved roads may be impassable during or after rainstorms. Contact the park for road and weather conditions. Driving backroads may require 4-wheel-drive vehicles. Off-road biking is prohibited. Gas stations are few and far between in this area; fill the gas tank before starting a long trip.

CAPITOL REEF NATIONAL PARK

Torrey, UT 84775, tel: 801-425-3791.
Access: The visitor center is 11 miles (18 km) east of Torrey via Route 24.
Seasons & Hours: The park is open daily year-round. The visitor center is open 8am–4.30pm, extended hours in summer; closed Christmas.
Entrance Fee: Yes.
Handicapped Access: Visitor center (with assistance), a campsite and part of the Fremont River Trail.
Activities: Scenic drive, camping, hiking, biking, backpacking, backroad driving, rock climbing, wildlife-watching, interpretive programs.
Permits & Licenses: Free backcountry camping permits required.
Camping: First-come, first-served.
Accommodations: None in the park. Lodging is available in Torrey, Bicknell and Hanksville. Contact Utah's Canyonlands Region, PO Box 550-R9, Moab, UT 84532, tel: 800-635-6622 or tel: 801-259-8825.

Food and Supplies: No services in the park. Food and supplies are available in Torrey, Bicknell and Hanksville.
Weather: Summer temperatures usually 60°F–95°F (16°C–35°C) with sudden thunderstorms causing flash floods; winter temperatures usually 15°F–45°F (–9°C–7°C) with occasional light snow. Spring and fall are the most moderate times to visit, but weather can change quickly.
General Information: If you plan on hiking, carry sunscreen, sunglasses, a hat and adequate water (a gallon/4 liters per person per day). Carry water in your car. Unpaved roads may be impassable during or after rainstorms. Contact the park for road and weather conditions. Driving back roads may require 4-wheel-drive vehicles. Off-road biking is prohibited. Gas stations are few and far between in this area; fill the gas tank before starting a long trip.

CEDAR BREAKS NATIONAL MONUMENT

82 N 100 East, Cedar City, UT 84720, tel: 801-586-9451.
Access: The monument is about 23 miles (37 km) from Cedar City via Routes 14 and 148.
Seasons & Hours: The visitor center is open 8am–5pm, June–September. The park road is open June–October, de-

pending on weather.
Entrance Fee: Yes.
Handicapped Access: Visitor center, select campsites and overlooks.
Activities: Scenic drive, camping, hiking, backpacking, wildlife-watching, interpretive programs.
Permits & Licenses: No.
Camping: First-come, first-served.
Accommodations: None in the park. Lodging is available in Cedar City, Parowan, Brian Head, Panguitch. Contact Iron County Travel Bureau, PO Box 1007, Cedar City, UT 84720, tel: 800-354-4849.
Food and Supplies: No services in the park. Food and supplies are available in Cedar City, Parowan, Panguitch.
Weather: Summer temperatures usually 40°F–70°F (4°C–21°C) with sudden thunderstorms; winter temperatures usually 5°F –40°F (–15°C–4°C) with heavy snowfall.
General Information: If you plan on hiking, carry sunscreen, sunglasses, a hat and adequate water (a gallon/4 liters per person per day). Carry water in your car. Contact the park for road and weather conditions. Off-road biking is prohibited.

NATURAL BRIDGES NATIONAL MONUMENT

Box 1, Lake Powell, UT 84533, tel: 801-259-5174.
Access: The monument is about 41 miles (66 km) from Blanding via Routes 95 and 275.
Seasons & Hours: The monument is open daily year-round. The visitor center is open daily 8am–4.30pm, extended hours in summer; closed Christmas and New Year's Day. Some trails may be closed by snow in winter.
Entrance Fee: Yes.
Handicapped Access: Visitor center and some overlooks.
Activities: Scenic drive, camping, hiking, wildlife-watching, interpretive programs.
Permits & Licenses: No.
Camping: First-come, first-served.
Accommodations: None in the park. Lodging is available in Blanding, Mexican Hat, Bluff, Monticello. Contact San Juan County Travel Bureau, PO Box 490, 117 S Main St, Monticello, UT 84535, tel: 801-587-3235.
Food and Supplies: No services in the park. Limited food and supplies are

available in Fry Canyon, otherwise you must travel to Blanding, Mexican Hat, Bluff, Monticello.
Weather: Summer temperatures usually 70°F–100°F (21°C–38°C) with sudden thunderstorms; winter temperatures usually 15°F–40°F (–9°C–4°C) with snowfall.
General Information: If you plan on hiking, carry sunscreen, sunglasses, a hat and adequate water (a gallon/4 liters per person per day). Carry water in your car. Contact the park for road and weather conditions in winter. Off-road biking is prohibited. Gas stations are few and far between in this area; fill the gas tank before starting a long trip.

TIMPANOGOS CAVE NATIONAL MONUMENT

RR 3, Box 200, American Fork, UT 84003, tel: 801-756-5238.
Access: The monument is about 30 miles (48 km) south of Salt Lake City via I-15 and Route 92.
Seasons & Hours: The visitor center is open May–September, 8am–4.30pm, extended summer hours.
Entrance Fee: A fee is charged for the cave tour.
Handicapped Access: Visitor center only; the cave is not wheelchair-accessible.
Activities: Cave tour, hiking, wildlife-watching, interpretive programs.
Permits & Licenses: No.
Camping: First-come, first-served.
Accommodations: None in the park. Lodging is available in Pleasant Grove, American Fork, Heber, Provo, Salt Lake City and surrounding area. Contact Utah Travel Council, Council Hall, Capitol Hill, Salt Lake City, UT 84114, tel: 800-200-1160.
Food and Supplies: No services in the park. Services are available in Provo, Salt Lake City and surrounding area.
Weather: Summer highs in the 90°F (32°C) with sudden thunderstorms; winter temperatures often dip below freezing with abundant snowfall. Cave temperature 43°F–47°F (6°C–8°C).
General Information: The cave tour takes about 3 hours and requires a steep 1½-mile (2-km) walk to the cave entrance. Cave tours fill early during busy summer season. Reservations can be made in advance by phoning monument headquarters.

ZION NATIONAL PARK

Springdale, UT 84767-1099, tel: 801-772-3256.

Access: The Zion Canyon Visitor Center is 46 miles (74 km) east of St George via I-15 and Route 9. The Kolob Canyons Visitor Center is 18 miles (29 km) south of Cedar City by way of I-15.

Seasons & Hours: The park is open daily year-round. Zion Canyon Visitor Center is open 8am–5pm, extended summer hours. Kolob Canyons Visitor Center is open 9am–4.30pm, extended summer hours.

Entrance Fee: Yes.

Handicapped Access: Visitor centers, some trails (with assistance) and some campsites.

Activities: Scenic drive, camping, hiking, biking, backpacking, backroad driving, horseback riding, rock climbing, wildlife-watching, interpretive programs.

Seasonal Events: September: The Southern Utah Folklife Festival is a celebration of Mormon pioneers with music, dancing, food, crafts and storytelling.

Permits & Licenses: Backcountry camping permits required.

Camping: First-come, first-served.

Accommodations: In the park: *Zion Lodge***, TW Recreational Services, Cedar City, UT 84720, tel: 801-586-7686 or tel: 801-772-3213.

Additional lodging is available in Springdale, Kanab, Hurricane, St George and Cedar City. Contact Washington County Travel Bureau, 425 S 700 East, St George, UT 84770, tel: 800-869-6635 or Kanab Chamber of Commerce, tel: 801-644-5229.

Food and Supplies: A restaurant is located in Zion Lodge. Additional food and supplies are available in Springdale, Kanab, Hurricane, St George and Cedar City.

Weather: Weather varies considerably depending on elevation. Summer temperatures usually 65°F–105°F (18°C–41°C) with sudden thunderstorms causing flash floods; winter temperatures usually 25°F–55°F (–4°C–13°C) with heavy snow at higher elevations. Spring and fall are the most moderate times to visit, but weather changes quickly in any season.

General Information: If you plan on hiking, carry sunscreen, sunglasses, a hat and adequate water (a gallon/4 liters per person per day). Carry water in your car. Unpaved roads may be impassable during or after rainstorms. Contact the park for road and weather conditions. Off-road biking is prohibited. Stay alert on the trail; some areas have steep dropoffs; canyons, ravines and other low-lying areas may flood during or after rainstorms. Shuttle bus service is scheduled to start in Zion Canyon as early as 1997.

THE ROCKY MOUNTAINS

COLORADO

BLACK CANYON OF THE GUNNISON NATIONAL MONUMENT

2233 E Main St, Suite 2, Montrose, CO 81401, tel: 303-249-7036.

Access: The monument is about 15 miles (24 km) northeast of Montrose via Highway 50 and Route 347.

Seasons & Hours: The monument is open daily year-round although occasionally closed by snow in winter. The visitor center is open daily in summer 8am–7pm, reduced hours in winter.

Entrance Fee: Yes.

Handicapped Access: Visitor center and some campsites

Activities: Scenic drive, backpacking, camping, hiking, fishing, wildlife-watching, interpretive programs.

Permits & Licenses: Free backcountry permits; Colorado fishing license.

Camping: First-come, first-served.

Accommodations: None in the park. Lodging is available in Montrose. Contact Montrose Chamber of Commerce, 1519 E Main St, Montrose, CO 81401, tel: 800-873-0244.

Food & Supplies: Limited food service on South Rim. Additional services available in Montrose.

Weather: Summer temperatures usually 40°F–90°F (4°C–32°C), winter temperatures usually –10°F–35°F (–23°C–2°C). Expect summer thunderstorms and heavy snowfall in winter.

General Information: The dark, sheer 2,000-foot (610-km) high walls of this narrow canyon make it one of the most dramatic sights in the West. Steep, unmarked trails leading to the canyon floor are recommended for experienced, fit hikers only. Stay on the trails and behind guard rails.

COLORADO NATIONAL MONUMENT

Fruita, CO 81521, tel: 303-858-3617.

Access: The monument is off I-70 near Grand Junction in western Colorado.

Seasons & Hours: The monument is open daily year-round. The visitor center is open 8am–4.30pm, extended hours in summer.

Entrance Fee: Yes.

Handicapped Access: Visitor center and several overlooks.

Activities: Scenic drive, backpacking, camping, hiking, horseback riding, wildlife-watching, interpretive programs.

Permits & Licenses: Backcountry permits are recommended.

Camping: First-come, first-served.

Accommodations: None in the park. Lodging is available in Grand Junction and Fruita. Contact Grand Junction Visitor & Convention Bureau, 360 Grand Ave, Grand Junction, CO 81501, tel: 303-962-2547.

Food & Supplies: None in the park. Services are available in Grand Junction and Fruita.

Weather: Hot, dry summers with temperatures 60°F–100°F (16°C–38°C). Winter temperatures are usually 25°F–45°F (–4°C–7°C) , with occasional dustings of snow.

General Information: This 20,450-acre (8,276-hectare) park features a 23-mile (37-km) scenic drive past small canyons and sandstone formations as well as an excellent network of hiking trails.

CURECANTI NATIONAL RECREATION AREA

102 Elk Creek, Gunnison, CO 81230, tel: 303-641-2337.

Access: The recreation area is 15 miles (24 km) west of Gunnison via Highway 50.

Seasons & Hours: The recreation area is open daily year-round. The visitor center is open 8am–6pm in summer, 8am–4.30pm in fall; closed January and February; open weekends only in

March.

Entrance Fee: No.

Handicapped Access: Visitor center, nature trails and select campsites.

Activities: Backpacking, camping, hiking, boating, water-skiing, fishing, wildlife-watching, interpretive programs.

Permits & Licenses: Colorado fishing license.

Camping: First-come, first-served.

Accommodations: None in the park. Lodging is available in Gunnison and Montrose. Contact Gunnison County Chamber of Commerce, PO Box 36, Gunnison, CO 81230, tel: 800-274-7580.

Food & Supplies: There are limited services at Elk Creek and Lake Fork Marinas in summer. Additional services available in Gunnison and Montrose.

Weather: Summer temperatures usually 40°F–90°F (4°C–32°C), winter temperatures –20°F–35°F (–30°C–2°C). Expect thunderstorms and afternoon winds in summer and snowfall in winter.

General Information: Three lakes created by dams on the Gunnison River are the centerpiece of this 42,114-acre (17,043-hectare) park, offering a variety of water sports and excellent backcountry hiking and birding. Boats can be reserved at Elk Creek Marina (tel: 303-641-0707) or Lake Fork Marina (tel: 303-641-3048).

DINOSAUR NATIONAL MONUMENT

4545 Highway 40, Dinosaur, CO 81610, tel: 303-374-2216.

Access: The monument is about 18 miles (29 km) east of Vernal, Utah, via Highway 40 and Route 149, and 112 miles (180 km) west of Craig, Colorado, via Highway 40.

Seasons & Hours: The monument is open daily year-round. The visitor center is open daily 8am–4.30pm, extended hours in summer; closed Thanksgiving, Christmas and New Year's Day.

Entrance Fee: Yes.

Handicapped Access: Lower floor of visitor center and some campsites.

Activities: Exhibits at dinosaur fossil quarry, backpacking, camping, hiking, boating, fishing, wildlife-watching, interpretive programs.

Permits & Licenses: Free backcountry camping permit; Colorado and/or Utah fishing licenses.

Camping: First-come, first-served.

Accommodations: None in the park. Lodging is available in Dinosaur, Craig and Vernal. Contact Craig Chamber of Commerce, 360 Victory Way, Craig, CO 81625, tel: 303-824-5689.

Food & Supplies: No services in the park. Services are available in Dinosaur, Craig and Vernal.

Weather: Summer temperatures usually 60°F–90°F (16°C–32°C), winter temperatures 20°F–60°F (–6°C–0°C); snowfall is common.

General Information: The Green and Yampa rivers have cut dramatic canyons and exposed an abundance of dinosaur fossils, many on display at the Dinosaur Quarry.

GREAT SAND DUNES
NATIONAL MONUMENT

11500 Highway 150, Mosca, CO 81146, tel: 719-378-2312.

Access: The monument is about 35 miles (56 km) northeast of Alamosa via Route 160 and 150.

Seasons & Hours: The monument is open daily year-round. The visitor center is open daily 8am–5pm, extended summer hours; closed Thanksgiving, Christmas, New Year's Day.

Entrance Fee: Yes.

Handicapped Access: Visitor center and a backcountry campsite.

Activities: Backpacking, camping, hiking, wildlife-watching, four-wheel-drive tours, interpretive programs.

Permits & Licenses: Free backcountry permit.

Camping: First-come, first-served.

Accommodations: None in the park. Lodging is available in Alamosa and Fort Garland. Contact Alamosa County Chamber of Commerce, Cole Park, Alamosa, CO 81101, tel: 719-589-3681.

Food & Supplies: There are no services in the park. Services are available in Alamosa, Fort Garland and at roadside stores outside of the park entrance.

Weather: Summer temperatures usually 45°F–85°F (7°C–29°C), winter temperatures –10°F–35°F (23°–2°C) with occasional snow. Surface temperature of dunes in summer can make hiking inadvisable.

General Information: At 700 ft (213 meters), the tallest dunes in America are preserved in this 38,662-acre (15,646-hectare) park at the foot of the Sangre de Cristo Mountains in southern Colorado.

MESA VERDE NATIONAL PARK

PO Box 8, Mesa Verde National Park, CO 81330, tel: 303-529-4465.

Access: The park entrance is about 8 miles (13 km) east of Cortez and 45 miles (72 km) west of Durango via Highway 160.

Seasons & Hours: The park is open daily year-round. The visitor center is open daily Memorial Day–Labor Day, 8am–5pm. The Chapin Mesa Archaeological Museum is open daily 8am–5pm, extended hours in summer. Ruins Road may be closed by snow in winter.

Entrance Fee: Yes.

Handicapped Access: Visitor center, museum and some overlooks.

Activities: Scenic drives, camping, hiking, interpretive programs.

Permits & Licenses: Hiking registration may be required depending on route; consult a ranger.

Camping: First-come, first-served.

Accommodations: Lodging is available in the park at:

Far View Lodge**, PO Box 277, Mancos, CO 81328, tel: 303-529-4421.

Additional accommodation available in Cortez, Mancos and Durango. Contact Cortez Chamber of Commerce, PO Box 968, Cortez, CO 81321, tel: 800-346-6528.

Food & Supplies: Food service and limited supplies are available in the park at Morefield, Far View and Spruce Tree Terrace. Additional services in Mancos, Durango and Cortez.

Weather: Summer temperatures usually 50°F–95°F (10°C–35°C), winter temperatures 15°F–50°F (–9°C–10°C). Expect summer thunderstorms and heavy snowfall in winter.

General Information: Visiting the ruins on foot may be strenuous. In general, overlooks and pullouts give adequate views. Disturbing artifacts is strictly forbidden. Tel: 303-529-4461 for road and weather conditions.

ROCKY MOUNTAIN NATIONAL PARK

Estes Park, CO 80517, tel: 303-586-1399.

Access: The park is about 65 miles (104 km) northwest of Denver via

Highway 36 and 15 miles (24 km) northeast of Granby via Highway 34.

Seasons & Hours: The park is open year-round. Visitor centers are open 8am–9pm in summer, 8am–5pm in winter; closed Christmas. Alpine Visitor Center, Moraine Park Visitor Center and Lily Lake Visitor Center are open summers only. Trail Ridge Road may be closed by snow mid-October–early June.

Entrance Fee: Yes.

Handicapped Access: Visitor centers, museum and select trails and campsites.

Activities: Scenic drives, camping, hiking, backpacking, fishing, horseback riding, cross-country skiing, snowshoeing, mountain climbing, rock climbing, wildlife-watching, interpretive programs.

Permits & Licenses: Colorado fishing license and free backcountry camping permits required.

Camping: Some sites can be reserved in advance by contacting Mistix, PO Box 85705, San Diego, CA 92186-5705, tel: 800-365-2267. Other sites available on a first-come, first-served basis.

Accommodations: None in the park. Lodging is available in Estes Park and Grand Lake. Contact Estes Park Chamber of Commerce, Estes Park, CO 80517, tel: 800-443-7837 or Grand Lake Chamber of Commerce, tel: 303-627-3402.

Food & Supplies: Services in the park are limited to a snack bar at Fall River Pass. Complete services are available in Estes Park and Grand Lake.

Weather: Weather varies considerably depending on elevation. Summer temperatures 40°F–75°F (4°C–24°C), colder (often much colder) in the high country. Winter temperatures –5°F–30°F (–20°C to –1°C). Expect summer thunderstorms and heavy snowfall in winter. Higher elevations are subject to freezing or near-freezing temperatures year-round.

General Information: For rock and mountain climbing instruction and guide service, contact Colorado Mountain School, PO Box 2062, Estes Park, CO 80517, tel: 303-586-5758.

IDAHO

CRATERS OF THE MOON NATIONAL MONUMENT

PO Box 29, Arco, ID 83213, tel: 208-527-3257.

Access: The monument is 18 miles (29 km) southwest of Arco via Highway 20/26.

Seasons & Hours: The monument is open daily year-round. The visitor center is open daily 8am–4.30pm, extended hours in summer; closed Thanksgiving, Christmas, New Year's Day and President's Day. Park road may be temporarily closed by snow November–April.

Entrance Fee: Yes.

Handicapped Access: Visitor center, nature trail and some campsites.

Activities: Camping, hiking, wildlife-watching, interpretive programs.

Permits & Licenses: Backcountry use permits required.

Camping: First-come, first-served.

Accommodations: None in the park. Lodging is available in Arco, Pocatello and Idaho Falls. Contact Idaho Travel Council, 700 W State St, Boise, ID 83720, tel: 800-635-7820.

Food & Supplies: Limited services are available in Arco. Additional food and supplies are available in Idaho Falls and Pocatello.

Weather: Summer temperatures usually 35°F–80°F (2°C–27°C) with occasional highs in the 90°F (32°C); winter temperatures 0°F–30°F (–18°C to –1°C) with extremes well below 0°F (–18°C) and with heavy snow November–March.

General Information: This 53,545-acre (21,669-hectare) park preserves a rugged landscape of lava flows, craters, caves and volcanic cones.

MONTANA

BIGHORN CANYON NATIONAL RECREATION AREA

PO Box 458, Fort Smith, MT 59035, tel: 406-666-2412 or tel: 307-548-2251.

Access: The recreation area is 43 miles (69 km) south of Hardin, Montana, via Route 313 and 58 miles (93 km) from Cody, Wyoming, via Routes 14A and 37.

Seasons & Hours: The recreation area is open daily year-round. The Bighorn Canyon Visitor Center is open 8.30am–5pm, extended hours in summer. The Fort Smith Visitor Center is open 9am–5pm in summer, hours are variable in winter. Visitor centers are closed Thanksgiving, Christmas and New Year's Day.

Entrance Fee: No.

Handicapped Access: Visitor centers.

Activities: Camping, hiking, backpacking, wildlife-watching, boating, fishing, interpretive programs.

Permits & Licenses: Backcountry camping permit; Wyoming and/or Montana fishing licenses.

Camping: First-come, first-served.

Accommodations: None in the park. Lodging is available in Hardin, Lovell and Fort Smith. Contact Custer Country, Route 1, Box 1206A, Hardin, MT 59034, tel: 406-665-1671.

Food & Supplies: Limited food and supplies are available in Fort Smith, Ok-A-Beh and Horseshoe Bend. Additional food and supplies available in Hardin and Lovell.

Weather: Summer temperatures 45°F–85°F (7°C–29°C), winter temperatures –15°F–40°F (–26°C–4°C), with occasional snow.

GLACIER NATIONAL PARK

West Glacier, MT 59936, tel: 406-888-5441.

Access: The West Glacier entrance is 33 miles (53 km) northeast of Kalispell via Highway 2. On the east side of the park, the St Mary entrance is 31 miles (50 km) northwest of Browning via Highway 89.

Seasons & Hours: The park is open daily year-round. Sections of the Going-to-the-Sun Highway are usually closed by snow mid-October–mid-June. Apgar Visitor Center is open daily 8.30am–4pm, extended summer hours. Other visitor centers are open seasonally.

Entrance Fee: Yes.

Handicapped Access: Apgar and St Mary visitor centers, one nature trail and select campsites.

Activities: Camping, hiking, backpacking, horseback riding, wildlife-watching, boating, fishing, cross-country skiing, snowshoeing, interpretive programs.

Permits & Licenses: Free backcountry camping permits required.

Camping: First-come, first-served.

Accommodations: Lodging in the park is managed by Glacier Park, Inc., PO Box 147, East Glacier, MT 59434, tel: 406-226-5551 or tel: 602-207-6000.

Glacier Park Lodge***.
Lake McDonald Lodge**.
Many Glacier Hotel***.
Rising Sun Motor Inn**.
Swiftcurrent Motor Inn**.
The Village Inn***.
Apgar Village Lodge**, PO Box 398, West Glacier, MT 59936, tel: 406-888-5484.

Additional lodging is available in East Glacier, St Mary and West Glacier. Contact Glacier Country, 945 4th Ave East, Kalispell, MT 59901, tel: 800-338-5072.

Food & Supplies: Food service and supplies are available in the park at Lake McDonald, Swiftcurrent, Apgar Village and St Mary Lake; outside the park in East Glacier, West Glacier and St Mary.

Weather: Summer temperatures usually 40°F–75°F (4°C–24°C), colder at higher elevations. Winters are very cold with heavy snow, temperatures usually 0°F–35°F (–18°C–2°C). Be prepared for high winds, sudden weather changes and violent storms anytime.

General Information: Never try to feed or approach wildlife. Glacier Park, Inc. (East Glacier, MT 59434, tel: 406-226-5551) offers a variety of guided bus tours. Glacier National Park SceniCruise (PO Box 5262, Kalispell, MT 59903, tel: 406-888-5727) offers cruises on McDonald, Many Glaciers, Two Medicine and St Mary lakes. For information about Waterton Lakes National Park in Canada, contact the park at Waterton Park, AB, T0K 2M0, tel: 403-856-2203.

NORTH DAKOTA

THEODORE ROOSEVELT NATIONAL PARK

PO Box 7, Medora, ND 58645, tel: 701-623-4466.

Access: The south unit is 36 miles (58 km) west of Dickinson via I-94. The north unit is about 70 miles (113 km) from Dickinson via I-94 and Highway 85, and about 60 miles (97 km) south of Williston via Highway 85. A 20-mile (32-km) dirt road runs from the south unit to the Elkhorn Ranch. Sections of park roads are closed by snow in winter.

Seasons & Hours: The park is open

daily year-round. The south unit visitor center is open 8am–4.30pm, extended hours in summer. The north unit visitor center is open 9am–5.30pm in summer, winter hours vary. The Painted Canyon Visitor Center is open April–November, 8.30am–4pm, extended hours in summer. Visitor centers are closed Thanksgiving, Christmas and New Year's Day.

Entrance Fee: Yes.

Handicapped Access: Visitor centers, select campsites and some nature trails.

Activities: Scenic drive, camping, hiking, backpacking, horseback riding, float trips, wildlife-watching, interpretive programs.

Permits & Licenses: Free backcountry camping permits required.

Camping: First-come, first-served.

Accommodations: None in the park. Accommodations are available in Medora, Dickinson and Williston. Contact Medora Visitors Bureau, tel: 701-623-4444.

Food & Supplies: No services in the park. Services are available in Medora, Beach, Belfield, Dickinson, Watford City and Williston.

Weather: Summer temperatures usually 40°F–90°F (4°C–32°C), with occasional highs in excess of 100°F (38°C) and sudden rainstorms. Winter temperatures –10°F–30°F (–23°C to –1°C) with severe snowstorms. Be prepared for sudden changes in weather, storms and windy conditions.

General Information: Never feed or approach wildlife.

SOUTH DAKOTA

BADLANDS NATIONAL PARK

PO Box 6, Interior, SD 57750, tel: 605-433-5361.

Access: The park is about 60 miles (97 km) east of Rapid City via I-90 and Route 240, and about 20 miles (32 km) west of Kadoka via I-90.

Seasons & Hours: The park is open daily year-round. The Ben Reifel Visitor Center is open daily 8.30am–5pm, extended hours in summer; closed Thanksgiving, Christmas and New Year's Day. White River Visitor Center is open in summer only. Roads may be closed by snow in winter.

Entrance Fee: Yes.

Handicapped Access: Visitor centers,

some campsites and nature trails.

Activities: Scenic drive, camping, hiking, backpacking, wildlife-watching, interpretive programs.

Permits & Licenses: No.

Camping: First-come, first-served.

Accommodations: In the park: *Cedar Pass Lodge**, PO Box 5, Interior, SD 57750, tel: 605-433-5460.

Additional accommodations are available in Wall and Interior. Contact the Wall Chamber of Commerce, PO Box 527, Wall, SD 57790, tel: 605-279-2665.

Food and Supplies: Limited food and supplies are available at Cedar Pass. Additional services in Wall and Interior.

Weather: Summer temperatures 50°F–90°F (10°C–32°C), with occasional highs in excess of 100°F (38°C) and sudden, severe rainstorms. Winter temperatures 0°F–40°F (–18°C–4°C) with occasional lows well below 0°F (–18°C) and blizzard conditions.

General Information: Never feed or approach wildlife. Be prepared for sudden changes in weather, high winds and sudden hail, rain or snowstorms. Hikers should carry adequate water – a gallon (4 liters) per day per person.

JEWEL CAVE NATIONAL MONUMENT

RR 1, Box 60AA, Custer, SD 57730. tel: 605-673-2288.

Access: The monument is 13 miles (21 km) west of Custer by way of Highway 16.

Seasons & Hours: The monument is open daily year-round. Daily cave tours are offered May–September. Cave tours may not be available during the remainder of the year; call ahead. The visitor center is open May–September, 8am–7.30pm, October–Apr 8am–4pm; closed Thanksgiving, Christmas and New Year's Day.

Entrance Fee: A fee is charged for the cave tour.

Handicapped Access: Visitor center and one room of cave.

Activities: Cave tour, hiking, wildlife-watching, interpretive programs.

Permits & Licenses: No.

Camping: No.

Accommodations: None in the park. Lodging is available in Custer, South Dakota, and Newcastle, Wyoming. Contact the Rapid City Convention and Visitors Bureau, PO Box 747, Rapid City, SD 57709, tel: 605-343-1744;

South Dakota Tourism, 711 Wells Ave, Pierre, SD 57501, tel: 605-773-3301.
Food and Supplies: No services in the park. Services are available in Custer, South Dakota and Newcastle, Wyoming.
Weather: Summer temperatures 45°F–90°F (7°C–32°C). Winter temperatures 0°F–45°F (–18°C–7°C) with heavy snow. The cave is 47°F (8°C) year-round.
General Information: Calcite "decorates" extensive limestone passages with sparkling, jewel-like crystals. The cave tour is offered on a first-come, first-served basis. You may have to wait for an opening during the busy summer season. Reservations are required for the "off-trail" caving tour.

MOUNT RUSHMORE
NATIONAL MEMORIAL

PO Box 268, Keystone, SD 57751, tel: 605-574-2523.
Access: The memorial is 2 miles (3 km) southwest of Keystone via Route 244.
Seasons & Hours: The orientation center is open daily 8am–10pm, mid-May–mid-September, until 5pm the rest of the year; closed Christmas.
Entrance Fee: No.
Handicapped Access: Orientation center.
Activities: Hiking, wildlife-watching, interpretive programs, exhibits.
Special events: March/April: Easter Service
July: Independence Day festivities
August 10: Gutzon Borglum Day is commemorated with presentations and music.
Permits & Licenses: No.
Camping: No.
Accommodations: None in the park. Lodging is available in Keystone, Hot Springs, Custer and throughout the Black Hills. Contact the Rapid City Convention and Visitors Bureau, PO Box 747, Rapid City, SD 57709, tel: 605-343-1744; South Dakota Tourism, 711 Wells Ave, Pierre, SD 57501, tel: 605-773-3301.
Food and Supplies: Food service is available in the park and surrounding towns.
Weather: Summer daytime temperatures 45°F–90°F (7°C–32°C). Winter temperatures –10°F–45°F (–23°C–7°C) with heavy snow.

General Information: The sculptor's studio is open May–September.

WIND CAVE NATIONAL PARK

Hot Springs, SD 57747, tel: 605-745-4600.
Access: The park is about 6 miles (10 km) north of Hot Springs via Highway 385, and 26 miles (42 km) east of Custer via Highway 16A and Route 87.
Seasons & Hours: The park is open daily year-round. Cave tours offered daily, limited schedule in winter. Visitor center and cave closed Thanksgiving, Christmas and New Year's Day.
Entrance Fee: For cave tour only.
Handicapped Access: Visitor center and portion of cave tour (see rangers at visitor center).
Activities: Cave tours, caving, scenic drive, camping, hiking, backpacking, wildlife-watching, interpretive programs.
Permits & Licenses: Free backcountry camping permits required.
Camping: First-come, first-served.
Accommodations: None in the park. Lodging is available in Custer, Hot Springs, Keystone and Rapid City. Contact the Rapid City Convention and Visitors Bureau, PO Box 747, Rapid City, SD 57709, tel: 605-343-1744; South Dakota Tourism, 711 Wells Ave, Pierre, SD 57501, tel: 605-773-3301.
Food and Supplies: Cafeteria at visitor center in summer only. Additional services in Custer, Hot Springs, Keystone and Rapid City.
Weather: Summer temperatures usually 50°F–90°F (10°C–32°C). Winter temperatures 0°F–50°F (18°C–10°C) with light snow. The cave is 53°F (12°C) year-round.
General Information: Never try to feed or approach wildlife. Bison may seem placid and slow-moving, but they can charge suddenly and at great speed if irritated. Call park headquarters to make reservations for off-trail caving tours.

WYOMING

DEVILS TOWER NATIONAL MONUMENT

PO Box 8, Devils Tower, WY 82714, tel: 307-467-5283.
Access: The monument is about 29 miles (47 km) northwest of Sundance via Highway 14 and Route 24.
Seasons & Hours: The monument is

open daily year-round. The visitor center is open May–October, 8am–5pm, extended summer hours.
Entrance Fee: Yes.
Handicapped Access: Visitor center and select campsites
Activities: Camping, hiking, rock climbing, wildlife-watching, interpretive programs.
Permits & Licenses: Climbing permits required. Climbers must register before a climb and sign out afterward.
Camping: First-come, first-served.
Accommodations: None in the park. Lodging is available in Sundance, Moorcroft and Spearfish. Contact Sundance Chamber of Commerce, PO Box 1004, Sundance, WY 82729, tel: 307-283-1000.
Food and Supplies: No services in the park. Services are available in Sundance, Moorcroft and Spearfish.
Weather: Summer daytime temperatures 70°F–85°F (21°C–30°C). Winter temperatures –10°F–40°F (–23°C to –1°C) with snowfall.
General Information: The nation's first national monument protects an 865-foot (264-meters) tower of volcanic rock, a favorite with rock climbers.

GRAND TETON NATIONAL PARK

PO Drawer 170, Moose, WY 83012, tel: 307-739-3300.
Access: The Moose Visitor Center is about 13 miles (21 km) north of Jackson via Highway 89/26/191. The Colter Bay Visitor Center is about 35 miles (56 km) south of Grant Village in Yellowstone National Park. Jackson Hole Airport, about 8 miles (13 km) from Jackson, is serviced by flights from Denver and Salt Lake City.
Seasons & Hours: The park is open daily year-round. Moose Visitor Center is open daily, 8am–5pm, extended summer hours; closed Christmas. Colter Bay Visitor Center is open seasonally only. Some park roads may be closed by snow November–May.
Entrance Fee: Yes.
Handicapped Access: Visitor centers, Indian Arts Museum and some ranger-led activities.
Activities: Scenic drive, camping, hiking, backpacking, fishing, float trips, boating, horseback riding, rock climbing, mountain climbing, cross-country skiing, snowshoeing, wildlife-watching, interpretive programs.

Special Events: July–August: Grand Teton Music Festival features performances at Teton Village by an international roster of musicians and orchestras.

Permits & Licenses: Free backcountry camping permits required.

Camping: First-come, first-served.

Accommodations: In the park:

Colter Bay Village (cabins)***.
Jackson Lake Lodge****.
Jenny Lake Lodge*****, Grand Teton Lodge Co., PO Box 240, Moran, WY 83013, tel: 307-543-2855.
Signal Mountain Lodge****, Teton Park Road, PO Box 50, Moran, WY 83013, tel: 307-543-2831 or tel: 307-733-5470.

Additional lodging is available in Jackson. Contact Wyoming Division of Tourism, I-25 at College Drive, Cheyenne, WY 82002, tel: 800-225-5996.

Food and Supplies: Restaurants and limited supplies are available in the park at Jackson Lake Lodge, Colter Bay Village and Signal Mountain Lodge. Additional services available in Jackson.

Weather: Weather varies considerably depending on elevation. Summer temperatures in lower elevations usually 35°F–80°F (8°C–27°C) with occasional highs in the 90°F (32°C); winter temperatures 0°F–30°F (–18°C to –1°C) with extremes well below 0°F (–18°C) and heavy snow November–April. Temperatures are much colder at higher elevations, where snow remains well into summer. Expect a variety of weather conditions in any season.

General Information: Do not approach or feed wildlife. Bison appear placid and slow-moving but can charge quickly and suddenly if irritated. Contact Grand Teton Lodge Co. (tel: 307-543-2855) for Jackson Lake cruises, float trips on the Snake River, boat rentals and horseback riding.

YELLOWSTONE NATIONAL PARK

PO Box 168, Yellowstone National Park, WY 82190, tel: 307-344-7381.

Access: The Fishing Bridge Visitor Center is 80 miles (129 km) west of Cody, Wyoming, via Highway 20/16/14. The Grant Village Visitor Center is about 75 miles (121 km) north of Jackson, Wyoming, via 191/89. The Old Faithful Visitor Center is about 145 miles (233 km) from Idaho Falls, Idaho, via Highway 20. Mammoth Hot Springs Visitor Center is about 48 miles (77 km) south of Livingston, Montana, via Highway 89.

Seasons & Hours: The park is open daily year-round. Many park roads may be closed by snow November–April. Mammoth Hot Springs Visitor Center is open daily 9am–5pm, extended hours in summer. Other visitor centers are open seasonally.

Entrance Fee: Yes.

Handicapped Access: Visitor centers, some campsites and some ranger-led activities.

Activities: Scenic drive, camping, hiking, backpacking, fishing, boating, horseback riding, rock climbing, mountain climbing, cross-country skiing, snowshoeing, wildlife-watching, interpretive programs.

Special Events: March: Rendezvous Ski Race in West Yellowstone, Montana.

Permits & Licenses: Free backcountry camping permits required.

Camping: Some sites can be reserved in advance by contacting Mistix, PO Box 85705, San Diego, CA 92186-5705, tel: 800-365-2267.

Accommodations: In the park:

Canyon Lodge (cabins)**.
Grant Village Motel**.
Lake Lodge & Cabins**.
Lake Yellowstone Hotel & Cabins**.
Mammoth Hot Springs Hotel & Cabins***.
Old Faithful Inn****.
Old Faithful Lodge & Cabins*.
Old Faithful Snow Lodge & Cabins**.
Roosevelt Lodge & Cabins**, TW Services, Inc., PO Box 528, Yellowstone National Park, WY 82190, tel: 307-344-7311.

Additional lodging is available in Jackson, Cody and Livingston. Contact Wyoming Division of Tourism, I-25 at College Drive, Cheyenne, WY 82002, tel: 800-225-5996 or Travel Montana, 1424 9th Ave, PO Box 200533, Helena, MT 59620, tel: 800-847-4868.

Food and Supplies: Restaurants and limited supplies are available in the park at Lake, Canyon, Tower Fall, Mammoth Hot Springs, Grant Village, Old Faithful. Additional services available in Jackson, Livingston, Cody, Cooke City, West Yellowstone and Gardiner.

Weather: Weather varies considerably depending on elevation. Summer temperatures in lower elevations usually 35°F–80°F (2°C–27°C) with occasional highs in the 90°F 932°C); winter temperatures 0°F–30°F (–18°C to –1°C) with extremes well below 0°F (–18°C) and heavy snow November–April. Temperatures are much cooler at higher elevations, where snow remains into summer. Expect a variety of weather conditions in any season.

General Information: Do not try to approach or feed wildlife. Bison appear placid and slow-moving but can charge quickly and suddenly if irritated. Contact TW Recreational Services, Inc., Yellowstone National Park, WY 82190, tel: 307-344-7311 for information on guided bus tours, cruises of Yellowstone Lake, snowcoach tours, boat rentals and horseback riding.

THE NORTHWEST

ALASKA

ANIAKCHAK NATIONAL MONUMENT AND PRESERVE

PO Box 7, King Salmon, AK 99613, tel: 907-246-3305.

Access: There are no roads to Aniakchak. Charter flights are available from King Salmon.

Seasons & Hours: The monument is open daily year-round.

Entrance Fee: No.

Handicapped Access: No.

Activities: Fishing, wilderness camping, float trips, wildlife-watching.

Visitor Facilities: None.

Camping: Wilderness camping only.

Permits & Licenses: Alaska fishing license.

Accommodations: None in the park; nearest lodging is in King Salmon. Contact King Salmon Visitor Center, PO Box 298, King Salmon, AK 99613, tel: 907-246-4250.

Food & Supplies: No services in the park; supplies are available in King Salmon.

Weather: Temperatures usually –30°F–30°F (–34°C to –1°C) in winter,

40°F–70°F (4°C–21°C) in summer; violent wind, rain and snowstorms in any season. Be prepared for extreme conditions.
General Information: Visitors must be completely self-sufficient and experienced in wilderness travel. Insect repellent is recommended. Most travelers arrive between June and August. Contact park headquarters well in advance of visit.

BERING LAND BRIDGE
NATIONAL PRESERVE

PO Box 220, Nome, AK 99762, tel: 907-443-2522.
Access: There are no roads to Bering Land Bridge. Charter flights are available from Nome and Kotzebue.
Seasons & Hours: The preserve is open daily year-round.
Entrance Fee: No.
Handicapped Access: No.
Activities: Fishing, wilderness camping, float trips, wildlife-watching, backcountry hiking.
Visitor Facilities: None.
Camping: Wilderness camping only.
Permits & Licenses: Alaska fishing license.
Accommodations: None in the park; nearest lodging is in Nome and Kotzebue. Contact Nome Visitor Center, PO Box 240, Nome, AK 99762, tel: 907-443-5535.
Food & Supplies: No services in the park; supplies and restaurants are available in Nome and Kotzebue.
Weather: Temperatures usually –30°F–30°F (–34°C to –1°C) in winter, 40°F–75°F (4°C–24°C) in summer; violent wind, rain and snowstorms in any season. Be prepared for extreme conditions.
General Information: Visitors must be completely self-sufficient and experienced in wilderness travel. Insect repellent is recommended. Most travelers arrive between June and August. Contact park headquarters well in advance of visit.

CAPE KRUSENSTERN
NATIONAL MONUMENT

PO Box 1029, Kotzebue, AK 99752, tel: 907-442-3890.
Access: There are no roads to Cape Krusenstern. Charter flights and boats are available from Kotzebue.

Seasons & Hours: The monument is open daily year-round.
Entrance Fee: No.
Handicapped Access: No.
Activities: Fishing, wildlife-watching, backcountry hiking and camping.
Visitor Facilities: Information is available from park office in Kotzebue.
Camping: Wilderness camping only.
Permits & Licenses: Alaska fishing license.
Accommodations: None in the park; nearest lodging is in Nome and Kotzebue. Contact Nome Visitor Center, PO Box 240, Nome, AK 99762, tel: 907-443-5535.
Food & Supplies: No services in the park; food and supplies are available in Nome and Kotzebue.
Weather: Temperatures usually –60°F–30°F (–51°C to –1°C) in winter; 30°F–75°F (–1°C–24°C) in summer; violent wind, rain and snowstorms in any season. Be prepared for extreme conditions.
General Information: Visitors must be completely self-sufficient and experienced in wilderness travel. Insect repellent is recommended. Most travelers arrive between June and August. Contact park headquarters well in advance of visit.

DENALI NATIONAL PARK AND PRESERVE

PO Box 9, Denali Park, AK 99755, tel: 907-683-2294.
Access: Rail, bus (summer only) and charter air service available from Fairbanks and Anchorage. The park is 121 miles (195 km) from Fairbanks and 237 miles (381 km) from Anchorage by car via Alaska Highway 3. Gas stations are few; fuel up at every opportunity. Automobile access to park interior is limited. Free shuttle buses run daily from Visitor Center between late May and mid-September. Shuttle-bus seats may be reserved in advance by calling 800-622-7275. Waiting two or three days for an unreserved bus seat is not uncommon during the summer.
Seasons & Hours: The park is open daily year-round. The visitor center is open 7am–6pm, September–May.
Entrance Fee: Yes.
Handicapped Access: Visitor enter, Eielson visitor center, park headquarters, Denali Park Hotel, park auditorium, several campsites, post office and shuttle bus.

Activities: Fishing, camping, wildlife-watching, hiking, float trips, mountain climbing, dogsledding, guided nature walks, cross-country skiing, bus tours.
Visitor Facilities: Visitor center and Eielson visitor center.
Camping: A portion of the park's tent and RV sites may be reserved in advance by calling 800-622-7275. The remainder are available on a first-come, first-served basis. 14-day summer limit; 30-day winter limit.
Permits & Licenses: Free backcountry permits are available on a first-come, first-served basis from the Visitor Center.
Accommodations:
Denali National Park Hotel****, ARA Denali Park Hotels, 825 W 8th Ave, Anchorage, AK 99501, tel: 907-276-7234.
Camp Denali (cabins)****, PO Box 67, Denali, AK 99755, tel: 907-683-2290.
Denali Cabins****, PO Box 229, Denali, AK 99755, tel: 907-683-2643.
Food & Supplies: Restaurants and supplies are available at park entrance and along Highway 3 outside the park.
Weather: Temperatures usually –40°F–30°F (–40°C to –1°C) in winter, 40°F–70°F (4°C–21°C) in summer; violent wind and storms in any season. Be prepared for extreme conditions. Snow may close the park road from late September to mid-May.
General Information: Backcountry travelers must be completely self-sufficient and experienced in wilderness travel. Insect repellent is recommended. Most travelers arrive between June and August. Contact park headquarters well in advance of visit for reservations and information.

GATES OF THE ARCTIC
NATIONAL PARK AND PRESERVE

PO Box 74680, Fairbanks, AK 99707, tel: 907-456-0281.
Access: There are no roads to Gates of the Arctic. Charter flights are available from Fairbanks to Bettles and Anaktuvuk Pass; charter flights are also available from Bettles into the park.
Seasons & Hours: The park is open daily year-round.
Entrance Fee: No.
Handicapped Access: No.
Activities: Fishing, wilderness camp-

ing, wildlife-watching, backpacking, mountain climbing, float trips.

Visitor Facilities: There are no facilities in the park; ranger stations are located in Bettles and Anaktuvuk Pass.

Camping: Wilderness camping only.

Permits & Licenses: Alaska fishing license.

Accommodations: There are a few small, rustic wilderness lodges: *Alatna Lodge & Wilderness Cabins****, Alatna Guide Service, PO Box 80424, Fairbanks, AK 99708, tel: 907-479-6354.

Walker Lake Lodge***, 930 9th Ave, Fairbanks, AK 99701, tel: 907-452-5417.

Limited accommodations are available outside the park in Coldfoot. Contact Fairbanks Visitor Information Center, 550 First Ave, Fairbanks, AK 99701, tel: 800-327-5774 or tel: 907-456-5774.

Food & Supplies: No services in the park; limited supplies are available in Bettles. Bring all food from Fairbanks.

Weather: Severe winter conditions and short summers; violent wind, rain and snowstorms in any season. Be prepared for extreme arctic conditions.

General Information: Visitors must be completely self-sufficient and experienced in wilderness travel. Insect repellent is recommended. Contact park headquarters well in advance of visit to plan your trip and to request a list of outfitters and guides.

GLACIER BAY NATIONAL PARK AND PRESERVE

PO Box 140, Gustavus, AK 99826, tel: 907-697-2230.

Access: There are no roads to Glacier Bay. Flights and charter boats are available from Juneau.

Seasons & Hours: The park is open daily year-round; facilities are limited mid-September–mid-May.

Entrance Fee: No.

Handicapped Access: Visitor center, Glacier Bay Lodge and Forest Loop Trail.

Activities: Fishing, camping, whale-watching, boat tours, wildlife-watching, glaciers, mountain climbing, backpacking, boating, guided tours, interpretive programs, nature walks.

Visitor Facilities: Information is available at Glacier Bay Lodge and Bartlett Cove.

Camping: First-come, first-served; 14-day limit.

Permits & Licenses: Alaska fishing license; boating permits.

Accommodations:

Glacier Bay Lodge***, Gustavus, AK 99826, tel: 907-697-2225, open seasonally.

A few basic accommodations are available outside the park in Gustavus. Contact Gustavus Visitor Association, c/o Bear Track Mercantile, PO Box 259, Gustavus, AK 99826, tel: 907-697-2358.

Food & Supplies: A restaurant is located in Glacier Bay Lodge. Limited supplies in Gustavus. Campers should bring food and supplies from Juneau.

Weather: Severe winter conditions and short summers; violent wind, rain and snowstorms. Be prepared for wet, cold weather even in summer.

General Information: Most travelers see the park by boat; tour boats leave daily in summer from Glacier Bay Lodge. Backpackers must be completely self-sufficient and experienced in wilderness travel. Insect repellent is highly recommended. Contact park headquarters well in advance of visit for reservations and information on guides and outfitters.

KATMAI NATIONAL PARK AND PRESERVE

PO Box 7, King Salmon, AK 99613, tel: 907-246-3305.

Access: A 10-mile (16-km) dirt road runs from King Salmon to Lake Camp just inside the park boundary. Flights connect Anchorage to King Salmon, where you can hike, boat or hire a charter bush plane into the park.

Seasons & Hours: The park is open daily year-round; facilities are limited June–mid-September.

Entrance Fee: No.

Handicapped Access: Auditorium, campground restroom, Brooks Lodge.

Activities: Fishing, camping, bear-watching, mountain climbing, backpacking, boating, guided tours, nature walks, interpretive programs.

Visitor Facilities: Information available at park headquarters in King Salmon and at Brooks Camp Visitor Center.

Camping: Brooks Camp; reservations required.

Permits & Licenses: Alaska fishing license; backcountry permits available

at Brooks Camp Visitor Center and park headquarters.

Accommodations: Katmailand manages rustic backcountry lodges and cabins including:

Brooks Lodge, Grosvenor Lodge and *Kulik Lodge*****, 4700 Aircraft Drive, Anchorage, AK 99502, tel: 800-544-0551.

Enchanted Lake Lodge****, PO Box 97, King Salmon, AK 99613, tel: 907-246-6878.

Limited accommodations are also available in King Salmon. Contact King Salmon Visitor Center, PO Box 298, King Salmon, AK 99613, tel: 907-246-4250.

Food & Supplies: Limited food and supplies are available in the park at Brooks and Grosvenor Lakes camp; outside the park at King Salmon.

Weather: Severe winter conditions and short summers with highs in the mid-60°F (mid-16°C); violent wind, rain and snowstorms. Be prepared for wet, cold weather even in summer.

General Information: Backpackers must be completely self-sufficient and experienced in wilderness travel. Insect repellent is recommended. Contact park headquarters well in advance of visit for reservations and information on guides and outfitters.

KENAI FJORDS NATIONAL PARK

PO Box 1727, Seward, AK 99664. Tel: 907-224-3175.

Access: Seward, about 6 miles (10 km) from the park boundary, is 125 miles (201 km) from Anchorage via Alaska Highway 9. A single unpaved road enters the park as far as Exit Glacier, about 8œ miles (14 km). The road may be closed by snow between mid-October and May. Train, bus, plane and ferry service available from Anchorage.

Seasons & Hours: The park is open daily year-round. The visitor center is open daily 8am–5pm, extended summer hours; closed Christmas.

Entrance Fee: No.

Handicapped Access: Visitor center and paved trail at Exit Glacier.

Activities: Fishing, camping, wildlife-watching, mountain climbing, glaciers, backpacking, cross-country skiing, boating, guided tours, nature walks, interpretive programs.

Visitor Facilities: Information is available at Seward visitor center and Exit

Glacier ranger station.

Camping: First-come, first-served.

Permits & Licenses: Alaska fishing license.

Accommodations: Hotels and motels are available outside the park in Seward. Contact Seward Chamber of Commerce, PO Box 749, Seward, AK 99664, tel: 907-224-3046.

Food & Supplies: There are no food or supplies available in the park. Restaurants and supplies are available in Seward.

Weather: Severe winter conditions and short, wet summers. Violent wind, rain and snowstorms.

General Information: Backpackers must be completely self-sufficient and experienced in wilderness travel. Insect repellent is recommended. Contact park headquarters well in advance of visit.

KOBUK VALLEY NATIONAL PARK

PO Box 1029, Kotzebue, AK 99752, tel: 907-442-3890.

Access: There are no roads to Kobuk Valley. Flights are available from Fairbanks to Kotzebue, where charter planes can be hired into the park.

Seasons & Hours: The park is open daily year-round.

Entrance Fee: No.

Handicapped Access: No.

Activities: Wilderness camping, wildlife-watching, backpacking, float trips, fishing.

Visitor Facilities: There are no facilities in the park. Information is available at park headquarters in Kotzebue.

Camping: Wilderness camping only.

Permits & Licenses: Alaska fishing license.

Accommodations: Rustic accommodations are available in Kotzebue, Ambler and Kiana. Contact Nome Visitor Center, PO Box 240, Nome, AK 99762, tel: 907-443-5535.

Food & Supplies: No services in the park. Limited supplies can be purchased in Kotzebue.

Weather: The park is subject to extreme arctic weather at any time of year.

General Information: Backpackers must be completely self-sufficient and experienced in wilderness travel. Insect repellent is recommended. Contact park headquarters well in advance of visit.

LAKE CLARK NATIONAL PARK AND PRESERVE

4230 University Drive, Suite 311, Anchorage, AK 99508, tel: 907-271-3751.

Access: There are no roads to Lake Clark. Charter flights are available from Anchorage, Kenai, Homer and Iliamna.

Seasons & Hours: The park is open daily year-round.

Entrance Fee: No.

Handicapped Access: No.

Activities: Wilderness camping, wildlife-watching, backpacking, float trips, fishing.

Visitor Facilities: Aside from a ranger station at Port Alsworth on the shore of Lake Clark, there are no facilities in the park. Information is available at park headquarters in Anchorage.

Camping: Wilderness camping only.

Permits & Licenses: Alaska fishing license.

Accommodations: There are a few rustic lodges in the park:

Alaska's Wilderness Lodge****, 1 Lang Road, Port Alsworth, AK 99653, tel: 907-781-2223.

Koksetna Wilderness Lodge***, General Delivery, Port Alsworth, AK 99653, tel: 907-781-2227.

Lakeside Lodge***, Port Alsworth, AK 99653, tel: 907-262-5245.

Silver Salmon Creek Lodge***, PO Box 3234, Soldotna, AK, tel: 907-262-4839.

For additional lodging contact Anchorage Visitor Information Center, 1600 A St, Suite 200, Anchorage, AK 99501, tel: 907-276-4118.

Food & Supplies: Food and supplies should be brought into the park from Anchorage or Kenai.

Weather: Severe winter conditions and short summers with high temperatures 60°F–75°F(16°C–24°C); violent wind, rain and snowstorms in any season. Be prepared for extreme conditions.

General Information: Visitors must be completely self-sufficient and experienced in wilderness travel. Insect repellent is recommended. Contact park headquarters well in advance of visit.

NOATAK NATIONAL PRESERVE

PO Box 1029, Kotzebue, AK 99752, tel: 907-442-3890.

Access: There are no roads to Noatak. Charter flights are available from Kotzebue.

Seasons & Hours: The preserve is open daily year-round.

Entrance Fee: No.

Handicapped Access: No.

Activities: Wilderness camping, wildlife-watching, backpacking, float trips, fishing.

Visitor Facilities: There are no facilities in the park. Information is available at park headquarters in Kotzebue.

Camping: Wilderness camping only.

Permits & Licenses: Alaska fishing license.

Accommodations: Limited lodging is available in Kotzebue. Contact Nome Visitor Center PO Box 240, Nome, AK 99762, tel: 907-443-5535.

Food & Supplies: Food and supplies are not available in the park. All supplies should be brought into the park.

Weather: Severe winter conditions and short summers; violent wind, rain and snowstorms in any season. Be prepared for extreme arctic conditions.

General Information: Visitors must be completely self-sufficient and experienced in wilderness travel. Insect repellent is recommended. Contact park headquarters well in advance of visit.

WRANGELL-ST ELIAS NATIONAL PARK AND PRESERVE

PO Box 29, Glennallen, AK 99588, tel: 907-822-5234.

Access: Two unpaved roads enter the park, one from Chitina in the central section of the park and the other from Slana in the northern section. The roads are usually passable in summer; they may be closed by snow September–mid-May. Regular passenger vehicles with high clearance can usually negotiate park roads in summer, but a four-wheel-drive vehicle may be necessary. Charter flights can be hired in Tok, Gulkana, Valdez, McCarthy, Anchorage and Fairbanks.

Seasons & Hours: The park is open daily year-round. The visitor center is open daily 8am–6pm, September–May.

Entrance Fee: No.

Handicapped Access: Visitor center.
Activities: Wilderness camping, wildlife-watching, backpacking, float trips, fishing, mountain climbing, cross-country skiing.
Visitor Facilities: Information is available at park headquarters in Glennallen just outside of park. Ranger stations are located outside park at Chitina (seasonal), Slana and Yakutat.
Camping: There are private campgrounds on the Chitina-McCarthy Road.
Permits & Licenses: Alaska fishing license.
Accommodations: *Kennicott Glacier Lodge***, PO Box 103940, Anchorage, AK 99510, tel: 907-258-2350.

McCarthy Wilderness Bed & Breakfast**, PO Box 111241, Anchorage, AK 99511, tel: 907-277-6867.

Tanada Lake Lodge****, PO Box 258, Fairbanks, AK 99707, tel: 907-452-1247.

There are limited accommodations in and around Glennallen and Chitina. Contact Greater Copper Valley Chamber of Commerce, PO Box 469, Glennallen, AK 99588, tel: 907-822-5555.
Food & Supplies: Limited food and supplies are available in Glennallen and Chitina.
Weather: Severe winter conditions and short summers; violent wind and snowstorms in winter, rainstorms are common in summer. High-quality rain gear is a must.
General Information: This is a 13 million-acre (5 million-hectare) wilderness park in southeastern Alaska with limited facilities for travelers. Visitors must be completely self-sufficient and experienced in wilderness travel. Insect repellent is highly recommended. Contact park headquarters well in advance for a list of outfitters and guides, and to plan your visit.

YUKON-CHARLEY RIVERS
NATIONAL PRESERVE

PO Box 74718, Fairbanks, AK 99707, tel: 907-456-0594.
Access: There are no roads in the park. Enter by boat or plane from Circle or Eagle, accessible by road from Fairbanks and Tetlin Junction. Flights are available from Fairbanks to both Circle and Eagle.
Seasons & Hours: The preserve is open daily year-round.

Entrance Fee: No.
Handicapped Access: No.
Activities: Wilderness camping, wildlife-watching, backpacking, float trips, fishing.
Visitor Facilities: Information is available at the seasonal visitor center in Eagle.
Camping: Eagle and Circle campgrounds; wilderness camping; no reservations required.
Permits & Licenses: Alaska fishing license.
Accommodations: None in the park. Lodging is available in Circle and Eagle. Contact Fairbanks Visitor Information Center, 550 First Ave, Fairbanks, AK 99701, tel: 800-327-5774 or tel: 907-456-5774.
Food & Supplies: Limited food and supplies are available in Circle and Eagle.
Weather: Severe winter conditions and short summers; violent wind and snowstorms in winter, rainstorms are common in summer. High-quality rain gear is a must. Local roads may be closed in winter.
General Information: This 2œ-million-acre (1-million-hectare) preserve along the Canadian border protects stretches of the Yukon and Charley rivers. There are no facilities within the park. Visitors must be completely self-sufficient and experienced in wilderness travel. Insect repellent is highly recommended. Contact park headquarters in advance for a list of outfitters and river guides, and to plan your visit.

OREGON

CRATER LAKE NATIONAL PARK

PO Box 7, Crater Lake, OR 97604, tel: 503-594-2211.
Access: The park is about 70 miles (113 km) northeast of Medford via Highway 62, 60 miles (97 km) north of Klamath Falls and 143 miles (230 km) southeast of Eugene via Routes 58, 97 and 138.
Seasons & Hours: The park is open daily year-round. The north entrance and sections of park roads may be closed by snow October–June. Steele Visitor Center is open daily 9am–5pm, closed Christmas. Rim Visitor Center is open in summer only, 10am–6pm.
Entrance Fee: Yes.
Handicapped Access: Visitor centers,

select campsites and most overlooks.
Activities: Scenic drive, camping, hiking, backpacking, boat tours, wildlife-watching, cross-country skiing, snowshoeing, interpretive programs.
Permits & Licenses: Free backcountry camping permit.
Camping: First-come, first-served.
Accommodations: In the park: *Mazama Motor Inn****, Crater Lake Lodge, Inc., Crater Lake, OR 97604, tel: 503-594-2511. The *Crater Lake Lodge* will reopen in 1995.

Additional lodging is available in Diamond Lake, Prospect, Fort Klamath, Chilioquin and Medford. Contact Klamath County Chamber of Commerce, PO Box 1867, Klamath Falls, OR 97601, tel: 800-445-6728.
Food & Supplies: Limited food service and supplies are available at Mazama Village and Rim Village. Additional services are available in Diamond Lake, Prospect, Fort Klamath, Union Creek, Chilioquin and Medford.
Weather: Summer temperatures 35°F–80°F (2°C–27°C). Winter temperatures 15°F–40°F (–9°C–4°C), with occasional lows well below 0°F (–18°C) and as much as 20 ft (6 meters) of snow.
General Information: Never try to feed or approach wildlife. Be prepared for cold weather in any season and snowy conditions October–April.

OREGON CAVES NATIONAL MONUMENT

19000 Caves Highway, Cave Junction, OR 97523, tel: 503-592-2100.
Access: The monument is 20 miles (32 km) southeast of Cave Junction via Route 46 in the southwestern corner of Oregon.
Seasons & Hours: The monument is open daily year-round. The visitor center (in Cave Junction) is open daily 9am–5pm. Cave tour and visitor center closed Thanksgiving and Christmas.
Entrance Fee: A fee is charged for the cave tour.
Handicapped Access: First room of cave only. Contact Park Service for assistance.
Activities: Guided cave tours, hiking, wildlife-watching, interpretive programs.
Permits & Licenses: No.
Camping: No.
Accommodations: Lodging is available in the park June–September at Oregon

Caves Chateau, PO Box 128, Cave Junction, OR 97523, tel: 503-592-2100. Additional lodging in Cave Junction. Contact Cave Junction Chamber of Commerce, tel: 503-592-2631.

Food & Supplies: Food service is available to guests at Oregon Caves Chateau June–September. Additional services available in Cave Junction.

Weather: Summer temperatures 35°F–80°F (2°C–27°C), with occasional highs in the 90°F (32°C). Winter temperatures 15°F–40°F (–9°C–4°C) with snowfall. Cave temperature is 42°F (6°C) year-round.

General Information: Ground water has carved the marble bedrock into chambers and a variety of fascinating flowstone formations. Guided tours are offered.

WASHINGTON

COULEE DAM
NATIONAL RECREATION AREA

1008 Crest Drive, Coulee Dam, WA 99116, tel: 509-633-9441.

Access: The recreation area can be entered at various places along Franklin D Roosevelt Lake, including Grand Coulee, Kettle Falls and Fort Spokane.

Seasons & Hours: The recreation area is open daily year-round. The Coulee Dam Visitor Arrival Center is open daily 9am–5pm, extended hours in summer; other visitor centers are open seasonally; closed Thanksgiving, Christmas and New Year's Day.

Entrance Fee: No.

Handicapped Access: Visitor centers and some campsites.

Activities: Camping, hiking, swimming, boating, water-skiing, fishing, wildlife-watching, interpretive programs.

Permits & Licenses: Washington fishing license.

Camping: First-come, first-served.

Accommodations: None in the park. For lodging in the area, contact Grand Coulee Dam Area Chamber of Commerce, PO Box 760, Grand Coulee, WA 99133, tel: 509-633-3074.

Food and Supplies: Limited food and supplies are available in the park. Additional services available in Grand Coulee, Kettle Falls, Colville, Northport.

Weather: Summer temperatures usually 50°F–100°F (10°C–38°C), cooler in the northern section of the lake. Winter is cold, with frequent fog and cloudiness, 5°F–40°F(–15°C–4°C).

General Information: 150-mile (241-km) long Franklin D Roosevelt Lake was created by Grand Coulee Dam. The recreation area offers a variety of water sports, hiking and camping.

MOUNT RAINIER NATIONAL PARK

Tahoma Woods, Star Route, Ashford, WA 98304, tel: 206-569-2211.

Access: The Paradise Visitor Center is 74 miles (119 km) southeast of Tacoma via Routes 7 and 706, 98 miles (158 km) southeast of Seattle via I-5, Route 7 and Route 706, and 87 miles (140 km) west of Yakima via Routes 12, 123 and 706. Gray Line of Seattle offers daily bus service between Seattle and Mount Rainier May–mid-October.

Seasons & Hours: The park is open daily year-round. Some roads may be closed by snow November–June. Paradise Visitor Center is open daily 9am–7pm, weekends only October–January.

Entrance Fee: Yes.

Handicapped Access: Visitor centers, Longmire Museum and some campsites; limited access to paved nature trails.

Activities: Scenic drive, camping, hiking, biking, backpacking, rock climbing, mountain climbing, cross-country skiing, snowshoeing, wildlife-watching, interpretive programs.

Permits & Licenses: Free backcountry camping permits required.

Camping: First-come, first-served.

Accommodations: In the park: *National Park Inn****.

Paradise Inn***, Mount Rainier Guest Services, PO Box 108, Ashford, WA 98304, tel: 206-569-2275. Additional lodging is available in Ashford, Packwood and Elbe. Contact Southwest Washington Tourism, PO Box 876, Longview, WA 98632, tel: 206-425-1211.

Food and Supplies: Available in the park at Longmire, Sunrise and Paradise. Additional services available in Ashford, Elbe, Packwood, Enumclaw.

Weather: Weather varies considerably depending on elevation. Summer temperatures usually 40°F–80°F (4°C–27°C), cooler at higher elevations; winter temperatures usually 10°F–35°F (–12°C–2°C) with heavy snow.

Weather can change quickly in any season.

General Information: Summer is generally crowded; consider visiting in early fall. Crossing snowfields may require special skills and equipment. Hiking in high elevations can be extremely difficult, causing dizziness, nausea and shortness of breath. Give yourself a few days to adjust. For mountain-climbing instruction and guide services, contact Rainier Mountaineering, 535 Dock St, Suite 209, Tacoma, WA 98402, tel: 206-627-6242. For cross-country skiing equipment, contact Longmire Ski Touring Center, tel: 206-569-2411.

NORTH CASCADES
NATIONAL PARK COMPLEX

(including Lake Chelan and Ross Lake National Recreation Areas), 2105 Highway 20, Sedro Woolley, WA 98284, tel: 206-856-5700.

Access: The park is 50 miles (81 km) east of Burlington and 70 miles (113 km) west of Twisp via Route 20. Stehekin (in Lake Chelan National Recreation Area) can be reached via boat or floatplane from Chelan on Highway 97 or by foot from the south unit of North Cascades National Park. The only ramp for private boats on Ross Lake (in Ross Lake National Recreation Area) is at the end of an unpaved road from Hope, British Columbia.

Seasons & Hours: The park is open daily year-round. Newhalem Visitor Center is open daily 8.30am–5pm, weekends only in winter; closed Thanksgiving, Christmas and New Year's Day. Route 20 may be closed by snow mid-October–April.

Entrance Fee: No.

Handicapped Access: Visitor centers, select campsites and some nature trails.

Activities: Scenic drive, camping, hiking, backpacking, rock climbing, mountain climbing, fishing, cross-country skiing, snowshoeing, wildlife-watching, interpretive programs.

Permits & Licenses: Free backcountry camping permits required.

Camping: First-come, first-served.

Accommodations: In the park: *Ross Lake Resort* (cabins)**, Rockport, WA 98283, tel: 206-386-4437.

North Cascades Stehekin Lodge**, PO Box 457, Chelan, WA 98816, tel:

509-682-4494.

Silver Bay Inn**, PO Box 43, Stehekin, WA 98852, tel: 509-682-2212.

Stehekin Valley Ranch**, PO Box 36, Stehekin, WA 98852, tel: 509-682-4677.

Additional lodging is available in Concrete and Chelan. Contact Lake Chelan Chamber of Commerce, PO Box 216, Chelan, WA 98816, tel: 800-424-3526.

Food and Supplies: Limited services available in the park at Newhalem and Stehekin. Additional services available in Marblemount, Concrete and Chelan.

Weather: Weather varies considerably depending on elevation. Summer temperatures in lower elevations usually 45°F–80°F (7°C–27°C); winter temperatures 25°F–45°F (–4°C–7°C) with heavy snow. Temperatures are much cooler at higher elevations, where as much as 20 ft (6 meters) of snow can accumulate before melting in summer. Weather can change quickly in any season.

General Information: Crossing snowfields may require special skills and equipment. Hiking in high elevations can be extremely difficult, causing dizziness, nausea and shortness of breath. Give yourself a few days to adjust. For information about Seattle City Light's tours of park and power facilities, tel: 206-684-3030.

OLYMPIC NATIONAL PARK

600 E Park Avenue, Port Angeles, WA 98362, tel: 206-452-4501.

Access: The Port Angeles visitor center is about 140 miles (43 km) northwest of Tacoma via Highways 5 and 101. The Hoh Rain Forest Visitor Center is about 100 miles (31 km) north of Aberdeen via Highway 101 and Hoh Road.

Seasons & Hours: The park is open daily year-round. Visitor centers and ranger stations are closed Christmas and New Year's Day. Some park roads may be closed by snow October–April.

Entrance Fee: Yes.

Handicapped Access: Visitor centers, some nature trails and campsites.

Activities: Scenic drive, camping, hiking, backpacking, fishing, rock climbing, mountain climbing, cross-country skiing, snowshoeing, wildlife-watching, interpretive programs.

Permits & Licenses: Free backcountry camping permits required.

Camping: First-come, first-served.

Accommodations: In the park:

Kalaloch Lodge***, 157151 Highway 101, Forks, WA 98331, tel: 206-962-2271.

Lake Crescent Lodge***, HC 62, Box 11, Port Angeles, WA 98362, tel: 206-928-3211.

Log Cabin Resort**, 3183 E Beach Road, Port Angeles, WA 98363, tel: 206-928-3245.

Sol Duc Hot Springs Resort**, PO Box 2169, Port Angeles, WA 98362, tel: 206-327-3583.

Additional lodging is available in Lake Quinault, Port Angeles, Sequim, Forks. Contact the Port Angeles Chamber of Commerce, 121 E Railroad, Port Angeles, WA 98362, tel: 206-452-2363 or the Forks Chamber of Commerce, PO Box 1249, Forks, WA 98331, tel: 206-374-2531.

Food and Supplies: Restaurants and limited supplies are available in the park at Kalaloch, Sol Duc Hot Springs and Lake Crescent. Additional services available in Port Angeles, Forks and Sappho.

Weather: Weather varies considerably depending on elevation. Summer temperatures in lower elevations usually 40°F–70°F (12°C–21°C); winter temperatures 20°F–45°F (6°C–14°C). Temperatures are much cooler at higher elevations, where snow is heavy well into May. Most of Olympic's precipitation falls October–March. Expect heavy rain, wind and fog in any season.

General Information: Crossing snowfields may require special skills and equipment. Hiking in high elevations can be extremely difficult, causing dizziness, nausea and shortness of breath. Give yourself a few days to adjust. Obtain a tide table before hiking on the beach; incoming tides can trap hikers between headlands. Look for floating logs, too. An unexpected wave can send them hurtling toward the beach, crushing anything that gets in the way. The ocean is cold and currents are fierce; swim in the lakes instead of the ocean.

HISTORIC AND ARCHAEOLOGICAL SITES

Contact these parks directly for hours, seasons, access, road and weather conditions.

CALIFORNIA & PACIFIC ISLANDS

CALIFORNIA

Cabrillo National Monument, PO Box 6670, San Diego, CA 92166, tel: 619-557-5450. This coastal park commemorates the voyage of Juan Rodriquez Cabrillo, the Portuguese explorer who "discovered" California in 1542.

Eugene O'Neill National Historic Site, PO Box 280, Danville, CA 94526, tel: 510-838-0249. The playwright wrote some of his best-known works at this home from 1937–1944.

John Muir National Historic Site, 4202 Alhambra Ave, Martinez, CA 94553, tel: 415-228-8860. Muir's home commemorates his life and career as a naturalist, organizer and writer.

San Francisco Maritime National Historical Park, Fort Mason, Building 201, San Francisco, CA 94123, tel: 415-556-1659. Several historic ships and a maritime museum on the San Francisco waterfront.

GUAM

War in the Pacific National Historical Park, PO Box FA, Agana, GU 96910, tel: 671-477-9362. The park commemorates all people involved in World War II's Pacific campaigns.

HAWAII

Kalaupapa National Historical Park. Kalaupapa, HI 96742. This is the site of a Hansen's disease (or leprosy) settlement founded in the late 1880s. A few residents still live at the settlement. Visitation is limited. Visitors must first obtain a permit.

Kaloko-Honokohau National Historical Park, c/o Pu'uhonua o Honaunau National Historical Park, PO Box 129, Honaunau, Kona, HI 96726, tel: 808-328-2326. The park preserves several pre-European archaeological sites.

Pu'uhonua o Honaunau National Historical Park, PO Box 129, Honaunau, Kona, HI 96726, tel: 808-328-2326. An ancient Hawaiian sanctuary, the park preserves prehistoric sites, and a lovely coastal landscape.

Puukohola Heiau National Historic Site, PO Box 44340, Kawaihae, HI 96743, tel: 808-882-7218. The park preserves the ruins of a temple built on the Big Isles by King Kamehameha the Great in 1791.

USS Arizona **Memorial**, 1 Arizona Memorial Place, Honolulu, HI 96818, tel: 808-422-2771. An underwater memorial at the site where the *USS Arizona* was sunk during the 1941 attack on Pearl Harbor.

THE SOUTHWEST

ARIZONA

Casa Grande National Monument, 1100 Ruins Drive, Coolidge, AZ 85228, tel: 602-723-3172. The monument preserves a 4-story ruin, part of a 15th-century Hohokam village.

Fort Bowie National Historic Site, PO Box 158, Bowie, AZ 85605, tel: 602-847-2500. This 1,000-acre (405-hectare) park preserves the ruins of Fort Bowie, established in 1862 to protect settlers from Apache Indians. The fort was an important military post during the US Army's campaign against Geronimo.

Hubbell Trading Post National Historic Site, PO Box 150, Ganado, AZ 86505, tel: 602-755-3475. A working, 100-year-old trading post on the Navajo reservation.

Montezuma Castle National Monument, PO Box 219, Camp Verde, AZ 86322, tel: 602-567-3322. A well-preserved, 5-story cliff dwelling built about 700 years ago by people of the Sinagua culture.

Navajo National Monument, HC 71, Box 3, Tonalea, AZ 86044-9704, tel: 602-672-2366. Dramatic and well-preserved cliff dwellings built by the Kayenta Anasazi in the mid-13th century.

Sunset Crater National Monument, Route 3, Box 149, Flagstaff, AZ 86004, tel: 602-556-7042. The monument features a 1,000-foot (305-meters) cinder cone created by the eruption of Sunset Crater Volcano in 1064–65 and subsequent lava flows.

Tonto National Monument, HC02, Box 4602, Roosevelt, AZ 85545, tel: 602-467-2241. Cliff dwellings built and inhabited by Salado farmers in the 1300s.

Tumacacori National Historical Park, PO Box 67, Tumacacori, AZ 85640, tel: 602-398-2341. Ruins of a Spanish mission dating to the late 1600s in southern Arizona.

Tuzigoot National Monument, PO Box 68, Clarkdale, AZ 86324, tel: 602-634-5564. A Sinagua pueblo in the Verde Valley inhabited from AD 1000–1400.

Walnut Canyon National Monument, Walnut Canyon Road, Flagstaff, AZ 86004-9705, tel: 602-526-3367. 13th-century Sinagua cliff dwellings.

Wupatki National Monument, HC 33, Box 444A, Flagstaff, AZ 86004, tel: 602-556-7040. Well-preserved pueblo structures built by the Sinagua people about AD 1120.

NEW MEXICO

Aztec Ruins National Monument, PO Box 640, Aztec, NM 87410, tel: 505-334-6174. Stabilized ruins and a reconstructed kiva originally built in the early 1100s by Chacoan Anasazi.

Bandelier National Monument, HCR 1, Box 1, Suite 15, Los Alamos, NM 87544-9701, tel: 505-672-3861. Paleo-Indians, Archaic Indians and Anasazi have left hundreds of ruins and other archaeological sites throughout Frijoles Canyon and the surrounding wilderness.

Capulin Volcano National Monument, PO Box 40, Capulin, NM 88414, tel: 505-278-2201. A symmetrical, 1,000-foot (305-meter) cinder cone created by a volcanic eruption between 2,500 and 8,000 years ago.

El Malpais National Monument, PO Box 939, Grants, NM 87020, tel: 505-285-4641. Designated in 1987, the monument encompasses an area of dramatic lava flows, cinder cones, spatter cones, lava tubes and ice caves as well as evidence of 12,000 years of human habitation.

El Morro National Monument, Route 2, Box 43, Ramah, NM 87321, tel: 505-783-4226, This 200-foot (61-meter) high sandstone formation was occupied by Anasazi farmers from AD 1275–1350. The monolith bears Anasazi petroglyphs as well as inscriptions of early Spanish and Anglo explorers.

Fort Union National Monument, PO Box 127, Watrous, NM 87753, tel: 505-425-8025. Ruins of a key way station on the Santa Fe Trail.

Gila Cliff Dwellings National Monument, Route 11, Box 100, Silver City, NM 88061, tel: 505-536-9461. Mogollon cliff dwellings occupied in the late 1200s.

Pecos National Historical Park, PO Box 418, Pecos, NM 87552, tel: 505-757-6414. The park preserves the remains of Pecos Pueblo and later Spanish missions.

Petroglyph National Monument, PO Box 1293, Albuquerque, NM 87103, tel: 505-768-3316. A wealth of prehistoric and historic rock carvings are protected on Albuquerque's West Mesa escarpment along the Rio Grande.

Salinas Pueblo Missions National Monument, Box 496, Mountainair, NM 87036, tel: 505-847-2585. The park preserves the remains of influential Pueblo Indian villages and 17th-century Spanish missions.

TEXAS

Alibates Flint Quarries National Monument, c/o Lake Meredith Recreation Area, PO Box 1460, Fritch, TX 79036, tel: 806-857-3151. The monument preserves the site where Native Americans quarried stone for tool making.

Chamizal National Memorial, 800 S San Marcial, El Paso, TX 79905, tel: 915-532-7273. The park commemorates the Chamizal Treaty of 1963, which ended a century-old border dispute between Mexico and the United States.

Fort Davis National Historic Site, PO Box 1456, Fort Davis, TX 79734, tel: 915-426-3225. A well-preserved fort established to protect pioneers in the mid- to late 1800s.

Lyndon B. Johnson National Historical Park, PO Box 329, Johnson City, TX 78636, tel: 210-868-7128. President Johnson's childhood homes, ranch, family cemetery and other structures.

San Antonio Missions National Historical Park, 2202 Roosevelt Ave, San Antonio, TX 78210, tel: 210-229-5701. The park preserves four Spanish colonial missions.

UTAH

Golden Spike National Historic Site, PO Box 897, Brigham City, UT 84302-0923, tel: 801-471-2209. The Union Pacific and Central Pacific Railroads met here in 1869, completing the first transcontinental railroad in the US.

THE ROCKY MOUNTAINS

COLORADO

Bent's Old Fort National Historic Site, 35110 Highway 194 East, La Junta, CO 81050-9523, tel: 719-384-2596. A reconstruction of the fort that served as a major meeting place for fur traders, Native Americans and pioneers on the Santa Fe Trail in the early 1800s.

Florissant Fossil Beds National Monument, PO Box 185, Florissant, CO 80816, tel: 719-748-3253. The monument preserves an abundance of fossil insects, leaves, fish and other creatures trapped by a volcanic eruption about 35 million years ago.

Hovenweep National Monument, McElmo Route, Cortez, CO 81321, tel: 303-529-4465. Extensive remains of Anasazi pueblos built and inhabited from AD 900–1300.

IDAHO

Hagerman Fossil Beds National Monument, PO Box 570, Hagerman, ID 83332-0570, tel: 208-733-8398. An active paleontological site newly acquired by the Park Service on the bluffs above the Snake River.

Nez Perce National Historical Park, PO Box 93, Spalding, ID 83551-0093, tel: 208-843-2261. The park interprets the history and culture of the Nez Perce Indians.

KANSAS

Fort Larned National Historic Site, Route 3, Larned, KS 67550, tel: 316-285-6911. The fort was established in 1859 to protect travelers and handle Indian affairs along the Santa Fe Trail.

Fort Scott National Historic Site, Old Fort Blvd, Fort Scott, KS 66701, tel: 316-223-0310. The fort was established in 1842 and played a vital role in Indian affairs, western expansion and the Civil War.

MONTANA

Big Hole National Battlefield, PO Box 237, Wisdom, MT 59761, tel: 406-689-3155. The park interprets the clash between the Nez Perce Indians and the US Army in 1877 during the dramatic and tragic Nez Perce War.

Little Bighorn Battlefield National Monument, PO Box 39, Crow Agency, MT 59022, tel: 406-638-2621. The site of "Custer's Last Stand," the fateful battle between the Seventh Cavalry and Lakota and Cheyenne warriors. Located on the Crow Reservation.

Grant-Kohrs Ranch National Historic Site, PO Box 790, Deer Lodge, MT 59722, tel: 406-846-2070. Once one of the largest ranches in the country, now a living museum of ranch life in the late 1800s and early 1900s.

NEBRASKA

Agate Fossil Beds National Monument, PO Box 27, Gering, NE 69341-0027, tel: 308-436-4340. The monument preserves a wealth of ancient fossil mammals.

Homestead National Monument of America, Route 3, Box 47, Beatrice, NE 68310, tel: 402-223-3514. The monument preserves the land and structures of an early claim made under the Homestead Act of 1862 and interprets the life of American pioneers.

Scotts Bluff National Monument, PO Box 427, Gering, NE 69341, tel: 308-436-4340. This 800-foot (244-meter) landmark on the Oregon Trail features living-history demonstrations and wagon ruts left by westering pioneers.

NORTH DAKOTA

Fort Union Trading Post National Historic Site, RR 3, Box 71, Williston, ND 58801, tel: 701-572-9083. This partially reconstructed fort was the center of fur trading on the upper Missouri River in the mid-1800s.

Knife River Indian Villages National Historic Site, PO Box 9, Stanton, ND 58571, tel: 701-745-3300. Preserves the site of Hidatsa and Mandan villages dating to 1845 and earlier.

WYOMING

Fort Laramie National Historic Site, PO Box 86, Fort Laramie, WY 82212, tel: 307-837-2221. The park preserves a military outpost established in 1849 to protect westering pioneers.

Fossil Butte National Monument, PO Box 592, Kemmerer, WY 83101, tel: 307-877-4455. The monument preserves a wealth of fish fossils as much as 60 million years old.

THE NORTHWEST

ALASKA

Klondike Gold Rush National Historical Park, PO Box 517, Skagway, AK 99840, tel: 907-983-2921. Historic buildings in Skagway and portions of the Chilkoot and White Pass Trail commemorate the gold rush of 1898.

Sitka National Historical Park, PO Box 738, Sitka, AK 99835, tel: 907-747-6281. Historic structures mark the site of the last major battle between Tlingit Indians and Russian colonists in 1804. Native art is exhibited and artists demonstrate their work.

OREGON

Fort Clatsop National Memorial, Route 3, Box 604-FC, Astoria, OR 97103, tel: 503-861-2471. A reconstructed fort occupies the site of the Lewis and Clark expedition's 1805-06 winter encampment.

John Day Fossil Beds National Monument, 420 W Main Street, John Day, OR 97845, tel: 503-575-0721. An abundance of plant and animal fossils from the Eocene to Pliocene epochs.

WASHINGTON

Fort Vancouver National Historic Site, 612 E Reserve St, Vancouver, WA 98661-3897, tel: 206-696-7655. The fort was the center of the Hudson's Bay Company's fur-trading network in the Northwest from 1825–1860.
San Juan Island National Historical Park, PO Box 429, Friday Harbor, WA 98250, tel: 206-378-2240. The park commemorates settlement of a boundary dispute between the US and Britain on the San Juan Islands from 1853–1872.
Whitman Mission National Historic Site, Route 2, Box 247, Walla Walla, WA 99362, tel: 509-529-2761. This mission, established by Marcus and Narcissa Whitman in 1836, was an important site on the Oregon Trail. The Whitmans were killed during an Indian uprising in 1847.

NATIONAL WILD AND SCENIC RIVERS

In addition to the parks and monuments covered in the color section of this book, the National Park Service administers a system of protected, free-flowing streams and rivers. Contact these units directly for information on hours, seasons, access, recreational opportunities, weather and road conditions.

Alagnak Wild River, c/o Katmai National Park and Preserve, PO Box 7, King Salmon, AK 99613, tel: 907-246-3305.
Alagnak River, Gates of the Arctic National Park and Preserve, PO Box 74680, Fairbanks, AK 99707, tel: 907-456-0281.
Aniakchak River, c/o Aniakchak National Monument and Preserve, PO Box 7, King Salmon, AK 99613, tel: 907-246-3305.
Charley River, Yukon-Charley Rivers National Preserve, PO Box 74718, Fairbanks, AK 99707, tel: 907-456-0594.
Chilikadrotna River, Lake Clark National Park and Preserve, 4230 University Drive, Suite 311, Anchorage, AK 99508, tel: 907-271-3751.
Flathead River, Flathead National Forest, PO Box 147, Kalispell, MT 59901,

tel: 406-892-4372.
John River, Gates of the Arctic National Park and Preserve, PO Box 74680, Fairbanks, AK 99707, tel: 907-456-0281.
Kobuk River, Gates of the Arctic National Park and Preserve, PO Box 74680, Fairbanks, AK 99707, tel: 907-456-0281.
Koyukuk River, North Fork, Gates of the Arctic National Park and Preserve, PO Box 74680, Fairbanks, AK 99707, tel: 907-456-0281.
Merced River, Yosemite National Park, PO Box 577, Yosemite National Park, CA 95389, tel: 209-372-0200.
Missouri River, c/o Midwest Region, National Park Service, 1709 Jackson St, Omaha, NE 68102, tel: 402-221-3471.
Mulchatna River, Lake Clark National Park and Preserve, 4230 University Drive, Suite 311, Anchorage, AK 99508, tel: 907-271-3751.
Noatak River, Gates of the Arctic National Park and Preserve, PO Box 74680, Fairbanks, AK 99707, tel: 907-456-0281.
Rio Grande River, Big Bend National Park, Big Bend National Park, TX 79834, tel: 915-477-2251.
Tinayguk River, Gates of the Arctic National Park and Preserve, PO Box 74680, Fairbanks, AK 99707, tel: 907-456-0281.
Tlikakila River, Lake Clark National Park and Preserve, 4230 University Drive, Suite 311, Anchorage, AK 99508, tel: 907-271-3751.
Tuolumne River, Yosemite National Park, PO Box 577, Yosemite National Park, CA 95389, tel: 209-372-0200.

NATIONAL TRAILS SYSTEM

The National Park Service in association with other state and federal agencies manages a system of scenic, historic and recreational trails, many of which pass through or between national parks and monuments. Contact these regional offices for maps and information on access, recreational activities and weather conditions.

Continental Divide National Scenic Trail, Forest Service, Region 1, Federal Building, PO Box 7669, Missoula,

MT 59807, tel: 406-329-3150.
Iditarod National Historic Trail, Anchorage District, Bureau of Land Management, 6881 Abbott Loop Road, Anchorage, AK 99507, tel: 907-271-5960.
Juan Bautista de Anza National Historic Trail, Western Region, National Park Service, 600 Harrison St, Suite 600, San Francisco, CA 94107, tel: 415-744-3975.
Lewis and Clark National Historic Trail, National Park Service, 700 Rayovac Drive, Suite 100, Madison, WI 53711, tel: 608-264-5610.
Mormon Pioneer National Historic Trail, Rocky Mountain Region, National Park Service, 12795 W Alameda Parkway, Lakewood, CO 80225, tel: 303-969-2875
Nez Perce National Historic Trail, Forest Service, Region 1, Federal Building, PO Box 7669, Missoula, MT 59807, tel: 406-329-3150.
Oregon National Historic Trail, Pacific Northwest Region, National Park Service, 83 S King Street, Suite 212, Seattle, WA 98104, tel: 206-553-5366.
Pacific Crest Trail, Forest Service, Region 6, PO Box 3623, Portland, OR 97208, tel: 503-326-2877.
Santa Fe National Historic Trail, Southwest Region, National Park Service, PO Box 728, Santa Fe, NM 87504, tel: 505-988-6888.

COOPERATING ASSOCIATIONS

Books, maps, special seminars, tours and other services are available from the following organizations:

Alaska Natural History Association, PO Box 230, Denali National Park, AK 99755, tel: 907-683-1258.
Badlands Natural History Association, PO Box 6, Interior, SD 57750, tel: 605-433-5361.
Big Bend Natural History Association, PO Box 68, Big Bend National Park, TX 79834, tel: 915-477-2236.
Bryce Canyon Natural History Association, Bryce Canyon, UT 84717, tel: 801-834-5322.
Canyonlands Natural History Association, 30 S 100 East, Moab, UT 84532, tel: 801-259-6003.
Carlsbad Caverns-Guadalupe Moun-

tains Association, PO Box 1417, Carlsbad, NM 88221, tel: 505-785-2318.

Crater Lake Natural History Association, PO Box 157, Crater Lake, OR 97604, tel: 503-594-2211.

Death Valley Natural History Association, PO Box 188, Death Valley, CA 92328, tel: 619-786-2331.

Glacier Natural History Association, PO Box 428, West Glacier, MT 59936, tel: 406-888-5756.

Grand Canyon Natural History Association, PO Box 399, Grand Canyon, AZ 86023, tel: 602-638-2481.

Grand Teton Natural History Association, PO Box 170, Moose, WY 83012, tel: 307-739-3404.

Joshua Tree Natural History Association, 74485 National Monument Drive, Twentynine Palms, CA 92277, tel: 619-367-1488.

Northwest Interpretive Association, 3002 Mount Angeles Road, Port Angeles, WA 98362, tel: 206-452-4501.

Point Reyes Natural History Association, Bear Valley Road, Point Reyes Station, CA 94956, tel: 415-663-1200.

Redwood Natural History Association, 1111 2nd St, Crescent City, CA 95531, tel: 707-464-9150.

Rocky Mountain Nature Association, Rocky Mountain National Park, Estes Park, CO 80517, tel: 303-586-1399.

Sequoia Natural History Association, HCR-89, Box 10, Three Rivers, CA 93271, tel: 209-565-3758.

Southwest Parks and Monuments Association, 221 N Court Ave, Tucson, AZ 85701, tel: 602-622-1999.

Yellowstone Association, PO Box 117, Yellowstone National Park, WY 82190, tel: 307-344-2293.

Yosemite Association, PO Box 230, El Portal, CA 95318, tel: 209-372-0420.

Zion Natural History Association, Springdale, UT 84767, tel: 800-635-3959.

Further Reading

General

Beyond the Hundredth Meridian, by Wallace Stegner. New York: Penguin, 1953.

Desert Notes: Reflections in the Eye of a Raven, by Barry Holstun Lopez. New York: Avon, 1981.

Desert Solitaire: A Season in the Wilderness, by Edward Abbey. New York: McGraw-Hill, 1968.

The Desert Year, by Joseph W. Krutch. Tucson: University of Arizona, 1990.

The Exploration of the Colorado River and Its Canyons, by John Wesley Powell. New York: Penguin, 1987.

A Fierce Green Fire: The American Environmental Movement, by Philip Shabecoff. New York: Hill and Wang, 1993.

Journey on the Crest, by Cindy Ross. Seattle: The Mountaineers, 1987.

National Park: The American Experience, by Alfred Runte. Lincoln: University of Nebraska Press, 1979.

PrairyErth, by William Least Heat-Moon. Boston: Houghton Mifflin, 1991.

The Quiet Crisis, by Stewart Udall. Salt Lake City: Peregrine Smith Books, 1988.

A Sand County Almanac, by Aldo Leopold. New York: Ballantine Books, 1966.

A Sense of Wonder, by Rachel Carson. New York: Harper & Row, 1965.

Silent Spring, by Rachel Carson. Boston: Houghton Mifflin, 1962.

Walden and Other Writings, by Henry David Thoreau. New York: Bantam Books, 1962.

Where the Bluebird Sings to the Lemonade Spring: Living and Writing in the West, by Wallace Stegner. New York: Random House, 1992.

Parks and Wildlife

Adventuring in the California Desert, by Lynne Foster. San Francisco: Sierra Club Books, 1987.

The Complete Guidebook to Yosemite National Park, by Steven P. Medley. El Portal: Yosemite Association, 1991.

Deserts, by James A. MacMahon. New York: Alfred A. Knopf, 1985.

Easy Access to National Parks, by Wendy Roth and Michael Tompane. San Francisco: Sierra Club Books, 1992.

Glacier and Waterton Lakes National Parks: A Traveler's Guide, by Thomas Schmidt. Jackson Hole: Free Wheeling Travel Guides, 1992.

Grand Canyon: An Anthology, by Bruce Babbitt. Flagstaff: Northland Press, 1978.

Grand Canyon: A Traveler's Guide, by Jeremy Schmidt. Jackson Hole: Free Wheeling Travel Guides, 1991.

Grand Canyon National Park: A Natural History Guide, by Jeremy Schmidt. Boston: Houghton Mifflin Company, 1993.

Grand Canyon: Today and All Its Yesterdays, by Joseph Wood Krutch. Tucson: University of Arizona, 1989.

The Guide to National Parks of the Southwest, by Nicky Leach. Tucson: Southwest Parks & Monuments Association, 1992.

In Denali, by Kim Heacox. Santa Barbara: Companion Press, 1992.

Inside Death Valley, by Chuck Gebhardt. Chelsea, MI: Bookcrafters, 1988.

In the House of Stone and Light: A Human History of the Grand Canyon, by Donald J. Hughes. Grand Canyon: Grand Canyon Natural History Association, 1978.

Joshua Tree National Monument: A Visitor's Guide, by Robert Cates. Chatsworth, CA: Live Oak Press, 1990.

Olympic National Park: Where the Mountain Meets the Sea. Del Mar: Woodlands Press, 1984.

Pacific Coast, by Bayard H. McConnaughey. New York: Alfred A. Knopf, 1985.

Texas' Big Bend Country, by George Wuerthner. Helena: American Geographic Publishing, 1989.

The Man Who Walked Through Time, by Colin Fletcher. New York: Random House, 1989.

This Curious Country: Badlands National Park, by Mary Durant and Michael Harwood. Interior: Badlands Natural History Association, 1988.

Western Forests, by Stephen Whitney. New York: Alfred A. Knopf, 1985.

Wildflowers of the American West, by

Rose Houk. San Francisco: Chronicle Books, 1987.

Wind Cave: An Ancient World Beneath the Hills, by Arthur N. Palmer. Hot Springs: Wind Cave/Jewel Cave Natural History Association, 1988.

Yellowstone and Grand Teton National Parks: A Traveler's Guide, by Steven Fuller and Jeremy Schmidt. Jackson Hole: Free Wheeling Travel Guides, 1991.

Yellowstone: In the Eagle's Eye, by Larry Mayer. Billings: The Billings Gazette, 1991.

The Yosemite, by John Muir and Galen Rowell. San Francisco: Sierra Club Books, 1989.

Other Insight Guides

The 190 books in the *Insight Guides* series cover every continent and include 28 titles devoted to the United States, from Alaska to Florida, from Seattle to Boston. A companion volume to this one is *Insight Guide: US National Parks East.*

Two other titles are also relevant to the present volume:

Insight Guide: American Southwest covers this culturally rich region in great detail, from Apache Junction to Albuquerque, from Los Alamos to Las Vegas, from ghost towns to the Grand Canyon.

Insight Guide: Native America provides a unique blend of absorbing text about the Native Americans' culture and a detailed guide to Indian reservations, historic sites, festivals and ceremonies, from the deserts of the Southwest to the lush woodlands of the east coast.

Insight Guides have always been ecologically aware and several "Discover Nature" titles in the series are written especially for those wishing to understand and appreciate nature and wildlife. They combine truly remarkable photography with an insightful and practical approach to travel.

Insight Guide: Amazon Wildlife brings together an impressive team of naturalists and top-class wildlife photographers to focus on the largest tropical rainforest on earth.

Insight Guide: East African Wildlife ranges across Kenya, Tanzania, Uganda and Ethiopia, combining informative essays on the wildlife with a practical travel guide, from the sparkling waters of the Indian Ocean to the ice-encrusted peaks of the Mountains of the Moon.

Insight Guide: Indian Wildlife is a comprehensive guide to the wildlife parks of India, Nepal and Sri Lanka. It provides both a broad background to the region's wildlife and a practical guide to the art and practice of observing animals, birds and reptiles in their natural state.

Photography by
Stewart Aitchison 151, 175, 192
James Ariyoshi 124
Dugald Bremner 1, 2, 47, 49, 76/77, 81, 140, 153, 159, 164/165, 169, 170, 187, 196, 232/233, 239, 248, 294/295, 297, 303, 330/331
Steve Bruno 98, 142, 144, 176, 189, 246/247, 251, 265, 291
Dave Edwards 42/43, 44, 185, 237
Bill Hatcher 46, 110L, 134/135, 186, 206/207, 280
Kim Heacox 33, 53, 137, 210R, 342, 345
Kerrick James 58, 110R, 152, 177, 183, 203L, 221, 260/261, 284, 301, 352
Gavriel Jecan 145, 149
Lewis Kemper 10/11, 41, 45, 67, 70, 73, 74, 82, 89, 99, 102, 103, 105, 107R, 108, 111, 167, 218, 219, 257, 263, 268/269, 270, 277, 286, 288, 292, 302, 312, 325, 328, 349
Tom and Pat Leeson Cover, 35, 36, 39, 79, 83, 93, 112/113, 118, 160, 174, 188, 193, 194, 197, 210L, 220, 224/225, 255, 256, 262, 273, 274, 276, 281, 283, 285, 293, 299, 313, 317, 319, 320, 321, 322/323, 326, 332, 333, 334, 336, 338/339, 344, 346, 347
Larry Mayer 24/25, 254, 278/279
Steve Mulligan 34, 107L, 158, 180/181, 236, 241, 266, 296
National Park Service, Grand Canyon National Park 16/17, 19
National Park Service, Yellowstone National Park 20, 22, 54
National Park Service, Yosemite National Park 18, 21, 55, 75
William Neill 69, 71, 72, 249
Oakland Museum 23
Joel Rogers 329
Eugene Rose 90/91, 95, 96
Galen Rowell/Mountain Light 120/121
John Running 48, 56/57, 123, 139, 141, 148, 198/199
Scott Rutherford 125
Tom Till 26, 27, 28, 29, 30, 31, 32, 64/65, 66, 97, 100/101, 106, 109, 126, 130/131, 136, 143, 146/147, 154/155, 156/157, 161, 162, 163, 166, 171, 178, 179, 184, 190/191, 201. 202, 203R, 204/205, 214/215, 216, 217, 222/223, 228, 229, 231, 234, 235, 238, 240, 242, 243, 252, 253, 258/259, 264, 267, 275, 282, 289, 300, 306/307, 335
Connie Toops 50/51, 80L
Pat Toops 122
Stephen Trimble 129, 172/173, 227
Larry Ulrich 78, 80R, 84/85, 92, 114, 115, 116, 119, 127, 128, 168, 182, 195, 200, 213, 226, 230, 287, 290R, 337
Art Wolfe 12, 15, 38, 40, 117, 208, 211, 308, 311, 314/315, 318, 324, 327, 340, 343, 348, 350/351
George Wuerthner 52, 86, 88, 212, 290L, 316

Maps Berndtson & Berndtson

Visual Consultant V. Barl

Index